A Cruising Guide to the Turks and Caicos Islands

Third Edition

Including Expanded Coverage of the Dominican Republic

Part I
The Caicos Islands

Includes
Providenciales, The Caicos Cays, West Caicos, French Cay, North Caicos, Middle Caicos, East Caicos, South Caicos, the Ambergris Cays, and Routes Across the Caicos Banks

Part II
The Turks Islands

Includes
Grand Turk, North Creek Anchorage, Hawksnest Anchorage, Salt Cay, and Great Sand Cay

Part III
The Dominican Republic

Includes
Luperón, Cofresi, Puerto Plata, Sosúa, Rio San Juan, Puerto El Valle, Samaná, Puerto Bahia Marina, Bahía de San Lorenzo (Los Haitises), Puerto de Haina, Santo Domingo, Boca Chica, Casa de Campo Marina, Isla Saona, and Cap Cana Marina

by
Stephen J. Pavlidis

Seaworthy Publications, Inc.
Cocoa Beach, Florida

A Cruising Guide to the Turks and Caicos Islands
Third Edition
Including Expanded Coverage of the Dominican Republic

Copyright © 2017 Stephen J. Pavlidis

ISBN 978-1-892399-40-3
7.0

Published in the USA by:
Seaworthy Publications, Inc.
2021 N. Atlantic Ave., Unit #226
Cocoa Beach, Florida 32931
Phone 321-610-3634
email orders@seaworthy.com
www.seaworthy.com - Your Bahamas and Caribbean Cruising Advisory

All rights reserved. No part of this book may be reproduced, stored in a retrieval system, or transmitted in any form, or by any means, electronic, mechanical, photocopying, recording, or by any storage and retrieval system, without permission in writing from the Publisher.

CAUTION: Sketch charts are not to scale and are not to be used for navigational purposes. They are intended as supplements for NOAA, DMA, or British Admiralty charts and no warranties are either expressed or implied as to the usability or the information contained herein. The Author and Publisher take no responsibility for their misuse.

A publication like this is actually the result of a blending of many people's talents, knowledge and experiences. I would like to take this opportunity to thank the following for their help in this effort: Capt. Lee Bakewell of the S/V *Winterlude* for his help with programming; Dean Bernal; *Caicos Marina and Shipyard* and manager David Taylor; Judd Clarence; Titus H. DeBoer of the *Bamboo Gallery*; Andy Lowe and Star Droshine for their help with the diving sections and areas around Provo; Captain Bob Gascoine of the M/V *Aquanaut*, whose years of experience in these waters made my job that much easier; Ralph Higgs of the Tourist Board; a special thanks goes to Carol Hochberg-Holker of the S/V *Alcyone*, for her dedicated editing; Captain Willis Jennings of South Caicos; Chuck and Alexis Kehn; John Lawson, *Caribbean Cruisin' Ltd.*; Dwayne and Denver Pratt; Josiah Marvel, Providenciales historian and proponent of the *Grand Turk Landfall Theory*; Captain David Matthews of the S/V *Tao* whose twenty-plus years of experience here are now available for all to benefit from; Beryl Nelson of *TACRA*; D.J. Piltingsrud; Nicolas Popov of *Island Expeditions School at Sea*; *Scooter Bob's*; Pierre Seymour, Deputy Chief Conservation Officer of the *DECR* in Provo; Jack and Pat Tyler; and Lenny Williams of *Lenny's Photo*. If there is anybody that I have neglected to mention here, rest assured that it is an oversight and I sincerely apologize.

Cover design by Ken Quant, Broad Reach Marketing, Milwaukee, WI

Library of Congress Cataloging-in-Publication Data
Pavlidis, Stephen J.
 [Turks and Caicos guide]
 A cruising guide to the Turks and Caicos Islands : including expanded coverage of the Dominican Republic / Stephen J. Pavlidis. -- Third edition.
      pages cm
 Revision of author's Turks and Caicos guide.
 Includes bibliographical references and index.
 ISBN 978-1-892399-40-3 (pbk. : alk. paper) -- ISBN 1-892399-40-7 (pbk. : alk. paper)
 I. Title.
 GV776.29.T94P38 2015
 917.296'104--dc23
                    2014049336

Introduction

There is an ancient bit of wisdom that has been passed down over the centuries about slowing down the maddening pace of one's travels through life long enough to appreciate what life has placed along your path. More commonly called stopping to smell the roses, this sage advice is often a way of life aboard some cruising boats, not all, just some and therein lies a sadness. All too often voyagers rush from one port to another seeing little of what lies between, save sea and sky. Most cruisers will tell you that it is the voyage itself that is important; your ultimate destination will still be there and you will arrive there eventually, at worst, a bit more fulfilled for savoring each and every tiny destination along your route.

The Turks and Caicos Islands are a perfect example of those tiny destinations. Like the lady who is always a bridesmaid and never a bride, the Turks and Caicos Islands are, more often than not, used as a stopover, a place to refuel and get some sleep, perhaps even wait out some weather, for those boaters sailing between the U.S. and the Caribbean. Some older publications have given the Turks and Caicos Islands, and especially Providenciales (usually just called Provo), the thumbs down in some regards for reasons I cannot fathom. Perhaps the authors of these publications were not treated well. Perhaps they had a bad attitude about the Turks and Caicos Islands and could not view the area objectively. That, my friends, is a sin for the author of a cruising guide. We must be objective, impartial. We have a tremendous responsibility that cannot be taken lightly. We must show off the best of the areas we visit, and yet, we cannot blindly ignore the worst. But if we have been treated badly at one time or another, we must hope that it was just a bad day. We must return a few days or weeks later, and see if things have changed. One must spend a lot of time in an area to notice trends, to get the feel for the way of life. Our written word is very often taken for "Bible truth" concerning the areas we write about. That is why I get so angry when I hear cruisers say that "So and so doesn't have anything good to say about Provo!" or "What's his name said that you can't do this or you can't do that there so why stop?" I know immediately that these people did not spend enough time in the Turks and Caicos Islands, that they did not stop to smell the roses, to savor each and every nuance of their aroma, going from flower to flower like a bee in search of droplets of tasty, sweet nectar. Instead they hastily grabbed the bunch and suffered a thorn. One must learn how to handle the thorns and to delight in the fragrant bouquet presented by the delicate petals.

With the help of this book you will learn how to handle the thorns. You will learn that there are several all weather anchorages, even a few good hurricane holes. Boats heading to the Caribbean will learn that you can provision in Provo for less than in Nassau or George Town with some prices being almost equivalent to those in the U.S. You will learn that there are quite a few National Parks where fishing is prohibited, the result is fantastic diving rich in marine life. Fishermen will come to know the Pinnacles and some of the other hot spots for piscatorial action. More important, you will come to understand that there is more to the Turks and Caicos Islands than simply being a rest stop on the superhighway to and from the Caribbean. The Turks and Caicos Islands can be a destination in themselves.

Stephen J. Pavlidis

Table of Contents

Introduction 3

The Basics 6
- Anchoring 6
- Charts 7
- Clothing 8
- Currency 8
  - The Turks and Caicos Islands 8
  - The Dominican Republic 8
- Customs and Immigration 8
  - The Turks and Caicos Islands 8
    - Ports of Entry 8
    - Departure Tax 10
    - eSeaClear/Sail Clear 10
  - Dominican Republic 10
    - Ports of Entry 10
    - Firearms 10
    - Pets 11
- Dinghy Safety 11
- Diving 11
- Fishing 12
- Garbage 13
- Ham Radio 13
  - Visitor's License 14
- Holidays 14
- Hurricane Holes 15
  - The Southern Bahamas 16
  - The Turks and Caicos Islands .. 16
  - The Dominican Republic 17
- JoJo the Dolphin 17
- Medical Emergencies 19
  - The Turks and Caicos Islands .. 19
  - The Dominican Republic 20
- National Parks 20
- Phoning Home 21
  - The Turks and Caicos 21
  - The Dominican Republic 21
- Provisioning 21
- Radio and TV 22
- Tides and Currents 22
  - The Turks and Caicos 23
  - The Dominican Republic 23
- Time 23
- VHF 23
  - The Turks and Caicos 23
  - The Dominican Republic 23
- Weather 23
  - Chris Parker 24

Using the Charts 26

List of Charts 27

Index of Charts 29
- Chart Legend 32

The Caicos Islands 33
- A Brief History 35
- The Caicos Islands 42
  - Ports of Entry 42
- Approaches 42
- Providenciales 44
  - North West Point, Sandbore Channel 45
  - Sandbore Channel, Sapodilla Bay 48
  - The Southern Shore 55
  - Northern Shore, Grace Bay 59
- The Caicos Cays 63
  - Leeward Going Through to N. Caicos 63
- West Caicos 70
- French Cay 72
- North Caicos 75
- Middle Caicos 77
- East Caicos 78
- Routes Across the Caicos Bank 80
- South Caicos 82
- The Southern Cays 86

The Turks Islands 89
- Ports of Entry: 89
- Approaches 90
- Grand Turk 92

Table of Contents

    North Creek Anchorage............................ 92
    Front Street Anchorage 96
        Cockburn Town, and South Base 96
    Hawksnest Anchorage 101
    Salt Cay... 104
    Great Sand Cay 107

The Dominican Republic............109

    The Dominican Republic........................ 110
        Ports of Entry: 110
        Places of Interest 112
    The Future... 112
    A Brief History 113
    Medical Help 114
    The Northern Coast................................. 114
        Luperón... 115
        Ocean World Marina 122
        Puerto Plata 124
        Sosúa 126
        Rio San Juan....................................... 129
        Puerto El Valle.................................... 130
    The Eastern Coast 130
        Samaná... 130
        Puerto Bahía Marina 132
        Bahía de San Lorenzo 134
    The Southern Coast 134
        Barahona... 134
        Las Salinas.. 136
        Puerto de Haina 138
        Santo Domingo 138
        Boca Chica.. 139
        (San Andrés) 139
        East of Boca Chica.............................. 141
        Casa de Campo Marina 142
        Isla Saona 142
        Cap Cana Marina 144

A Little Basic Spanish 146

Appendices 149

    Appendix A: Navigational Lights 149
    Appendix B: Marinas............................... 149
    Appendix C-1: Services Dominican Republic 150
    Appendix C-2: Services Turks and Caicos 153
    Appendix D: Waypoints 155
    Appendix E: Protected Areas 157
    Appendix F: Metric Conversion 157
    Appendix G: Flags................................... 158

Index 159

About the Author 163

About Don Reynolds 163

The Basics

Anchoring

Just as important as getting your vessel moving and keeping her heading along your chosen courseline quickly and efficiently is the fine art of keeping your vessel from moving. Many of the anchorages in this book are swept by swift tidal currents, sometimes up to 3 knots, and to avoid bumping into your neighbor in the middle of the night or putting your vessel on the rocks or beach, two anchors, such as in a Bahamian Moor, are required.

Anchor choice is basically a personal preference. Some skippers prefer *CQRs*, while others swear by a *Bruce*, a *Rocna*, a *Mantus*, or a *Danforth*. Of the lot, you will find that a *Danforth* holds as well or better than a *CQR* or *Bruce* in sandy bottoms while the *CQR* or *Bruce* is preferred when anchoring in rocky bottoms. Whatever your choice of anchor, you must deploy your anchor correctly and with sufficient scope to hold you when the tide changes, if a front approaches, or if a squall should blow through at 2:00 a.m. (which seems to be the time they choose to blow through). Your anchor should have a length of chain (at least 15') shackled to your anchor to keep your rode from chafing against coral or rocks and to create a catenary curve that helps absorb shock loads while lowering the angle of pull on your anchor. Too high an angle may cause your anchor to pull up and out of the bottom. Some cruisers prefer all chain rodes with a nylon snubber to absorb the shock loads. This is an excellent arrangement but a windlass may be needed unless you prefer the workout involved with hauling in the chain and anchor every time you move.

In many of the leeward anchorages in The Turks and Caicos Islands you will find that you can lie quite comfortably to only one anchor. When setting your anchor do not just drop it and let your rode run out, piling itself on top of your anchor. Lower your anchor to the bottom and deploy the rode as you fall back with the current or wind until you have at least a 5:1 scope out, 7:1 is preferable but not always possible. When calculating the amount of scope required, be sure to allow for high tide as well as the height of your anchor roller or fairlead above the water. Without being precise, you can figure on a 2½'-3' tidal rise in The Turks and Caicos Islands although occasionally you may find a 4½' rise, and in general a little more rise during a full moon and a little less with no moon (remember that the soundings in this guide are at *MLW, Mean Low Water*, this means that it is possible to have a lower tide with less depth that what is shown). When you have secured your rode, back down with the engine at about ½ throttle to set the anchor. If you have not succeeded in securing your anchor, try again. To check the set it is best to dive on your anchors or at the very least, look at their set through a glass bottom bucket from your dinghy. You may find that you will have to set them by hand, especially in rocky areas.

If there are other boats in the anchorage when you arrive and they are riding to two anchors, or if you are in an area beset by tidal currents, it is best to set two anchors in a Bahamian Moor. Although one anchor may be fine if you have the swinging room, when the tide changes it may pull out and fail to reset. These anchorages are often very crowded and while you may swing wide on your one anchor and not find yourself endangered by the rocks or beach, you and your neighbor may go bump in the night because his two anchors have kept him in one spot. If unsure the best thing to do is follow the lead of those boats that are there before you. Conversely, if you arrive at an anchorage and everyone is on one anchor and you choose to set two, do so outside the swing radius of the other boats. If you are riding on one anchor and find that you are lying to the wind but that the swell is rolling you, position another anchor at an angle off the stern so as to align your bow into the swell making for a more comfortable night. Another option is to rig a bridle which allows your vessel to lie to the swells and not the wind.

To set a *Bahamian Moor*, you must first decide where you wish for your vessel to settle. You will lay out two anchors, one up-current and one down-current of that spot which will keep you swinging in a small circle. Head into the current to where you will drop your first anchor and set it properly. Let out as much scope as you can, setting your anchor on the way by snubbing it, until you are at the spot where you are to drop your down-current anchor. If the wind has pushed you to one side or the other of the tidal stream, you will have to power up to the position where you will set your second anchor. Lower your second anchor and pull your vessel back up current on your first rode, paying out the rode for the second anchor and snubbing it as you maneuver back up current to your chosen spot. You may want to dive on your anchors to check their set. Keeping your rodes tight will keep you swinging in a tighter circle. Check your anchor rodes daily as they will twist together and make it extremely difficult to undo them in an emergency.

In some tight anchorages you will be unable to set your anchors 180° apart. An alternative is to set them 90° apart in a "Y" configuration perpendicular to the wind. A skipper with a large swing radius in very tight quarters is apt to find out what his neighbors think of his anchoring technique as soon as the wind shifts. Responsible anchoring cannot be over-stressed.

Always set an anchor light. Some cruisers feel this is unimportant in some of the more isolated anchorages. What they do not understand is that many locals run the islands at all hours of the night, even on moonless nights, and an anchor light protects your vessel as well as theirs. There are no "designated anchorages" in the Turks and Caicos Islands.

It is important to note that lee-side anchorages can get rolly at times. The *North Atlantic Ocean* surge seeks out any way it can to round the tips of these islands to cause you seemingly no end of discomfort and there is not much you can do about it except possibly use a second anchor or bridle arrangement to keep your bow or stern into the swell. If using a bridle, set up your line on the opposite side that you wish to turn your vessel. For instance, if you need to turn your bow to port to face the incoming swells and make for a calmer ride, run your bridle line from a winch to a block on your starboard quarter and then forward outside your shrouds to your anchor line. Either tie it to your rode or, if you use all chain, attach it to the shackle where your nylon snubber (be sure to use a long one, at least 10'-20' if you are setting up for a bridle arrangement) hooks to your chain. After your anchor is set, simply crank in your bridle line bringing your bow to port and off the wind.

Never anchor in coral, even with your dinghy anchor. An anchor can do a great deal of damage to a very fragile ecosystem that will take years to recover if it is to recover at all. Besides, sand holds so much better anyway.

In summer months and on into the early fall, or when there is no wind, you may wish to anchor a good distance from shore to keep away from the relentless biting insects. Cays with a lot of vegetation or mangroves will have a higher concentration of biting insects.

Proper anchoring etiquette should by practiced at all times. For instance, if the anchorage is wide and roomy and only one boat is at anchor, do not anchor right on top of them, give your neighbor a little breathing room and some solitude. You would probably appreciate the same consideration should the situation be reversed. Cruisers often exhibit a herding instinct where they seek the comfort of other nearby cruisers, anchoring much too close at times. Many boaters, after a long, hard day in rough seas or bad weather, anxiously await the peace and tranquility of a calm anchorage. The last thing they want is noise and wake.

If you have a dog aboard that loves to bark, be considerate of your neighbors who do not wish to hear him. They do have that right. Jet skis can be a lot of fun, but only when you are astride one. Many cruisers have little tolerance for the incessant buzzing back and forth of high speed jet skis. It is a good show of manners to slowly leave the anchorage where you can have your high speed fun and games and not disturb anyone. The same can be said of water skiing which is prohibited within 200' of the shoreline in The Bahamas unless the skier is approaching or leaving the shore at a speed of 3 knots or less. If at all possible, try not to run your generators at sunset or after dark. At sunset, many cruisers are sitting in their cockpits enjoying cocktails and watching the sun go down and do not want a generator disturbing their soft conversations. Courtesy shown is usually courtesy returned.

Charts

The best charts that you can buy for the Turks and Caicos Islands, besides the ones in this publication, are TC-001, TC-002, and TC-003 by Captain Bob Gascoine, (*Wavey Line Publishing*, http://www.waveylinepublishing.com/). Bob, the dean of Turks Islands divers, has done a remarkable job and created some truly accurate and reliable charts that also show all the major dive sites along the shores of the Turks and Caicos Islands. His charts go into a bit more detail in the area of the *Caicos Bank* where he shows the *Damn Fool Channel* route, a small boat or shallow draft route through an incredibly beautiful area that I do not cover for the simple reason that the vast majority of cruising boats are restricted from entry by their draft. Captain Gascoine also has a new chart out for Hispaniola and several for The Bahamas.

Clothing

If you are heading to the Turks and Caicos Islands or the Dominican Republic, you will enter a tropical climate where the theme for clothing is light. You will most likely live in shorts and T-shirts (if that much). Long pants and sturdy, comfortable shoes are preferred when hiking for protection from the bush and the rugged terrain. Long sleeved shirts (or old cotton pajamas) and wide brimmed hats are important in keeping the sun off you. Polarized sunglasses (helpful for piloting) and suntan lotion (suntan oil tends to leave a long lasting greasy smear all over everything) should be included in your gear. In winter months it is advisable to bring something warm to wear, especially in the evenings. Long pants and sweaters are usually adequate and a light jacket would be a good idea as some frontal passages will occasionally drop the temperature to 60° F.

It is important that men and women dress appropriately when entering settlements. Skimpy bathing suits for men as well as women are excellent for the beach or boat but in town they are not apropos. Men should wear shirts in town as some local inhabitants are quick to remind you to cover up. Remember, you are a visitor here and that entails a certain responsibility.

Currency

The Turks and Caicos Islands

The legally acceptable currency of the Turks and Caicos is the American dollar. The treasury also issues a Turks and Caicos crown and quarter. If you are arriving in the Turks and Caicos from the Bahamas you will want to cash in your Bahamian money in the Bahamas prior to your arrival at Provo. The banks in the Turks and Caicos will not accept Bahamian money and you'll be stuck with it unless you find a cruiser heading north. Traveler's checks are accepted almost everywhere and many places, including some grocery stores, take major credit cards. If you are coming from someplace without a sales tax such as the Bahamas, restaurant and grocery bills will take some getting used to as the Turks and Caicos charges a 10% sales tax on food items. There are no company or personal income taxes in the Turks and Caicos Islands. The government's budget is derived from the 10%-30% customs duty on incoming goods.

The Dominican Republic

In the Dominican Republic the currency in usage is the Peso (RD$) and you may change your dollars into pesos at *Claró* in Luperón (you may also withdraw pesos on your credit or debit card here). At the time of this writing in 2014 the exchange rate was RD$43.49=US$1. Some other locations will give you a slightly higher rate.

Please note that the rate mentioned will certainly have changed by the time this guide is published. It is the nature of this work that business listings change and rates fluctuate, I can only give you a guideline here. If you would like a good online currency converter, visit the *XE Universal Currency Converter* web site (http://www.xe.com/ucc/full.shtml).

Foreign currency can also be changed into Dominican pesos at *Banco de Reservas* booths at the airports, major hotels, or at commercial banks. Banking hours are 0830 to 1500, M-F. Airport booths remain open to service all incoming flights, up to 24-hours if necessary.

Traveler's checks and major credit cards are widely accepted. Cash advances are available at some commercial banks. When tipping, a 10% gratuity (as well as an 8% sales tax) is often included in the bill. Please note that the practice of tipping taxi drivers is not the custom in the DR but it is widely practiced.

Don't change very much more money than you plan to spend, only 30% of Dominican currency exchanged by visitors can be changed back into dollars upon departure (a tip - save your currency exchange receipts). Although it's extremely tempting, one should avoid changing money on the black market. Absolutely no more than US$5,000 may be taken out of the country when you leave. Arrests have been made for even small currency-law violations.

Customs and Immigration

The Turks and Caicos Islands

Ports of Entry
Providenciales: South Dock, *Turtle Cove Marina*, Caicos Marina and Shipyard, Blue Haven Marina, Southside Marina
South Caicos: Cockburn Town
North Caicos: airstrip (not for boaters)

Grand Turk: Marine Police Dock at *South Base*, Cockburn Town dock

All vessels entering the waters of the Turks and Caicos must clear in with *Customs* (http://customs.gov.tc/) and *Immigration* officials at the nearest port of entry listed above. Failure to report within 24 hours may subject you to a penalty and make you liable for confiscation and forfeiture of your vessel. When approaching your selected port of entry be sure to fly your yellow "Q" flag. Only the captain of the vessel may go ashore to arrange clearance and no other shore contact is permitted until pratique is granted. Normal working hours are 0800 to 1630, Monday through Friday. If arriving outside normal hours or on holidays you may expect to pay overtime charges, usually a $6.00 overtime fee Monday through Friday, and an $8.00 fee overtime if you clear in on Sundays and holidays.

Vessels staying in the islands for 7 days or less must pay a fee of $100, ($130 on the weekends) even if the stop is to purchase fuel. If you intend to stay more than seven days you must get a cruising permit from *Customs* at a charge of $300 for 90 days (renewable for 90 days too). But first you must report to *Immigration* to secure a visa. Visas are granted for periods not to exceed 30 days and can be renewed twice, each renewal costs $50 per passport. If your cruising permit expires you can renew it for another 90 days. If you wish to stay in the Turks and Caicos for longer than 180 days must pay an *Import Duty* that is currently 11% of local valuation or leave the country and not return until the following calendar year. Vessels over 60' LOA will need a special anchoring permit from DEMA; the price is $100 for 30 days.

North Americans need proof of citizenship. If you are flying in and returning by way of a boat in transit you need some proof that you are able to leave the country. It is suggested that you purchase a round trip ticket and leave the return reservation open. When you return aboard your boat you may then cash in your unused ticket or use it for a future flight. Check with the airline when buying your ticket as to their policy in this matter. As soon as the captain has cleared *Customs*, you must take down your yellow "Q" flag and replace it with the British courtesy flag. Canadian citizens need a valid passport or some proof of identity such as a birth certificate along with a photo ID and a return ticket if arriving by air and a visa is not required. Australian, New Zealand, EU, and Japanese citizens need a valid passport and a return ticket, but no visa is required. Citizens of countries not listed above should check with the embassy or consulate in their home country for details on entry requirements.

Vessels leaving the Turks and Caicos are now required to clear out 24-hours in advance of their scheduled departure time. If you're in a marina, have the dockmaster notify *Customs* for you and an officer will soon arrive to clear you out of the country. If you're in *Sapodilla Bay* you can go to South Dock for your outward clearance. If you clear out and must wait on weather in some place like Great Sand Cay (if you're bound for the DR) it is fine to await weather at the cay, however you cannot clear out and then anchor at an inhabited cay. If you are in *Turtle Cove Marina* or Leeward Going Through and wish to stopover at *Sapodilla Bay* before heading to Luperón, do not call *Customs* to come to you for an outward clearance, instead, when you arrive at *Sapodilla Bay*, go to *South Dock* to clear.

Most vessels heading across the banks and venturing south to the DR or Puerto Rico leave Provo and head to Ambergris Cay and then Sand Cay. As long as you do not stop at any other inhabited islands in the Turks and Caicos Islands, you may proceed straight across the banks and stage your trip from Sand Cay. When clearing out of *Sapodilla Bay*, you can clear out in the afternoon and not actually leave until the next morning, as long as you are gone before *Customs* opens. This enables you to have an early morning start to get to Ambergris before dark. There are no fees to clear out unless you choose to do so outside of normal working hours. The same rates for overtime are charged as for clearing in. If you or your guests are flying out, be advised that the airport departure tax is US$15 for visitors over the age of twelve.

Firearms, including those charged with compressed air, must be declared and brought in to *Customs* with you when you clear. Unless you have prior approval in writing from the *Commissioner of Police*, *Customs* will impound them and store them for you at the police station until your departure. Spear guns are also illegal and must be brought in to *Customs* when you clear.

There is no quarantine period on pets, but approval must be obtained from the *Department of Environmental Health* (649-946-2152) at least two weeks prior to arrival. All pets must be declared and have a recent bill of health (dated within one month of the date of your departure) from a certified veterinarian. Pets must also have a recent rabies shot. The importation of controlled drugs and pornography is illegal in the Turks and Caicos Islands.

Anyone over the age of 17 may bring certain items duty free including personal effects such as wearing apparel and ship's stores. If you are staying seven days or less each crew member is permitted 50 cigarettes, 25 cigarillos, or 60 grams of smoking tobacco, plus one liter of wine (less than 25% alcohol by volume), or .5 liters of potable spirits. If you are staying in the country for less than 24 hours you are permitted 25 cigarettes, 12 cigarillos, 6 cigars, or 30 grams of smoking tobacco. Crew who are staying in the Turks and Caicos Islands for more than 7 days receive the full statutory allowance of tobacco and spirits: 1 liter of alcohol or 2 liters of wine, 200 cigarettes, 100 cigarillos, 50 cigars or 125 grams of pipe tobacco. Fifty grams of perfume or .25 liters of toilet water is also permitted.

Dutiable goods, up to a value of $200.00 and purchased outside the Turks and Caicos, may be brought in by visitors as gifts and must be declared when clearing in. Persons arriving in the islands with the intention of working are allowed to bring in personal effects duty free, providing they intend to remain in the islands not less than 12 months. Duties on imported goods run in the neighborhood of 10%-33% depending on the particular item.

In the spring of 1998, the government of the Turks and Caicos dropped all duties on computer products so you might not have to pay duty for parts shipped into the country. For more information you may telephone the Collector of Customs on Grand Turk at 649-946-1176, 649-946-1805, or 649-338-2426.

Departure Tax

There is a $35 departure tax when flying out of the Turks and Caicos Islands.

eSeaClear/Sail Clear

eSeaClear has been replaced by Sail Clear which is a service that provides vessel operators the ability to submit electronic notifications of arrival to participating *Customs* offices in the Caribbean. Registered users can access the system via the Internet to enter and maintain information about their vessel and crew. Prior to arrival at a new country the vessel operator simply insures that the information is accurate and submits a new notification. Upon arrival, *Customs* can access the notification information to process your clearance more efficiently and without the need for the Ship's Master to fill out the declaration forms. Sail Clear is now operating in the Cayman Islands, Grenada, St. Kitts, Nevis, Montserrat, Anguilla, Curaçao, Bermuda, St. Lucia, the BVI's, Dominica and the Turks and Caicos.

Dominican Republic

Ports of Entry
Barahona, Manzanillo, Luperón, Cofresi (*Ocean World Marina*), Puerto Plata, Samaná, *Puerto Bahia Marina*, Salinas, Santo Domingo, Boca Chica, Casa de Campo

Firearms

Firearms must be declared upon arrival and the *Commandante* will keep them for you until you are ready to depart DR waters. Pets must have a valid rabies inoculation and a health certificate.

In 2009, the Dominican Republic passed a new law that pertains to cruisers arriving and clearing in at marinas only. The law states that only two officials may board your vessel and they are not permitted to ask for compensation of any sort. After the officials leave you must go to the *Immigration* office to have your passports stamped. For a typical 90-day stay some new fees have been set up. The vessel must pay 5% of the dockage fee as a tax and 2% of any fuel bill as a tax.

In most places the officials involved with clearance will come aboard your vessel (and no, they will not remove their shoes in most instances) to grant clearance and inspect your vessel. Generally, but not always, you will be visited by *Immigration, Customs, Agriculture, Drug Enforcement* (you are permitted to accompany this official as they inspect your vessel), the Dominican *Coast Guard (Marina de Guerra)*, and occasionally *M-2*, the *Dominican Intelligence Agency*.

If you opt to clear at a government dock you will also deal with someone representing *Portuario* (*Ports*). I have experienced *Ports* trying to hit me up for a fee when I cleared at Luperón, you must be careful and not be afraid to say "No." You may even be asked for a tip for the *Commandante* or for a T-shirt.

If you clear at a marina you will pay more for their services since they are taking care of everything for you. You will still be boarded by a gang of officials.

Pets

Pets are permitted in the DR though you will be asked for a health certificate in some places.

The Dominican Republic requires that vessels transiting her waters obtain a *despacho* for moving from one harbor to the next (obtained from the *Marina de Guerra*). If you ask for a *despacho* with *puntos intermedios* you will not get one. That means if you go from Samaná to Cap Cana you cannot stop anywhere in between unless it is a "rest stop," a provisioning stop, bad weather, or the stop is required for "repairs." A *despacho* will not be issued for harbors that are NOT a port of entry. You must also obtain a *despacho* when you clear out.

Dinghy Safety

Most cruisers spend a considerable amount of time in their dinghies exploring the waters and islands in the vicinity of their anchorage. It is not unknown for a dinghy engine to fail or a skipper to run out of gas miles away from the mother vessel. For this reason I urge boaters to carry some simple survival gear in their dinghies. First, I would recommend a handheld VHF radio for obvious reasons. If there are any other boats around this may be your best chance for getting some assistance. A good anchor and plenty of line are also high on the list. I do not mean one of those small three pound anchors with thirty feet of line that is only used on the beach to keep your dinghy from drifting to Cuba. It may pay to sacrifice the onboard room and use a substantial anchor with a couple of feet of chain and at least 100' of line. Just as you would go oversize on your mother vessel do the same with your dinghy. If you are being blown away from land a good anchor and plenty of line gives you a good chance of staying put where someone may find you.

Next, a dinghy should have a supply of flares. Local boaters often carry a large coffee can with a rag soaked in oil lying in the bottom. If they get in trouble lighting the rag will produce an abundant amount of smoke that can be seen from a quite a distance. A dinghy should be equipped with survival water, a bottle or some small packages manufactured by a company called *DATREX*. It would be a good idea to throw in a few *MRE*'s. These are the modern, tastier version of *K-Rations* that our armed forces survived on for years. Each *MRE* also contains vital survival components such as matches and toilet paper. Another handy item that does not take up much room is a foil survival blanket. They really work and take up as much space as a couple of packs of cigarettes.

Please don't laugh at these suggestions. I have seen people forced to spend a night or two in a dinghy and these few items would have made their experience much more pleasant if not entirely unnecessary. I have run out of gas and used flares to attract some local attention even though one of my boat mates was ready to dive in and swim for the nearest island to fetch some help. Now, I never leave in my dinghy without my little survival bag stashed away in the dink. It doesn't take much effort to prepare a small bag for your dinghy and it will be worth its weight in gold should you need it.

One final word, if you find the need to skirt a large sandbank lying to leeward of a cay remember that even though the sandbanks stretch out quite a way to the west, there is usually a channel of slightly deeper water nearer the shoreline of the cays.

Diving

From shallow water reef dives to deep water wall drop-offs, the diving in the Turks and Caicos Islands is as good as it gets anywhere and much better than most places. You don't need scuba equipment to enjoy the undersea delights that are available; many reefs lie in less than 30' and are easily accessible to those with snorkels, dinghies, and curiosity.

Providenciales is a hotbed of diving activity with more than a half-dozen different diving shops offering dive trips, charters, and complete instructions. Here you can dive with *Dive Provo*, *Art Pickering's Turtle Divers*, *Flamingo Divers*, *Beaches Resort*, *Club Med*, and *Caicos Adventures*. For those wishing a longer dive, the liveaboard dive boat *Turks and Caicos Aggressor* is based at *Turtle Cove Marina*, while Peter Hughes' *Sea Dancer* is based out of the *Caicos Marina and Shipyard* (800-9DANCER).

In the waters between *Grace Bay* and Pine Cay you'll find wonderful spur & groove coral reefs, which consist of central reefs with arm-like lateral extensions and grooves. The spur and groove coral generally runs perpendicular to the wall, which runs parallel to the shoreline. West Caicos is known for its many great dives just off its dramatic limestone cliffs. In *Sapodilla Bay* you'll find the 65' M/V *Island Diver* offering snorkel and SCUBA trips. For more on

Island Diver and their *Ocean Outback* services visit their web site at http://www.oceanoutback.com/.

Grand Turk represents a wealth of tremendous experiences for the diver. Less than a quarter of a mile off shore and starting in just 25'-45' of water, a coral wall runs the full length of the island, with profiles ranging from steeply sloping terrain to interesting coral undercuts and perfectly vertical drop-offs.

The sponge growth and fish populations are spectacular and distinctively different from the other Turks and Caicos sites. You can expect manta rays in the summer, turtles year-round and humpback whales in the winter, this is a primary corridor for migrating humpback whales from December through April.

Some of the world's best wall diving can be found within 300 yards of the western shore of Grand Turk. Here coral cliffs drop from 30' below the surface to over 7,000' deep. Mooring buoys protect the delicate coral structure and there are several dive operations working these waters. In Grand Turk try *Blue Water Divers*, *Sea Eye Divers*, or *Oasis Divers*, all located on Front Street in Cockburn Town.

Although the waters in The Turks and Caicos are crystal clear and the obstructions plainly visible in the ambient light, divers must take proper precautions when diving in areas of current. Experienced divers are well aware of this, but it must be stated for novices and snorkelers. Tidal fluctuations can produce strong currents that must be taken into account when diving. Waves breaking over and around inshore reefs can create strong surges that can push or pull you into some very sharp coral. Only experienced divers should penetrate wrecks and caves.

Most of the dive sites in the Turks and Caicos have moorings installed by the *National Parks Committee* and maintained by the many dive boats that use them. Please do your part to protect these fragile coral eco-systems and don't anchor on the reefs; anchor nearby in sand, it holds better anyway.

While summer waters run about 82°F-84°F at the surface, it is certainly warm enough for swimsuits though most divers welcome protection in the form of a light cover-up. In the winter, water temperatures of 74°F-78°F would suggest the use of a wetsuit. Dive computers are an advantage owing to the multi-level nature of the diving in the Turks and Caicos.

A must for divers in the Turks and Caicos Islands is the *Diving, Snorkeling, & Visitors Guide to the Turks and Caicos Islands* by Captain Bob Gascoine. Bob is the dean of all Turks Islands divers and his excellent guide has loads of useful information about the cays as well as about the diving surrounding them.

Fishing

The drop-offs around the Turks and Caicos Islands offer fishing that is as good as it gets anywhere. The annual mid-summer *Caicos Classic IGFA Billfish Release Tournament* (http://caicosclassic.tc/) results in a great number of billfish including blue marlin and swordfish being weighed-in. In 1996 for example, a 599 lb. blue marlin was hauled in, the largest ever caught in the Turks and Caicos Islands. Of course you can also find dolphin, wahoo, kings, yellowfin, and bonita in large numbers when trolling offshore. The *Caicos Banks* are ideal bonefishing grounds and there are several guides on Provo.

There are several different categories of fishing permits. Most visiting skippers only need a regular sportfishing license. Tournaments and charter sportfishing boats have separate categories. If you intend to fish on the *Mouchoir Banks* you will need a special permit for that privilege. A regular sportfishing permit cost $15 for thirty days and is renewable. They can be purchased at the *DECR*, the *Department of the Environment and Coastal Resources* (sometimes just referred to as *Fisheries*), upstairs from the *Public Treasury* in Provo or at their office on Grand Turk. Licenses can also be picked up at *Turtle Cove Marina* ($16 as of this writing) at Sellar's Pond on Provo, and at *J & B Tours* at *Leeward Marina,* also on Provo. Remember that you are not allowed to fish within the boundaries of any national park in the Turks and Caicos Islands, and especially at the drop-off along the reefs bordering Provo.

Fishing permits are only valid for hook and line fishing, the use of spear guns, pole spears, and Hawaiian slings are not permitted in the Turks and Caicos Islands. Every July the *Minister* must go before the *Executive Council* to lift the ban on the use of hooks to catch lobsters for the local licensed commercial fishermen. This allows the commercial fellows to use a hook on the end of a pole to snag the lobster and also to have a Hawaiian sling in the water with them for protection (visiting skippers may also have a Hawaiian sling with them in the water for protection but if caught the burden is on you to prove its necessity; fines for violations of Turks and Caicos fishing regulations can go as high as $50,000 and/or 12 months in jail and yes, *Fisheries* does patrol their waters!).

Lobster and conch may not be taken from the waters of the Turks and Caicos by visitors to these islands. The use of SCUBA and hookah rigs for fishing are also not permitted in the Turks and Caicos Islands. Even with a fishing permit, you are only allowed 10 pounds of fish per day for consumption. In other words, you are not allowed to fill your freezer. Skippers holding a valid license may remove one fish from the Turks and Caicos for trophy mounting purposes.

Garbage

When I first began cruising I had this naive idea that all cruisers lived in a certain symbiosis with nature. My bubble finally burst with the bitter realization that many cruisers were infinitely worse than common litterbugs. So often they have the attitude of "out of sight, out of mind." I sometimes wonder if they believe in supernatural beings, hoping that if they dump their trash somewhere imaginary garbage fairies will come along and take care of the disposal problems for them. One cruiser leaves a few bags of garbage in some secluded (or not so secluded) spot and the next cruiser says "My, what a good spot for a garbage dump. Ethel, bring the garbage, I've found the dump!" This is why you often go ashore on otherwise deserted islands and find bags and piles of bags of garbage. Nothing is worse than entering paradise only to discover some lazy, ignorant, slob of a cruiser (no, I have not been too harsh on this type of person, I can still think of plenty of other adjectives without having to consult a thesaurus) has dumped his bags of garbage in the bushes. Please do not add to this problem. Remember, your garbage attracts all kinds of foul creatures such as rats (and other careless cruisers).

Nobody likes storing bags of smelly garbage aboard but if you cannot find a settlement nearby to take your garbage for free, you will have to make an allowance in your budget to pay for the local garbage disposal service. If you are nowhere near a garbage facility you should stow your trash aboard separated into three groups for easier disposal. First cans and bottles (wash them first to remove any smells), then into another container stow the organic stuff such as food scraps, rinds, and eggshells, and finally paper and plastic trash. Your food scraps, stored in a large coffee can with a lid, can be thrown overboard on an outgoing tide. Paper and plastic should be burned completely and the ashes buried deep and not on the beach. Cans and bottles should be punctured or broken and dumped overboard in very deep water at least a few miles offshore. Cut off both ends of the cans and break the bottles overboard as you sink them. If you cannot implement a garbage disposal policy aboard your vessel, stay home, don't come to these beautiful islands. Do not abuse what we use.

Ham Radio

The following is a listing of ham nets you may wish to participate in during your cruise through the waters of The Bahamas, the Turks and Caicos Islands, and the Dominican Republic.

Net Name	Time ET	Freq. KHz
Bah. Am. Radio Society	0830 Sundays	3,696
Bah. Wx Net	0720	3,696 or 7,096
Caribbean Net	1100-1200 UTC	7,420*
Computer Net	0900 Fridays	7,268
CW Net - slow	0630 M,W,F	7,128
CW Net - fast	0630 T, T, S, S	7,128
Hurricane Net	As needed	14,325; 14,275; 14175
Intercontinental	1100 UTC	14,300, 14216*
Maritime Mobile	After Intercon.	14,300, 14216*
TACARS	0800 Sundays	3,780
Waterway Net	0745	7,268

*This frequency changes often

All visitors to the Turks & Caicos Islands on production of a valid Amateur Radio License from their own country, with the necessary application form and fee, will receive a VP5/HomeCall License. Maritime Mobile visitors within 12 nautical miles of the Turks & Caicos Islands must apply for and have a Visitors License before operating

The Wireless Telegraphy (Amateur Radio Operator Licensing) Regulations 2004 designates the Turks and Caicos Amateur Radio Society, ("TACARS") as the certifying organization of qualified persons to operate amateur radio in the Turks & Caicos Islands. Qualified persons are those that hold a valid un-expired amateur license from another country and have complied with the necessary application processes. Additionally, residents who have passed a properly administered test of TACARS and have complied with the necessary application processes may also be qualified to operate amateur radio in the Turks and Caicos Islands. Every license issued is valid for the calendar year in which it is granted and expires on 31 December in that year (except special event licenses, see below).

Visitor's License

To get a visitor's license, you will need to submit a completed application form (you can download one at http://www.tacars.org/license.pdf), a copy of your current home amateur radio license, and a check payable to T.A.C.A.R.S. for $35.00 in U.S. currency (if a Special Event license is requested include an additional $35.00). Send all of this via *FedEx* to Jody Millspaugh (the *FedEx* recipient phone number is 649-946-4436), *Cherokee Road,* Providenciales, Turks and Caicos Islands, B.W.I.

If you wish to check on the status of your application via the Internet, Jody's email address is jody@carbisurf.com. Reciprocal licenses may be collected by the operator upon arrival in Providenciales or Jody will send you a copy prior to your departure, your regular license will still need to be picked up in person after your arrival in Provo. You can phone Jody Milspaugh, VP5JM, at 649-946-4436 to arrange for pickup. If you arrive in the Provo without a reciprocal, you can call Jody at the above mentioned number and she will arrange to meet you so you may apply for your license. Jody will give you a receipt that will allow you to transmit until your regular license arrives.

The Turks and Caicos do not have a third-party agreement with the United States; this means that you cannot make a phone patch from the Turks and Caicos Islands to the U.S.

Amateur radio operators visiting the Dominican Republic can get a 30-day reciprocal (HI) for no charge upon clearing in.

Holidays

The following public holidays are observed in the Turks and Caicos:

New Year's Day - January 1
Commonwealth Day (March; date varies)
Good Friday
Easter Sunday
Easter Monday
National Hero's Day (May; date varies)
Her Majesty The Queen's Official Birthday (usually the second Sunday)
Emancipation Day - August 1
National Youth Day (September; date varies)
Columbus Day
International Human Rights Day - October 24
Christmas Day
Boxing Day - December 26

Holidays that fall on Sunday are always observed on Monday. Holidays that fall on Saturday are also usually observed on Monday. The following public holidays are observed in the Dominican Republic:

New Year's Day - January 1
Epiphany - January 6 (usually celebrated on the closest Friday or Monday)
Our Lady of Altagracia Day - January 21
Juan Pablo Duarte's Birthday - January 26 (usually celebrated on the closest Friday or Monday)
Independence Day - February 27
Good Friday
Easter Sunday
Easter Monday
Labor Day - May 1
Ascension Day - varies
Feast of Corpus Christi - varies in May and June
Restoration of the Republic Day - August 16
Our Lady of Mercedes Day - September 24
Columbus Day
Christmas Day

Dominicans love festivals and the calendar year has several for you to enjoy. Carnival in Santo Domingo takes place along the Santo Domingo Malecón the week of February 27 during the *Independence Day* celebrations. The famous *Merengue Festival* is a lively celebration of the country's national music, with *Merengue* bands performing at most major hotels and along the Santo Domingo Malecón. This huge party takes place from the last week in July through the first week of August.

The term *Merengue* refers both to the music and the dance, which evolved in the Dominican countryside among the happy people of a divided island. The history of the *Merengue* is woven into the fabric of Dominican history itself. This Afro-Caribbean dance became part of country life and is still danced today around the squares of small villages, next to bonfires on secluded beaches, in ballrooms, and in nightclubs throughout the world. In the traditional countryside settings, the music is provided by a *Perico Ripiao*, a small band made up of an accordion, a drum, a guiro and a box bass. Puerto Plata's *Merengue Festival* is held during the second week of October. Christmas celebrations begin in early December and end on *Epiphany Day* on January 6.

One of the biggest celebrations in Luperón is the huge *St. Patrick's Day* party, a great mix of locals and cruisers which has started drawing crowds of 1,000. There's music and a pig roast on the beach and each boat contributes a few pesos to cover the cost of the food they eat.

Hurricane Holes

THERE IS NO SUCH THING AS A HURRICANE HOLE! There is no anchorage so secure that it cannot be decimated by a strong hurricane and a high storm surge. There are no guarantees; there is no Fort Knox to hide in when a named windstorm threatens. Now, with that out of the way we can discuss how to protect yourself in those special places that offer the best hurricane protection. Let's begin our discussion with what constitutes protection and pass along a few hints as to how to secure yourself as well as get along with your neighbors.

First, make sure your fuel is topped off and you have enough food and water for an extended period. Also, make sure you have enough cash to see you through as phone lines may be down for a while which would prohibit credit card usage. Once your tanks, lockers, and wallet are topped off, you can head for protection. Some skippers prefer to head to sea when a hurricane threatens. Some will take off at a ninety-degree angle from the hurricane's forecast path, usually heading south to Venezuela. I cannot advise you as to what course to take, but I for one, unless absolutely necessary, will not gamble with racing a storm that is unpredictable (no matter what the forecasters claim).

For protection, most of us would prefer a narrow creek that winds deep into the mangroves where we will be as snug as the proverbial bug-in-a-rug. These creeks are rare, and to be assured of space you must get there early. When a storm threatens, you can bet that everybody will soon be aware of it and the early birds will settle in the best places. Sure, those early birds might have to spend a night or two in the hot, buggy mangroves, but isn't that better than coming in too late and finding the best spots taken and your choices for protection down to anchoring in the middle of a pond with a bit of fetch and no mangroves to offer protection? Hint number one...get to safety early and secure your vessel.

So how do you secure your vessel? Easy! First, find a likely looking spot where you'll be safest from the oncoming winds. Try to figure out by the forecast path of the storm where the wind will be coming from as the storm passes and plan accordingly (remember that the winds blow counterclockwise around the center in the northern hemisphere). If your chosen spot is in a creek that is fine. Set out bow and stern anchors and tie off your vessel to the mangroves on each side with as many lines as you can, including lines off the bow and stern to assist the anchors. Use plenty of chafe gear (I like old fire-hose, leather, and towels) as the lines lead off your boat and rig your lines so that they don't work back and forth on the mangroves as well. If chain can be used to surround the mangroves that will help. If other boats wish to proceed further up the creek past your position, remove your lines from one side of your boat to allow them to pass. Courtesy amongst endangered vessels will add to the safety factor of all involved, especially if somebody needs to come to somebody else's aid later on.

If your only choice is to head into the mangroves bow or stern first, always go in bow first; it stands to reason that if you place your stern into the mangroves serious rudder damage could result. I prefer to go bow-in as far as I can, until my boat settles her keel in the mud (trying to keep the bow just out of contact with the mangroves), tie off well, and set out at least two stern anchors. If other boats will be tying off into the mangroves in the same manner on each side of you, courtesy dictates each skipper assist the other in the setting of anchors (so that they don't snag on each other) and the securing of lines in the mangroves (and don't forget to put out fenders).

If you must anchor in the open, away from the mangroves, place your anchors to give you 360° protection. The greatest danger to your vessel will likely be the other boats around you, and in the Caribbean there's going to be a better than average chance that you'll be sharing your hole with several unattended boats, often times charter boats that are not secured in the best of manners. A good lookout is necessary for these added dangers.

Once secure, your next step is to strip everything off your boat and stow it below. Sails, bimini top, dodger, awnings, rail-mounted grill, wind-generators, solar panels, jerry cans, and anything small and loose that can become a dangerous object should it fly away at a hundred plus miles an hour. And, don't forget to secure your dinghy as well! Keep a mask and snorkel handy in the cockpit, you might need it to stand watch. Also, keep a sharp knife close at hand; you never know when you might need it. Pack all your important papers in a handy waterproof container, and in the most severe of circumstances, use duct tape to secure your passport, wallet, and/or purse to your body. Plan ahead as you secure your vessel so that you will not have to go on deck if you don't absolutely have to, it is most difficult to move about in 100-knot winds.

If you are going to be cruising in The Bahamas from June through November, hurricane season, you should always keep a lookout for a safe hurricane hole. In the northern and central Bahamas you're never too far away from some sort of refuge, some holes are better than others but like the old adage advises: Any port in a storm. With that in mind let me offer a few of the places I consider hurricane holes. Bear in mind that if you ask ten different skippers what they look for in a hurricane hole you're likely to get ten different answers. Some of these holes may not meet your requirements. I offer them only for your consideration when seeking safety for your vessel. The final decision is yours and yours alone. For the best information concerning hurricane holes always check with the locals. They'll know the best spots.

The Southern Bahamas

If you are cruising the southern Bahamas from Crooked-Acklins to Mayaguana or Inagua you will not find a truly safe hole. Although I have heard about a large sailboat riding out *Hurricane Klaus* lying between Samana and Propeller Cay I would not attempt to test my luck. I would head to better protection at George Town, Exuma.

The Turks and Caicos Islands

In the Caicos Islands, Providenciales offers several dredged canals that offer an opportunity to get well inland, hopefully away from any damaging seas though you may still be affected by a storm surge. On the south side of Providenciales, the canals at *Cooper Jack Bight* are a favorite place for local boaters and are well protected. A 6½' draft can enter here at high water. Bear in mind that when anchoring in any of the dredged canals around Provo, that the bottom will likely be poor holding; you'll have to set some of your anchors on shore here.

A small, narrow, shallow canal, leads northward from *Caicos Marina and Shipyard* to some private residences in the *Long Bay Hills* section of Provo and offers excellent protection but draft is limited to 3'-4' at low water; the canal entrance, through a small bascule bridge, prohibits wide multihull vessels.

In Leeward Going Through there is a small canal leading into the Leeward community. The bar at the entrance restricts entry to vessels with drafts of less than 5' at high tide. Leeward Going Through has often been used as a hurricane hole by some skippers and should also be considered as well as the cuts between Pine Cay and Fort George Cay, Ft. George Cay and Dellis Cay, and between Dellis Cay and Parrot Cay. A word of warning about the tides here during hurricanes. When a storm surge approaches from the south across the banks, the water rushes in the southern sides of these cuts at a good clip. One past hurricane raised the water level in Leeward Going Through by over 6'. You can probably imagine the current involved with the movement of that much water, so use extreme care when securing your vessel. On the northern shore, folks were walking around in knee-deep water in the central portion of *Turtle Cove Marina* during *Hurricane Frances* in 2004, that's an approximate surge of 6'-8'.

On the northern shore of Providenciales, skippers should consider *Sellar's Pond* and *Turtle Cove Marina*, a very well protected spot. But check with the marina first for space availability; they might not want to take on any other boats. Just west of *Sellar's Pond* is small *Thompson's Cove*, a private dredged community with a sign warning that all unauthorized boats will be removed. Drafts of less than 5' can work their way in here on a high tide. There are several undeveloped lots and if one did not have permission to tie up inside, one would have to hope that the landowners would understand that a life threatening storm chased you inside and you would not leave until the danger passed. As well protected as *Thompson Cove* is, I would probably make it my last choice.

Shallow draft boats, those with drafts of less than 3', could work their way into some of the creeks between North Caicos, Middle Caicos, and East Caicos if needed. South Caicos' Cockburn Harbour is excellent in most conditions but it is unsuitable to me as a hurricane shelter.

In the Turks Islands, the only choice for shelter is to round the northern tip of Grand Turk and seek shelter inside North Creek if conditions allow entry (see text in *Part II, The Turks Islands, Grand Turk, The North Creek Anchorage*). The entrance channel is limited to about 6½' on a normal high tide but once inside the water deepens to over 12' in places. There is quite a bit of north/south fetch to take into consideration.

The Dominican Republic

Along the northern shore of the Dominican Republic the best hurricane hole is in the harbor at Luperón, which is probably one of the best hurricane holes in the entire Caribbean.

Although the rivers on the southern shore of the Dominican Republic look inviting and offer good protection, caution must be exercised as torrential rains will cause flooding and very strong currents, not to mention all manner of flotsam and jetsam floating down on you.

JoJo the Dolphin

JoJo is a very, very unique Atlantic bottlenose dolphin. Since 1980 JoJo has been plying the waters of the Turks and Caicos Islands centering on the Provo area. This friendly dolphin has become a powerful symbol for nature conservation in the Turks and Caicos Islands.

JoJo is one of the few dolphins around the world who have chosen to voluntarily interact with human beings in his own natural habitat. Much loved by the islanders, the government has proclaimed JoJo a National Treasure and in 1987 appointed a special Warden, Dean Bernal, to protect him. Dean first met

JoJo and Dean

JoJo in 1985 when JoJo began following Dean on his long swims out to the reefs off Providenciales. At that time JoJo was already a popular figure along the beachfront but he was known to bite people and he had a dangerous reputation. What most people did not know is that JoJo only bit those who tried to touch him as he cavorted in the shallows. It seems that for some wild dolphins, a human's attempt to touch the mammal is considered a threat and JoJo was simply defending himself.

At the time, Dean was employed as a Dive Instructor on Providenciales and each day after Dean's dive instructions, usually about 5:00 P.M., JoJo and Dean would begin their reef swim. They would swim out to the reef where Dean would meet a dive boat to conduct a night dive, and then Dean and JoJo would swim back to shore in the dark. Their nightly dives became a regular part of Dean's daily regimen and the relationship between Dean and JoJo grew stronger steadily. If JoJo showed up before the SCUBA lessons ended, he would playfully pull on Dean's regulator hose trying to drag him away from his students. Sometimes he would swim in high-speed circles around the group, effectively reducing the visibility to zero and canceling the instruction. Occasionally he would patiently wait, hovering just over Dean's shoulder, for the lessons to end. One time JoJo herded an 8' shark into the middle of the group to break up the day's class. Knowing that Dean will stay in the water with him for hours when they are with other marine life, JoJo has brought Dean fish, lobsters, turtles, manta rays, whale sharks, an occasional bull and nurse shark, and he has even herded in a baby humpback whale along with its mother. JoJo's playful antics are often aimed at others. Quite often water skiers in the waters off Provo would suddenly find themselves paddling water. JoJo likes to come up underneath the ski and butt it skyward throwing the skier. JoJo once took a diver's $3,000 camera and hid it in the reef but playfully returned it 15 minutes later.

Through patient observation since 1987, Dean has compiled an impressive collection of data providing a rare and complete look into a wild dolphin's life in the open ocean. Diaries, data sheets, video and film materials now form a library and a wealth of information on the behavior of dolphins in their natural habitat. Dean has been fortunate to witness and document JoJo's behavior and interaction with whales, sharks, manta rays, other dolphins, numerous other forms of marine life, submarines, people and even terrestrial animals. Over the years, Dean has documented JoJo's growth through puberty, his competing for his position in a pod, his sickness and his well-being. Because of the Dean's ongoing *Dolphin Project*, the development of trust in his and JoJo's relationship, and Dean's position as a Warden, JoJo's life has been saved on numerous occasions. Dean has been able to treat JoJo's wounds caused by such incidents as entanglement in turtle nets, infections from stingray barbs, confrontations with sharks, and impacts from water ski boats. Dean has contacted *Club Med* about putting guards on their ski boats at a cost of about $200. *Club Med* refused and hired a lawyer for $400 to fight the case. Doesn't make sense, does it? It shows where *Club Med's* priorities lie. JoJo's first and worst injury came from a jet ski and Dean is fighting the new PWC rental business that just opened in Leeward Going Through.

As JoJo grows older, Dean's research is becoming far more complex. Since JoJo has expanded his 26-square mile home range around Provo to 260 miles (in 1997 JoJo was seen off Grand Turk, thirty miles across the deep Columbus Passage), it makes the research much more challenging, not to mention interesting and rewarding. JoJo is now mating and travelling with other dolphins intermittently, finding new feeding grounds, utilizing new habitats and migratory routes, and continuing to expand his experiences of what a young free-roaming, wild dolphin should be living and experiencing.

Thanks to the *JoJo Dolphin Project (http://www.marinewildlife.org/jojoproject.php)* the importance of this information from a conservation and animal welfare perspective has given Dean the opportunity to develop his work into a full-time research project. Never before has the chance to learn about the behavior, interaction, health, habitat and needs of a single wild dolphin been so clearly available for study. The information is vital to the conservation of all dolphins because it provides a rare, intimate and relatively complete look at the dolphin's life in the wild.

JoJo is easily recognized. JoJo prefers the waters between *Grace Bay* and Pine Cay on the northern shore of Providenciales, but may be seen just about anywhere. If a dolphin approaches your vessel, sticking his head out of the water to look at you, or perhaps circling your boat at anchor, the chances are that this is JoJo. If you're diving and a large dolphin approaches you it will likely be JoJo. JoJo has numerous prop marks and scars on his body and fins and this makes him almost unmistakable.

JoJo has been known to approach divers very closely, getting as close as a foot or two away to satisfy his curiosity. If you are in the water and JoJo appears, there are several things you need to remember for your protection and his. First, understand that although JoJo is a wild creature, he is capable of expressing his feelings and his personality as well as aggression and anger. Never reach out to touch him, especially around the blowhole at the top of his head; this is his nose and he breathes through it. Do not approach JoJo, remain passive and let him come to you. Don't swim after him, he might perceive it as a threat and act defensively. If provoked he may bite or use his tail to slap you. If JoJo shows any behavior that you are uncomfortable with, do not panic; exit slowly from the water. Dean reminds us not to lie on our backs in the water as JoJo gets unpredictable at this. Actually he gets very amorous (if you follow my drift). He once tried to mate with the SCUBA tank of a female dive instructor I know in Provo.

JoJo is now a commercial entity as well. You can choose from the *JoJo Collection* of jewelry at the *Royal Jewels Duty Free* shop in Provo.

Medical Emergencies

The Turks and Caicos Islands

Provo has a few medical centers to fill most any need. On Leeward Highway is the Menzies Medical Practice, phone 941-4242/4321, email menzies@tciway.tc, and Grace Bay Medical Center, phone 941-5252. Here are three full-time physicians, a dentist, an optometrist, a chiropractor, a psychologist, and a pharmacy. Services include an emergency room and ambulance, general family practice, and trauma care. Divers will be happy to know that Menzies has a hyperbaric chamber on site staffed by trained personnel. Menzies offers a Florida lab linkup and obstetric ultrasound. The Myrtle Rigby Health Clinic (941-3000) is a government run facility with a full-time physician and nursing staff that is also located on Leeward Highway. Rigby's offers family practice, X-ray, obstetrics and ultra-sound, lab services, casualty reception, and a maternity unit. The New Era Medical Centre (941-5455/3233) is located in Blue Hills and is staffed by one doctor offering family practice, a pharmacy, lab, emergency defibrillation and EKG units, delivery and post-natal care. New Era is open 24 hours and monitors VHF ch. 82. Other medical services include Dr. Steve Bourne (231-0000; bourne@tciway.tc), Dr. Dawn O'Sullivan (231-1350, dawnos@tciway.tc); the Associated Medical Practices on Leeward Highway in Provo (946-4242); Dental Services Ltd. (946-4321), an optometrist (941-5842), and a chiropractor, Dr. Kathleen Sims (941-3391). If you need a veterinarian call Which Doctor on VHF ch. 16, or call 946-4353.

On North Caicos there are three government clinics at Bottle Creek, Kew (https://www.visittci.com/kew-clinic), and Sandy Point. There are two resident nurses and three nurse's aides, and a government doctor visits weekly. Two environmental health officers work weekdays from 0800 to 1630. In case of emergency call 941-3000 or 946-5422.

There is a clinic on South Caicos (946-3216) with a visiting doctor and two full-time nurses (https://www.visittci.com/south-caicos-clinic).

On Middle Caicos there is a government clinic at Conch Bar (946-6985) with a trained nurse. At Lorimars and Bambarra there are community health aids. A doctor visits every two weeks.

On Grand Turk you will find the *Grand Turk Hospital* (946-2040/2110) north of the *Front Street Anchorage*. The hospital is staffed by four physicians and can handle emergency cases, general medicine, surgery, geriatric care, obstetrics, and pediatrics. Also on Grand Turk is the government-run *Downtown Clinic* (946-2328) open from 0800 to 1230 and from 1400 to 1630.

You will find that all government offices, from post offices to these government clinics are all closed for lunch from 1230 to 1400. Just south of Grand Turk at Salt Cay you will find a government clinic (946-6985) with a full-time nurse and a doctor that visits every two weeks.

National Air Ambulance (http://www.nationaljets.com/air-ambulance.html) out of Ft. Lauderdale, Florida (954-359-9900 or 800-327-3710), can transport patients from the Turks and Caicos to the United States. You might also try *AAA Air Ambulance*; call collect to 612-479-8000. If you join *DAN*, the *Divers Alert Network*, for a small yearly fee you are covered under their *Assist America Plan*. This program offers emergency evacuation for any accident or injury, diving related or not, to the nearest facility that can provide you with adequate care. After you have been stabilized to the satisfaction of the attending physician and the *Assist America* doctor, *Assist America* will arrange your transportation back to the United States, under medical supervision if necessary.

The Dominican Republic

In the DR, the phone number for a medical emergency is 911, but don't count on it working all the time. Most medical centers are bi-lingual, many accept international insurance, and the costs can be 1/3 of the prices in the U.S. All the clinics are free to residents of the Dominican Republic and cruisers, but the more serious medical problems, such as those that require a visit or a stay at one of the hospitals in Puerto Plata or Santiago can cost quite a bit. Most medical insurance is accepted throughout the DR and drugs that can only be acquired by prescription in the US, are available without a prescription in the DR, and most are very inexpensive. It helps to know the Spanish translation of the drug when you head for the *pharmacia*.

There is a medical clinic in Luperón where two of the three doctors in residence speak passable English. The clinic is located at the end of *Calle Luperón*, two blocks south of *Verizon* and then three blocks southwest. While the clinic can deal with most basic health problems, for testing you will be referred to the *Laboratory Luperón*, just across from the *guagua park*. If you have your samples in before 1200 you can usually get the results by 1700. If you need a dentist try the *Medicon Dental Implant Center, Independencia No. 9*, (phone 888-848-7639, ext: 24368).

If you need medical attention in Puerto Plata visit *Centro Médico Bournigal* (809-586-2342, Fax: 809-586-6104 or email them at info@bournigal-hospital.com, http://www.centromedicobournigal.com/).

In Santiago you can find medical attention at *HOMS*, the *Hospital Metropolitano de Santiago, Duarte Highway* Km 2.8 (829-947-2222 Ext. 5000, Fax: 829-947-2223, or you can reach them by email at info@homshospital.com, http://www.homshospital.com/).

In Sosúa or Cabarete you can visit the *Medical Center Carretera Sosua-Cabarete* Km 1, Sosúa, 809-571-4696, or you can reach them by email at cmc.sosua@gmail.com. In Cabarete visit *Servi-Med* Dr. Gidion or Dr. Naurio Carretera, *Cabarete 25* (809-571-2903). If you need a vet in Sosúa or Cabarete, visit *Dr. Bob's*, on the main road from Sosúa to Cabarete. (24-hour phone number 809-430-5503). After *El Choco Road* you will come to a *Coastal* gas station, just past the station is the *Dr. Bob's* sign.

In Samaná, Dominican Republic, quality medical care can be found at the *Centro Medico de Especialidades Samaná* (with ambulance service), located at *Calle Coronel Andrés Díaz No.06*, phone: 809-538-3999, 809-538-3888, or fax them at 809 538-2424 (http://cmes.com.do/). The *International Medical Center* (info@internationalmedicalcenter.com) is located in the *Plaza Pueblo Principe*, Local 4, in the heart of downtown Samaná and is open 24/7 (809-552-1117, Fax: 809-538 2675). If you need a dentist in Samaná, visit Dr. Elizabeth Frias de Martinez, her clinic (*Miami Family Dental*) is located at *Calle Peter Vander Horst No.2* (809-538-3180, Cell: 809-988-1705.

In Santo Domingo, *Clinica Abreau*, (http://clinicaabreu.com.do/) at *Calle Arzobispo Portes No. 853*, has 24-hour emergency service and free treatment for foreigners (809-688-4411). the *El Hospital Docente Padre Billinil* is located on *Calle Padre Billini y Santomé, Zona Colonial*, and offers free consultations (809-333-5656). If you need an ambulance call *Movi-Med Ambulance Evacuation Service* at 809-532-0000.

National Parks

One of the largest misrepresentations that visiting cruisers have of the Turks and Caicos concerns its national parks system. I consistently hear misinformed cruisers moaning and groaning to themselves, and others, that they cannot anchor or fish in the Turks and Caicos Islands because of the many national parks. The worst part is that they often impart their lack of knowledge to other cruisers, who may be considering a Turks and Caicos cruise, often ruining their cruise before it even begins.

In 1992, the Government of the Turks and Caicos Islands created a national park system and set aside 33 specific protected areas to protect their scenic environments and habitats, both to preserve and conserve them for future generations as well as make them available for public recreation. The listing includes 11 national parks, 11 nature reserves, 4 sanctuaries and 7 historical sites totaling more than 325 square miles. Two hundred and ten square miles of this total amount are sensitive and ecologically essential wetlands ratified under the Switzerland based *International Ramsar Bureau*. Some of these protected areas include marine replenishment areas as well as breeding grounds for turtles, seabirds and other creatures. All the national parks are under the supervision of the *DECR*.

The Turks and Caicos have five different classifications for their protected areas. At the top of the list is the *UNESCO* (*United Nation Educational, Scientific, and Cultural Organization*) *Heritage Site*. Next is the *National Park* allowing access, recreation, and some development. A *Nature Reserve* allows limited use, recreation, and development. A *Sanctuary* does not allow development and only allows limited access with a permit issued by the *DECR*. A *Historical Site* allows access and limited development. For a complete listing of all protected sites in the Turks and Caicos Islands see *Appendix E: Listing of Protected Areas*. If you are unsure if you are within the boundaries of any protected area, please check this listing.

Vessels under 60' in length may anchor in any national park on any clear sand bottom. Damaging any coral by misuse of your anchoring privileges may result in a fine. Vessels over 60 in length may not anchor or take a mooring. Moorings must be vacated at the request of a dive boat. If bad weather is threatening or repairs must be made, vessels over 60' may anchor anywhere except in coral. Water skiing and jet skis are not permitted in any protected area in the Turks and Caicos Islands.

Phoning Home

The Turks and Caicos

Cable and Wireless, Ltd. International, handles all phone and fax communications in the islands. If you see what appears to be a pay phone booth, it is a card booth. There are no pay phones on any of the islands. These phone booths take either *MasterCard*, *Visa*, *American Express*, or local *Cable and Wireless* phone cards. Phone cards can be purchased at the *Cable and Wireless* offices on *Leeward Highway* in Provo and on *Front Street* in Grand Turk in increments of $10-$25 (add $1 per $10 increment, a $10 card will actually cost you $11 and a $20 card, $22). Phone rates to the U.S. have dropped significantly.

Cruisers from North America who bring *TDMA* or *GSN* phones, and who have overseas roaming set up with *AT&T* or *Cingular*, will find that they can use their cell phones in the Turks and Caicos Islands. For more information about cell phone usage in the Turks and Caicos contact *Cable and Wireless* at 800-804-2994, or visit any of their offices, one is on *Leeward Highway* in Provo.

The area code for the Turks and Caicos is 649. Dial 119 for police, hospital, or fire.

The Dominican Republic

The DR's phone communications are handled by the privately owned telephone company *Claró*. Direct dialing to and from the DR is quick and easy using the 809 area code. The DR's phone system is one of the most sophisticated telecommunications systems in Latin America with capabilities such as international direct dialing, faxing, teleconferencing, electronic mail and now videoconferencing. The area codes for the Dominican Republic are 809, 829, and 849.

If you would like a cell phone while in the DR, there are several providers including *Claró*, *France Telecom* (*Orange*), *Tricom*, and *Centennial*.

The Dominican Republic postal service boasts over 190 branches and is the least expensive (although slowest) way of sending and receiving international mail. The postal service also has a higher priced express mail service similar to the *USPS Priority Mail*. Private couriers include *DHL*, *Fed Ex*, *UPS*, *CPS*, and several local P.O. Box courier services such as *Express Parcel Service*.

Provisioning

If you are on a tight budget, it might be best for you to stock up on provisions in the United States or at Puerto Plata or Santiago in the Dominican Republic prior to your Turks and Caicos cruise. Take enough for the length of your cruise and then some. Although the prices in the Dominican Republic are increasing, there are still plenty of deals to be had, especially on locally made products.

With few exceptions, prices in The Turks and Caicos are a little higher than American prices but generally lower than Bahamian prices on most goods. Food items are taxed in the Turks and Caicos. Beer and cigarette prices will seem outrageous with cigarette prices some 2-3 times higher than in the

States. The Dominican beer *El Presidente* is very good and more reasonably priced than foreign beers.

Rum, as one would think, can be very inexpensive while American whiskies and certain scotches are very high. Staples such as rice, beans, flour, and sugar are just slightly higher than U.S. prices. Vegetables can be quite reasonable in season. Meats, soft drinks, and milk all are considerably higher than in America. As you shop the various markets throughout the Turks and Caicos you will find some delightful items that are not sold in the U.S., foreign butter and meats, for example. The shopping experience will give you the opportunity to purchase and enjoy some new treats. Of course, the prices on fresh fish, conch, and lobster are all open to bargaining with the local fishermen, with the South Caicos fishermen giving you the best deal.

If you plan to dine out while in the islands, you will find the prices to be comparable to or higher than at home. I have found that it is difficult for two people to have a decent lunch in Provo with a couple of sodas or beers for under $20.00. It is common for dining establishments in the Turks and Caicos to include a 10%-15% gratuity on the check on top of the 10% government tax.

Radio and TV

The official Government radio station is *Radio Turks and Caicos* (FM) located on Grand Turk and broadcasting on 106 MHz with 7,000 watts of power 24 hours a day.

WIV-FM Radio on Providenciales broadcasts 24 hours a day on four FM stations with 500 watts of power. Local ads and community announcements are aired seven days a week at various times between 7am and 7pm. Stereo 92.5 MHz has contemporary easy rock, 90.5 MHz plays country and western music, 89.9 MHz plays classical music, and "soft sounds" is on 89.3 MHz.

WPRT Radio can be found on the FM band at 88.7 MHz broadcasting with 1,000 watts of power. They provide local programming and community announcements seven days a week and Gospel music on Sundays.

Also found on the FM band at 96.7 MHz with 1,000 watts is VIC FM Radio. This is a religious station broadcasting seven days a week with live programming on Sunday mornings and Wednesday and Sunday evenings.

There are 12 cable channels in Grand Turk and 42 in Provo, with some locally produced programs. However, you can only receive these if you are tied up at a marina that offers a cable service. There are no television broadcasting stations in the Turks and Caicos Islands.

There are over 120 AM radio stations in the Dominican Republic along with 6 HF stations, and 18 television stations scattered about.

Tides and Currents

When attempting to predict the state of the tide at any time other than at slack tide, you can use the *Rule of Twelfths* for a generally reliable accuracy. To do this, take the amount of tidal fluctuation and divide it into twelfths. For example, if high tide in Nassau is expected to be 3.0' and the low water datum is 0.0', the tidal fluctuation is 3', and each twelfth is 0.25' or 3". To predict the state of tide at different times you can use the *Rule of Twelfths* in the following table. The table is merely to demonstrate a point and uses an imaginary charted high tide of 3'. Always consult your chart tables or listen for tide information broadcasts and calculate accordingly.

Time of Low Water	Tide Datum - 0 Feet
1 hr after low, add 1/12	¼' above datum-3"
2 hr after low, add 3/12	¾' above datum-9"
3 hr after low, add 6/12	1½' above datum-18"
4 hr after low, add 9/12	2¼' above datum-27"
5 hr after low, add 11/12	2¾" above datum-33"
6 hr after low, add 12/12	High Water-3'*

*Caution: assumes a 3' tidal fluctuation.

Chart tables give the times and heights of high and low water but not the time of the turning of the tide or slack water. Usually there is little difference between the times of high and low water and the beginning of ebb or flood currents, but in narrow channels, landlocked harbors, or on tidal creeks and rivers, the time of slack water may vary by several hours. In some places you will find that it is not unusual for the currents to continue their direction of flow long after charted predictions say they should change.

Strong winds can play havoc on the navigator attempting to predict slack water. The current may often appear in places as a swift flowing river and care must be taken whenever crossing a stretch of strong current to avoid being swept out to sea or onto a bank or rocks. Some of the currents may flow from 2.5 to over 4 knots in places and in anchorages with tidal flow two anchors are a must. Some cuts may be impassable in adverse wind conditions or in heavy swells that may exist with or without any wind. Even in moderate conditions, onshore winds against an outgoing tide can create very rough conditions.

The Turks and Caicos

The islands of the Turks and Caicos are affected by the west setting *North Equatorial Current* on both their northern and southern extremities.

As a rule of thumb, you can estimate the tidal rise and fall in the Turks and Caicos to be about 2'-4' at most times with a mean rise of 2.6'. Neap tides, those after the first and last quarter of the moon, rise approximately ½' less, while tides after new and full moons rise approximately ½' more. During spring tides, when the moon is nearest the Earth, the range is increased by another ½'. Cruising through the Turks and Caicos during spring full moon tides will give you some of the lowest lows and highest highs. It is quite easy to run aground at this time on some of the Banks routes. Boats with drafts of 5' have reportedly run aground in what is normally a 6' depth at low water during this time. To receive tidal information while in the Turks and Caicos see the section *Weather*.

Tides in the Turks and Caicos use *Hawk's Nest Anchorage* at Grand Turk as their datum location. Low tides at this location are usually 14 minutes before Nassau tides and high tides at Grand Turk are 19 minutes before Nassau tides. Both high and low tides run generally .5' less than Nassau tides. Tides at Provo and Leeward Going Through are approximately one hour later than tides at Grand Turk. Tides on the *Caicos Banks* are generally northwest on the flood and southwest on the ebb with an average strength of approximately 1 knot.

Printed tide tables can be purchased for $5 in Providenciales at the *DECR*, just above the *Public Treasury*, across from *Island Pride Supermarket*. The *DECR* also has an office on Grand Turk.

Tides are sometimes unpredictable around Providenciales. Strong northeast winds will sometimes keep the tides on the southern side of Provo low for days at a time while strong southern winds will give the southern shore higher tides than normal. The tides at Leeward Going Through are erratic at best. While the tides in Provo are generally thought to be about ½ hour after Nassau, this is not the case in Leeward. I have seen tides there occur three hours after Nassau tides and the floods generally tend to flow for a shorter period than the ebbs. I have seen the flood tide only last three hours during strong southeast winds.

The Dominican Republic

In the passage between Great Sand Cay and Luperón in the Dominican Republic, you can expect to find a west/northwest setting current of about ½ - ¾ knots, and sometimes a bit stronger in periods of easterly winds.

Time

The Turks and Caicos Islands observe *AST, Atlantic Standard Time.*

VHF

The Turks and Caicos

In the Turks and Caicos, Channel 16 is the designated channel for hailing and distress. Please shift all traffic to a working channel when you have made contact with your party. Most of the local marine interests usually monitor VHF ch. 68, so if you can't find somebody on 16, then try 68 and move off to another channel after making contact.

The Dominican Republic

In Luperón, the primary hailing channel is 68. There is a boater's net every Sunday and Wednesday on VHF ch. 72 at 0800. Here you can hear the latest goings on in Luperón such as who has what deal on this or that, who has a dinner special, and what time the nautical flea market begins at *Puerto Blanco Marina* on Sunday. An announcement will be made on ch. 68 prior to the net.

Weather

The weather throughout the Turks and Caicos Islands is sub-tropical with a rainy season from June through October, coinciding with hurricane season. In the winter, temperatures in the Out Islands rarely fall below 60°F and generally are above 75°F in the daytime. During the summer months the lows are around 75°-78°F while the highs seldom rise above 90°F. Seawater temperatures normally vary between 74°F in February and 84°F in August. Humidity is fairly high all year long, especially during the summer months, but there is usually a breeze to lessen the effect. In the summer, winds tend to be light, 10 knots or less from the southeast with more calms, especially at night. In the winter, the prevailing winds tend to be more easterly or north of east and stronger. It is not unusual to get a week of strong winds, 20 knots or better, during the winter months as fronts move through. Depending on its speed and strength, a front passing off the southeast Florida coast will usually be in Nassau in about 12-24 hours; from there it may arrive in the Exumas within 12-36 hours, and the Turks and Caicos about 12-36 hours later.

In the summer the weather pattern is typically scattered showers with the occasional line squall. Although the main concern during June through November is hurricanes, The Bahamas are more often visited by a tropical wave with its strong winds and drenching rains. Tropical waves, sometimes called easterly waves, are low-pressure systems that can strengthen and turn into a tropical depression or hurricane. Cruisers visiting The Bahamas during hurricane season are advised to monitor weather broadcasts closely and take timely, appropriate action (also see previous section on *Hurricane Holes*).

Staying in touch with weather broadcasts presents little problem in the Bahamas and southward, even if you don't have SSB or ham radio capabilities. On Grand Turk, *Flagstaff* comes on VHF ch. 16 at 8:00 a.m. local time and informs those who want to hear the latest southwest North Atlantic weather forecast to shift to VHF ch. 13. You can frequently pick up *Flagstaff's* weather transmissions as far away as South Caicos. When *Flagstaff* is off the island Brian Riggs (of the *National Museum*), handles the weather broadcasts using the call *Bluewater*.

If you have ham radio capabilities you can pick up the *Bahamas Weather Net* every morning at 0720 on 3.696 MHz, lower sideband. The net begins with the local weather forecast and tides from the *Nassau Met. Office*. Next, hams from all over the Bahamas check in with their local conditions which are later forwarded to the *Nassau Met. Office* to assist in their forecasting. If you are interested in the approach of a front you can listen in and learn what conditions hams in the path of the front have experienced. The local conditions in the weather reports follow a specific order so listen in and give your conditions in the order indicated.

The *United States Coast Guard* in Portsmouth, Virginia weather broadcasts can be received on your SSB on 4428.7 KHz (ch. 409), 6506.4 KHz (ch. 601), 8765.4 (ch. 816), 13113.2 KHz (ch. 1205), and 17307.3 (ch. 1625) at 0600, 0800, 1400, and 2200.

Chris Parker

Chris Parker's weather nets are conducted 6 days a week, Monday through Saturday, but also Sundays when Tropical or other severe weather threatens. Chris' summer schedule, April to October, begins on 4.045 MHz at 0630 AST/EDT; then Chris moves to 8.137 MHz at 0700 AST/EDT; Chris is back on 4.045 MHz at 0800 AST/EDT; then Chris moves to 8.104 MHz at 0830 AST/EDT; Chris moves up to 12.350 MHz at 0915 AST/EDT; and finishes up at 6.221 MHz at 0930 AST/EDT. When severe weather or tropical weather systems threaten Chris will also transmit in the evenings, usually on 8.104 MHz at 2000 AST/EDT and Chris will usually announce this on the morning net.

Chris' winter schedule, November to March, begins at 0700 AST/0600 EST on 8.137 MHz; Chris then moves to 4.045 MHz at 0730 AST/0630 EST; Chris can then be found on 8.104 MHz at 0830 AST/0730 EST; Chris them moves up to 12.350 MHz at 0930 AST/0830 EST; Chris then finishes on 6.221 MHz at 1000 AST/0900 EST. Quite often during the winter months Chris may be late in getting to the 12 meg frequency. When severe weather or tropical weather systems threaten Chris will also transmit in the evenings, usually on 8.104 MHz at 1900 AST/1800 EST and Chris will usually announce this on the morning net. Chris begins the net with a 24-48 hour wind and sea summary followed by a synoptic analysis and tropical conditions during hurricane season. After this, Chris repeats the weather for those needing fills and finally he takes check-ins reporting local conditions from sponsoring vessels (vessels who have paid an annual fee for this service). Those who seek more information about weather, weather patterns, and the forecasting of weather, should pick up a copy of Chris Parker's excellent publication: *Coastal and Offshore Weather, The Essential Handbook* (visit http://www.mwxc.com).

Using the Charts

For the soundings on the charts I use the mothership, or my dinghy, both with a computer-based hydrographic system consisting of an off-the-shelf GPS and sonar combination that gives a GPS waypoint and depth every two seconds including the time of each observation. The software used records and stores this information in an onboard computer. When I begin to chart an area, I first put my dinghy's bow on a well-marked, prominent point of land and take GPS lat/longs for a period of at least ten minutes. I use the average of all these positions to check against the lat/longs shown on the topos that I use to create the charts. I also use cross bearings to help set up control points for my own reference. At this point I begin to take soundings.

My next objective is to chart the inshore reefs. Then I'll plot all visible hazards to navigation. These positions are recorded by hand on my field notes as well as being recorded electronically. I rely primarily on my on-site notes for the actual construction of the charts. The soundings taken by the system are later entered by hand but it is the field notes that help me create the basis for the chart graphics. Next I will run the one-fathom line as well as the ten-fathom line and chart these. Here is where the system does most of the work. Finally, I will crisscross the entire area in a grid pattern and hopefully catch hazards that are at first glance unseen. It is not unusual to spend days sounding an area of only a couple of square miles.

Due to the speed of *Brokedown Palace* as well as my dinghy, each identical lat/long may have as many as ten or twenty separate soundings. Then, with the help of *NOAA* tide tables, the computer gives me accurate depths to one decimal place for each separate lat/long pair acquired on the data run. A macro purges all but the lowest depths for each lat/long position (to two decimal places). At this point the actual plotting is begun including one fathom and ten fathom lines. The charts themselves are still constructed from outline tracings of topographic maps and the lat/long lines are placed in accordance with these maps. The soundings taken are shown in feet at MLW, *Mean Low Water*, the average low tide. Since MLW is an average, cruisers must be aware that there are times that there will be less water than shown, particularly on Spring low tides, during the full moon and new moon.

These charts are as accurate as I can make them and I believe them to be superior to any others. However, it is not possible to plot every individual rock or coral head so piloting by eye is still essential. On many of the routes in my guides you must be able to pick out the blue, deeper water as it snakes between sandbanks, rocky bars, and coral heads. Learn to trust your eyes. Remember that on the banks, sandbars and channels can shift over time so that what was once a channel may now be a sandbar. Never approach a cut or sandbar with the sun in your eyes, it should be above and behind you. Sunglasses with polarized lenses can be a big help in combating the glare of the sun on the water. With good visibility the sandbars and heads stand out and are clearly defined. As you gain experience you may even learn to read the subtle differences in the water surface as it flows over underwater obstructions. Yes, I could have included lovely color photographs of the different water colors and label them accordingly lulling you into thinking that you know the depth of the water by looking at the photos, but I chose not to. The only true way to gain the ability to read the water is to get out there and do it. Explore. Keep one eye on your depth sounder and one on the water around you. Soon you'll be an expert.

All courses shown are magnetic. All waypoints for entrances to cuts and for detouring around shoal areas are only to be used in a general sense. They are meant to get you into the general area, you must pilot your way through the cut or around the shoal yourself. You will have to keep a good lookout; GPS will not do that for you. The best aids to navigation when near these shoals and cuts are sharp eyesight and good light. The charts will show both deep draft vessel routes as well as some shallow draft vessel routes. Deep draft vessel routes will accommodate a draft of 6' minimum and often more with the assistance of the tide. Shallow draft vessel routes are for dinghies and small outboard powered boats with drafts of less than 3'. Shallow draft monohulls and multihulls very often use these same routes.

Not being a perfect world, I expect errors to occur. I would deeply appreciate any input and corrections that you may notice as you travel these waters. Please send your suggestions to Stephen J. Pavlidis, C/O Seaworthy Publications, 2023 N. Atlantic Ave., Unit 226, Cocoa Beach, Florida, 32931, or email me at stevepavlidis@hotmail.com.

List of Charts

**The prudent navigator will not rely solely on any
single aid to navigation, particularly on floating aids.**

CAUTION:

*The Approach and Index charts are designed strictly for orientation, they are not to be used for navigational purposes. All charts are to be used in conjunction with the text.
All soundings are in feet at Mean Low Water. All courses are magnetic.
Projection is transverse Mercator. Datum used is WGS84.*

Differences in latitude and longitude may exist between these charts and other charts of the area; therefore the transfer of positions from one chart to another should be done by bearings and distances from common features.

The author and publisher take no responsibility for errors, omissions, or the misuse of these charts. No warranties are either expressed or implied as to the usability of the information contained herein.

Note: Some *NOAA* and *DMA* charts do not show some of the reefs and heads charted in this guide. Always keep a good lookout when piloting in these waters.

Chart #	Chart Description	Page #
	The Caicos Islands	
TCI-C1	The Caicos Islands	45
TCI-C2	Providenciales	46
TCI-C3	North West Point, Malcolm Roadstead	49
TCI-C4	West Harbour to Wiley Point	49
TCI-C5	Sandbore Channel, Western Entrance	51
TCI-C6	Sandbore Channel, Sapodilla Bay	51
TCI-C7	Five Cays to Long Bay	58
TCI-C8	Cooper Jack Bight, Discovery Bay	60
TCI-C9	Juba Point Creek, Caicos Marina & Shipyard	60
TCI-C10	Sellar's Cut, Turtle Cove Marina	62
TCI-C11	Stubbs Cut to Pine Cay	64
TCI-C12	Leeward Going Through	66
TCI-C13	The Caicos Cays, Pine Cay to Parrot Cay, Ft. George Cut	70
TCI-C14	West Caicos	73
TCI-C14A	West Caicos Marina	73
TCI-C15	French Cay	75
TCI-C16	North Caicos	77
TCI-C17	Middle Caicos	79
TCI-C18	East Caicos, South Caicos	80
TCI-C18A	Jacksonville Cut	81
TCI-C19	South Caicos, Cockburn Harbour	85

Chart #	Chart Description	Page #
TCI-C20	Six Hills Cays to Long Cay	89
TCI-C21	Ambergris Cays, Fish Cays	90
The Turks Islands		
TCI-T1	The Turks Islands	91
TCI-T2	Grand Turk	93
TCI-T2A	Grand Turk, North Creek Entrance	95
TCI-T3	Grand Turk to Dunbar Shoals	104
TCI-T4	Dunbar Shoals to Salt Cay	104
TCI-T5	Salt Cay	108
TCI-T6	Great Sand Cay	110
The Dominican Republic		
DR-1	Luperón	118
DR-2	Ocean World Marina at Cofresi	125
DR-3	Puerto Plata	127
DR-4	Sosúa	130
DR-5	Rio San Juan	131
DR-6	Puerto El Valle	132
DR-7	Samaná	133
DR-8	Puerto Bahía Marina	135
DR-9	Bahía de San Lorenzo	135
DR-10	Barahona	137
DR-11	Las Salinas	139
DR-12	Puerto de Haina	139
DR-13	Santo Domingo	141
DR-14	Boca Chica	142
DR-15	Casa de Campo Marina	145
DR-16	Isla Saona	145
DR-17	Cap Cana Marina	147

Index of Charts

A Cruising Guide to the Turks and Caicos Islands

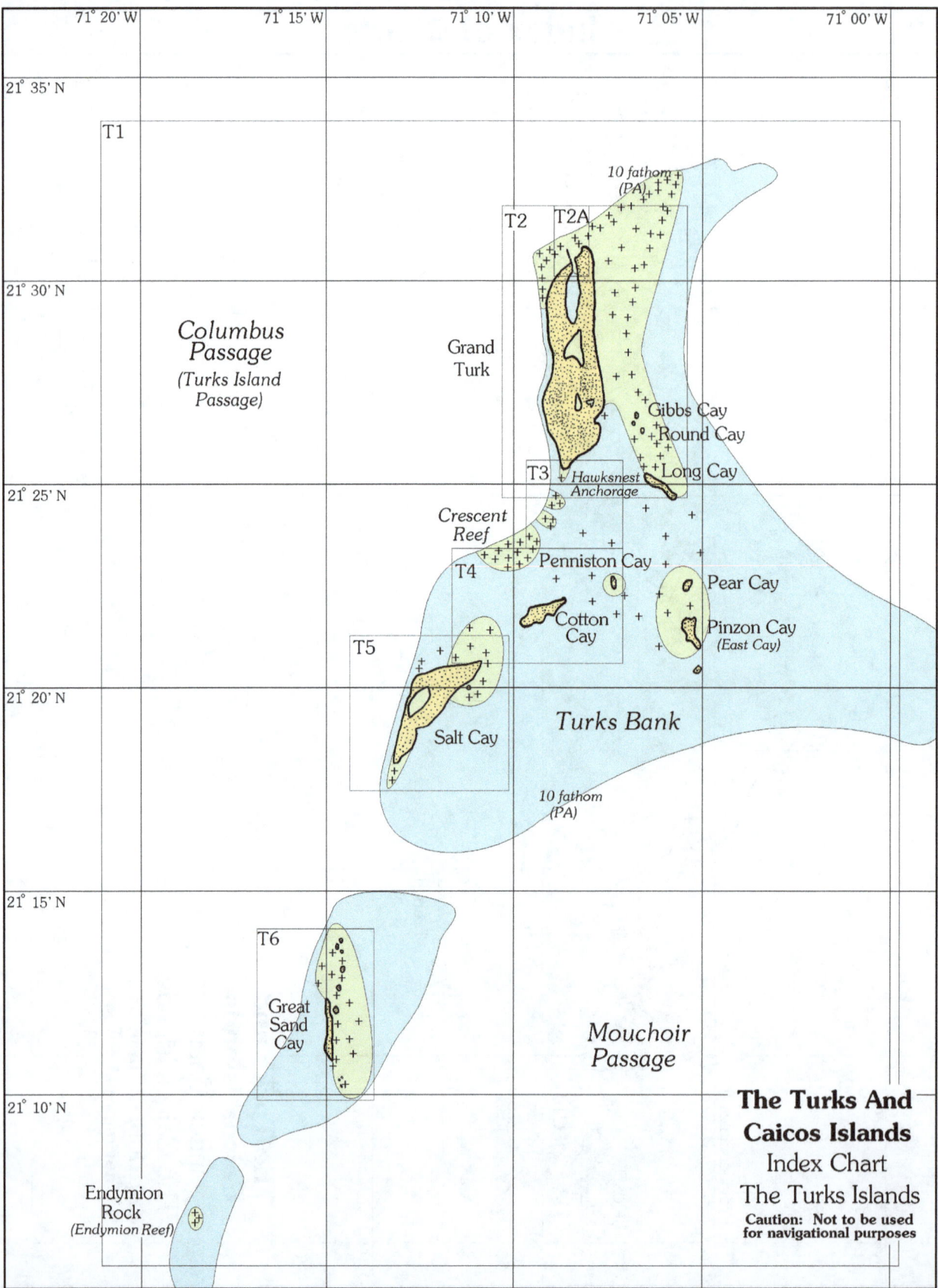

Dominican Republic
North Coast
Index Chart
Caution: Not to be used
for navigational purposes
DR-1
DR-2
Cofresi
Luperón
DR-3
DR-4
Cabo
Macorıs
Puerto Plata
Sosúa
DR-5
Cabo
Francés
Viejo
Dominican Republic
Rio San Juan

North Atlantic Ocean
Cabo Cabrón
Bahia
del Rincon
Cabo
Samaná
Puerto
El Valle
DR-6
Dominican Republic
Puerto
Bahía
Marina
DR-8
Samaná
DR-7
Punta Balandra
Bahía de Samaná
Cayo Levantado
Dominican Republic
East Coast
Index Chart
Caution: Not to be used
for navigational purposes
DR-9
Bahía de
San Lorenzo
Punta
El Negro
Punta Yabón

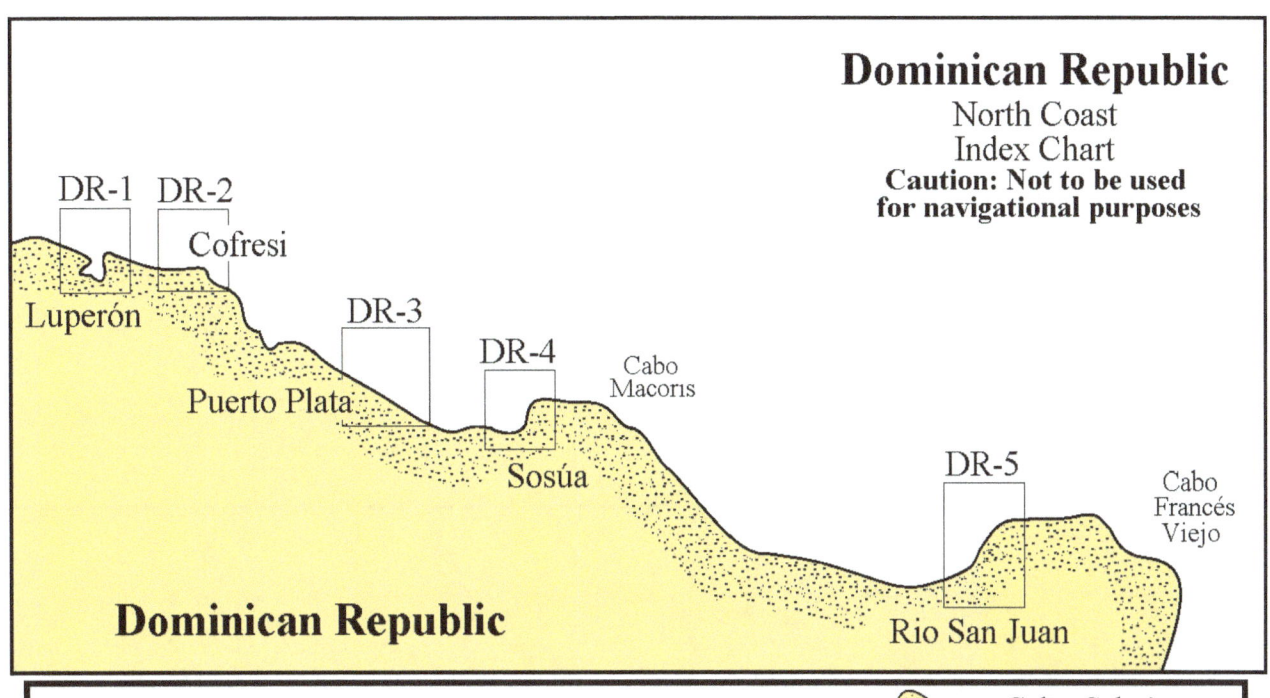

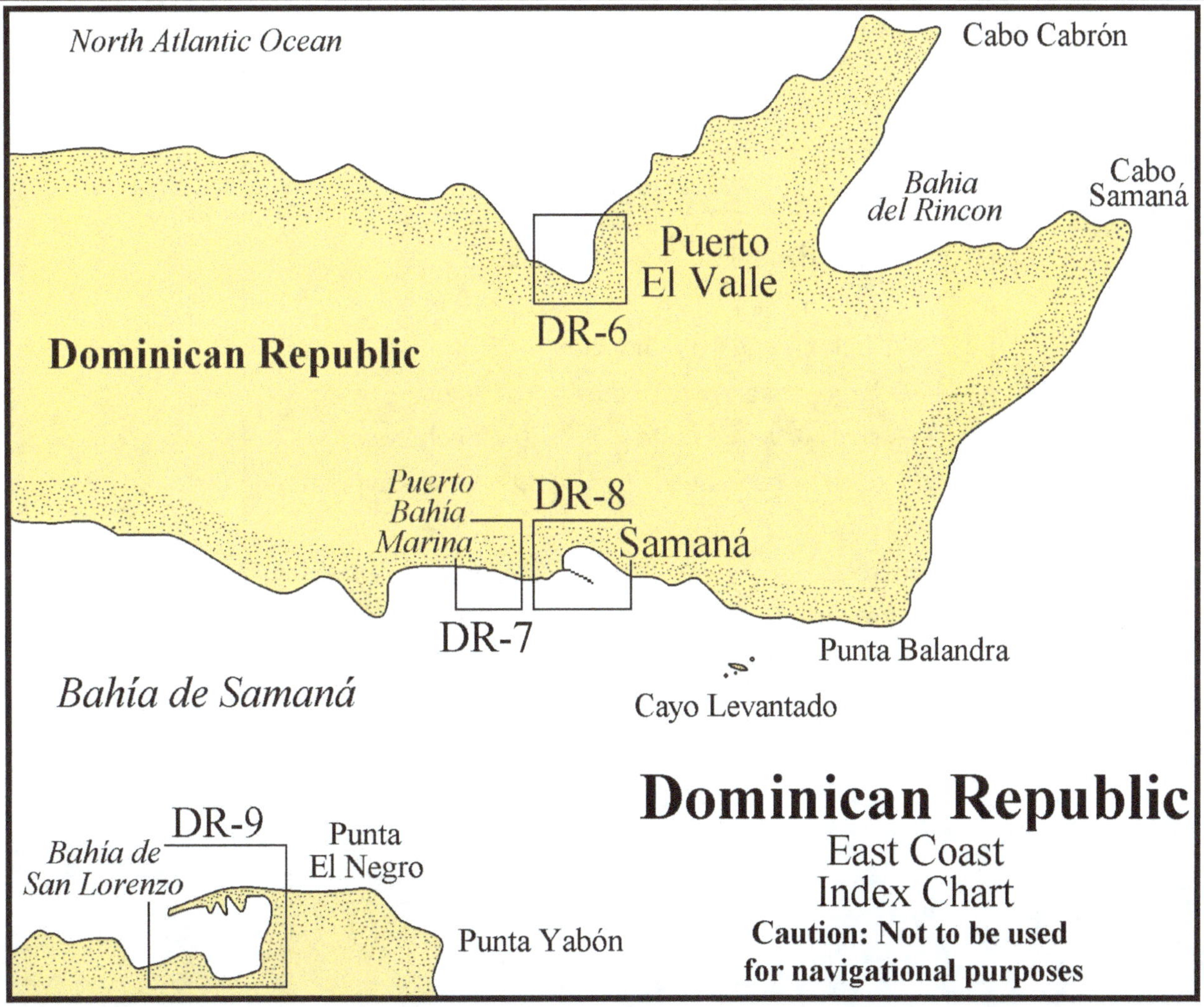

A Cruising Guide to the Turks and Caicos Islands

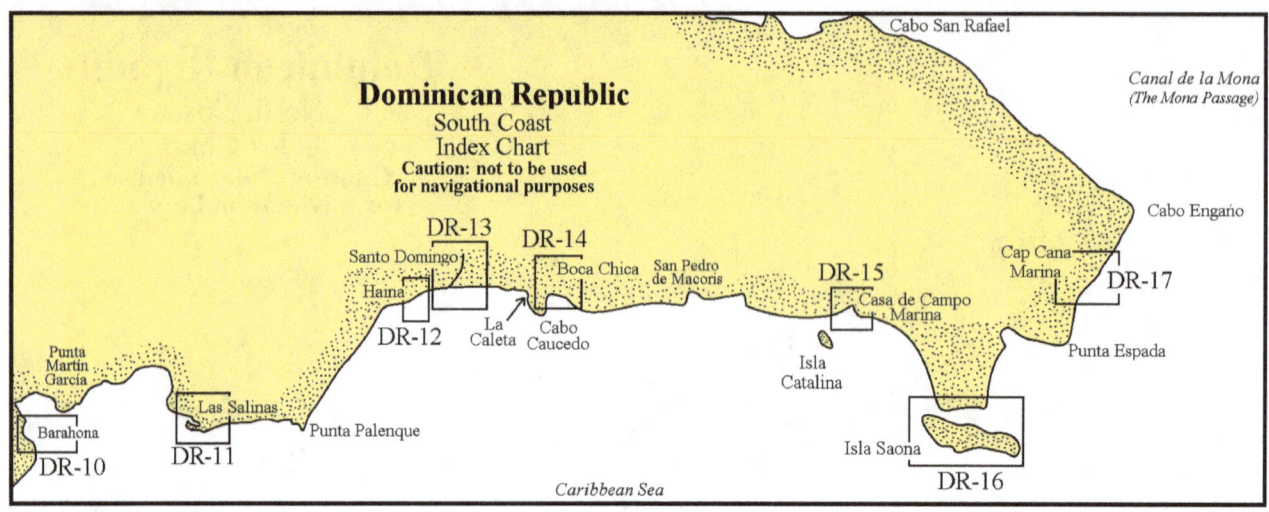

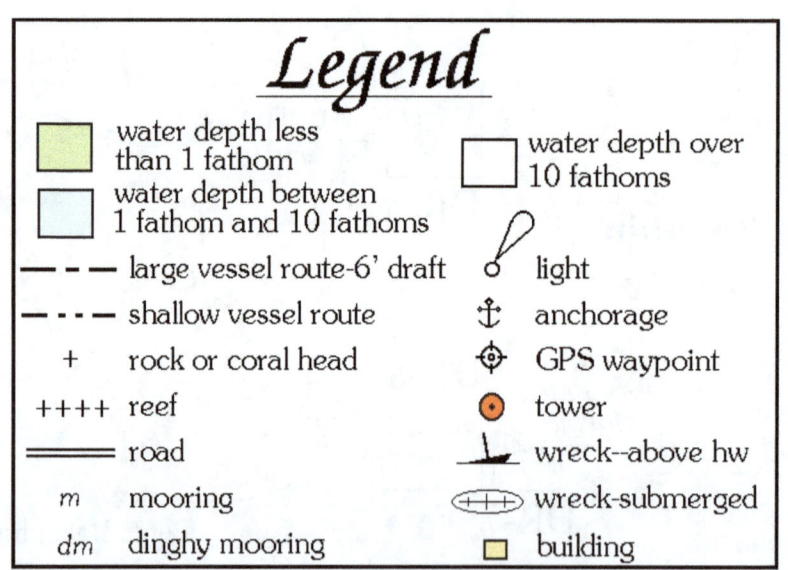

The Caicos Islands

Thornless Escape
A Prescription

By Captain David Matthews
S/V *TAO*

When you've done Stocking Island, up the hill
And told your lies at Chat and Chill,
Checked Peace and Plenty, Two T's in turn,
Now put Chicken Harbour to the stern.

Dreaded cold front's on the way,
Wind's gone south, it's time to say,
"Conception Island here we come,
Your eastern side will be some fun."

Feeling smug's a wee bit catching
Wind a' howling, but seas not matching
Raise a glass, boat's set to go
All waiting for Herb's weather window.

Frontal passage does its thing,
Back of the front has a certain ring.
Reefed main and spitfire is our dream,
Just love that breeze abaft the beam.

Now we're out where the big boys play,
Making easting it's safe to say,
It sure beats slogging it under power,
Rum-time soon passing Bird Rock tower.

Shore-leave over, diesel to the top,
Ready now for the next wee hop.

Attwood thirty seems slow to close,
Motorsailing madness, wind on the nose.

Northeast Breakers to starboard side,
West Plana's fine after this wild ride,
Barrel sponges, big guys, stories told,
Best SCUBA in the western world.

Behold a miracle, the sea got smooth,
Get this wagon in the groove.
On to Mayaguana's northwest side,
West wind coming, nowhere to hide.

Wind and current, the choppy situation,
Acknowledge Caicos Passage's reputation.
But we're smokin' now and doing fine,
Ticking miles off the ole rhumb line.

Following sea and sails are light,
Surf Sellar's Cut and hang a right.
Customs' coming out and hooks are down,
Passage complete with nary a frown.

Marine sunrise, hot water we've got,
Tiki Hut breakfast hits the spot.
IGA shopping and e-mail that works,
Welcome to Provo, Toast of the Turks!

A Brief History

The *Bahamas Platform*, of which the Turks and Caicos are a part, was created by the shifting of the Earth's plates, a process known as *plate tectonics*, approximately 11-25 million years ago during the era known as the *Miocene*. During the *Pleistocene Era*, about two million years ago, the rise and fall of the sea level segregated the islands of this archipelago. The cays themselves are basically limestone that was laid down as windblown deposits during the *Tertiary*, approximately 1 to 2 million years ago. Most of the current aspect of The Turks and Caicos Islands has been produced in geologically recent times by coral formation. The cays themselves are generally flat with few hills over a hundred feet high and their external limestone is worn razor sharp by the action of wind and wave. Several of the cays are honeycombed with caves and cave holes.

The first inhabitants of the Turks and Caicos Islands of which there is any record of were the Tainos. The Tainos were Arawakan in origin and sprang from South America where their descendants are still to be found in parts of Venezuela and the Guianas. The Arawaks colonized the Caribbean in dugout canoes, a specimen of which in Jamaica was 96' long with an 8' beam and may have carried as many as 150 rowers.

The relatively peaceful Tainos, although they were brave warriors, were forced to keep on the move by the presence of the far fiercer Caribs. The Caribs were a cannibalistic group whose chief purpose seemed to be murdering the Arawakan men, enslaving their women, and castrating the young Tainos and fattening them with rich diets and preventing them from engaging in any form of labor to ensure their tender flesh. The Carib religion promised a paradise for the courageous warrior wherein the Arawaks he killed would serve him as slaves while assuring the coward that he would be doomed to a hell wherein he would eternally serve a Taino master. A handful of Caribs survive to this day in Dominica though even less is known of their early culture than the Arawakans.

In their search for peace, the Tainos pushed their canoes northward into the Caribbean, reaching Hispaniola around 200 A.D. and then settling in Cuba and Jamaica over the next two hundred years. They reached the Turks and Caicos and The Bahamas sometime around 700-900 A.D. in the last wave of their migration. Here they became known as *luddu-cairi* or *luko-kayo,* meaning *island people*. We know them today as the Lucayans.

The Caribs were never far behind the Lucayans. By the time Columbus reached the New World, the Caribs had conquered the Lesser Antilles and were raiding Puerto Rico and Hispaniola. Columbus noted scars on the bodies of some of the Lucayans and through sign language was told that people on neighboring islands wanted to capture them and that they had defended themselves.

The Lucayans built circular, conical houses of wood and thatch, and survived on conch, fish, native game and plants. They were basket makers and were adept at manufacturing polished stone implements. Lucayan pottery is called *palmettoware* and it was tempered with bits of conch shell to improve the quality (Lucayan pottery has turned up at several archaeological sites throughout the Turks and Caicos Islands since 1912, unfortunately, most of these early finds were removed from the country or simply turned up missing). With the exception of some small gold decorations, the Lucayans had no knowledge of the use of metal. They slept in hammocks, a habit that Spanish seamen soon picked up. And there seems to have been some commerce between the Lucayans on Middle Caicos and their Taino cousins in Cuba and Hispaniola.

The Lucayans were a handsome people, almost oriental in appearance, with broad faces and foreheads flattened in infancy by tying them to boards. This practice was designed to add distinction to their appearance as well as hardening the bone as protection against blows. Mayans and Egyptians shared this unique custom at one time, as did an Indian tribe in Montana called the Flatheads. Lucayans wore their coarse hair in bangs in the front and long in the back. For the most part they wore no clothing, although they painted their faces and sometimes their entire bodies with red, black, and white pigments. They decorated themselves with tattoos, necklaces, bracelets, bones, and feathers. Their chiefs, or *caciques*, were allowed to practice polygamy and served as chief, judge, and priest in their culture. The Lucayans had a class structure and the *caciques* enjoyed all the benefits afforded to their position. The *cacique*'s canoe was the only one that was painted; when traveling by land, they were borne on litters while their children were carried on the shoulders of their servants. After death, the *cacique* was buried along with sufficient supplies for the journey to *Coyaba* along with one or two of his favorite wives.

The Lucayans were lovers of peace and simple pleasures with a gentle and generous nature, sharing anything they had with Columbus and his men. Next to singing and dancing, the Lucayans loved *batos*, an organized ball game similar to volleyball and soccer. The remains of a Lucayan ball court were found on the island of Middle Caicos. Ball courts have been found in Puerto Rico and points farther south but never this far north.

Though they had no written language, their spoken language was described as "soft and not less liquid than Latin." Some 20 Lucayan words and their derivatives survive to this day. Avocado, barbecue, canoe, Carib, cannibal, cassava, cay, guava, hammock, hurricane, iguana, maize, manatee, pirogue, potato, and tobacco all are Lucayan in origin. The Lucayans had their own names for the islands of the Turks and Caicos as well. The Caicos Islands were referred to as *Yucayo* while Providenciales was *Yucacanuco*, West Caicos was *Macubiza*, Middle Caicos was *Aniana*, East Caicos was *Quana*, and South Caicos was known as *Caciba*. The Turks Islands were called *Babueca* by the Lucayans while Grand Turk was known as *Amuana* (and if you accept the *Grand Turk Landfall Theory*, it was known as *Guanahani*), Salt Cay was called *Canamani*, Cotton Cay was *Macarei*, and Great Sand Cay was known as *Cacina*.

It was the Lucayans who taught Columbus' crew their custom of smoking the *cohiba* plant in their strange y-shaped pipes called *tobacco*. The tubes of the Y were inserted in their nostrils and the smoke inhaled until the smoker fell into a stupor. The Spaniards quickly picked up this habit although they did not inhale to the point of intoxication. Although Columbus never reported seeing the Lucayans smoke, in his log he described a leaf that he found a native carrying in his canoe as being highly valued by the Lucayans.

Columbus originally thought the Lucayans had no religion and believed that they would readily become Christians. But the Lucayans actually had a highly developed religion with two supreme beings, a male and a female, and a belief in an afterlife. They also believed in numerous spirit beings called *zemis* who lived in sacred trees, carved images, and in the relics of the dead. These *zemis* had to be appeased with great festivals in their honor. To induce visions of the future, the Lucayans ground into a powder a potent narcotic called *yopo* that they then snorted up the nostrils. A similar drug is still in use by Amerindians in Venezuela to this day (I'll give you three guesses as to what drug this may be). A Lucayan chief under the influence of *yopo*, foresaw the destruction of his civilization by "...strange blonde men in winged canoes."

The discovery of the New World by Columbus (who had blonde, almost white hair) in 1492, sounded the death knell for the Lucayan civilization. Columbus brought back seven Lucayan captives in chains, but two escaped en-route, some say on Providenciales. One returned to Europe with Columbus and was baptized at the Cathedral of Barcelona with the King and Queen of Spain standing as godparents. He took the name Diego Colón and returned with Columbus to the New World in the fall of 1493, where he served as Columbus' interpreter.

It was not long before King Ferdinand of Spain authorized raiding parties to the "useless islands." The Spaniards made some 500 journeys to the islands of The Bahamas and the Turks and Caicos to enslave the Lucayans for their mines and plantations in Cuba and Hispaniola. By 1513, within one generation, no Lucayans were estimated to be left in the Turks and Caicos Islands. The Spanish historian Herrera tells us that when Ponce de León arrived in Grand Turk in late 1512 he could only find one Lucayan to assist him in his search for the fountain of youth on Bimini. Maps of that period show Grand Turk called *Del Viejo* or *Old Man*. By contrast, in 1517 there were an estimated 20,000-40,000 Lucayans in The Bahamas and their price fluctuated at about 4 gold pesos each. The asking price skyrocketed to 150 gold pesos each for these excellent divers when rich pearl beds were discovered off Venezuela and Trinidad. The Spaniards played upon an Arawak superstition and enticed many Lucayans to board ships with promises of returning them to South America, their ancient homeland and the place where their souls would go when they died; *Coyaba*. Many Lucayans did not go willingly, choosing instead to fight the heavily armed Spaniards. Others, even mothers with small children, committed suicide by drinking the juice of the cassava plant to avoid a life of wretchedness at the hands of the cruel Spaniards. The rest died of starvation and ill treatment while in bondage and only a very few lived to old age. By the early 1520s, this peaceful, innocent civilization, that had lived only to satisfy nature without all the trappings of laws and governments, was obliterated from the face of the earth and sadly reduced to a footnote in history.

After the time of the Lucayans, the Turks and Caicos had few visitors save a few Spanish ships stopping in the Turks Islands for salt. The first Englishman to make mention of the island group was Captain John Hawkins of Plymouth, a well-known privateer who passed by the Caicos group in 1564 in search of salt. The islands re-entered history in the middle of the 17th Century when salt rakers from Bermuda decided to use three of the Turks Islands for an entrepreneurial venture. In the 1640s they created salt ponds on Salt Cay, Grand Turk, and South Caicos, and their endeavor was successful enough to create the basis for the local economy for the next two centuries. Even today, some consider the fine, white Turk's Island salt the preferred preservative and seasoning. From about 1678 onwards, Bermudian salt rakers of British descent were populating the islands, at first only in the dry season, and later on, living on the islands full-time. They immediately set out to destroy all the trees, seeking to increase salt production.

At first the salt rakers collected salt for their own use, but as their commodity increased in value it became the backbone of the Bermudian economy for over 100 years. Settlers on these islands during this time lived primarily off their salt production, fishing, and wrecking. While The Bahamas severed its ties with Bermuda in 1663, the salt rakers in the Turks and Caicos continued to maintain a link with the island. Several petitions were submitted to Parliament to annex these islands to Bermuda but all were turned down.

As Spanish shipping activity increased in the New World, the era of privateering began. Spanish ships laden with the riches of the New World would pass through the waters of the Turks and Caicos and The Bahamas on their way back to Spain making wrecking very profitable in these waters. It was said that if a crewman were lucky enough to survive the wreck, it was uncertain as to whether he would survive the wreckers. If the Spanish knew of the location of their wrecks they would send crews to salvage the valuables. Bahamian and Turks Island wreckers would drive off the intruders and loot what they had salvaged. As Captains became wise to the ways of the wreckers, wrecks became fewer and fewer, the privateers had to find other uses for their talents. This was not difficult, the era of the buccaneers was in full swing.

The original buccaneers (*boucaniers*), the forerunners of the pirates, were based just south of the Turks and Caicos Islands at Tortuga. They were a wild group of men from France, Holland, and England, indentured servants, seafarers, and adventurers. They wore colorful, picturesque garb and hunted the semi-wild cattle and pigs on the island, descendents of escapees from Spanish farms. They roasted the meat over fires called *boucans* and would sell this smoked meat product, along with hides and tallow, to passing ships. Hispaniola soon became the location of a huge illicit meat and hides trade. The *boucaniers* quickly learned to live less off hunting and rely more on their commerce with Spanish ships, first in canoes, then "acquiring" ships, and finally in small flotillas.

From 1629 to 1641, English buccaneers were organized as a company, using the island of Providence off the Nicaraguan coast as a base. The 1630s were a prosperous era for the Providence based buccaneers. Their prosperity ended abruptly in 1641, when the Spanish invaded the island and massacred every settler they could find. The few who escaped shifted their base of operations to Tortuga, an island off the northern coast of Hispaniola just south of the Turks and Caicos Islands. Recruits from every European trading nation began to pour in. By the middle 1600s the buccaneers formed armed bands who were accustomed to hardship, had strong codes of honor that they chose to live by, and were extremely well led. For over 75 years these buccaneers were the scourge of the Spanish fleet. In the 1640s, a buccaneer from Normandy who called himself Pierre Le Grand, often called the "Father of Piracy in the West Indies," boldly captured a Spanish galleon in the passage between Tortuga and the *Caicos Bank* while her crew slept. Le Grand and his 28 men approached the galleon in an old dilapidated raft, not far from sinking when the captain of the galleon spied their craft. Laughing at the condition of their vessel and the ragtag crew, the captain said he would not fear them even if they were the size of his own galleon. Le Grand had bored holes in the bottom of his boat to insure that his men were properly motivated, that either they would take the galleon or the sea would take them. Le Grand and his men pulled alongside the galleon and wedged the big ship's rudder and climbed aboard just as their own little boat sank beneath the waves. Le

Grand and his men took the ship without a shot and Le Grand himself burst into the officer's cabin in the midst of a quiet card game. Le Grand took the ship to France after allowing those of the galleon's crew who would not join his ranks to depart on the island of Hispaniola. Pierre Le Grand is believed to be the only pirate to have ever taken a galleon. After Le Grand and his men divvied up their spoils, they retired from the sea and Le Grand was said to have lived happily to a ripe old age.

Most prominent of the buccaneers were Edward Mansfield and the legendary Sir Henry Morgan. In 1664, Mansfield and Morgan set up a base in Nassau and were received quite favorably. Nassau came to be quite the haven for the wandering buccaneers. Mansfield's early and untimely death created confusion in the leadership of the buccaneers and Morgan set them off on a course of plunder and profit. The years between 1671 and 1686 were a time of buccaneer ascendancy as the buccaneers gained major European finance against the Spanish Empire. After the capture of Jamaica in 1655, Port Royal, just outside of Kingston, became the headquarters for English buccaneers and remained so for 20 years. Under Sir Thomas Modyford and Sir Henry Morgan their achievements reached a climax. The *Treaty of Madrid* with Spain in 1670, the death of Sir Henry Morgan in 1688, and finally the destruction by earthquake of Port Royal in 1692 dispersed these Jamaican-based buccaneers.

There is no fine line as to when the buccaneers became pirates. *Webster's* offers little difference between the two. History suggests that the code of honor of the early buccaneers was forgotten and the bands degenerated into piracy. The buccaneers had articles called *chasseparties* that allocated duties, rewards, and compensations. In all things, their brotherhood was expected to observe a rigid code of honor called *la coutume de la côte*, which roughly translated means, *the custom of the coast*. Despite their code and the *chasseparties*, the English and French buccaneers were always quarrelling. The number of English buccaneers at Tortuga having to rely on French protection increased year by year. The Jamaica and Carolina legislatures passed severe acts against them and the buccaneers became less and less particular about their prey. By 1685 their own people were even calling them pirates. Whatever unity there was between the British and French buccaneers dissolved when their two countries went to war after William of Orange ascended the English Throne in 1689. This struggle was to last 126 years with only one long break. Loyal English were no longer welcome in Hispaniola and when the Anglo-French fighting reached the Caribbean in 1691, the last of the English pirates left the safety of Tortuga and settled in areas of The Bahamas and the Turks and Caicos. Most of their activity was centered in the Nassau area but roaming pirates are said to have consistently used areas such as Parrot Cay, French Cay, and Grand Turk as bases from which to stage raids. By 1713, there were an estimated 1,000 active pirates operating in the waters of The Bahamas and the Turks and Caicos. One interesting theory about how the Turks Islands received their name suggests that in the 16th and 17th centuries, under the leadership of the two Barbarosa brothers, a band of Barbary pirates operated out of these waters. Originating in Constantinople, the brothers eventually settled on an uninhabited salt island that the Spanish later referred to as Grand Turk.

Some of the most notorious pirates to be found in the pages of history have been reported as lurking in Turks and Caicos waters over the years. Mary Read and Anne Bonney, the "lady" pirates who sailed with Calico Jack Rackham, Stede Bonnet the Gentleman Pirate, Benjamin Hornigold, Charles Vane, Captain Kidd, L'Olonnois, and Edward Teach who was much better known as Blackbeard. If any one pirate could embody the spirit of the era and of piracy itself, none would be better suited for it than Blackbeard. From 1713 until 1716 he teamed up with Benjamin Hornigold and was based in Nassau along with Captains Jennings, Burgess, and White. Blackbeard's independent pirate career lasted only two short years, from 1716 when he acquired his first ship, the *Queen Anne's Revenge*, until his death in the Carolinas in 1718.

Jean-David Rau, who named himself L'Olonnois after his birthplace in les Sables D'Olonne in Brittany, was one of the old guard, one of the last of the original *boucaniers* of Tortuga, and one of the most ruthless psychopathic pirates in history. He is said to have used French Cay, just south of Providenciales, as a hideout to wait on Spanish vessels heading northward through the *Windward Passage*. Recently the gentleman who started that rumor has since withdrawn his original statement though it is possible that L'Olonnois actually might have stayed there. Such a reputation did he create for himself that Spanish sailors would rather die fighting or drowning than to fall into his hands. If a captive would not tell L'Olonnois what he wished to know, L'Olonnois would often cut him to pieces and pull out his tongue. He had been known to hack a man to pieces one slice at a time, first a finger, then a hand, then an arm, until there was nothing left to remove, or the poor fellow died. He also practiced *woolding*, that is, tying a piece of rope around a man's head and twisting it tighter and tighter with a stick until his eyes popped out. L'Olonnois was the scourge of Central and South America from the Yucatan to Venezuela. His most famous torment involved a Spanish crew that remained silent concerning a route into a town in Central America, the main road being blocked and heavily protected. L'Olonnois ripped open one man's chest and began to gnaw on his still beating heart telling the rest of his hostages "I will serve you alike if you do not show me another way."

L'Olonnois met a fitting end. After an engagement with a Spanish flotilla that nearly decimated his band of buccaneers, he and some of his crew took to land working their way into the jungles of the Central and Southern America. Here cannibals made a meal of him and all but five of his surviving crew.

A stranger piratical trio than Calico Jack Rackham, Anne Bonney, and Mary Read would be hard to find. Anne Bonney and her penniless sailor husband moved to Nassau seeking employment. There she meet Calico Jack Rackham who soon swept her off her feet. She eloped with Rackham, heading off to sea in men's clothes. Calico Jack put her ashore with friends in Jamaica when she became pregnant until such time as she gave birth and could rejoin him. She later accompanied Rackham on all his later exploits. Mary Read, raised as a boy by her grandmother, joined an army unit as a cadet and fought bravely. She fell in love and eventually married another soldier, who at first did not realize that she was a woman. After her husband died she again dressed up as a man and went on board a vessel bound for the West Indies.

Read soon joined up with a band of privateers under Woodes Rogers on the island of Providence. Mary Read claimed she detested the life of the pirate; however, when some of the crew mutinied and returned to their former lifestyle, with them went Mary Read. She wound up on board Calico Jack's ship and no one had guessed she was a woman. And then along came Anne Bonney. Bonney thought Read was a rather handsome fellow and became enamored of her, forcing her to reveal her secret.

Jealous Calico Jack, noticed the partiality Bonney was showing to Read and threatened to shoot him/her. Once again her secret was revealed. Mary Read later fell in love with another crew member and revealed herself to him. When her lover fell into a disagreement with another crew member and the two were to duel ashore in two hours, Read found out and engaged the crew member in an argument and promptly killed him.

In 1719, Calico Jack was finally captured and removed from his ship. During the battle Anne Bonney, Mary Read, and one other crew member were the last fighters on deck, the rest of the crew fleeing below. Mary Read tried in vain to rouse the crew, finally killing one and wounding another before the lady buccaneers were captured. Rackham, who at this point was estranged from his mate, had taken to enjoying a bush hallucinogen and was removed from his below decks hiding place in a stupor. In court, when asked how they pled, Mary Read and Anne Bonney promptly announced, "My Lord, we plead our bellies!" Both women were pregnant and English law at the time forbade hanging a mother to be, no matter how serious her crime. Mary Read later became ill and died in prison, thereby cheating the hangman. Anne Bonney, through the intercession of some notable Jamaican planters, escaped the noose and was never executed. Calico Jack, while awaiting execution, was allowed a brief visit from Anne Bonney. Instead of consoling Rackham, she only told him that she was sorry to see him here and that if he had fought like a man he would not have to die like a dog. Anne Bonney wound up in Virginia, married with children. Parrot Cay, a corruption of Pirate Cay, is said to be one of Rackham, Bonney's, and Read's favorite hideouts. Legend also had it that in 1850, the English Captain Delaney recovered over $130,000 in pirate loot from Sand Cay. When Woodes Rogers began to break up the pirate presence in The Bahamas, fewer and fewer brethren of the coast visited the nearby Turks and Caicos Islands. Some privateering and wrecking continued through the remainder of the 18th and into the 19th centuries. Details of this era are sketchy at best, but it is known that in 1725 Grand Turk was seasonally occupied by upwards of 1,000 laborers raking salt, fishing for turtles, and wrecking.

Spain occupied the Turks Islands in 1710, even as the salt rakers prospered. France claimed the Turks and Caicos Islands in 1753 and erected wooden columns on them bearing her coat of arms. The crew of a British vessel from Charleston,

Carolina, destroyed these columns the following year. France later occupied Grand Turk and Salt Cay from 1778 to 1783 as the salt rakers continued their flourishing enterprise. During the American Revolution, Bermudian salt rakers ignored the British blockade and shipped salt to Washington's armies.

In 1766, in spite of the Bermudian's objections, The Bahamas government extended its jurisdiction to the Turks and Caicos Islands, while on the North American continent a rebellion was brewing. The *Stamp Act* of 1765 was the beginning of the end of British rule in the colonies. The American Revolution was getting underway and it was as much a revolt as it was a civil war. An estimated 20% of the population of the colonies was fiercely loyal to the Crown and hostile to the American cause.

Known as Tories, the Loyalists favored reconciliation with the Crown. Many stood to lose jobs, commerce, or prestige if the upstart rebels were victorious. Many Loyalists suffered greatly at the hands of the Patriots. Some were socially ostracized and their businesses boycotted; others who refused to sign loyalty oaths to the rebellion were accused of treason and often had all their land and possessions confiscated. Still more were tarred and feathered in the name of Patriotism. Many Loyalists were sent to the notorious *Simsburg Copper Mines* in Connecticut. They worked in holes 150' below the surface and so many died there that the mine was known as the "Catacombs of Loyalty." The Patriots became even more hostile and vengeful after the defeat of Cornwallis at Yorktown in 1781. Many Loyalists sought refuge in eastern Florida, as Florida was not involved in the American Revolution.

In 1783, just before the end of the American Revolution, a French contingent seized the Turks Islands. They successfully repelled a counter attack by the Captain of the *HMS Albemarle,* the young Horatio Nelson. The French had little influence on the islands and *Treaty of Versailles* on January 20, 1783 restored The Bahamas and the Turks and Caicos to England and gave Florida to Spain. The Loyalists in Florida felt cheated that Florida was being traded for The Bahamas and were irate at having to move again. No longer feeling safe in the colonies, the Loyalists looked elsewhere for safe haven.

Most of the Loyalists that arrived in the Turks and Caicos had holdings in the South Carolina and Georgia area. Probably the best known of these Loyalists was Wade Stubbs who emigrated from Gasworth in England's County Cheshire to East Florida, near St. Augustine between 1775 and 1778. When the Loyalists fled the mainland, the Crown granted 72 of them approximately 18,000 acres on North and Middle Caicos. Stubbs received 860 acres, the second largest of the 332 grants given, fashioned from the 10,090 acres on North Caicos. He initially called his plantation "Bellefield." In 1790 Wade Stubbs convinced his brother Thomas to leave Cheshire and join him. Thomas built a plantation called Cheshire Hall on Blue Caicos, what is today known as Providenciales

Thomas Stubbs started out growing Anguilla or long staple Sea Island cotton. Anguilla cotton grew to the size of small, bushy trees and produced a high quality cotton. Many of these plants still survive today in the bush on North and Middle Caicos. For several years the plantations flourished and were producing large yields; land values soared from £9,450 for a tract to over £70,000 per tract. Soon yields began getting smaller and smaller. The problems in production came from removing the sticky seeds from the cotton bolls, the chenille bugs that devoured the sweet leaves, and the fact that cotton quickly strips the soil of nutrients mandating long fallow periods of manuring to maintain yields. Eli Whitney's cotton gin solved the first problem in 1793, but the other two problems caused the downfall of the cotton business in the Turks and Caicos Islands. Also, a devastating hurricane in 1813 added to the abandonment of the plantations. Thomas Stubbs' *Cheshire Hall* cotton plantation was hit harder than most by the chenille bug and fertilization problems, and in 1810 he sold Cheshire Hall.

In 1791, Wade Stubbs was named a *Justice of the Peace* and as the years went by, added to his holdings of land and slaves, he was quite the Loyalist success story. He had purchased other plantations from other Loyalists who were deserting them and had so much land that he could leave vast tracts of land to fallow as yields fell. He purchased the Haulover Plantation on Middle Caicos after the original owners left. Cotton on that estate was still being raised within the memory of people still living today. Stubbs success was in part due to the fact that he raised enough stock to supply his fields with manure. So successful and important was this cotton trade that after the independence of Haiti in 1799, the British government built Fort George on a small cay just southwest of North Caicos to protect the cotton industry.

In 1800, 14 of Wades Stubbs' slaves stole one of his sloops and escaped. After 1806, Stubbs referred to *Bellefield* as *Wade's Green*, a name indicating his affection for the land and his prosperity. Wade Stubbs died in 1822 and was buried in a stone crypt behind *St. Thomas' Church* on Grand Turk. At the time of his death Wade Stubbs owned over 3,000 acres on North Caicos, 5,000 acres on Providenciales, and even more land on Middle Caicos, including Haulover. He had 384 slaves, all but 8 of whom were in the Caicos Islands. Some of his estate went to his nephew Henshell Stubbs, a Grand Turk salt producer, but most went to his namesake cousin, another Wade Stubbs, who continued living at *Wade's Green* until about 1850. After emancipation in 1833, the Stubbs slaves, some farming and some working in salt in the Turks, were freed and the plantations came to disrepair and disuse. In 1882 the government of the Turks and Caicos Islands purchased 1,800 acres of *Wade's Green* for division into 25-acre parcels to encourage farming. In 1885 the Stubbs house was refurbished as a combination courthouse, jail, and quarters for a magistrate who was posted there to stimulate the faltering settlement.

Between the years of 1827 and 1847 a salt tax was producing a quarter of the revenue of The Bahamas and Turks islanders were indignant. None of the money they paid in taxes was going to help their islands and the price of salt dropped considerably though the Salt Tax stayed the same. Though they were represented in Nassau, the distance and travel time involved limited the time a representative actually sat in Assembly. Although a mailboat reached Long Cay once a month and Grand Turk only four times a year, the only Bahamians they ever saw were tax collectors. Several boats bound for Jamaica passed through on a regular basis however and the Turks islanders grew to feel more kinship with Kingston than with Nassau.

After continuing complaints to the Crown an investigation was in order. The Governor of The Bahamas, George B. Matthew, made a perilous 18-day voyage from Nassau to Grand Turk which convinced him of the difficulties in transportation, communication, and life in general in these harsh islands. Separation was recommended. In 1848, the Turks and Caicos Islands were granted a separate charter providing for internal self-government subject to the Governor of Jamaica, a more pleasing proposition for the Turks islanders than continuing Bahamian rule.

The next few years were marked by prosperity in the salt business and the new government seemed to be working well. Then, in the evening of September 30, 1866, a devastating hurricane hit Grand Turk. By morning 63 were dead, over 750 homes destroyed, and more than a million bushels of salt were washed away. The country and its economy were literally left in ruins and the salt market became depressed in the ensuing years. In 1872 the islanders petitioned Queen Victoria to annex the Turks and Caicos Islands to Jamaica, which she did in 1873.

Over the following years the Turks and Caicos islanders continued to run their own affairs to a large extent. Unfortunately, Jamaican rule became no more popular than the preceding Bahamian rule. In reality, little was gained in the islands by their bond to Jamaica. When Jamaica became independent in 1962, the people of the Turks and Caicos Islands overwhelmingly wished to become a British Crown Colony. They got their wish. Also in 1962, John Glenn, after his famous space flight, first set foot back on planet Earth at Grand Turk.

Today the islands enjoy autonomous internal rule although the Governor is appointed by the Queen. Since undergoing massive economic development from 1967, the Turks and Caicos Islands have emerged as a world-class tourism destination and a major offshore financial center.

In 1976, the first constitution was granted to the islands creating a ministerial form of government. The present constitution did not come into being until March 4th, 1988. The Turks and Caicos Islands are a parliamentary democracy implementing the traditional Westminster model. The government consists of a governor, appointed by the Crown, who acts as the Queen's representative and is responsible for internal security, external affairs, defense, and certain judicial matters. The Legislative Council (LegCo) consists of 13 elected members serving four-year terms, three appointed members, a Speaker who is selected from outside or from the elected or appointed members who are not Executive Council (ExCo) members. The Executive Council, which is responsible for the day-to-day business of government, consists of the Governor, Attorney General, Chief Secretary, Financial Secretary, and the Chief Minister and his cabinet of four appointed ministers selected from the elected members of the Legislative Council.

In recent decades many Turks and Caicos islanders left their homes to find work in The Bahamas leaving huge gaps in the work force at home which are quite often filled by workers from Haiti and the Dominican Republic. With the huge tourism boom on Providenciales, this is slowly changing, as more and more native sons and daughters are finding adequate employment in their homeland. The tourism boom is increasing steadily with each passing year; one can only foresee prosperous times ahead for the Turks and Caicos islanders.

The constitution of 1976 was amended in recent years, but in any case has now been suspended since August 2009 and the Islands are now under the direct rule of Great Britain pending a further revision.

The Caicos Islands

Ports of Entry

Providenciales, South Caicos, North Caicos
Fuel: Providenciales, South Caicos
Haul-Out: Providenciales
Diesel Repairs: Grand Turk, Providenciales, Salt Cay, South Caicos
Outboard Repairs: Grand Turk, Providenciales, South Caicos
Propane: Grand Turk, North Caicos, Providenciales, South Caicos
Provisions: Grand Turk, North Caicos, Middle Caicos, Providenciales, South Caicos
Important Lights:
North West Pt., Providenciales: Gp Fl (3) W 15s
Providenciales, Bird Cay: Fl W ev 10 sec
Cape Comete, E. Caicos: Gp Fl (2) W ev 20 sec
West Caicos, Southwest Point: Q R
French Cay: Fl R
South Caicos: Fxd W
Long Cay, east end: Fl R ev 2.5 sec
Dove Cay, west end: Fl G ev 2.5 sec
Bush Cay: Gp Fl (2) W ev 10 sec

The Caicos Islands, for the most part, lie on the northern edge of the huge *Caicos Bank* west of the Turks Islands and separated from their sister cays by the ocean deep *Turks Island Passage*. The Turks and Caicos archipelago lies approximately 575 miles southeast of Miami and about 450 miles northeast of Jamaica. The majority of the land area, population, tourist industry, and yachting scene in the Turks and Caicos Islands are located in the Caicos Islands themselves, specifically on Providenciales.

Some say the Caicos Islands derived their name from *Caya Hica*, the Lucayan words for *String of Islands*, while others say the term is said to be derived from the Spanish *cayos* meaning rocky islands, while still others say the name *Caicos* is Lucayan in origin.

Limestone caves abound in the Turks & Caicos Islands where spelunking is becoming a popular activity. Some of the best caverns are on East and Middle Caicos, the latter of which is also home to some dazzling surface formations of limestone. Several valuable archaeological sites containing pre-Columbian artifacts have recently been found in some of the caves on Middle Caicos.

A very unusual and interesting phenomena occurs on a monthly basis after a full moon throughout the Caicos Islands. Look for an ebb tide about 3-6 nights after a full moon. About 1 hour after sunset, for around 15 minutes, the marine worm *Odontosyllis enopia* performs a sparkling mating ritual. Simply called *Glowworms*, the female of the species releases an egg mass that spirals to the surface emitting a pulsating pale green luminescence. The male, also glowing, does a zigzag sort of maneuver until he encounters these egg masses, causing an even brighter green flow. The number of mating displays may change from month to month but the spawning cycle is dictated by the lunar and solar patterns happening only a few nights of the month. This is a fascinating ritual to watch and most charter boat operators offer sunset glowworm cruises complete with dinner and drinks.

Approaches

Waypoints
Abraham's Bay - ¼ nm SSE of E entrance:
22° 20.80' N, 72° 58.30' W

Southeast Point - 1 nm WSW of anchorage:
22° 16.70' N, 72° 48.40' W

Vessels approaching the Caicos Islands from The Bahamas usually make Mayaguana their last stop in this island chain as they work their way south to Provo. From the waypoint at the eastern entrance to *Abraham's Bay*, 22° 21.70'N, 72° 58.45'W, the entrance to *Sandbore Channel* lies 46.6 miles away on a course of 150° while *Leeward Cut* bears 134° at 54.1 nautical miles distant. Bruce Van Sant, in his

The Caicos Islands

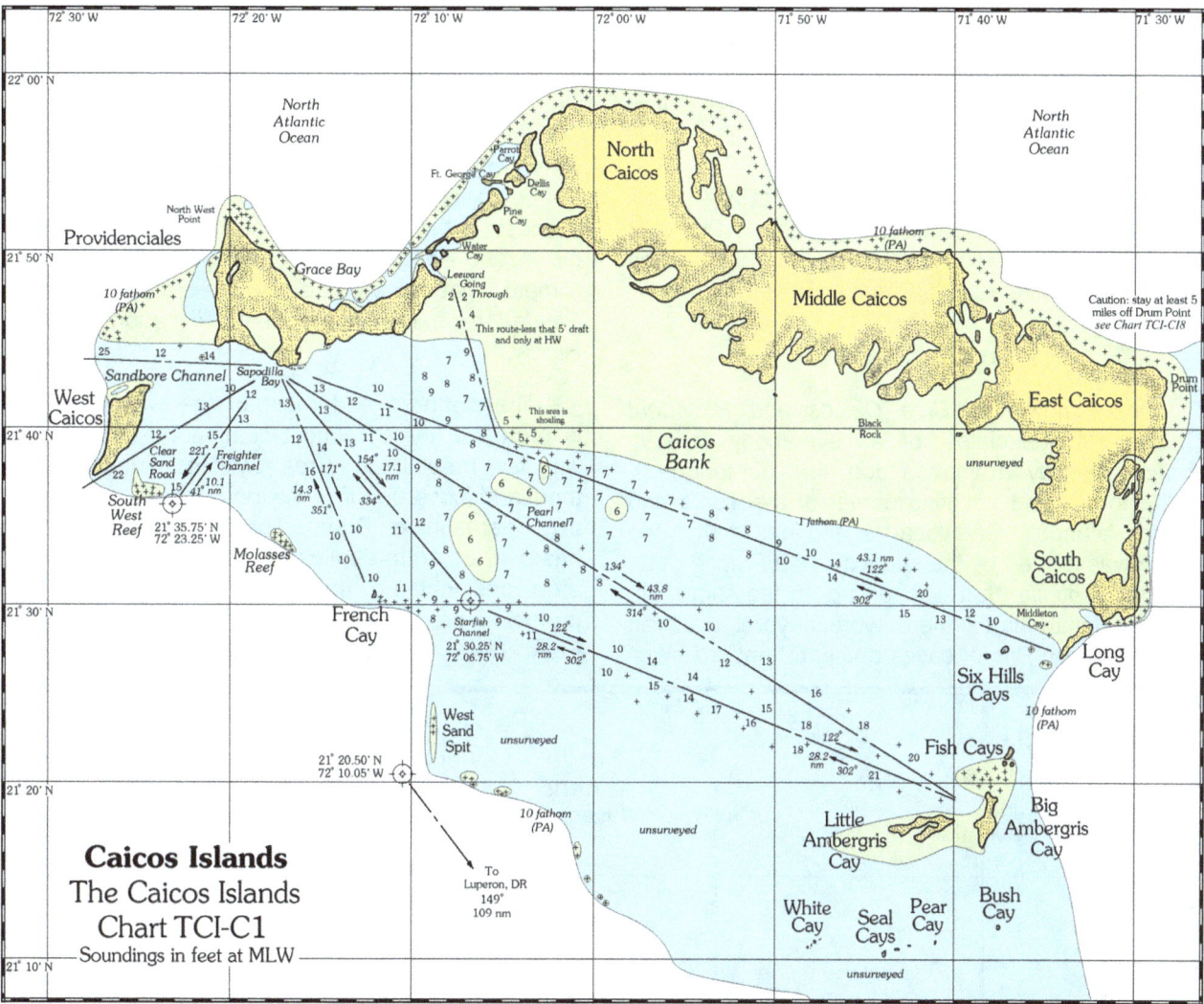

Gentleman's Guide to Passages South, suggests using Southeast Point as a staging area and leaving from there instead of the slightly longer run from *Abraham's Bay*. This is not a bad idea, but perhaps a bit outdated for today's crop of cruisers. Although staging at Southeast Point gives you a better angle on the wind and shortens the overall distance (if you don't count the over 11 miles traveled from *Abraham's Bay* to Southeast Point), most cruisers today don't bother with wind angles and simply turn on the engine and motorsail from *Abraham's Bay* or *Start Bay* to Provo. In southeast winds the reef at Southeast Point gives you no protection whatsoever, and the only protection you have at Southeast Point is from winds from the northeast to east (unless you want tuck into the northerly part of the bay in northerly winds). From the waypoint at Southeast Point, Mayaguana, 22° 16.70'N, 72° 48.40'W, *Sandbore Channel* bears 157° at a distance of 37.6 nautical miles while *Leeward Cut* bears 135° at 44 miles. The primary hazards on the route from Mayaguana to *Sellar's Pond*, *Stubbs Cut*, or *Leeward Cut* are the reefs off North West Point on Providenciales. A waypoint at 21° 53.10'N, 72° 19.90'W, will place you approximately ½ mile north of the reefs in deep water. If your route takes you to *Sellar's Pond*, *Stubbs Cut*, or *Leeward Cut*, especially at night, do not venture south of this waypoint until east of 72° 17' W. Also, bear in mind that when you head towards *Sandbore Channel*, once at the entrance you still have more than nine miles of easting to make before you reach the safety of the anchorage at *Sapodilla Bay*.

Vessels heading for the *Caicos Banks* from the Turks Islands must first cross the deep *Turks Island Passage*, sometimes called the *Columbus Passage*. From the *Front Street* anchorage at Grand Turk, the waypoint at the entrance to Cockburn Harbour

43

on South Caicos bears 281° at a distance of 21.1 nautical miles. From Salt Cay, Cockburn Harbour bears 306° at 19.3 miles, while from Great Sand Cay it bears 328° at 22.7 miles distant. *Long Cay Cut* at the south end of Long Cay bears 275° at 23.4 miles from the Front Street anchorage at Grand Turk, 298° at 20.6 miles from Salt Cay, and 320° at 22.9 miles from Great Sand Cay. Vessels heading to Provo or from across the *Caicos Bank* should see the section entitled *Routes Across the Caicos Bank*.

Providenciales

Once known as *Blue Caicos* and *Provident Caicos*, Providenciales, or as everybody calls it, Provo ("Just say Provo mon, don' hurt your tongue."), is the tourist and yachting center of the Turks and Caicos Islands. One local legend has it that the island was named by the survivors of a French boat, *La Providentielle*, that washed up on the shore. In pre-Columbian times there were several Lucayan settlements on Provo; caves dating to that era await your discovery in the Long Point and West Harbour Bluff areas. In later years, Provo, like many of its neighboring cays, such as French Cay, and Parrot Cay, was said to be a stopping place for pirates waiting to ambush treasure laden vessels plying the waters of the *Caicos Passage*. As in The Bahamas, the Loyalists came and went next. They found less success in the Turks and Caicos Islands than they did in The Bahamas, primarily due to its more arid climate. The ruins of the Loyalist era *Cheshire Hall Plantation* lie near the *Market Place* on Leeward Highway.

The northern and most of the western shore is protected by an almost continuous fringing reef with few breaks. This reef, with its almost vertical thousand foot drop-off, is the focus for the multitude of dive operations on Provo. The 38 square mile island has over 30 square miles of protected land and sea areas designated by the National Parks system. The protected areas include the *Chalk Sound National Park*, *North West Point Marine Park*, the *North*

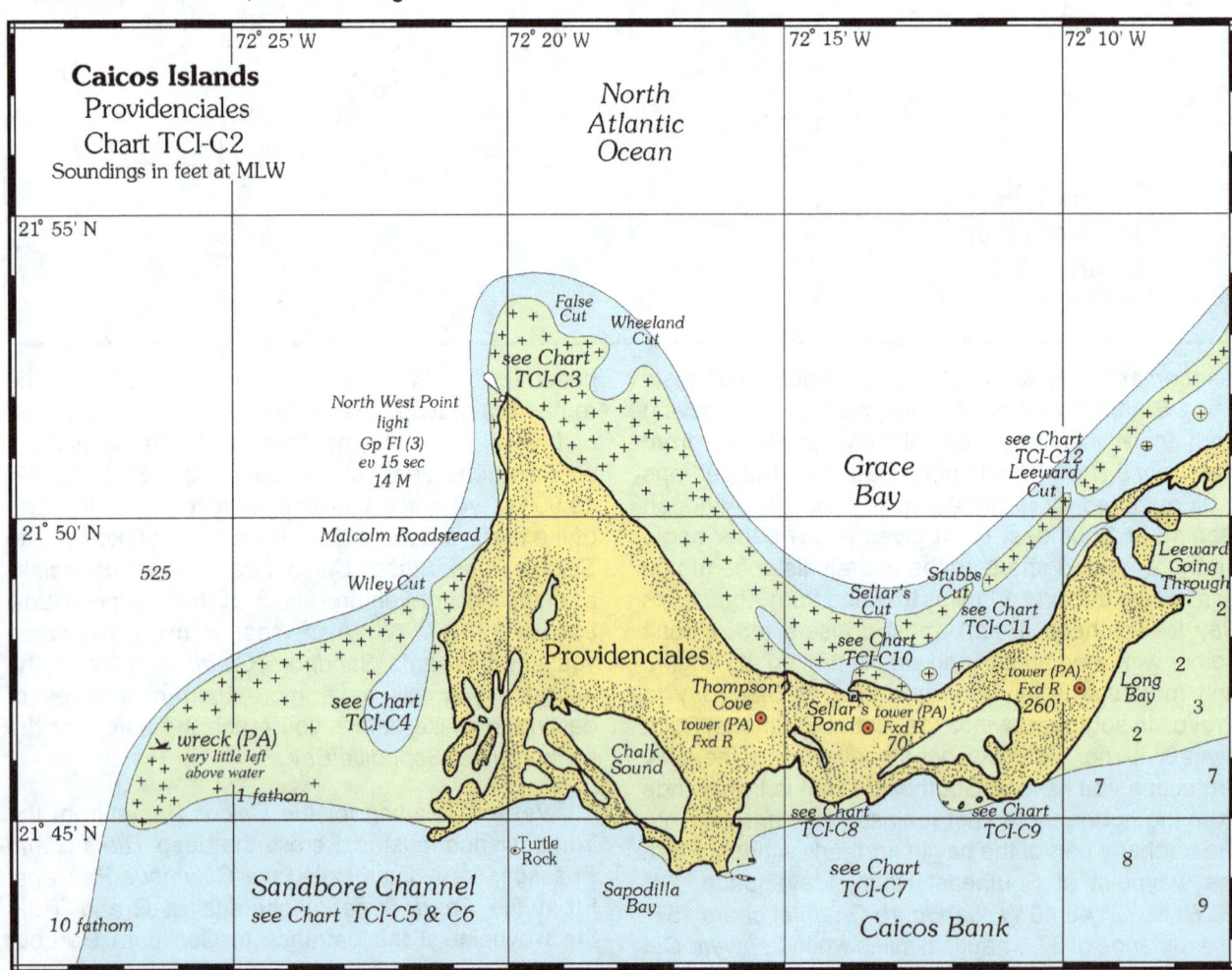

West Point Nature Reserve, the *Princess Alexandra Land and Sea Park*, the *Princess Alexandra Nature Reserve*, the *Pigeon Pond and Frenchman's Creek Nature Reserve*, the *Cheshire Hall Loyalist Ruins*, and *Sapodilla Hill*, with its stones engraved by shipwrecked sailors.

The three oldest settlements on the island are The Bight and Blue Hills on the northern shore and Five Cays on the southern shore. The Bight and Blue Hills were built around fresh water supplies and these locations give one a real feeling of a Caribbean settlement. Blue Hills had a notorious reputation as the wrecking capital of the island until just after the American Civil War. Nearby *North West Reef* contributed much to this profession and to the reputation of the community. Five Cays is primarily a fishing settlement with a large Haitian population. As recently as 1960, these three villages were all there was to Providenciales. It was on Provo that the economy of the Turks and Caicos first experienced its rebirth in the late 1960s, as tourism began to take over from the steadily declining salt industry.

In 1966, a Swedish surveyor named Bengt Soderqvist met with Fritz Luddington, who had been flying over the island for many years. Fritz was once the owner of the Two Turtles Inn in George Town, Exuma, Bahamas. These two shared their interests with other developers of vision. The government allowed the group to lease/purchase some 4,000 acres on Providenciales. In October of 1966, the seven investors, affectionately called the *Seven Dwarfs*, arrived on Providenciales on a boat of the same name. Tommy Coleman was the advance man for Fritz Luddington and his *Provident Ltd.* group. The other five investors were Julia Barber, Rogers Morton, Peter Thompson, Theodore Roosevelt III, and Richard DuPont. *Provident Ltd.* had certain obligations to meet to satisfy the government in order to receive the acreage, and these were met by 1971, scarcely five years from the inception of the project. This included the dredging of *Sellar's Pond* (now home to *Turtle Cove Marina*) and the creation of a channel to the sea, the building of roads to connect the three settlements of Blue Hills, The Bight, and Five Cays, the construction of a hotel and jetty at Five Cays, and the employment of a certain number of the local population. The jetty was actually constructed at *South Dock* as Five Cays was too shallow.

Provident Ltd. laid the early groundwork for the boom that was to come, and Provo is still right in the midst of that tourism boom. Resorts, marinas, restaurants, condos, residential projects, dive operations, a casino, and several shopping centers have all sprung up in recent years, and the end is nowhere in sight. Provo serves more than 100,000 visitors annually and it is a truly cosmopolitan island where you will find native Turks and Caicos islanders (*Belongers*), American, European, and Canadian expatriates, Haitians, Dominicans, and a variety of other nationalities and cultures. There are several major resorts, a casino, and one posh golf course.

Many cruisers have a love/hate relationship with Provo. Just as you cannot judge The Bahamas by Nassau, if you don't like Provo don't judge all the islands of the Turks and Caicos group by her standards. You'll find that many residents on the other islands in the Turks and Caicos archipelago often say that Provo is too cosmopolitan, that it tries to be too American. Indeed, Provo has a livelier nightlife, and more hustle and bustle than Grand Turk and South Caicos, and may give one the impression of being more of a suburb of Florida than a Caribbean hideaway. You will find that the rest of the islands of the Turks and Caicos have a much more laid-back out-island feel to them. A final note; if you are having any packages or mail sent to you in the Turks and Caicos and especially Provo, have them sent by *UPS* or *FedEx*, never by regular mail delivery, don't even think of sending it first class or airmail. It might take weeks. Even going by *UPS* or *FedEx* may pose a danger, although not common. I once ordered a part from a major marine supplier and told them to *FedEx* it to me in the Turks and Caicos Islands. Somehow, I still don't know how, it got to me even though it was addressed to the Cocos Keeling Islands. I've had other friends who found their mail had been forwarded to St. Kitts instead of the Turks and Caicos Islands, while others have had packages shipped to Turkey. You'd think that in this modern age…

North West Point, Sandbore Channel

Waypoints
North West Point, Provo - ½ nm N of reef:
21° 53.10' N, 72° 19.90' W

Malcolm Roadstead - ½ nm W of anchorage:
21° 49.85' N, 72° 20.80' W

Wiley Cut - ¼ nm NNW of cut:
21° 48.85' N, 72° 21.35' W

A Cruising Guide to the Turks and Caicos Islands

Navigational Information

Vessels approaching *Sapodilla Bay* and the western shore of Providenciales from Mayaguana or the Plana Cays will have no obstructions. If headed to Leeward Going Through or *Turtle Cove Marina* at *Sellar's Pond* on the northern shore of Provo on *Grace Bay,* you must take care to avoid the reefs off North West Point as shown on Chart TCI-C2. A good rule of thumb is not to head south of 21° 53'N until east of 72° 17'W.

South of North West Point on the western shore of Providenciales is a great anchorage in prevailing winds with quite an amusing history. *Malcolm Roadstead* offers a deep, reef-clear entrance right up to the beach as shown on Chart TCI-C3. Columbus is said to have anchored here in October of 1492. You too can anchor right off the beach in 8'-15' of water just off the new resort (don't try to anchor here with winds or seas with any northerly component to them.). A waypoint at 21° 49.85'N, 72° 20.80'W will place you approximately ½ mile west of the anchorage. From this position simply head in towards shore and anchor wherever your draft allows just off the beach. A good landmark to look for is the first large hill south of North West Point: it has a very distinctive white sandy road running vertically down its western face and the anchorage lies about ¼-½ mile south of the hill.

There are several mooring balls here that are suitable for boats of 60' in length and larger. These are primarily for the local dive boats but cruisers are permitted to use one if no commercial vessel requires it. There is good diving at, around, and near each mooring so be sure to avail yourself of the opportunity to view steep walls alive with corals.

Until recent years, this area was home to the *Tiki Huts*, shown on some charts as *Atlantic Village*, which were originally the set of a French game show called *Pago Pago*. The theme was a South Pacific island where contestants could win various prizes by completing several tasks. Just offshore is a dive site that consists of a large metal cage left over by the show. Contestants were required to dive down into the cage to catch small plastic pearls that were released into the water by a huge artificial "sponge" inside this cage. Nearby were several mermaids with SCUBA tanks to offer air to the divers when they needed a breath, bracelet-like rings that the divers earned were traded underwater for breaths of air. However there was one bad mermaid who would signal a diver over for a breath and then swim away.

This was done to add a bit of excitement to the show. You can imagine the problems they might have had with this format. The show filmed less than a dozen episodes that are sometimes still shown today on the local cable TV station.

Today, this area is the home to the *Amanyara Resort*, a private, world class resort featuring individual villas, each with a private chef and swimming pool!

Just south of *Malcolm Roadstead* is narrow *Wiley Cut* just north of Wiley Point. Vessels with drafts of less than 6' can, with the tide, work their way along the western shore of Provo from *Wiley Cut* to West Harbour Bluff on the inside of the reef, but I do not recommend this route for the average cruiser. This route is dangerous and should only be attempted by the skilled reef-navigator with excellent visibility and calm conditions. By using this route you'll save only a little time by not going around the reef to the mouth of the *Sandbore Channel* and the risk involved is not worth the few minutes saved. I only show this passage because it can be done and several local charter and dive boats use this reef-strewn route.

A waypoint at 21° 48.85'N, 72°, 21.35'W, will place you approximately ¼ mile north/northwest of *Wiley Cut* as shown on Chart TCI-C4. Never, I repeat NEVER, attempt this route with the sun directly in your eyes, with heavy following seas, or during periods of poor visibility and cloudy, murky water. Head in through the cut on a heading of SSE-SE keeping between the two very visible reefs. Work your way around Wiley Point as shown on Chart TCI-C4 steering between the numerous shallow heads and patch reefs that are strewn across the northern section of this route and, believe me, they are thick through here. Keep working your way southward, zigzagging between the heads, reefs, and shallow bars that begin to thin out along with the water around *North Creek*. Do not attempt to follow the courseline exactly as drawn on Chart TCI-C4: it is only for reference. Your actual route will be a little more winding with little resemblance to the courseline on the chart. Use your eyes through here, nothing else will get you through. Just north of *North Creek*, boats drawing less than 4' have the option of continuing southward paralleling the shore closer in to work your way through the shallows west of the area between *Well Creek* and Bone Fish Point. Vessels drawing over 5' are advised to head further west (as shown on the chart) around the shallows and through *Turtle Channel*. Vessels can anchor on the western side of West Harbour Bluff in prevailing winds but you

The Caicos Islands

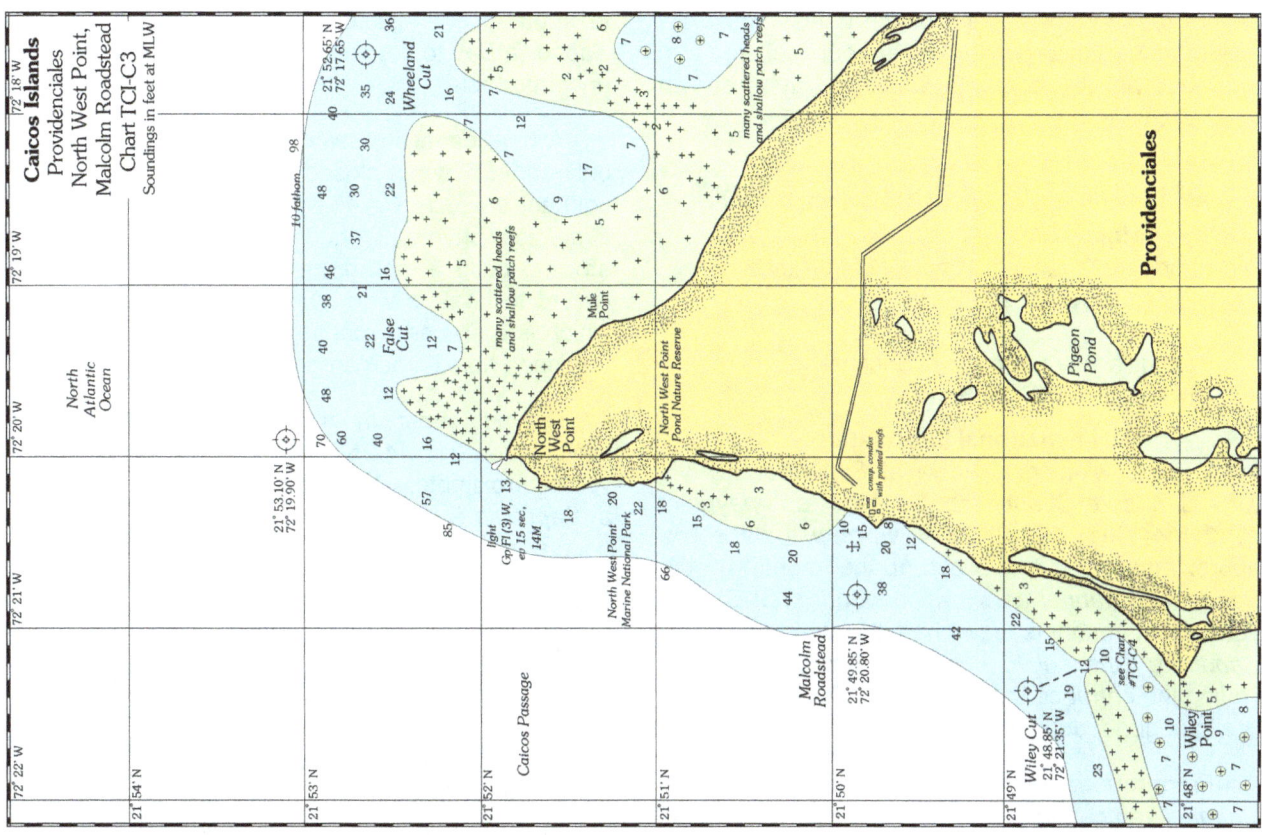

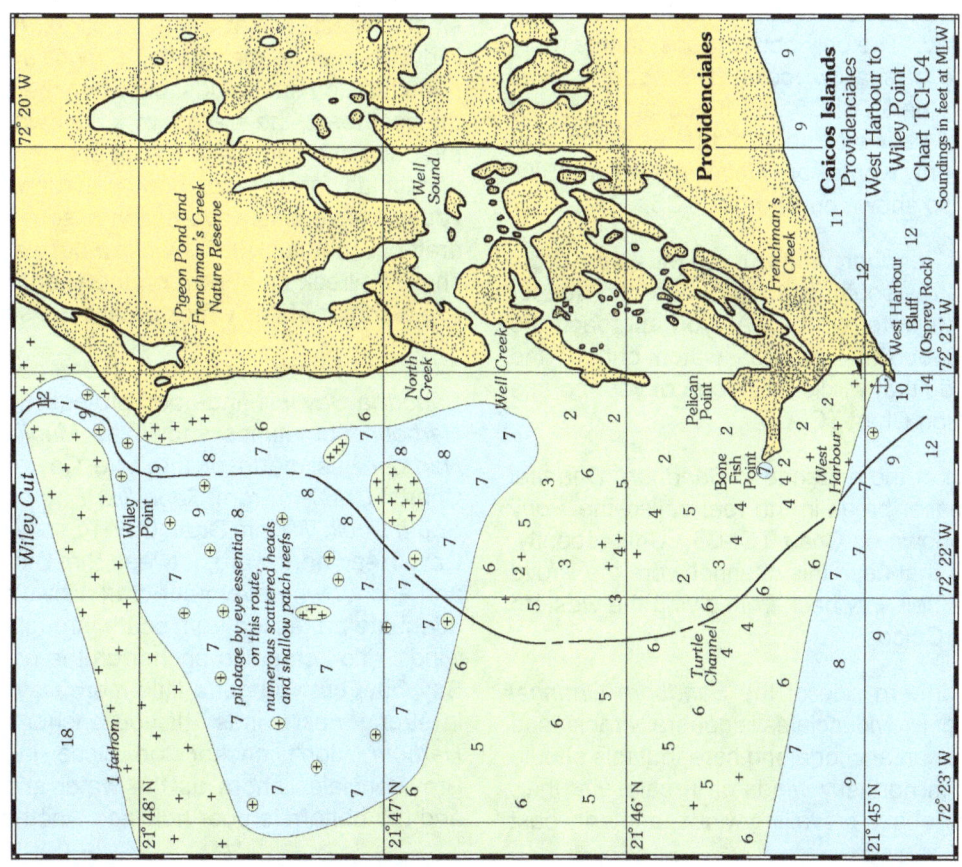

47

cannot tuck in close to the beach unless you draw less than 3'. Once past West Harbour Bluff you can turn eastward to proceed to *Sapodilla Bay* as shown on Chart TCI-C6.

Sandbore Channel, Sapodilla Bay

Waypoints

Sandbore Channel - ¾ nm W of entrance:
21° 44.50' N, 72° 27.25' W

Sapodilla Bay - ¼ nm S of anchorage:
21° 44.25' N, 72° 17.40' W

Navigational Information

Vessels wishing to arrive at *Sapodilla Bay* via wide *Sandbore Channel* should head to a waypoint at 21° 44.50'N, 72° 27.25'W, which will place you approximately ¾ mile west of the mouth of the *Sandbore Channel* as shown on Chart TCI-C5. In years past mariners have had the wreck north of *Sandbore Channel* to use as a navigation aid in finding the entrance to the channel. Today the wreck is all but gone, don't count on using it for a landmark.

From this waypoint at the entrance to *Sandbore Channel* you can take up your course of 100° for the 9.17 miles to the waypoint just south of the anchorage at *Sapodilla Bay*. The only obstructions on this route are the couple of shallow rocks at *Sandbore Shoal* as shown on Chart TCI-C5, but if you stay on your course you will pass well north of these. Once past this area your only worries are *Halfway Reef* and *Bluff Shoal*, both also shown on Chart TCI-C5.

Once past *Sandbore Shoal*, if you must stray from your course, stray south as that is where the deeper obstruction-free water will be. As you approach the Turtle Rock/*Sapodilla Bay* area watch out for the scattered heads that will lie well north of your course line as shown on Chart TCI-C6.

Just south of the entrance to *Sandbore Channel* is another smaller break in the reef called the *Pony Channel*, as shown on Chart TCI-C5. Until recently, the only boats that used this channel were the Provo dive boats on their way back from diving the western shore of West Caicos.

On the northern side of the *Sandbore Channel* the shoreline of Providenciales is generally rocky and steep-to. One can anchor along here, but this should only be done in northerly winds or in calm weather. In moderate or above prevailing winds, primarily east to southeast, a considerable chop builds up from *Sapodilla Bay* to the west and makes this shore very uncomfortable.

A small canal and swing bridge (vertical clearance only about 5' when closed) has been constructed to connect the *Silly Creek* area to *Proggin Bay*. *Silly Creek* is a private planned community and plans are afoot to build a marina inside. Currently access is limited to boaters who own property at *Silly Creek*, which is a shame because *Silly Creek* is a fantastic hurricane hole if you can get in there.

Heading east in the *Sandbore Channel*, a waypoint at 21° 44.25' N, 72° 17.40' W, will place you approximately ¼ mile south of the anchorage at *Sapodilla Bay*. It is not necessary to keep on the course line all the way from the entrance to *Sandbore Channel* to this waypoint. Once past Turtle Rock you can begin to adjust your course more north of east to arrive at the anchorage in *Sapodilla Bay* but you must keep an eye out for a few scattered, shallow heads.

The anchorage at *Sapodilla Bay*, as shown on Chart TCI-C6, although shallow, has very good holding in soft sand, but I see so many skippers anchoring too far south and west, virtually out of the small protection that the point offers, most likely this is due to their deeper drafts. *Sapodilla Bay* is good in north through east winds, but when the wind goes into the southeast, the waves work their way right around the point and can make it a bit uncomfortable. If you anchor as far as your draft will allow to the north; you will have less wave action in southeast winds. A draft of 5' can tuck in fairly close but watch out for the shallow wreck on shown on the chart; on a very low tide a corner of this wreck breaks the surface.

If a frontal passage threatens, cruisers in *Sapodilla Bay* will find good protection in *Bermudian Harbour*, sometimes shown as *Mudjian* or *Mudjon Harbour*, just north of the Five Cays as shown on Chart TCI-C7. From *Sapodilla Bay* head east past *South Dock*, William Dean Cay, Pussey Cay, and Sim Cay. Head northward between Sim Cay and Bay Cay and anchor wherever your draft allows and you'll find adequate protection from south through west to north winds. You can also anchor on the northern side of Bay Cay, but you get a little more wave action there in strong west winds. If you anchor in *Bermudian Harbour*, don't anchor too close in towards the Providenciales shore as the water shallows quickly and the bottom is poor holding. Another option is to

The Caicos Islands

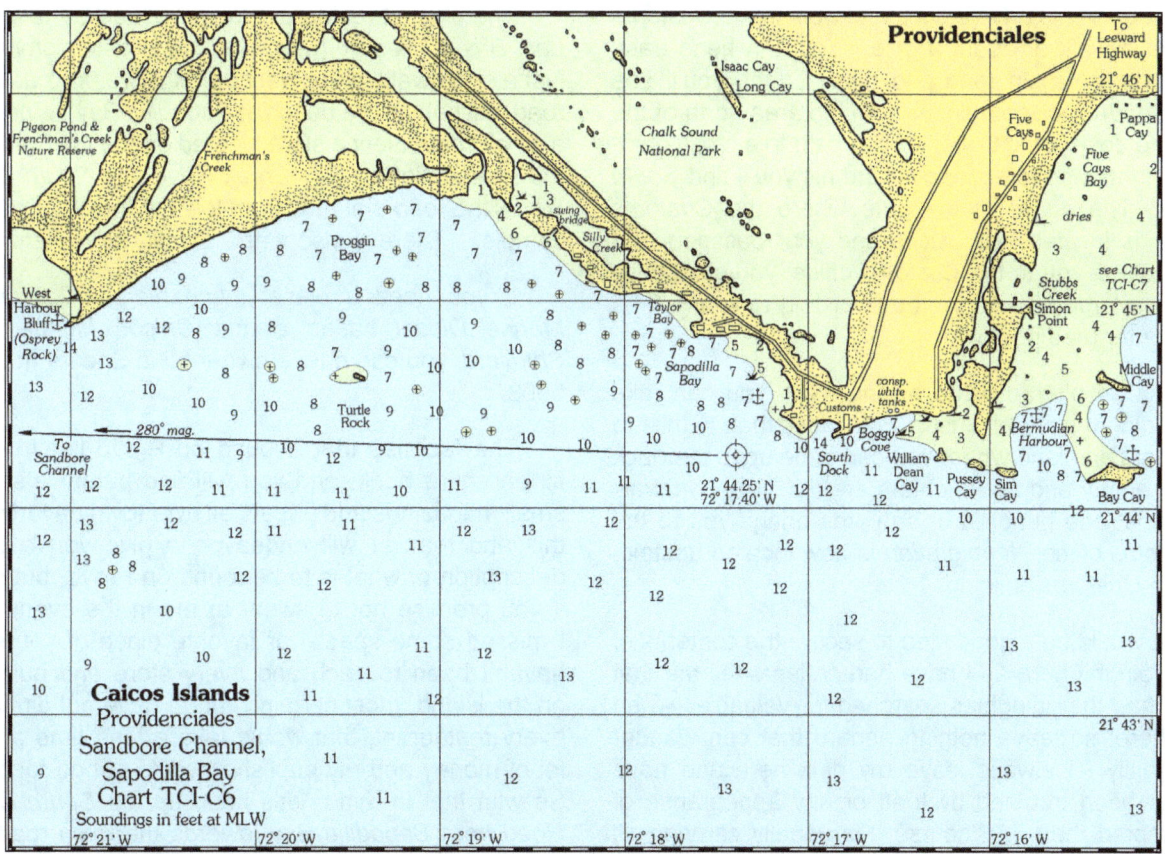

anchor in the lee of Middle Cay, also shown on Chart TCI-C7. Again, when the wind moves into the north it will be time to move back to *Sapodilla Bay*.

What You Will Find Ashore

It is possible to pick up local *Wi-Fi* service in *Sapodilla Bay* if you have a good, long range antenna.

On the hill overlooking *Sapodilla Bay* is the old *Provo Aquatic Center* at the southeastern end of the bay. The center has not been open in a few years and many cruisers are under the mistaken idea that they can clear in there or use the dock. The building is private now and the dock is reserved for the occasional dive boat to load and unload passengers, but several cruisers have been using the dock to tie up while in town. Please note that the property, including the dock, are private and off limits to cruisers.

On the top of *Sapodilla Hill* are several stones that were engraved by shipwrecked sailors and can be accessed from the hotel side of the hill or from the gravel road by the old *Aquatic Center* using a steep, rocky trail.

Vessels arriving at *Sapodilla Bay* and wishing to clear *Customs* are now advised to dinghy in to shore just north of the private dock and walk to the *Customs* office, a walk of about a mile. You can head east, towards the main road and take a right, you'll see the *South Dock* complex. From the area north of the private dock you can walk to the path to a cross path, turn right, then left, and over the hill you'll find *South Dock*. The guard at the gate where the *Customs* office is located, will ask to see your passport and then direct you to the *Customs* office, you can't miss it, it's a large two-story green building to your left as you enter (see photo).

As an alternative to a long walk, you can take your dinghy around Gussie Point, less than ½ mile to the east and land where you can or tie up to the dock if it's empty and no freighters are due. A short walk of about one hundred or so yards brings you to the *Customs* office. *Immigration* is now located upstairs in the *Customs* building.

It would be a good idea to secure the contents of your dinghy here as I have had cruisers tell me that they had their dinghies searched for valuables when left here; so leave nothing aboard that can wander off easily. I always leave my dink here and have never been troubled by theft or any appearance of attempted theft. Of course, I'm usually carrying all sorts of weapons to leave at *Customs* and that could be why my dink isn't bothered by whoever is messing around in our boats (you must leave your weapons with *Customs* for safe-keeping until you clear out of the Turks and Caicos).

Clearance itself is usually painless and quick; for more information on clearing in see the section *Customs and Immigration* in the chapter *The Basics*.

The *Customs* office is manned Monday through Friday and on weekends if commercial traffic is expected. You can try to contact *Customs* by calling *Harbourmaster* on VHF ch. 16, but you may or may not receive a reply. More than likely you'll receive a response from *South Side Marina* (east of *Sapodilla Bay* at *Cooper Jack Bight*) who monitor VHF ch. 16, 24/7, and are more than happy to help cruisers. *South Side Marina* also hosts a daily VHF net every morning at 0730 on VHF ch. 18.

Some of the buses and jitneys will try to get as much as they can for their service from the unwary tourist. By all means, agree on a price before boarding the bus or taxi or you will find that you may have made a grievous and expensive error.

The closest restaurant to *Sapodilla Bay* is at the *Las Brisas Resort* (http://neptunevillastci.com/wp/), just a short walk to the west on *Silly Creek Road* (the road just behind the beach at *Sapodilla Bay*). There is a small convenience store located on the town side of the intersection of *Silly Creek Road* and *South Dock Road,* the road that runs from town to the *South Dock* complex. There is also a new *Quality* store here.

If you need a diesel mechanic try *Caribbean Marine Diesel* based at the *Caicos Marina and Shipyard*; you can phone owner Mike Speers at 941-5903.

The facilities that abound on Provo itself could fill an entire book, and you will find pamphlets and small magazines and papers all over town advertising this and that. I will endeavor to give you a brief description of what is to be found on Provo, but only if you promise not to swear at me in the event that I missed some special or favorite place of yours. I haven't been to each and every store and building on the island, most certainly, and I have not dined at every restaurant; that would take a long time and a lot of money and my publisher would not go for that! So with that in mind, let's head up the *South Dock Road* from *Sapodilla Bay* towards the main road on

The anchorage at *Sapodilla Bay*

the island, *Leeward Highway*, and I'll try to give you a mini-tour of what's available on Provo.

From *Sapodilla Bay* and the docking facilities at *South Dock,* the *South Dock Road* winds up and over the gentle hills northward toward *Leeward Highway.* Heading north from the intersection of the *South Dock Road* and the road leading up to the *Aquatic Center* and *Silly Creek,* you'll find a small road that leads off to the right. The road does not look inviting and it appears to only lead into the parking lot of a small plant, but if you see a small sign that says "The Learning Center," that's your road, follow the signs. Take a right and walk up the hill as the small, rough road curves a bit to the right. At the top of the hill you'll see the greenhouses of *Island Fresh Produce*, the Provo hydroponics center. Fantastic hydroponic vegetables are grown here and sold to restaurants and grocery stores all over the island. *Island Fresh* (941-3903) does not sell retail, only wholesale, but they are happy to sell to the cruiser (what a great attitude!); you'll have to purchase a small minimum quantity, at least a pound of whatever you choose (restaurants must purchase a minimum of two pounds). The hydroponics center can be hard to find but fret not, their produce can usually be found at the *IGA* on *Leeward Highway*.

As you pass over the hills you'll get an absolutely gorgeous view of beautiful *Chalk Sound* and its vivid green waters. About a mile or so north of the *Shell* complex is a *Texaco* station on your left. Just before the *South Dock Road* joins the *Leeward Highway* you'll see *Kishco* on the right. This is a small dry-goods store with all sorts of home-related goodies for sale. The main *Kishco* store is now located on *Leeward Highway* and although it does not supply foodstuffs, it is the cheapest place on the island to buy wine. A couple of years ago *Kishco* purchased the entire contents of a hurricane damaged wine warehouse and today they are able to sell good wine with damaged labels at two bottles for the price of one!

Before long you'll come to the intersection at the *Leeward Highway*. The *Leeward Highway* is the main road that stretches from the airport on the western end of the cay all the way to the *Conch Farm* at the eastern end of Provo and you'll find located along this 4-lane highway the bulk of the business on Provo. To your right at the intersection of *South Dock Road* and *Leeward Highway* is *Lamont's Barbecue and Grill* for takeout food, or if you choose, eat outside at one of their tables.

If you take a left at *Leeward Highway* you will be on the *Old Airport Road* where immediately on your right you will see *The Wine Cellar* (http://winecellar.tc/) a barber shop, and a beauty parlor as well. For good island cuisine try the *Hole in the Wall Restaurant* and Bar at *William's Plaza* on the *Old Airport Road*. *Hole in the Wall* specializes in local cuisine and offers free pickup and drop off, just phone 941-4136

If you take a right on *Leeward Highway* from *South Dock Road* you will have several miles of stores and restaurants before you. On the left, just past *The Wine Cellar* is *Airport Road* which leads (where else?) to the *Fritz Luddington International Airport*. At the airport you can rent a car, visit any of several small shops, or, if you're hungry, you might want to stop at *Fast Eddies* for seafood and native dishes. At the *Airport Inn Plaza* you'll also find the *Indian Plaza Restaurant* with exotic Indian dishes and vegetarian delights.

Proceeding eastward on *Leeward Highway* from the *Airport Road*, you will now enter the downtown area and *Leeward Highway* widens from two lanes to four and is very well lit at night. "Downtown" is little more than a few stores and small mall-like centers along the *Leeward Highway* at what is known as *Butterfield Square*. On the north side of *Leeward Highway* you will see the yellow *TCI First Bank Building* which also houses some government offices, and several other shops. Next door is the *American Airlines* office and *Immigration*. A must stop is *Tasty Temptations*, open at 6:30 every morning until mid-afternoon serving fresh buns, rolls, bread, croissants, and sandwiches.

Across the street, on the southern side of *Leeward Highway*, is the *Town Center Mall* where you'll find *Rosie's Place* (the old *KFC* building), a computer service shop, and the *Island Pride Supermarket*, a great provisioning stop with a good deli and everything from frozen foods to fresh meats and veggies as well as fresh milk, orange juice, and ice cream. Next door to *Island Pride* is the new *Immigration* office in a large orange building that simply says "*Sam's*" on the front.

Just past *Butterfield Square* on the northern side of the road a *Shell* station just before the intersection with *Blue Hills Road*. *Blue Hills Road* takes you northward along the gorgeous *Grace Bay* shoreline through Blue Hills and northwards to North West Point via the new *Millenium Highway*.

Blue Hills is a lovely little community, the oldest one on the island, located on the edge of *Grace Bay* and bordering Blue Hills Road from *Leeward Highway* all the way to where the road turns into a sandy track past *Reef Harbour*. As you turn onto *Blue Hills Road* at the roundabout you'll see a black building on your left. Just behind this building is a gentleman who rebuilds electrical equipment, particularly alternators.

Here you'll find the *Government Clinic*, the *Provo Food Fair*, *Rigby's Variety Store*, and *Where It's At* where you can find fine Jamaican and native dishes. Along here you'll find *Computer Line*, a good spot for computer parts and Internet access.

As a cruiser, your primary stop might well be *Walkin Marine*, the only boating supply store on the island (but it is a good one). *Walkin Marine* is an *OMC* dealer and carries a good supply of outboard parts as well as most anything you need such as wire, 5200, stainless steel nuts and bolts, line, anchors, fishing supplies, and frozen bait. They also perform service work on all outboard motors. For more info ask at the store or call *Walkin Marine* on VHF ch. 16 and ask for Sherlock.

Just past where *Blue Hills Road* does a 90° at *Grace Bay* you'll find *Da Conch Shack* (http://daconchshack.com/Conch_Shack/Home.html), the only true island style beach front restaurant on Provo. Here you can have the freshest conch and conch salad found almost anywhere, right out of the bay to your plate. *South Side Marina* offers a weekly trip to *Da Conch Shack* from their marina at *Cooper Jack Bight*.

A bit west sits *Pub on the Bay* offering excellent native cooking and "just catched" seafood served to you right on the beach under palm thatched tiki huts. You've gotta try *Pub on the Bay*. Another fine eatery is *Henry's Road Runner Restaurant and Bar* specializing in local dishes. There is a strong Haitian influence in Blue Hills; one gentleman I talked to estimated it to be about 50% Haitian. Further west on *Blue Hills Road*, just past the *Three Queens Bar*, look to seaward and you will see several sailboats in various stages of construction. The Dean family, primarily James Pringle Dean and James Dean, has been building sloops here on the beach for over 30 years and racing them regularly in the local regattas.

Back on the *Leeward Highway*, as you continue east you'll come to a *First Caribbean Bank Branch* (https://www.cibc.com/fcib/) on the right. Across the street is the *Market Place* where you will find several nice gift shops, a jeweler, and a DVD rental store.

Continuing down *Leeward Highway* the shops begin to spread out more and more. You'll pass places like *Provo Building Supply* and the *Rigby*

Medical Center. Look for the medical center to be replaced soon by a new hospital just behind the current center.

South of *Leeward Highway*, where, on the hills above Five Cays, you'll find *TC Gas* where you can get your propane filled while you wait, and *Tibor's Machine Shop* (http://tiborsmachineshop.com/?page_id=41), who used to be on the *Old Airport Road*.

Heading east from *Market Square* you'll come to a huge *DO-IT Center* (http://www.doitcenterprovo.com/), much like a *Home-Depot* in the United States. Moving eastward once again on *Leeward Highway*, those provisioning might want to visit *Price Club Supermarket* (http://priceclubsupermarket.wix.com/priceclubprovo) with its huge stock of groceries and dry goods sold in bulk. *Price Club Supermarket* moved here from *South Dock Road* and their new large building houses even more goodies than their old place. If provisioning in Provo, you'll find the prices generally equivalent to Nassau prices, with some items priced close to stateside prices.

A little more eastward and you will come to *Quality Food Centre* (scheduled to move to *South Dock Road* and become the closest grocery store to the *Sapodilla Bay* anchorage; http://www.qualityfc.com/), *Menzies Medical Center*, and the former site of *Chez Woo Chinese Restaurant*, formerly *Hey Jose's Mexican Restaurant*. There are several small gift shops next to *Chez Woo* and at the end of the small strip mall and a photography studio. Heading westward, from *Hey Jose's* to *Sapodilla Bay*, take your first left, just past *Quality Supermarket* and *Menzies Medical Center* (a top quality medical center), and then take your first right.

A little east of *Chez Woo* you will come to *Suzie Turn* at *Suzie Turn Plaza*. The area around the turn-off from *Leeward Highway* to *Turtle Cove Marina* and the *Miramar Resort* is called *Suzie Turn*, because Suzie, a secretary who used to work in *Turtle Cove*, could never remember where the turn was. Her friends felt for her and put up a sign that read "Suzie, turn!" Both the sign and Suzie are long gone but the area still bears her name, as does *Suzie Turn Plaza*, home of *CompTCI*, a good spot for Internet access. More on *Turtle Cove Marina* a little later.

On the southern side of *Leeward Highway*, next door to *Bayview Motors*, you'll find a *NAPA* auto parts store if you need any items that may be useful on a boat (I can think of plenty). One word of warning however: no refunds, all sales are final, even if they gave you the wrong part. Next door to NAPA is *Angela's Top O' The Cove Deli* serving breakfast and lunch, and dinner (all to go), along with baked goods, meats, beverages, gourmet coffees, homemade desserts, pizza, soups and sandwiches, and quiche. Just past *Suzie Turn Plaza*, on the left side of *Leeward Highway* is the office of *Lime*, the local cable and wireless company. Further east on *Leeward Highway* is *PizzaPizza* at the new *Multiplex Cinema Plaza*. The cinema shows the latest movies on four screens.

On the right hand side of *Leeward Highway* is the huge *Graceway IGA* supermarket, a great place for provisioning in Provo. The store is large, even by US standards, and has just about anything you could want including a deli with fresh baked goods. Cruisers buying $50 or more in groceries get free delivery. Located in the same complex is a bank and the new location of *The Unicorn Bookstore*, THE place to go for reading materials (lots of kid's stuff too!), recent periodicals, used and new books, and lots of guides for the Caribbean. They also carry Bob Gascoine's charts and *The Turks and Caicos Guide*.

About ¾ mile past *IGA*, on the left, is *Pablo's Laundromat* where you can drop off your laundry for same day service (currently $6 per load, it's cheaper at *South Side Marina*). If you're staying at *Turtle Cove Marina*, there is a man that will pick up your laundry for you and drop it off at *Pablo's* for about $4 per load. Just past *Pablo's* as you head east is *A&J's Groceries*.

By the time this guide is published, *FedEx* will likely have moved to their new location near *IGA*. You can have your items shipped here and pick them up, just remember to mark all incoming supplies as ship's stores for a *Vessel in Transit*.

Just past *Pratt Road* on the northern side of *Leeward Highway* is the large *Business Solutions* store, sort of an "Office Depot" type of establishment. *Business Solutions* not only sells office and computer supplies, they also repair computers and can even print boat cards for you.

Still eastward on *Leeward Highway* is *Kathleen's Seven Eleven Convenience Store*, though it is much more than its name implies. *Kathleen's* is more like a regular grocery store than a convenience store as you might be used to in the U.S. or Canada. Here you can find lots of veggies, packaged foods, drinks, ice cream, and frozen meats, but the prices are slightly higher than *IGA* and *Island Pride*. Nearby, on the northern side of *Leeward Highway*, by the electrical power station, is *Neely's Restaurant and Bar*. *Neely's*, formerly *Dora's*, serves up delicious native seafood and chicken dishes for breakfast, lunch, and dinner and the seafood buffet on Mondays and Thursdays is not to be missed.

The turnoff to *Grace Bay* is well-marked, as are all the side roads leading off *Leeward Highway*. The *Grace Bay* turnoff is at the roundabout where *Leeward Highway* goes from 4-lanes down to 2-lanes. Continuing eastward, *Leeward Highway* is a 2-lane road but it is now paved all the way to the *Conch Farm* at Leeward Going Through. Taking a right on *Long Bay Hills Road* will take you to the *Caicos Marina and Shipyard*. As you drive down the rough road you'll crest a hill and on the right is *Sea Sage Hill Drive* where you'll want to visit *The Hole*, a naturally formed limestone hole 40' across and over 80' deep. There's a swimming hole at the bottom for those who dare to climb down the ropes to reach it.

Leaving *Leeward Highway* (before the Long Bay Hills turnoff at the roundabout where the highway goes from 4-lanes to 2) and going north towards the resorts on *Grace Bay* you'll find the *Grace Bay Pharmacy* (http://www.gracebaypharmacy.com/) where you can access the Internet, or visit an art gallery. Here too is the new *IGA Gourmet Store* where the upper end market items are beautifully presented. Just before where this road meets the highway you'll find *Almara's Craft Centre*, a colorful collection of small shops selling all manner of T-shirts, hats, and non-island made crafts.

This road ends rather quickly at the intersection of the *Bight Road*, where, if you turn left, you'll find *Bella Luna*, a multi-storied, Italian restaurant with a huge area for outside dining and glass walls permitting a wonderful view of *Grace Bay* even in inclement weather. *Bella Luna* is the place to go for true Italian food and good service in an elegant atmosphere.

Heading westward you will find the *Saltmills Mall*, and *Danny Buoy's Irish Pub and Sports Bar* (http://www.dannybuoys.com/db/). The mall boasts the *Big Al's Burgers* (http://bigalsislandgrill.com/) and several boutiques and gift shops such as *Peaches*, *Step in Style*, *Blue*, *Treasures*, and *Caribbean Creations*. On the upper floor is the National *Health Insurance Board* and the *Athletic Club Gym*. Nearby, *La Petite Place* is undergoing a makeover and remains mostly vacant.

Further west on the *Bight Road* you will pass the area known as Kingston (where *Annie's* is the place to go for local cooking although they maintain irregular business hours) and the *Beaches Resort* (http://www.beaches.com/main/tc/tc-home/) and *Le Deck* resorts. *Beaches* has a good deal for divers. For a set fee you get to go on a two-tank dive as well as have the complete use of the *Beaches* complex for one day. Swimming pool, beach, tennis court, and the opportunity to sample some outstanding dining are all yours for this one low price. Keep heading west and the *Bight Road* will bring you through the settlement of The Bight and onward to the *Turtle Cove Marina* complex, which we will discuss in a moment.

If you were to turn to the right, eastward, at the intersection of the *Bight Road*, immediately on your right is the *Ports of Call* shopping and dining area. This is one of the most popular stops on Provo and the highlight for most is *Barefoot Café* with their *Sunday BBQ Bash*. Wednesday nights they serve up an all-you-can-eat buffet, and not to be outdone, *Calico Jacks'* offers an All-You-Can-Eat Pasta Night on Mondays. Shoppers will delight at the offerings of the *Night and Day Boutique*, and *Provo Fun Cycles*. If you wish to work off the fancy meals you've been dining on, there is a gym upstairs at *Ports of Call*. Right next door to *Ports of Call*, just a bit to the east, is another shopping/dining mall, *La Petite Place*, where you can visit Juice, serving all sorts of freshly squeezed fruit and vegetable juices, fruit and herbal teas, and smoothies. Nearly all of the restaurants here at Ports of Call have free *Wi-Fi* for their customers, just ask for the password.

Heading east from Ports of Call you will pass many of the Grace Bay resorts such as the elegant *Grace Bay Club* with its extremely formal Anacaona Restaurant (formal attire only, no children under 12). Opposite the *Grace Bay Club*, behind the beautiful grounds of the Sunshine Nursery, is the Coco Bistro (http://www.cocobistro.tc/) where you can dine under the palms. All the brochures about this place never mention the mosquitoes and no-see-ums. If you plan to dine here, and you should, choose a very windy night. Even better, maybe the bistro should put a can of insect repellent on every table.

Along the same road are the *Wymara, West Bay Club* (http://www.thewestbayclub.com/), the *Turks and Caicos Club*, and *Coral Gardens* where the *Somewhere Café* serves Tex-Mex food and breakfast all day.

A little further east is the huge *Club Med* complex. Club Med is very private, it is not open to the general public, but for a fee you can become a member for a day and have access to their complex. If you just want to visit for a meal, I can recommend the Sunday All-You-Can-Eat Lunch Buffet. For $35 per person, 18 and older, you get to help yourself to a huge buffet, enjoy a Mimosa, and drink unlimited beer, wine, juices, and sodas. That's unlimited beer and wine folks! People should be beating a path for this one.

Just east of *Club Med* is the *Provo Golf Club*, an 18-hole championship course with an attractive clubhouse that is open to members and non-members alike (http://www.provogolfclub.com/). The golf course uses over 300,000 gallons of RO water a day to maintain its lush fairways and greens. The Arab backers that financed the golf course had to do something for the island to be allowed to construct the golf course so he built the *Provo Water Company* which benefits the course as well as the islanders. In 1996 the course was rated one of the top ten golf courses in the Caribbean. If you don't want to play golf, but want to dine at the club, stop in at the *Fairways Bar and Grill* and watch the duffers hard at play.

Across the street is the *Ocean Club*, a luxury condominium project. Now you will enter the Leeward area where a huge planned community development project is ongoing. The Leeward Highway ends at Leeward Marina and Leeward Going Through which we will discuss in greater detail in the section The Caicos Cays-Leeward Going Through to North Caicos.

The Southern Shore

Waypoints
Cooper Jack Bight - ½ nm SW of entrance:
21° 45.05' N, 72° 14.00' W

Caicos Marina/Shipyard - 1 nm SSE of entrance:
21° 44.80' N, 72° 10.30' W

Bay Cay - 1 nm ESE of:
21° 43.75' N, 72° 14.00' W

There are two good marine facilities on the southern shore of Providenciales including the only haul-out yard in the Turks and Caicos at this time. These services are easily accessible from *Sapodilla Bay* with only a few small reefs and shoals, easily seen in good light, to avoid. Don't try to head eastward to the marinas at *Discovery Bay* or Juba Point with the sun right in your eyes first thing in the morning. Bear in mind that strong northeast winds for a day or two can keep the tides low on the southern shore of Providenciales while strong southerly winds will give the area higher tides than normal.

Navigational Information
As of this writing the closest marina facilities to *Sapodilla Bay* are at the *South Side Marina* and *Harbour Club Marina*, both located in *Cooper Jack Bight*, sometimes called *Discovery Bay* (a draft of 7' can enter the marina at high tide). While *South Side Marina* is a full-service marina, *Harbour Club Marina* is private and is usually filled up with local dive boats.

To reach *South Side Marina* and *Harbour Club Marina* head east from *Sapodilla Bay* past the Five Cays, William Dean Cay, Pussey Cay, Sim Cay, Middle Cay, and Bay Cay, passing south of them as shown on Chart TCI-C6 and Chart TCI-C7. Once past Bay Cay you can take up an approximate northeast heading to a waypoint at 21° 45.05' N, 72° 14.00' W, placing you approximately ¼ nautical mile southwest of the entrance channel into the canals of *Cooper Jack Bight* and the marina as shown on Chart TCI-C8. Before heading out from *Sapodilla Bay* for either *South Side Marina* or *Caicos Marina and Shipyard* it might be a good idea to hail them on the VHF to let them know you are headed their way.

This area is often called *Discovery Bay*, primarily by the realtors and developers responsible for such things. From the waypoint in *Cooper Jack Bight* you will be able to look northeastward and see the marina complex hiding just inland. At this point, you can head generally NE past Cooper Jack Rock until you pick up the markers leading in to the marina. Watch out for scattered heads and shallow bars on this route, the whole southern shore of Providenciales has numerous scattered heads and bars strewn about that are easily seen in good light and avoided. Be sure to take the point and its shallow sandbar well to starboard. Round into the deeper water of the entrance channel (there is a small range set up on shore for this purpose, if you're confused contact

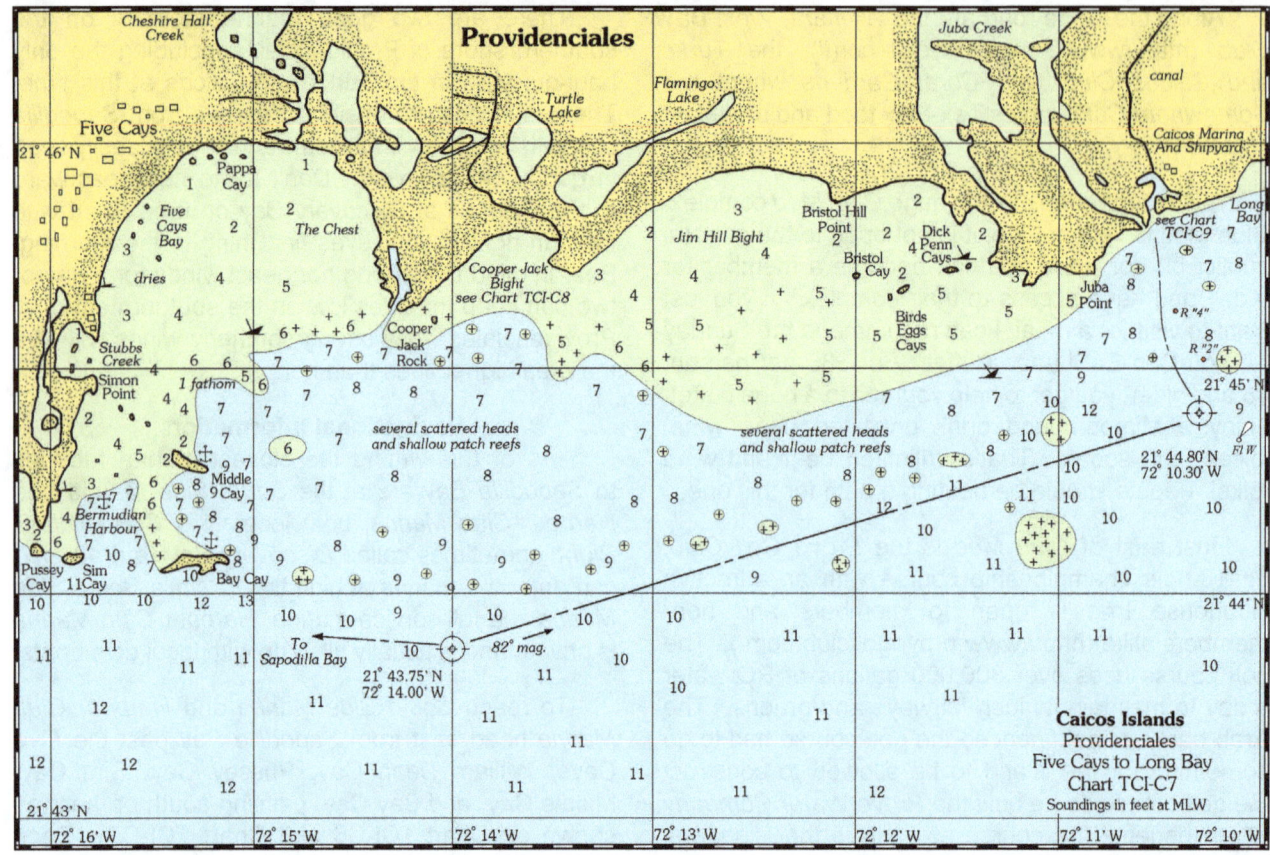

South Side Marina on VHF for instructions) and proceed to the marinas that lie straight ahead.

South Side Marina suggests using the following route and waypoints (unverified by me). First, hail the marina on VHF ch. 16 (working channel 18) to advise the marina staff of your approach. Starting at a waypoint at 21° 43.50' N, 72° 14.65' W, set a course of 30° magnetic for 1.8 nm to a second waypoint at 21° 45.26 N, 72° 13.98' W. At this point the marina's marker buoys (lit at night) should be visible over your starboard bow. Keep close to the buoys (red, right, returning), and then pass through between the red and green markers and immediately turn 90° to port to enter the marina.

What You Will Find Ashore

To your left, as the canals of *Discovery Bay* bear away, you will see the new *Provo Marine Biology Education Center*. *Turtle Lake* at the end of the canals is a good bonefishing spot. *South Side Marina* and *Harbour Club Marina* lie just ahead and to starboard. As I mentioned earlier, *Harbour Club* is private, but *South Side Marina* (http://www.southsidemarina-tci. com/) is a full-service cruiser-friendly marina (run by cruisers for cruisers).

Owner Bob Pratt and Manager Simon Anderson have worked overtime to upgrade the services at the marina and make it a true cruiser's destination, clean, quiet, and with a "family" atmosphere. One of their services is the voluntary monitoring of VHF ch. 16 on a 24/7 basis in case of emergencies. We all can feel safer knowing that the marina is listening and able to arrange assistance. The marina also hosts a daily VHF net on ch. 18 at 0730.

South Side Marina offers diesel and gas, as well as dockside electric and RO water. They have floating docks with 20 slips capable of handling vessels up to 65' LOA with a 6' draft (and in fact have docked two vessels of over 90' LOA). Ashore you will find bathrooms and showers, a laundry room with a self-service washer and dryer, Wi-Fi, a book exchange, ice, showers, TV hook up, temporary local phone rental, daily happy hours in the gazebo, and weekly barbeques with free transportation for cruisers at *Sapodilla Bay* and *Turtle Cove Marina*. Simon also offers free rides to the grocery store for guests of

South Side Marina. Cruisers are welcome to use the dinghy dock at the marina for a fee of $5 per day. The use of holding tanks while in the marina is mandatory but the marina does not have a pump out facility so you will have to go elsewhere for that.

The marina is home to *Bob's Bar* (open nightly from 1700-2100), a popular eating and drinking establishment where you will meet lots of locals and ex-pats and hear their tales. Their marina store sells *Wavey Line Charts*, courtesy flags, and T-shirts, and the marina staff can help with onward voyage planning. Next day propane fills are available.

Well east of *Cooper Jack Bight* is Juba Point and the well-marked entrance to the *Caicos Marina and Shipyard* (http://www.caicosmarina.com/) where a draft of 6' can enter just past low tide. In 1986, Canadian investor Ted Trump built this marina with the goal of making it the largest marina complex in the Caribbean, and today new owners are in the process of upgrading and expanding the services with plans for more slips and even a playground for the kiddies. *Caicos Marina and Shipyard*, the only place to haul a boat (a 75-ton travel-lift and a 20-ton forklift) between Stella Maris and George Town in The Bahamas, and Puerto Rico. They also sell diesel, gas, ice, sodas, and RO water. The marina has a small laundry, public telephone, Internet access, and they can handle your mail and fax needs. The yard can handle all sorts of hull related work such as fiberglass repairs, strut work, welding, painting, interior repairs, and even motor work in their newly refurbished eco-friendly yard.

Dockage is side-to along their 500' dock and with the installation of their new floating docks, *Caicos Marina and Shipyard* is able to accommodate approximately 24 vessels with full electric, Wi-Fi, pump out, and RO water. Their large shed has now been converted into stacked dry-storage for smaller boats and the marina now offers long-term wet and dry storage of cruising boats including a care-taking service to run your engine, pump the bilge, and charge the batteries. The *Caicos Marina and Shipyard* can be reached by VHF on Ch. 16, or by phone at 649-946-5600, by fax at 649-946-5390, and by email at caicosmarinashp@tciway.tc. The Providenciales *Police Marine Division* is based at the *Caicos Marina and Shipyard*. The marina is also an agent for *Grace Bay Car Rentals* (http://www.gracebaycarrentals.com/). Look for the marina to open a bar and restaurant in the near future.

Housed on the marina property is Mike Speer's *Caribbean Marine Diesel* where you can have your engine serviced or replaced, welding done, and have your prop straightened. You can telephone *Caribbean Marine Diesel* for service if your boat can't make it to the marina at 941-5903. If you need welding and/or fabrication in steel, aluminum, or stainless steel, call Mike Robertson at *Osprey Marine Services* at 946-5122. Mike is one of the best welders and fabricators on the island and can also help you with any woodworking repairs as well as minor rigging and hull repairs.

Navigational Information

To find Juba Point and the *Shipyard* from the Sapodilla waypoint steer 108° for 3.2 miles, past the Five Cays, William Dean Cay, Pussey Cay, Sim Cay, Middle Cay, and Bay Cay, to a waypoint at 21° 43.75'N, 72° 14.00'W, as shown on Chart TCI-C7. The best way to describe the route to the *Shipyard* is to use the natural land formations themselves instead of waypoints. From the waypoint southeast of Bay Cay, look to the north and east. That last point of land that you see to the east is Juba Point. Heading just north of east on a course of approximately 82°, a line of dark spots, shallow patch reefs and rocky bars, will lie parallel to this route. Keep south of all the dark spots that you see (the line of shallow reefs) keeping them well off your port side as the deeper, obstruction free water lies to their south. The actual course line has you passing north of one of the dark reefs, but it is fine to pass it to the south as well. The course here is not as important as staying in the clear blue/green water and avoiding any dark patches that you see.

As you approach Juba Point you will notice what looks like a huge white "I" seemingly carved into the hillside. Actually it is a sandy road with a vertical trail leading down to a sandy beach. As you take the huge white "I" on your port beam, the *Shipyard* entrance channel lies approximately ¾ mile to the east. At this point you should be able to make out the cranes and perhaps even the entrance channel markers of *Caicos Marina and Shipyard*. From here you can work your way to a waypoint at 21° 44.80' N, 72° 10.30' W, which will place you a little over 1 nautical mile south of the entrance channel leading into the *Caicos Marina and Shipyard* as shown in the blow-up on Chart TCI-C7 and Chart TCI-C9. From this waypoint you should see the outer sea buoy (white light atop) and the two red markers between it and the shore. From this position, the entrance channel is approximately 1 nautical mile distant on

A Cruising Guide to the Turks and Caicos Islands

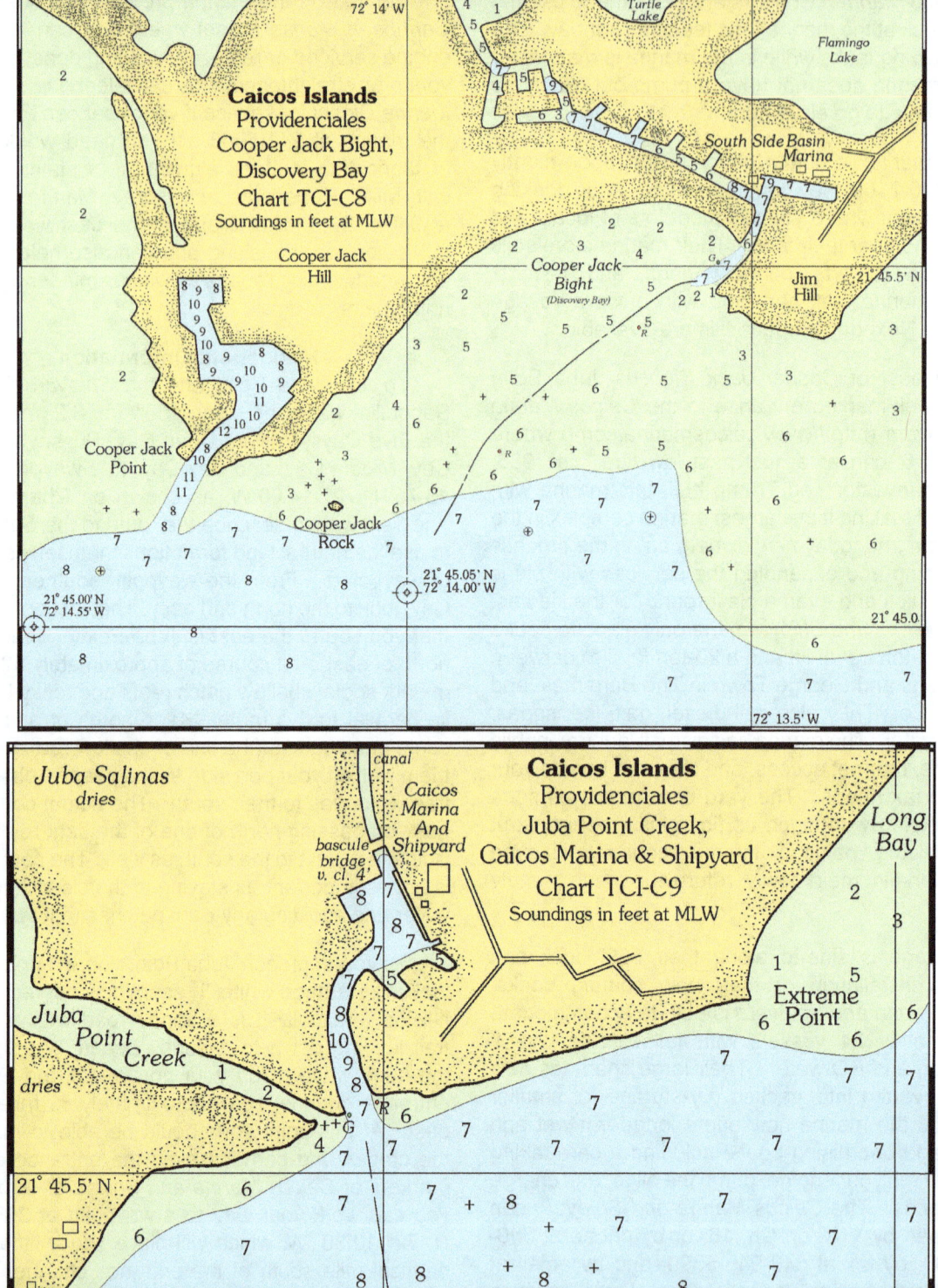

an approximate course of 345° magnetic (but as you will notice, the course actually bends more northward after R "4").

The channel mouth is marked by tall red and green striped pilings (red-right-returning), and as you approach the entrance keep a lookout for any stray heads in the surrounding waters. There is a shallow spot between the channel markers that carries 6' at low water. The channel curves to the east as you approach the marina complex with its huge building and tall cranes that are usually the first sight of the marina from seaward. The two small coves southeast of the marina dock and lift are private and are not part of the marina complex; they would make a fair hurricane hole if needed. A canal heads northward from the marina past a small bridge towards a number of private homes in the Long Bay Hills area, but draft is limited to about 3'-4' at MLW. This too would be a nice spot to ride out a hurricane.

Now if you insist on waypoints for this route then here you are: from the *Sapodilla Bay* waypoint head 108° for 3.2 nautical miles to a waypoint southeast of *Bay Cay* at 21° 43.75'N, 72° 14.00'W, as shown on Chart TCI-C7. From this waypoint steer 82° for 3.6 nautical miles to a waypoint at 21° 44.80' N, 72° 10.30' W. This is the outer waypoint for your route to the *Shipyard*. From this waypoint keep the red markers to starboard as you approach the entrance channel as shown on Chart TCI-C9. Keep a sharp lookout for the reefs that abound on the N side of this courseline.

Northern Shore, Grace Bay

Waypoints
North West Point - ½ nm N of reef:
21° 53.10' N, 72° 19.90' W

Wheeland Cut - ½ nm NNE of cut:
21° 52.65' N, 72° 17.65' W

Stubb's Cut - ¼ nm NW of cut:
21° 48.93' N, 72° 11.30' W

Grace Bay, the large body of water on the northern shore of Providenciales, is the location for most of the tourism infrastructure as well as being a fantastic sailing ground in its own right. Here you can get the full effect of the prevailing east/southeast winds, but with very little sea. *Grace Bay* is named after Gracie Jane Hinson, usually just called Grace, who was born in Grand Turk in 1873. In 1892 Grace married Hugh Houston Hutchings, also a native of Grand Turk. The couple spent their honeymoon at a small cottage on the beach on the north shore of Providenciales near the settlement called *The Bight*, then called *Blue Hills*. Grace was a very beautiful woman and the couple's visit was quite an occasion for the few inhabitants of the area. After the couple returned to Grand Turk, the people of Blue Hills referred to the beach as *Grace Beach* and the waters as *Grace Bay*, as they are known today.

Navigational Information
As mentioned earlier, vessels approaching *Sapodilla Bay* and the western shore of Providenciales from Mayaguana or The Plana Cays will have no obstructions. If headed to Leeward Going Through or *Turtle Cove Marina* at *Sellar's Pond* on the northern shore of Provo on *Grace Bay*, you must take care to avoid the reefs off North West Point as shown on Chart TCI-C2. A good rule of thumb is not to head south of 21° 53'N until east of 72° 17'W. A waypoint at 21° 53.10'N, 72° 19.90'W, will place you approximately ½ mile north of the reefs in deep water. If your route takes you to *Sellar's Pond*, *Stubbs Cut*, or *Leeward Cut*, especially at night, do not venture south of this waypoint until east of 72° 17' W.

Just east of North West Point as shown on Chart TCI-C3, is *Wheeland Cut*. Vessels drawing less than 4' can enter this cut and pass eastward between the outer reef and the northern shore of Providenciales, that is if they can pick their way through the shallow reef that winds itself from Provo out to the barrier reef just southeast of *Wheeland Cut*. I do not recommend this route as there is nothing to gain by taking it, but everything to lose. There are numerous shallow patch reefs, coral heads, and rocky bars between the reef and the shore that you must avoid along this route. The best water is just inside the reef, staying north of the shoreline until in the vicinity of the high hills just west of Sellar's Pond. The only boats that actually use this route are the local fishermen and a few of the dive boat operators. And by all means stay out of *False Cut*- it is exactly that. It can lead even small outboard powered boats (yes, I mean dinghies) to destruction. From *False Cut* to North West Point the area is literally STREWN with dangerous *shallow* reefs, many of which dry out at low water or lie just inches below the surface.

This area is a great snorkel spot in settled weather, but use extreme caution; these waters are thick with heads just waiting for the unwary dinghy.

A Cruising Guide to the Turks and Caicos Islands

The heads are especially thick close to the point. The *North West Point Light* (*Gp Fl-3 W, ev 15 sec, 15M*) is once again out of operation and when it will be repaired is anybody's guess.

The center of the yachting scene in *Grace Bay* is located at *Turtle Cove Marina* in *Sellar's Pond*. There are two routes to *Turtle Cove Marina* from outside the reef, but the best one is the primary route through *Sellar's Cut* as shown on Chart TCI-C10. A secondary route - and this one is usually only used by those skippers with good weather, even better visibility, and a fearless desire to sail around and through reefs paralleling the beach - is to pass through the reef via *Stubbs Cut* and head westward towards *Sellar's Cut* on the inside of the reef. We will discuss entering *Stubbs Cut* in a moment, but for now, let me just say that once inside *Stubbs Cut*, the skipper can parallel the beach close in, keeping all the white dive site buoys to starboard as you approach *Sellar's Cut*. Off the *Beaches Resort* you will have to keep further offshore and steer between several small patch reefs and heads to gain *English Cut* as shown on Chart TCI-C10.

For those skippers wishing to enter through *Sellar's Cut*, a waypoint at 21° 48.40'N, 72° 12.40'W, will place you approximately ¼ mile north of the green daymark that defines the entrance channel through *Sellar's Cut* as shown on Chart TCI-C10. There are supposed to be a matching set of red and green markers here, but wind and wave seems to remove one or the other every year. Remember that as you approach the cut and find yourself wondering where the other marker is. Always remember that any floating aid to navigation mentioned in this book is subject

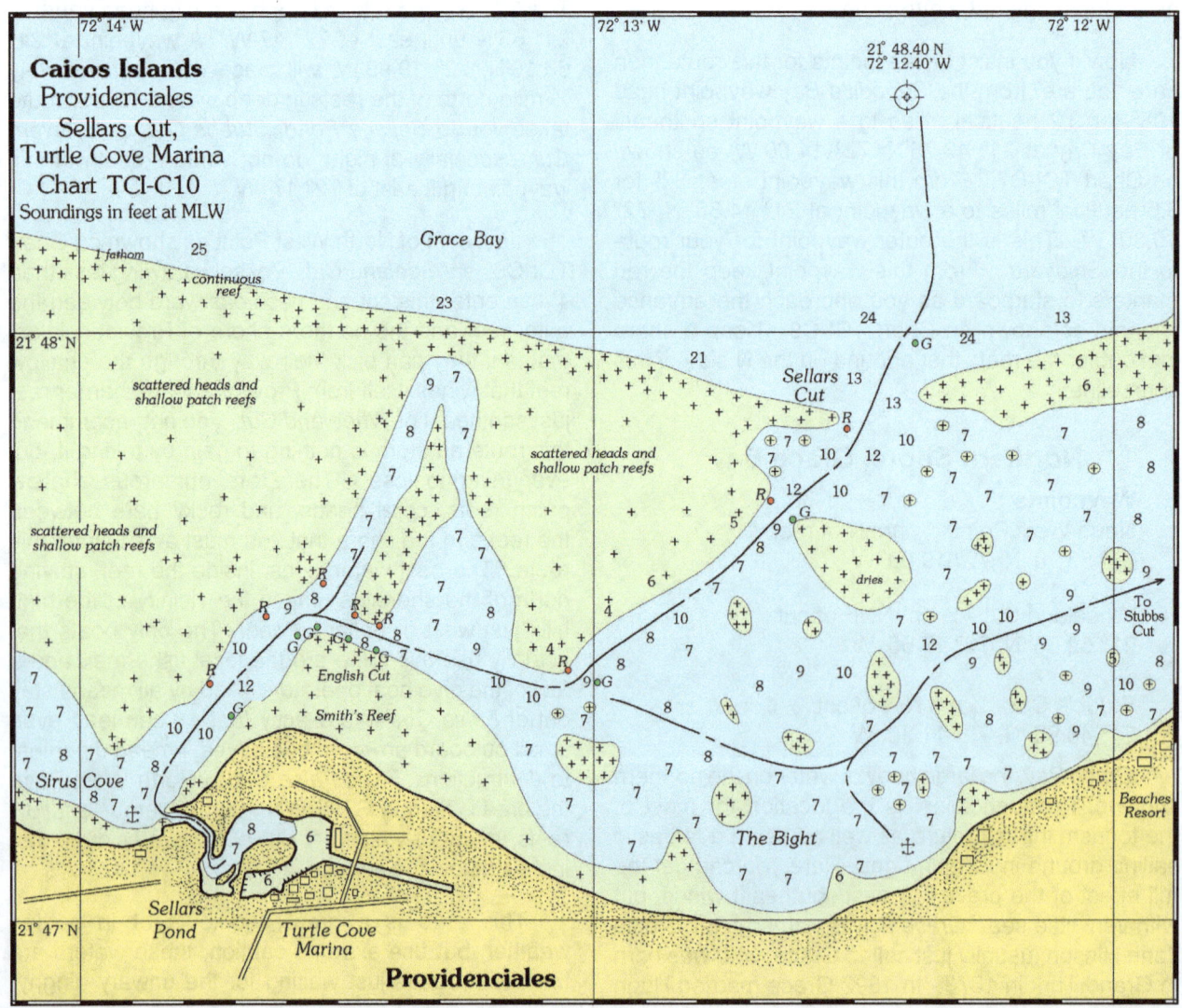

to disappearing or moving between the time we go to print and the time you arrive at your destination. Storms, high winds and seas, all combine to play havoc on floating aids along the northern shore of Provo from *Sellar's Cut* to *Leeward Cut*.

From the waypoint at *Sellars Cut* head generally southward until you can pass between the outer green daymark (red right returning), in 13'-22' of water and follow the rest of the markers in as shown on the chart. At one time you had a choice of two routes to take when inside the reef, the more northerly route has been discontinued and the markers removed in favor of the far easier *English Cut*. I have run both routes and much prefer *English Cut*, which, though narrow (a 52' long by 30' wide trimaran can make it through with no problem) has a minimum depth of 7' and is far shorter. Once through *English Cut* keep the green markers to port as you head towards the marina entrance. Watch out for the shallow heads lying just north of the shoreline about 100 yards northeast of the entrance to the pond. The winding entrance channel itself is narrow and has a shallow sandbar at its eastern entrance, on your port side when entering, and a rocky bar across the channel on your starboard side. Once inside, give the final inner turn on your port side a wide berth before rounding to port into the pond itself.

Never attempt *Sellar's Cut* with a strong northerly swell; in these conditions the cut will break all the way across and any mishap at this point could be disastrous. If unsure about how to enter *Sellar's Cut* and the entrance to *Turtle Cove Marina*, call the marina on VHF ch. 16 and the dockmaster will be happy to have someone come out to lead you in. At this time there is no charge for this service but a tip is expected, and very well deserved as you will see.

There used to be a nice anchorage in *Sirus Cove* just west of the entrance to *Sellar's Pond* and *Turtle Cove Marina*. It's a calm spot in moderate prevailing conditions, though the bottom is a bit grassy, and it offered an excellent opportunity for cruisers to avail themselves of all that *Turtle Cove* has to offer by dinghy. There is some question as to whether the National Park Wardens will allow you to anchor there even though the dive boats use the anchorage for their guests.

Another good anchorage is in *The Bight* just south of the *Beaches Resort*. This spot has good holding and adequate protection from the prevailing wind and swell. Snorkelers will love to investigate *Smith's Reef*, the large area lying between *English Cut* and the shoreline. *Smith's Reef* is a favorite local dive spot where you can explore several shallow water patch reefs and numerous scattered heads that are frequented by snorkelers from both the resorts and the local dive operations. In fact, between the barrier reef and the shoreline are many shallow reefs marked by white buoys. These are all active dive sites and the buoys are for the dive boats to tie to. You can take your dinghy out to these reefs and see for free what the charterers and other tourists pay a lot of money to view.

What You Will Find Ashore

Turtle Cove Marina has 106 slips, sells diesel and gas, and can handle a 188' vessel with a 7.5' draft. The marina is a port of entry so if you need to clear in the dockmaster can arrange for a *Customs* officer to visit your boat. The marina offers *Wi-Fi*, propane fills, and hosts the annual *Provo International Billfish Tournament* in mid-summer and sells fishing licenses year-round. In years past cruisers could anchor in *Sellar's Pond*, but the sandbar that once filled the center is now part of the marina, and docks have been constructed around its circumference effectively ending the anchoring in the pond.

The complex surrounding the marina has just about anything a cruiser could want; what isn't there is only a short taxi ride away, or perhaps you would rather rent a scooter or car from *Scooter Bob's* (http://scooterbobstci.com/) on the marina grounds. *Scooter Bob's* has some of the most competitive rental prices on the island and also has a good line of fishing tackle and baits. Scooter Bob's is one of four auto rental companies on the island who will deliver to any marina. The others are *Tropical Auto Rental* (http://www.tropicalautorentalci.com/index.php), *Grace Bay Autos*, and *Rent a Buggy* (http://rentabuggy.tc/).

Also on site is *The Tiki Hut* (http://tikihut.tc/), a very nice outdoor bar and grill combo, and *The Anchorage Restaurant* serving economical lunches and eloquent dinners with great homemade ice cream. The *Tiki Hut* is very popular and offers a *West Indian Curry Night* on Mondays, and a *Chicken and Rib Night* on Wednesdays, while the *Anchorage* offers *Peking Duck Night* on Mondays, *Mussels Night* on Tuesdays, and a *Sushi and Sashimi Night* on Saturdays, and a *Sunday Brunch* until 1400. The *Anchorage* also offers Internet access.

Provo Turtle Divers (http://provoturtledivers.com; formerly *Art Pickering's Turtle Divers*) operates out of *Turtle Cove* for those wanting to explore the fine reef diving in Grace Bay or West Caicos. There are numerous other small gift shops, boutiques and salons in the surrounding complex including *Tipsy's Liquors*.

Across the street from the marina you'll find the steep natural stone stairs that lead up to the *Miramar Resort*, formerly the *Erebus Inn* (when it was named after a giant butterfly which when touched brings you good luck), is truly elegant and its *Magnolia Wine Bar and Restaurant* (http://www.magnoliaprovo.com/default.html) is nothing short of first class with an absolutely stunning view of *Grace Bay*. I suggest going there just for the view, but I personally avoid the staircase from *Turtle Cove Marina*. Perhaps if I made better use of *Bodywise*, the complete gym that is located at the *Miramar Resort*, the steep staircase known as *Cardiac Hill* might not be so exhausting.

Of course, the time I spend at *Turtle Cove* in *Sharkbites* probably doesn't help. Situated on the eastern end of the marina property, the Friday evening happy hour with two for one drinks and complimentary munchies is a regular stop for me when I'm on Provo. *Sharkbites* also offers a Wednesday night *Fish & Chips Night*. I sincerely believe, and I may have tried them all, that *Sharkbites* has <u>THE BEST</u> chicken wings on the island of Providenciales. I've heard it said that they also have the island's best hamburgers but I can't seem to get past the wings to try the burgers. Check out the money shark and the card shark hanging from the ceiling in *Sharkbites*. Nearby is a DVD rental store, Tropical Upholstery (for canvas and upholstery repairs) and *Baci*, an Italian style eatery with excellent espresso.

About a mile to the west of *Sellar's Pond*, around the next point (Cove Point), lies the almost hidden entrance to the dredged creeks of *Thompson Cove* as shown on Chart TCI-C2, a very, very private residential community. The sign that welcomes you

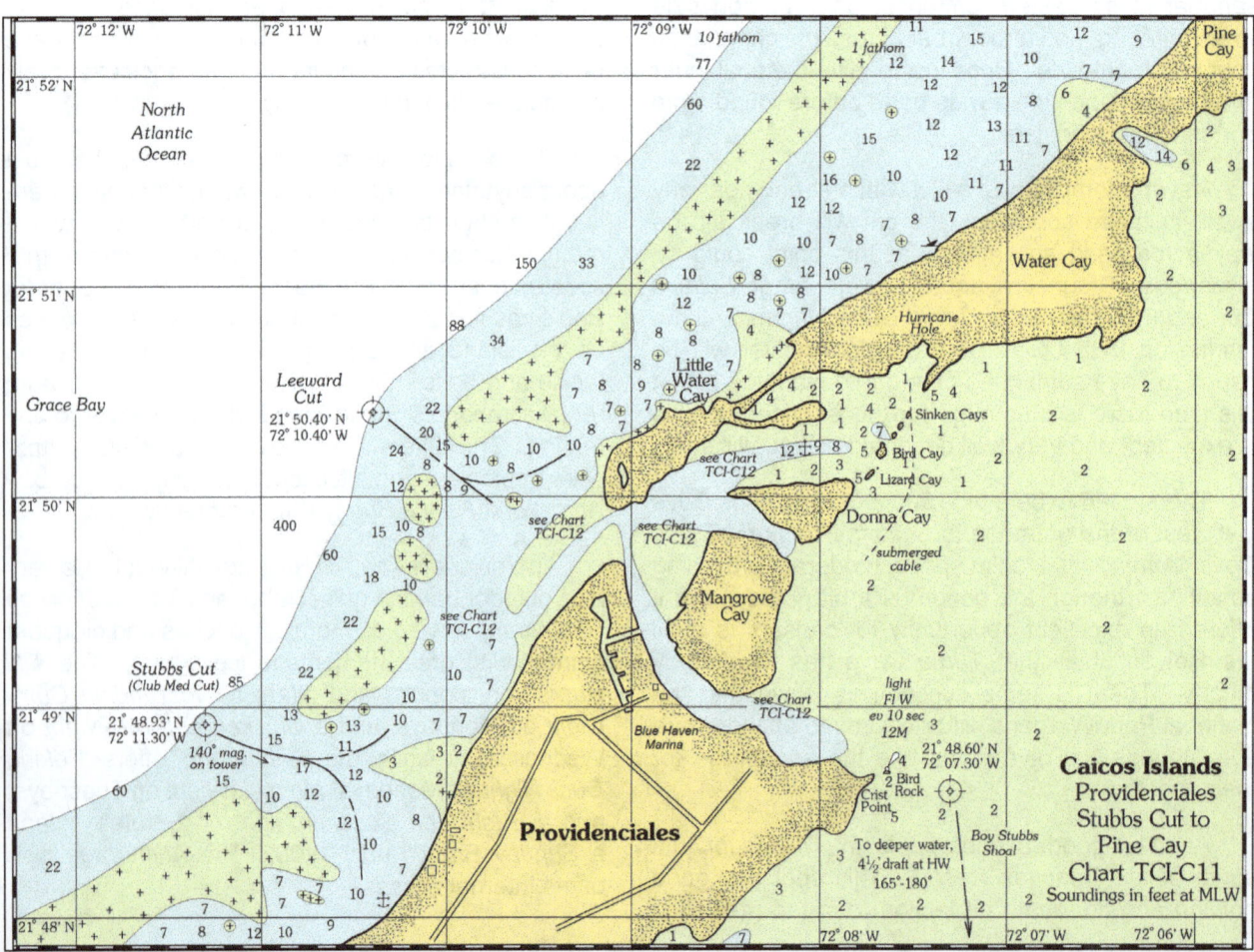

at the entrance says it all: *"Private. Unauthorized boats will be removed."* *Thompson Cove* would make a great hurricane hole with excellent protection in its narrow creeks (5'-7' at MLW) that are protected on all sides by high hills. If you had permission you could probably tie up to someone's unused dock or simply head up one of the channels to secure yourself.

Drafts of less than 5' can wiggle their way into *Thompson Cove* on a high tide by heading west from Sellar's Pond in 7' of water dodging the occasional head or small reef that you will come across. As you approach the next point there will be a rocky bar that works its way west/northwest from the point. A small white buoy marks a narrow cut through the reef to port. Enter the cut at high tide and work your way in towards the narrow entrance to *Thompson Cove*. Five feet can make it in with a good visibility and a high tide of at least 2 ½'; needless to say the ability to read the water is essential here.

Navigational Information

To the east of *Sellar's Cut* is the wide and deep *Stubbs Cut*, sometimes called *Club Med Cut*. When *Leeward Cut* and *Sellar's Cut* are breaking, *Stubb's Cut* may still be passable. A waypoint at 21° 48.93'N, 72° 11.30'W, will place you approximately ¼ mile northwest of the cut as shown on Chart TCI-C11. From this waypoint look ashore and you will see a large red and white tower, the *Cable and Wireless* tower that sits in the Long Bay Hills area (260' with a fixed red light at night). Put the tower on your bow and steer 140° magnetic to enter the cut. An alternative method of entry is to line up the tower and the red roofed building that lies just below it on the beach. The eastern end of this building is elevated and pointed. Line up the tower directly behind this raised portion of this roof or slightly to the east of it, between the roof and the trees, and come in on that heading.

Once inside, watch out for the shallow bars to starboard. Once inside *Stubb's Cut* you can head northeastward to Leeward Going Through as shown on Chart TCI-C12 or southwest towards *English Cut* as shown on Chart TCI-10. If heading to *English Cut* you can cruise close in to shore keeping the line of white dive buoys to starboard. Once in the vicinity of the *Sandal's Beaches Resort* you will have to keep offshore a little more as shown on the chart. If headed to Leeward Going Through there are fewer obstructions as shown on the charts.

Every Thursday night there is a huge new party for locals, ex-pats, and tourists, *The Turks and Caicos Fish Fry*. The party begins about 1730 and lasts till 2130 or later at *Bight Park* on *Lower Bight Road*. A US$10-per-person taxi ride from any *Grace Bay* resort will help you get to this family friendly event. The food, served up by several small vendors and residents is unbeatable as is the steel band music!

The Caicos Cays

Leeward Going Through to North Caicos Waypoints
Ft. George Cut - ½ nm NW of cut:
21° 53.70' N, 72° 07.90' W

Leeward Cut - ½ nm NW of cut:
21° 50.40' N, 72° 10.40' W

Deep water on Banks for shortcut to Leeward:
21° 45.50' N, 72° 07.00' W

Stretching from the northeast tip of Provo to the tip of North Caicos lie a small group of barrier islands. These unassuming little gems surrounded by settings of finely powdered beaches and warm, blue waters, are some of the prettiest sites in the entire archipelago. From the air, they take on the appearance of a delicate necklace suspended between the two points of land. Little Water Cay, Water Cay, Pine Cay, Fort George Cay, Dellis Cay, and Parrot Cay: these names include both uninhabited wild life preserves (the domain of the *Turks and Caicos National Parks*) as well as award-winning and internationally recognized luxury resorts.

Each island is blessed with gorgeous beaches, swirling sand flats, and plenty of shallow coral reefs. The most beautiful and protected anchorages in the Caicos Islands can be found in between these cays and all are within a short dinghy ride of each other. A word of warning: the ability to read water is essential here as you will travel over some shallow sandbars before you will be able to enjoy the deeper protected water of the anchorages. Never try these entrances with the light in your eyes; you'll have little chance of discerning the shallow water from the deeper water.

The area that is sometimes called the Caicos Cays, stretches from the northeast end of Providenciales to North Caicos. The best anchorage for those wishing to spend time on Provo is at Leeward Going Through as shown on Charts TCI-C11 and Chart TCI-C12. A 7½' draft, sometimes 8' (if you've got a really high tide), can enter this harbor at high tide and the protection is

A Cruising Guide to the Turks and Caicos Islands

excellent in all conditions short of a hurricane (even though I know of several skippers who have ridden out one here). Here you'll find the *Blue Haven Marina* and the *S. Walkin and Sons Marina*.

Navigational Information

The entrance to Leeward Going Through is tricky and it changes frequently. What is shown today may be different tomorrow or next week, however the entrance channel was dredged in late 2004, but who knows how long it will last before it silts in to its original state. With the opening of the *Turks and Caicos Yacht Club* new buoys were installed, but with the closing of the marina the buoys are no longer maintained and may be off position or even gone entirely when you try to enter.

As a general rule, the tides around Providenciales are approximately ½-1 hour after tides at Nassau, but this is not always the case at Leeward. The tides here are erratic at best. For the most part, the flood tide does not flow as long as the ebb tide. I have seen the flood last only three hours in strong southeast winds. Use caution if attempting to figure the tides.

If bound for the anchorage at Leeward Going Through there are several entrances through the reef. *Leeward Cut* is the closest but in a strong northerly swell it breaks all the way across, effectively closing the cut. *Stubbs Cut* or *Fort George Cut* would be better in those conditions, though not much better. A waypoint at 21° 50.40'N, 72° 10.40'W, will place you approximately ½ mile northwest of Leeward Cut as shown on Chart TCI-C11. This is where it begins to get tricky. At last report, new markers were installed on this route, but the markers have a reputation for disappearing shortly after they are set in place, often moved or destroyed by huge northerly swells. Use your eyesight and depthsounder to get you through here. If in doubt call *Blue Haven Marina* for assistance. From time to time there will be a combination of red and green markers through here. Bear in mind that buoys may or may not be there as you approach. As I mentioned earlier, if in doubt, call *Blue Haven Marina* on VHF for the latest information.

From the waypoint, enter *Leeward Cut* on an approximate heading of 135°-140° magnetic. The heading here is not as important as staying south of the very shallow reef on the north side of the cut. This reef is easily seen in good visibility and is usually

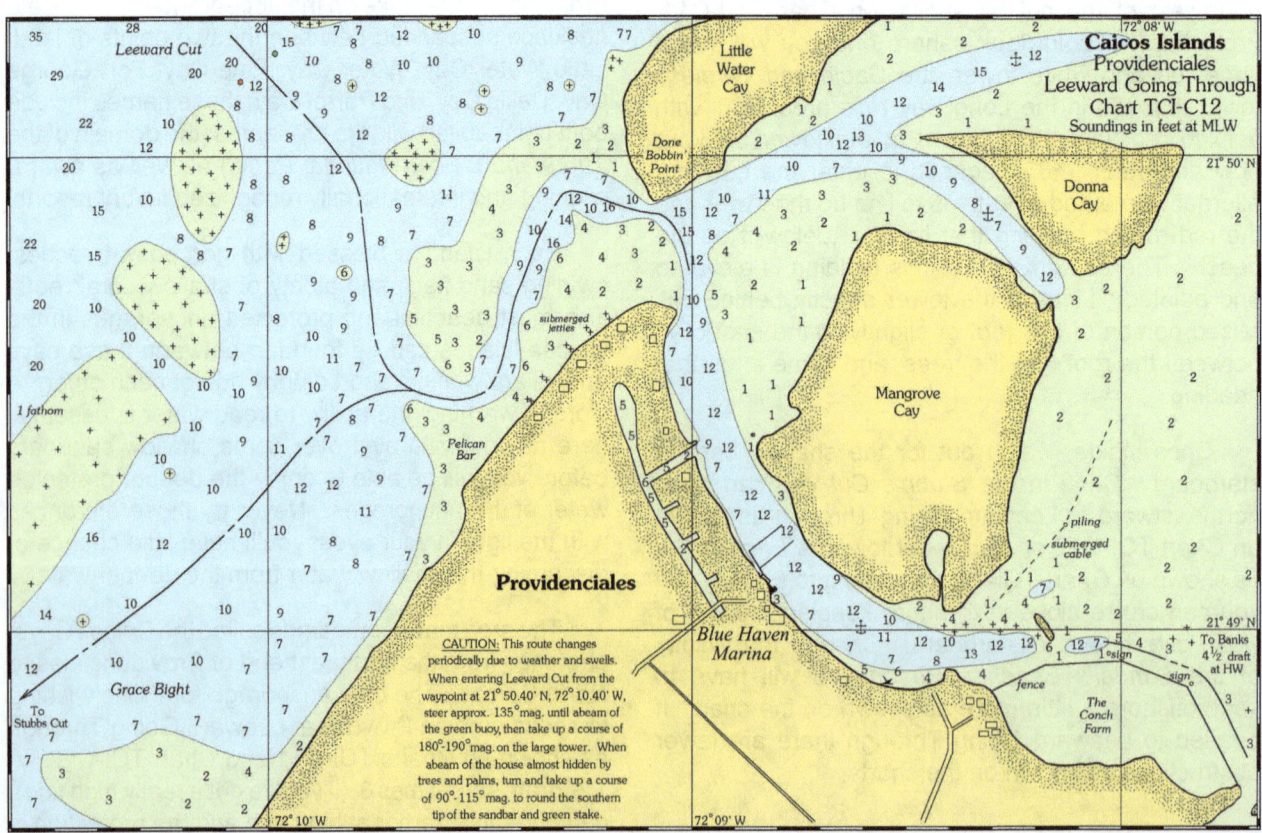

64

breaking. Once inside the reef you will see a small patch reef as shown on Chart TCI-C12. Keep this reef to port and turn to starboard to steer towards the huge red and white striped *Cable and Wireless* tower (260', Fxd R) to the south on a heading of approximately 180°-190°. As you are heading south look ashore and you will see a string of houses leading south from the northeast tip of Providenciales. There is one residence that is almost hidden by trees with several palms lining the shoreward side of the home. Just in front of this house is a shallow sandbar that works southward from Little Water Cay. Round this shoal well to the south and head northeastward between the sandbar and the shore. If you can't discern the shoal, head in on the house that I just mentioned on an approximate heading of 90°-115° keeping an eye out for the shallow bar to port. Pass between the shallow bar to port and then, swinging wide back towards *Leeward Cut,* avoid the shallows off the beach as shown on the chart and work your way towards the cut between Little Water Cay and Providenciales. Pass between the two and then you can turn to starboard to head into Leeward Going Through and the anchorage.

The best anchorage used to be just to the north of the newly expanded marina docks. If you wish to anchor south of the docks, be advised that about 150 yards south of the docks the bottom gets rocky with scattered coral heads littering the bottom. There are small, scattered heads throughout the anchorage at Leeward Going Through, even north of the marina, but they are a little thicker south of the docks. Diving to check on your anchor here is advised.

There is a fair bit of current in Leeward Going Through and two anchors set in a Bahamian moor are absolutely necessary, unless you like to untangle your lines when they get wrapped around the stray head.

When anchored at Leeward Going Through and bad weather threatens, you will need to keep an eye out for incoming vessels, as the skippers of many of the local dive boats bring their craft in here to anchor when inclement weather threatens. While many of these skippers have a captain's license and are in fact veteran seamen, a captain's license is not required in the Turks and Caicos Islands and a few of these "captains" have little concern about where and how they anchor their unattended boats. Some of these skippers simply drop an anchor and head to shore.

What You Will Find Ashore

The large *Blue Haven Marina and Resort* complex (the former *Niki Beach Resort and Marina*) dominates the area and offers slips for vessels to 220' LOA with full electric, a fuel dock, water, pump outs, cable TV, restaurant and bar, a volleyball court, horseshoe pit, large scale chess set, and a pool with a swim-up bar. The marina monitors VHF ch. 16 and 14 and can be reached by phone at 649-946-9910, or you can visit their website at http://www.bluehaventci.com/ or email them at contact@bluehaventci.com.

Just south of the docks at Leeward Going Through is *Walkin Marina*. The marina is only suitable for shallow draft vessels, and small powerboats and has no fuel dock. You can reach the marina by phone at 649-946-8898. Here you can take a ferry to North Caicos where you can rent a car to visit both North Caicos and Middle Caicos (connected by a causeway), and have lunch at any of several restaurants on the island before returning on the last ferry to Provo at 1630. You can also visit the growing tourist and marina complex on the north side of North Caicos.

South of Heaving Down Rock, the ramp where the small barges load and unload about ½ mile south of the marina, you will notice a large area with pilings in the water and nets stretched between them. This is the *Conch Farm*, established in 1984 to commercially grow the queen conch, *strombus gigas*. The life cycle from egg to adult takes about four years. The *Conch Farm* has successfully developed hatchery and juvenile rearing techniques, and the *Farm* has a current inventory of approximately 1.5 million conch in all stages of their growth cycle. Theirs is the only such facility in the world. The *Conch Farm* has guided tours and a *Conch Boutique* and restaurant. South of Mangrove Cay and east of the Conch Farm is a submerged cable in 1'-3' of water at low tide. This cable is easily seen and definitely something to avoid.

From the dock at *Leeward* you can get on any one of several charter boats for a wonderful day trip to North Caicos or if you desire, any other island in the chain from Middle Caicos, to South Caicos and even Grand Turk. Here you can find *Silver Deep* (http://www.silverdeep.com/fishing/scubadiving.htm) who will take you just about anywhere you want to go in these islands: North Caicos, Middle Caicos, East Caicos, South Caicos, Grand Turk, and even to Salt Cay. Owner Arthur Dean and his brothers will be happy to take you to any of these spots from Leeward.

TURTLE COVE MARINA
your port of entry to providenciales, turks + caicos

Turtle Cove Marina features 65 deep water slips and full dockside services including cable tv, free wifi, water, power, gas and diesel. Our prime location offers access to the most nearby amenities of any marina in the TCI with hotels, restaurants, diving, car rentals, tour operators and more, all right off the dock - just steps away from your slip! Call us on VHF 16 and we'll be there to welcome you with our complimentary Marina Guide Boat.

(649) 941.3781 • tcmarina@tciway.tc • www.turtlecovemarina.com • follow us

For more information call 941-5595 or check in at the *Silver Deep* office at *Leeward*. Not to be outdone, *J & B Tours*, also at *Leeward*, has several Island exploration charters that will take you in and around Provo and all the way to South Caicos if you like. For more info, check their office or call 946-5047. *J & B Tours* also sells fishing licenses. Both *Silver Deep* and *Big Blue* (http://bigblueunlimited.com/) offer charter dive trips.

Navigational Information

Vessels drawing 5' or less and wishing to head out onto the *Caicos Bank*s from Leeward Going Through can do so at high tide, and only at high tide. The last year or so has seen a supply boat with a 5' draft enter Leeward Going Through from the *Caicos Bank*, this has helped this route a lot since the supply boat has basically "dredged" a 5' deep channel for us. Since it is easy to get Nassau tides by SSB and ham radio (see the section on *Weather* in the chapter *The Basics*). A vessel drawing 4½' will need a tide of over 2'-2½', that is a 2.6'-3.1' above datum Nassau tide or equivalent. Remember that tides here are generally .6' less than tides in Nassau and approximately one hour later. A 5' draft needs a tide of the equivalent of a Nassau above datum tide of 3.6' and more, not rare, but definitely not common. I have traveled this route with a Nassau tide of 3.8' above datum and saw nothing less than 5' the entire route. Bear in mind that wind direction sometimes affects the tides on the banks south of Provo. A few days of northwest through northeast wind may cause an unusually low tide on the southern shore of Provo while a strong southeast to southwest wind will have the reverse effect. The prudent mariner will likely check the route at high tide by dinghy the day prior to his planned departure.

From Leeward Going Through, head south toward the *Conch Farm* as shown on Chart TCI-C12, passing between the small unnamed cay and the *Conch Farm* (don't try this route in the early morning with the sun in your eyes; you won't be able to see a thing). Keep the first sign and the conspicuous brown shoal that parallels the *Conch Farm* fence to starboard. Once past the first sign, head for the second sign staying about 75'-100' off the fence. There are a couple of shallow heads on this part of the route, but they should lie well to port if you keep your course close to a line between the two signs that parallel the fence. Once past the second sign, keep parallel to the fence as you head towards Bird Rock keeping about 50-

100 yards east of the rock. As you come abeam of Bird Rock steer approximately southeast until about two hundred yards or so south of the rock, to avoid a shallow sand patch lying just south and southeast of Bird Rock. From this position you can take up a course of anywhere between 165°-200° to cross shallow *Boy Stubbs Shoal*; the deeper water seems to be on a course of about 180°-200°. The shallowest part of this route lies between ½ mile and 2 miles south of Bird Rock across shallow *Boy Stubbs Shoal*. The bottom is not quite flat through here, there are several "humps" in the bottom and if you are too early or if the tide is too low, you will likely keep bumping over them as you power your way through, but don't worry as they're all soft sand.

Keep on your course for several miles, dodging any black or brown patches you see, until you reach deeper water, anywhere from 7' and above, generally in the area of 21° 45.50' N-21° 46.00' N. This route is a terrific shortcut if you're headed to *Sapodilla Bay*. I believe that if enough sailboats come through here we'll eventually have a pretty nice channel dredged (but don't try it with a winged keel, they tend to act as an anchor).

If you are in *Sapodilla Bay*, *South Side Marina*, or *Caicos Marina and Shipyard* and wish to avail yourself of this shortcut to Leeward, head ENE past the shipyard to a waypoint at 21° 45.50'N, 72° 07.00'W. Watch out for scattered heads and shallow patch reefs along this route. Once in the general vicinity of the waypoint, head for a waypoint at 21° 48.60'N, 72° 07.30'W, approximately ¼ mile east/southeast of Bird Rock. From this position simply follow the above mentioned directions in reverse.

What You Will Find Ashore

Just North of Leeward Going Through lies Little Water Cay, a very popular picnic spot for locals and cruisers; logs show that the island is visited annually by over 17,000 tourists. The island lies within the boundaries of the *Princess Alexandra National Park* and has been set aside as a nature preserve for about 1,500-2,000 of the rare and endangered Turks Island rock iguanas (*Cyclura carinata*) as well as a variety of bird life. When Loyalists and Salt Rakers first inhabited the Turks and Caicos Islands, their pet dogs decimated the indigenous iguana population on these cays, until the only place you can find them today is on the uninhabited cays such as Little Water Cay. As the *Meridian Club* (http://www.meridianclub. com/) was being built on Pine Cay in 1973, an iguana survey showed a population of 15,000 on the cay.

By 1976 nearly all the iguanas were gone due to predation by cats and dogs introduced during construction. A 1995 survey showed only one iguana, a few burrows, and several tracks along the northeast coast. A new problem has occurred by the creation of the sand bridges between Little Water Cay, Water Cay, and Pine Cay over the last several decades. Speculation concerning the feral cats on Pine Cay suggests that it is only a matter of time before they work their way down to Little Water Cay.

From the small beach on the southern shore of the cay there is a nice boardwalk that takes you through the interior of the cay to view the local vegetation and the island's population of iguanas. The nature trail on the northern shore of the island, best reached from the *Grace Bay* side of the cay and within easy dinghy distance from Leeward, is the most scenic in terms of animal life. If you visit the cay, please stay on the boardwalk; do not feed, touch, or harass the iguana in anyway, and please do not bring a cat or dog ashore. A bit of Turks and Caicos Island folklore that has to be seen to be believed has it that the iguanas in these islands will dance to music. Try it and see, grab a few cans or bottles and tap out a rhythm, or perhaps bring along a boom box with your favorite CD and play DJ for these creatures. The waters between Little Water Cay, Donna Cay, and Mangrove Cay as shown on Chart TCI-C12 are deep and make for a very good though current-ridden anchorage. Two anchors are a must here. The only problem with this anchorage area occurs on the weekends when the locals tend to water ski through here. Donna Cay was once part of Mangrove Cay until Hurricane Donna changed the landscape along these islands, hence the name of the cay.

North of Little Water Cay, and connected to Little Water Cay since Hurricane Donna, is the uninhabited Water Cay. Just off its western shore, as shown on Chart TCI-C11, is the wreck of an old barge in 4' of water. The barge was being towed along the shore when it broke loose and came to rest in its current location. On the northern shore of Water Cay are some very nice beaches and sheer rock ledges that are wonderful for snorkeling or just swimming. In prevailing winds these beaches are very calm, though sometimes a swell can work its way over the reef to push your anchored dinghy ashore. These very beaches were the background for the 1987 *Sports Illustrated Swimsuit Edition*.

Pine Cay lies just to the north of Water Cay and is named after the Cuban Pine which thrives on the edges of the island's freshwater ponds. Once a separate cay, Pine Cay was joined to Water Cay by Hurricane Donna, as was Little Water Cay. Pine Cay is best known for being the home of the *Meridian Club*, an extremely exclusive total-getaway resort constructed in 1973. No phone, no TV, just peace and quiet and pristine beach. No loud vehicles are allowed, only golf carts and bicycles. The island itself has several distinctive zones of vegetation, shared mainly by palmettos and pines. On the islands northern end there are a few brackish lakes inhabited by several species of (once) saltwater fish, also a legacy of Hurricane Donna.

Pine Cay was also the site of an ancient Lucayan settlement, and in the 18th and 19th centuries is said to have been used as a hideout for pirates. Pine Cay is private and visits ashore must be by invitation only, although access to the beach up to the dune line is allowed. You can anchor off the beach, a somewhat surgy anchorage at times, on the western shore of Pine Cay wherever your draft allows, but only in prevailing winds. You can also pick up a dive boat mooring if they are available and not needed by a commercial vessel. If you're interested in name-dropping, it is said that Bill Cosby and Denzel Washington frequent Pine Cay, and that Jimmy Buffet has a passion for bonefishing in the nearby waters.

Navigational Information

Further north, the Pine Cay, Fort George Cay, Dellis Cay, and Parrot Cay anchorages can be easily accessed by sea via *Fort George Cut* as shown on Chart TCI-C13. Vessels wishing to visit the area from Leeward Going Through can do so by venturing northeast inside the reef. As shown on Chart #'s TCI-C11, Chart C12, and chart C13, the route lies between the reef and Water Cay and Pine Cay. There are only a few shallow reefs and a couple of sandbars to watch out for. Stay away from any dark spots you see; these will likely be heads or small patch reefs.

For skippers entering through *Fort George Cut*, a waypoint at 21° 53.70'N, 72° 07.90'W, will place you approximately ½ mile northwest of *Fort George Cut*.

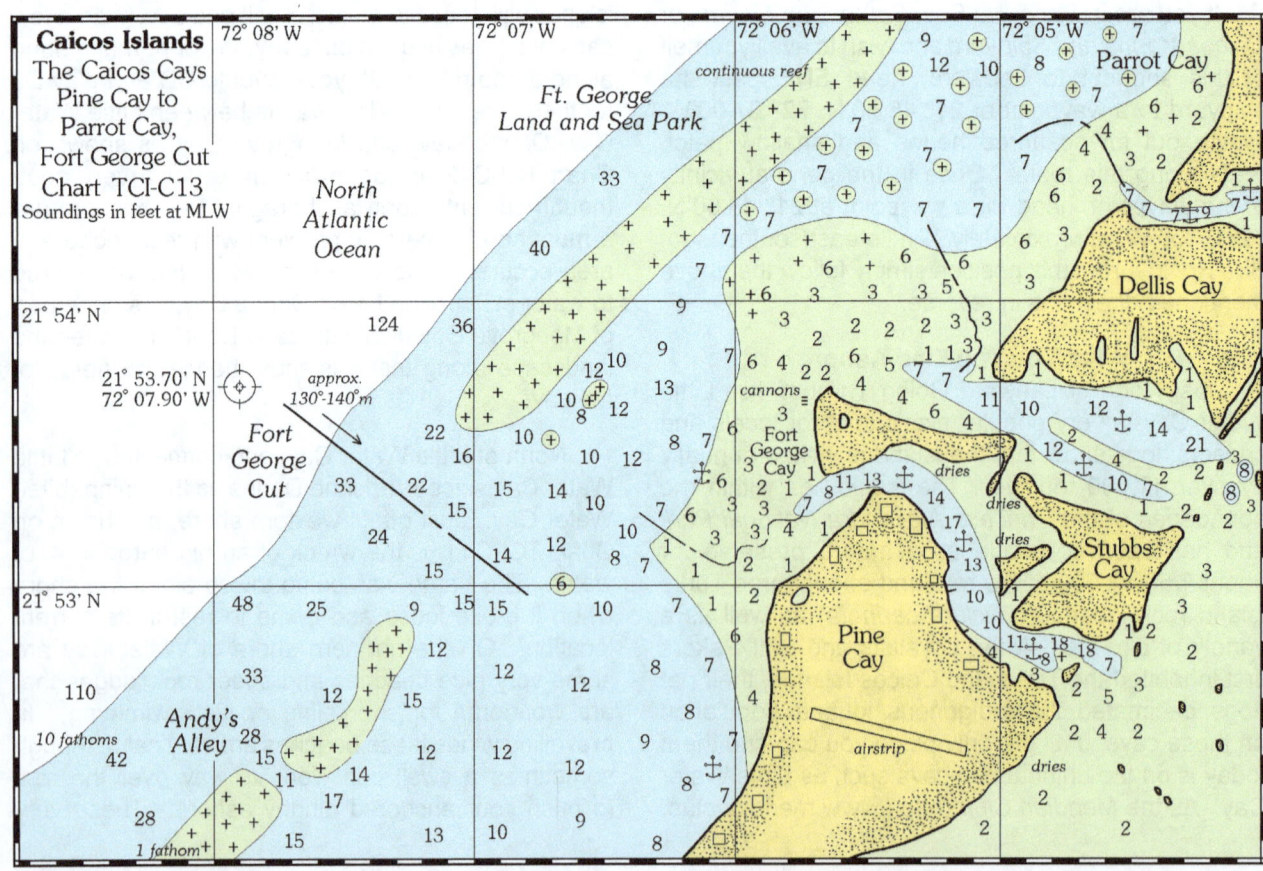

Enter the cut on an approximate heading of 130°-140° magnetic. The heading here is not so important as simply staying between the reefs, but not to worry, *Fort George Cut* is wide and deep. Once inside you can head southward to Leeward or Water Cay, or northward to Dellis Cay and Parrot Cay. About a mile southwest of Fort George Cay is another smaller break in the reef known as Andy's Alley. This very visible bright blue cut is about 100 yards wide and has a minimum depth of 11'. To find Andy's Alley look for the southern end of the beach on Pine Cay, and when approaching the usually breaking reef, look for the bright blue cut.

What You Will Find Ashore

Fort George Cay is a *National Historic Site* that dates back to 1798-1812. To protect the cotton production on North and Middle Caicos, settlers built Fort George and set up cannons to defend their main port of export in anticipation of attack by pirates and Americans. Today, thanks to *Hurricane Donna*, the same cannons that were poised to protect the islands now lie in about 3'-4' of water, making for an excellent snorkel. Look for them about 50 yards south of the small beach on the northwestern tip of Fort George Cay about 50' offshore. There are three of these two hundred-year-old cannons, all pointing to seaward; you can't miss them. You can anchor west of Fort George Cay wherever your draft allows, but only in settled weather, and watch out for a surge coming in over the reef. There is a wonderful, deep, uncrowded anchorage between Fort George Cay and Pine Cay that only sees some small boat traffic from the resort on Pine Cay. This is an extremely difficult anchorage to enter: it has shallowed to the point that only drafts of less than 5' can enter, and that's on a high tide.

As little as three or four years ago, drafts of 5'-6' could enter here, but as with all the cuts along this section of the Caicos Cays, what is deep today may be quite shallow tomorrow. After entering Fort George Cut head northeastward until you can take up an approximate southeast heading towards the point on Pine Cay as shown on Chart TCI-13. There is really no way to describe the entrance here other than to say that it curves around generally back towards the northeast until you reach the darker, deeper water between the cays. A high tide, excellent visibility and the ability to read water are what will get you through here. There are several sandbars that you must zigzag between and some shallow grassy patches that give a false impression of being deeper than they look. Once inside you will find a deep anchorage that goes well eastward between Pine Cay and Stubbs Cay and even out onto the Caicos Bank a bit. As usual, put down two anchors for the current.

Dellis Cay, named after a Greek sponger from Hydra named John Dellis, was the center of a small but thriving sponging industry on the cay in the late 1800s. The cay is subject to a unique pattern of tide and current, giving this island the nod when it comes to some of the best beachcombing in the Turks and Caicos Islands. Beautiful white sandy beaches surround Dellis Cay; ashore you may find the ruins of an old fish processing plant. There is a good, deep anchorage between Dellis Cay and Fort George Cay that can be accessed by vessels with drafts of less than 5'. Excellent, and I do mean excellent, visibility as well as a healthy dollop of patience is required to find the channel, as the sandbars change often and you will have to do quite a bit of zigzagging. Only try this just before high tide and remember that there may be no one around to help you should you run aground.

Navigational Information

As shown on Chart TCI-C13, head northeastward from *Fort George Cut* between the reef and Fort George Cay, avoiding the large shallow bar that sits northwest of Fort George Cay and the small shallow reefs between the bar and the outer barrier reef. Line up the southwestern tip of Dellis Cay and head in on it on a heading of 140° magnetic. You will probably have to dodge some shallow spots as all these sandbars change frequently in this stretch of cays. As you approach the southwestern tip of Dellis Cay you will find that you also have to pass between two shallow yellow colored sandy bars, 1'-2' at MLW. One works out westward from Dellis Cay, the other also lies east/west just a little northwest of the first bar. You will have to turn to starboard to pass between the two to make it into the deeper water at the entrance to the anchorage. The anchorage itself has two arms, one on the Dellis Cay side, one on the Stubbs Cay side. Both offer good protection, though I prefer the anchorage on the Dellis Cay side.

In recent years, Dellis Cay was acquired by a Turkish developer and became part of an elaborate Ponzi scheme. Wealthy clients were offered exclusive homes yet no infrastructure was ever completed. The developer has had his assets frozen pending investigation.

North of Dellis Cay and southwest of North Caicos lies Parrot Cay. Some say that Parrot Cay is a corruption of "Pirates Cay," where legendary pirates such as Calico Jack Rackham, Annie Bonney, Mary Read, and Blackbeard are said to have visited. An 18th century house still stands on this 300-acre private island. There was an attempt at growing cotton on Parrot Cay in 1918, but it lasted only a few years. Along Parrot Cay's northern shore you will see the red roofs of a prestigious modern resort that was deserted but is now being reopened.

There is an nice anchorage lying between Parrot Cay and Dellis Cay that is much easier to access than the anchorage between Fort George Cay and Pine Cay. A vessel with a draft of 5'-6' can enter here with the tide; the only dangers are the numerous (though easily seen in good light) shallow heads and small patch reefs that dot the waters between the reef and Dellis Cay and Parrot Cay. Good visibility is essential but a cool head and nerves of steel are just as important. As shown on Chart TCI-C13, work your way north inside the reef from Fort George Cut, taking care to avoid the many shallow heads and patch reefs. When you are north of the cut between Parrot Cay and Dellis Cay you will notice the darker water inside the cut and a small arm of it heading out north/northwest towards the reef. You will want to line up the northern point of Dellis Cay and take up an approximate heading of south/southeast on it. The heading here is not as important as trying to picture how the deeper water flows out over the sandbar. This channel, 4' in places at MLW, is your only way in if you draw 5'-6'. Once inside, the deeper water goes well eastward to the eastern end of Dellis Cay, with only a slight zigzag.

West Caicos

Waypoints
Pony Channel - ¼ nm W of:
21° 43.40' N, 72° 27.30' W

Pony Channel - ¼ nm E of:
21° 43.40' N, 72° 26.75' W

West Caicos Marina - ¼ nm NW of entrance:
21° 42.00' N, 72° 28.00' W

West Caicos - ¾ nm S of Southwest Point:
21° 36.75' N, 72° 29.00' W

Freighter Channel - SW waypoint:
21° 35.75' N, 72° 23.25' W

West Caicos, lying approximately 10 miles southwest of Providenciales and *Sapodilla Bay*, was originally called *Macubiza* by the Lucayans and *Petite Caique* by the French. The waters off the western shore of the island offer miles of superb wall-diving and imposing limestone cliffs, a favorite spot for the numerous dive boats operating out of nearby Provo. In years past, West Caicos was allegedly a haven for pirates that would attack homeward bound French boats returning from Haiti. A French Captain in 1753 wrote that West Caicos was "abounding in the white beaked Bahamian parrot." It is said that Nelson captured a French sailing vessel off West Caicos in 1777 when he commanded the sloop *Little Lucy*. The tourist brochures say that Delvin's Cove at the northern end of West Caicos was a hideout for the infamous pirate Delvin or Dulien but I was unable to find any reference to a pirate by that name.

On the western shore you will find the ruins of Yankee Town where in the mid-1800s a flourishing community of sisal workers lived. In 1849, 18 acres were planted at Spencerville on the northern coast of West Caicos and proved so successful that over 1,000 acres of sisal were eventually being grown on the island. If you look around you will find the ruins of a sisal press, railway, steam engines, and several limestone buildings dating to the late 1800s and early 1900s when 70 salt and sisal workers lived and worked here. At a cost of over $30,000, the government constructed the railway and a saltwater canal to the salinas but the sisal project was halted at the beginning of the American Civil War. The old railway stretches across West Caicos in an east/west direction and if you hike the causeway you may see some of the pink flamingos, osprey, and herons that live along the shores of Lake Catherine, a nature reserve. The Dominican dictator Trujillo tried to buy West Caicos a few years prior to his assassination. It is believed that he wanted the island for a hideaway, but the deal fell through when clear title could not be found. In 1973 *Esso* planned to build a huge oil refinery on the cay, but plans were abandoned when the owner suddenly died. You can anchor off Yankee Town in settled weather or in light to moderate prevailing east/southeast winds. Stronger winds create a bit more surge in the anchorage.

Navigational Information
Vessels approaching *West Caicos Marina* from *Sapodilla Bay* should head west, out *Sandbore Channel* to the waypoint shown and then turn southward to the waypoint off the marina. There is

The Caicos Islands

another option, *Pony Channel*, just north of the reef that borders the northwestern shore of West Caicos, but this route is not recommended except for the experienced reef navigator with good visibility, and calm conditions. Approaching from *Sapodilla Bay* you'll have deep water all the way to a waypoint at 21° 43.40' N, 72° 26.75' W, which places you approximately ¼ mile east of *Pony Channel* as shown on Chart TCI-C5. From the waypoint head west passing north of the reef and south of a smaller shoal as shown on the chart. Vessels heading for *Sapodilla Bay* from *West Caicos Marina* can follow this route in reverse. From *West Caicos Marina* parallel the reef north/northwest to a waypoint at 21° 43.40' N, 72° 27.30' W, which places you approximately ¼ mile west of *Pony Channel*. Head east through the channel for about ½ mile and then set your course for *Sapodilla Bay*.

The entrance to the *West Caicos Marina* itself lies through a natural break in the reef just west of Company Point. A waypoint at 21° 42.00' N, 72° 28.00' W, will place you approximately ¼ nautical mile northwest of the entrance channel leading into the marina as shown on Chart TCI-C14A. From the waypoint pass between the entrance jetties and enter the marina basin. **Use extreme caution**, there are shallow reefs on both sides of the channel, and if that were not enough to worry about, Provo dive boats use the channel to pass to and from the western shore of West Caicos. The dive boats usually don't slow down for cruising vessels and a dangerous situation could come about if one was headed outward from *Bernard Bay* as you were headed into the marina. Keep your eyes open here and let's avoid any problems. The marina is just part of a much larger project involving condos and all the amenities, most located near the southern end of West Caicos.

There is a nice lee anchorage off the northwestern tip of West Caicos that is often used by locals as well as the dive boat operators working out of Provo. The anchorage in *Bernard Bay* that is shown on Charts TCI-C5 and Chart TCI-C14 lies just off a beautiful beach and is a great spot in settled weather and in east to southeast winds. The anchorage can be gained through a small winding break in the reef off Company Point as shown on Chart TCI-C14 and in greater detail on Chart TCI-C14A. You can also reach *Bernard Bay* from the *Sandbore Channel* area directly from *Sapodilla Bay* as shown on Chart TCI-C5. Both routes require good light and you'll have to dodge several coral heads and small patch reefs in water that is less than 6' deep (at MLW) in places, but you may find that the end result is worth your effort. If you don't wish to try the cut at Company Point, you might consider anchoring south of Company Point along the western shore of West Caicos as shown on the chart and taking a short dinghy ride in to the beach.

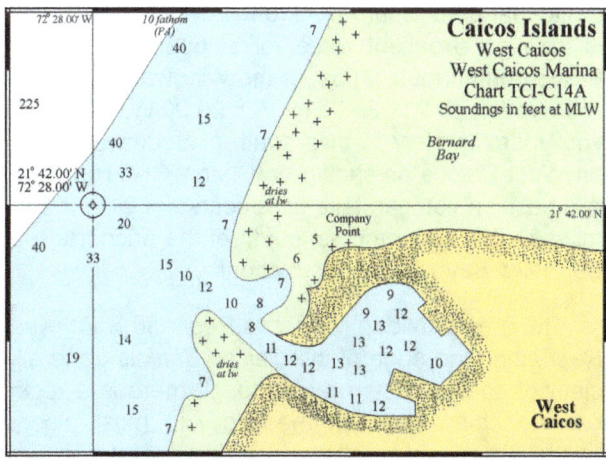

What You Will Find Ashore

The *West Caicos Marina* started out well but along the way something went awry. It seems that funding was lost with the demise of the financing company and the entire project was on hold for almost the last two years. The current situation is that the marina is closed and nobody is permitted ashore on the marina grounds, however the owners have no problem with transient vessels anchoring inside the marina's basin. It is just as easy to use the dive buoys just off the marina but they must be made available for dive boats during daylight hours. For the latest info on the status of *West Caicos Marina* contact Simon, the manager at *South Side Marina* on Provo.

The eastern and northern shores of West Caicos offer miles of beautiful sandy beaches with a few rocky cliffs at the northeastern and southern tips and the rusty ruins of an old freighter about midway down the eastern shore. It is said that when this freighter was wrecked, the crew opened the safe aboard and removed a quantity of silver bars. Atop a bluff on the southeastern shore of West Caicos stands Star Town, the ruins of an old *DEA* base during the 1970s and early 1980s. The site got its name from the two Quonset hut style buildings that are laid out in a star pattern. At the northeastern end of West Caicos, just south of Cove Point, it is possible for a draft of less than 6' to work its way within a few hundred yards of shore to gain some lee from west through north/northwest winds. Caution: if the wind shifts at night you won't be able to find your way out. On the northern shore you'll find the *Molasses Reef Hotel*, part of the *Ritz-Carlton* empire.

Navigational Information

Along the eastern shore of West Caicos is the popular *Clear Sand Road,* the channel from the ocean across the banks that is often used by the freighter traffic that uses *South Dock* on Providenciales. This is also an excellent route for skippers heading to Provo from Inagua, Cuba, or the *Windward Passage*. A waypoint at 21° 36.75'N, 72° 29.00'W, will place you approximately ¾ mile south of Southwest Point on West Caicos as shown on Chart TCI-C14. From this position you can take up a course of 64° for 13.1 miles to the waypoint just south of the anchorage at *Sapodilla Bay* with no obstructions.

The area between *Molasses Reef* and *Southwest Reef* along the edge of the *Caicos Bank* is generally clear of shallow patch reefs though there is a rocky bar stretching between the two. In most places this bar has 15'-20' over it and does not pose a navigational hazard to the average cruising boat. There is a channel through here as shown on Chart TCI-C1 that is simply called the *Freighter Channel*. It is often used by commercial vessels headed to *South Dock* on Provo and leads in from the sea between *Southwest Reef* and *Molasses Reef* with a least depth of 12' near *South Dock*.

Capt. Dave Matthews of the trimaran *Tao* has been sailing these waters for over 25 years and suggests that if you are off the southern end of West Caicos and cannot find refuge from strong northeast winds you can tuck up under the lee of *Southwest Reef* for some protection from the seas (parts of the reef and bars to its north dry at low water). For shelter from west/northwest winds and seas you can anchor in the lee of Sandy Point as shown on the chart.

French Cay

Waypoints
French Cay - ½ nm W of anchorage:
21° 30.60' N, 72° 12.70' W

French Cay - ¾ nm SW of anchorage:
21° 29.75' N, 72° 12.65' W

French Cay was originally called Cay Blondell at the beginning of the 1600s. Blondell was a French surveyor in Haiti who was commissioned to study the feasibility of building a navigational landmark on the cay to assist those vessels en route to and from the *Windward Passage*. The French lost several ships in the vicinity over the years, including one three-decked merchantman laden with treasure from Hispaniola. Blondell stressed the importance of building some sort of structure on French Cay to keep mariners from confusing it with West Caicos and West Sandspit, but nothing ever came of his efforts. Over the intervening years, French Cay's greatest claim to fame is that the pirate Francoise L'Olonnois is said to have occasionally used the island as a base from which to raid ships en route to and from the nearby *Windward Passage*.

Today French Cay is a protected bird sanctuary and you will understand why when you visit. Hundreds of gulls, boobies, and terns call this tiny sliver of rock and sand on the edge of the *Caicos Bank* home, swarming over and around it throughout the day. Until recently, a permit from the *DECR* was required to set foot upon the island, today however landing on French Cay is prohibited.

The Caicos Islands

In the waters surrounding French Cay nurse sharks mate each summer so give them a wide berth if you happen to be there at the same time; they are usually not aggressive unless molested. The island itself is rather low-lying and sandy, with excellent snorkeling along its southwest side. French Cay has gotten quite popular with dive boats operating on a daily basis out of Providenciales.

Navigational Information

As you approach French Cay, you will probably not sight this low-lying island until about five miles away. Your first sight of it will probably be the top of the light standing on the southwestern part of the cay (Fl R, 10'). From the waypoint just south of the anchorage at *Sapodilla Bay*, steer 171° for 14.3 miles to a waypoint at 21° 30.60'N, 72° 12.70'W, which places you approximately ½ mile west of the anchorage on the western shore of French Cay as shown on Chart TCI-C15. On this route the water depths range from about 16' just south of *Sapodilla Bay* to about 10' just north of French Cay, and there are no obstructions. As you approach French Cay from these 10' depths, the water gets progressively deeper as you head for the edge of the *Caicos Bank*.

If arriving from offshore head to a waypoint at 21° 29.75'N, 72° 12.65'W, which places you approximately ¾ mile southwest of the anchorage area and on the edge of the *Caicos Bank*. From the entrance waypoint to *Caicos Marina and Shipyard* at Juba Point, French Cay bears 197° at a distance of 14.8 nautical miles.

If headed to *Sapodilla Bay* from French Cay you will begin to make out the hills of Providenciales from more than 10 miles away. The conspicuous twin white fuel tanks at the *Texaco* yard east of the green

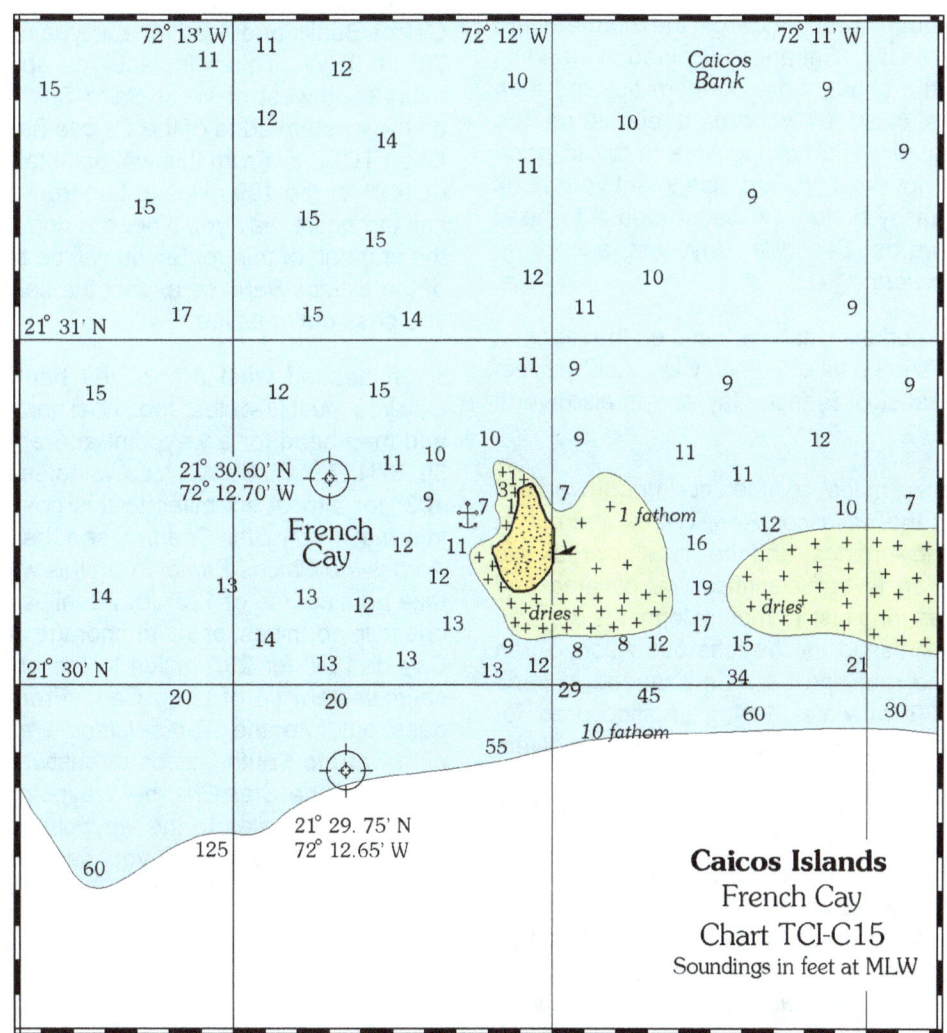

Caicos Islands
French Cay
Chart TCI-C15
Soundings in feet at MLW

customs building at *South Dock* are your landmarks if you are making for *Sapodilla Bay*, but don't confuse them with the several white houses that lie to the east of *Sapodilla Bay*. Another good landmark as you get closer is the huge crane at South Dock just west of the white tanks. As I said, there are no obstructions on this route; I have run this route at night from French Cay to *Sapodilla Bay*, but I cannot recommend that others do so.

What You Will Find Ashore

The northern section of the anchorage area tends to be rocky and grassy, but if you set your anchor well in the surrounding sand you will stay put. The best holding is in the sandy holes in the grassy areas in the center of the anchorage area. In moderate east/southeast winds you might get a bit of a surge around the southwestern tip of French Cay, if so, it's very easy to rig a bridle for a comfortable night.

A bit of a lee anchorage is available from southwest through west winds off the northeastern shore of French Cay. Entrance is gained by heading north around the shoal of the northern tip, and then heading in as close as your draft allows on the northeastern side. The holding here is fair to good depending on how well you are able to set your hook in the rocky/grassy bottom. A better idea is to head northward towards *Sapodilla Bay* and anchor in *Bermudian Harbour.*

Excellent snorkeling can be found on the reef that lies south and southeast of French Cay. Another reef lies well southeast of French Cay and is also worth exploration.

Just a few miles to the north/northwest of French Cay is the *Molasses Reef Wreck,* the oldest shipwreck in the Americas and the first shipwreck site in the Caribbean to be scientifically excavated and exhibited. Measuring just 19 meters long, the caravel, having safely crossed the treacherous Atlantic, ran aground on the reef and became stranded in sand in about 15'-20' of water, laying undiscovered for some 400 years until it was found by treasure divers in 1976. Some unscrupulous salvager tried to gain financially from the excavation by claiming the ship was the *Pinta*, Columbus' flagship on his 1492 voyage of discovery. The claim was soon proven to be false and the government of the Turks and Caicos Islands took over the salvage and identification process. A government permit was issued to the *Institute of Nautical Archaeology* at Texas A&M's *National Museum* under the direction of Dr. Donald H. Keith. Irate treasure hunters then tried to dynamite the site with, fortunately, minimal damage. Dating of Lucayan pottery pieces found on the site placed the ship on the reef prior to 1513 (remember, all the Lucayans were forcibly removed from the Turks and Caicos Islands by 1513) and researchers speculated that the ship was a slaver en route to Hispaniola. The ship was armed with state-of-the-art weapons of the period and the national museum on Grand Turk now displays the largest selection of 16th century wrought iron breech loading cannons in the world.

Navigational Information

From French Cay, with the right wind, you can sail right off the bank for Inagua, Little Inagua, Haiti, Manzanillo or Luperón in the DR, or to the *Windward Passage* and Cuba. If you are bound for Manzanillo, a course of 179° for 101.5 nautical miles will bring you to the entrance to Manzanillo. If bound for Luperón from French Cay, head out into the deeper water off the Caicos Banks and head for a waypoint at 21° 20.50'N, 72° 10.05'W. This will place you approximately two miles southwest of *West Sand Spit*, a shallow area on the western edge of the *Caicos Bank* as shown on Chart TCI-C1. From this waypoint take up a heading of 149° for the 109 miles to Luperón. If you intend to sail the entire way you'll need a northeast wind. For the first half of this route you will be sailing in the lee of the *Caicos Bank* so expect the seas to build once you pass out of its lee.

If headed west across the banks from French Cay you must first clear the shoal north of French Cay and then head for a waypoint at *Star Channel* at 21° 30.25'N, 72° 06.60'W. You will steer approximately 102° for almost six miles to this position. For more information on *Star Channel* see the section *Routes Across the Caicos Bank*. From this waypoint you can take up a course of 123° for 28 miles to the waypoint one mile northwest of the anchorage at Big Ambergris Cay or 104° for 29.7 miles to the anchorage at the southwestern tip of Long Cay. From here you can pass out into the *Turks Island Passage* to head northward to South Caicos or eastward to the Turks. Also from the *Star Channel* waypoint you can steer 113° for 28.1 miles to the waypoint just north of the Fish Cays. From here you can head out across the *Turks Island Passage* to Great Sand Cay if you choose.

North Caicos

North Caicos, located only 12 miles from Provo, is about 44 square miles in area. Its 1,500 inhabitants primarily live in the four settlements that are connected by the King's Highway, which runs the length of the island. The southern shore of the island is primarily mangroves and tidal flats, home to flocks of flamingos, bonefish, and tarpon. Thanks to its abundant rainfall, North Caicos is known as the garden center of the Turks and Caicos Islands. At one time, extensive farms fed all of the islanders with crops transported by inter-island trading sloops.

Navigational Information

There are no deep draft anchorages at North Caicos; the closest for a 5'-6' draft is between Parrot Cay and Dellis Cay as shown on Chart TCI-C13. There are several day charters that run out of *Leeward Marina* that can provide lunch and transportation, either scooters or jeeps, for those interested in taking a tour of this beautiful cay. The entire northern shore of North Caicos is protected by an offshore barrier reef, but a vessel with a draft of less than 6' can work its way through the reef at *Ropier Cut* (see Chart TCI-C16) in an emergency. That route, as are almost all the inshore routes between Parrot Cay eastward to East Caicos, is literally strewn with shallow coral heads and shoals. If you choose to dinghy to the island you can rent a car from Pat Hamilton at 946-7141 or from *Old Nick Rental Cars* at 946-7358.

What You Will Find Ashore

Along the northwestern shore of North Caicos, Three Mary's Cays is a great snorkeling spot near Sandy Point where you'll also find ospreys and their nesting sites. The cays are a protected sanctuary and visits ashore are by *DECR Permit* only. Sandy Point is a small fishing/farming community of only about 40-50 residents, where, in the early 1900s, guano miners discovered a cave containing ancient Lucayan artifacts, including a stone idol. The community is tucked in behind the lush vegetation of the cay and the casual visitor might not even see the buildings. At the dock by the small harbor sits an old rusting crane, while to the right sits a huge old wooden hull. There used to be a blue hole tucked into the mangroves right off this harbor, but it was filled in during a hurricane. Located here is the *North Caicos Yacht Club and Marina*, a small but very nice marina built to support the condos and home owners here. Basically it is just a dredged canal with concrete sides, there are no amenities (except for a small local

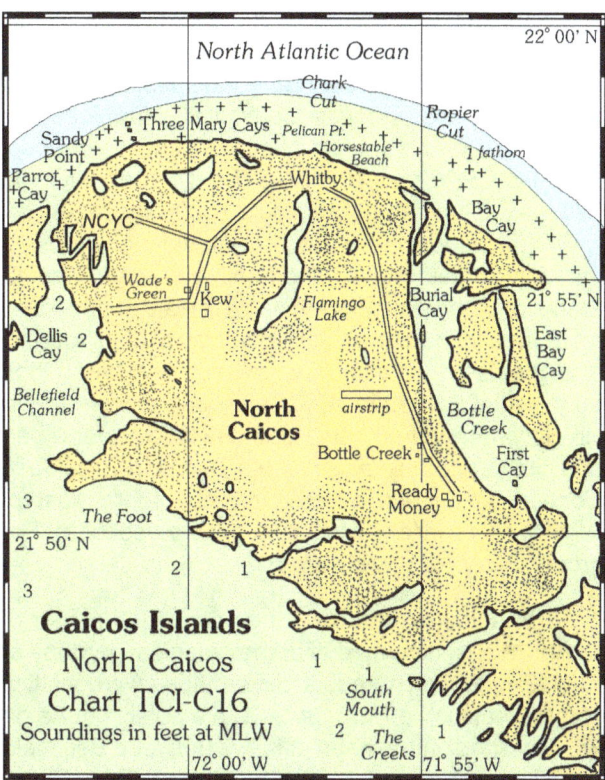

store selling basic food and drinks) and the marina is not open for cruisers at the time of this writing.

Most visitors make their first stop at Whitby where you'll find *Whitby Plaza*, a resort area located along the northern shore. Three hotels here offer fine lodging and meals to those who wish to get away from the hustle and bustle of Provo. Here you'll find a tourist information center; a great spot to begin your exploration of North Caicos. You'll probably want to check out the *North Caicos Art Center*, where you can find great buys on very nice native arts and crafts as well as silk paintings and pareos by local islanders. You might want to call ahead to make sure they'll be open as they really don't stick to a schedule. Call Alveira at 946-7120 or Regina at 946-7360.

Don't miss dining at *Papa Grunt's Seafood Restaurant* for great food. You might also want to sample the choices at *Marina View* and the *Ocean Club*. Directly across from *Whitby Plaza* is *Flamingo Pond* where you can view and photograph hundreds of West Indian flamingos. To find the pond, take the *Whitby Highway* heading east to the beach roads and you will come to *Flamingo Lookout* with its sign and small covered viewing platforms. Aircraft flying out of the nearby airstrip have been restricted from flying across the pond to the delight of the flamingos and flamingo enthusiasts. The *Prospect of Whitby Hotel* serves Italian cuisine with dinner reservations requested at what is really *Club Vacanza*, a mini *Club Med* for Italians just west of Whitby. The *Prospect of Whitby Hotel* is named after the famous *Prospect of Whitby Pub* that overlooks the Thames River in London. The nearby *Pelican Beach Resort* (http://www.pelicanbeach.tc/) has a great view overlooking the pine-fringed shore. The family-run resort has 12 rooms and serves excellent native meals in a modern restaurant. The bar attracts locals as well as tourists and guests on the cay. If you need fresh bread look up Wealthy Forbes in Whitby; just ask anyone in the village where to find her. For those who prefer a bed and breakfast inn, try *Joanne's Bed and Breakfast*. *Horsestable Beach* on the northern shore east of Whitby offers miles of beautiful private beaches. For groceries try *KJ Variety Store*.

The settlement at Kew, the agricultural center of North Caicos, is named after the botanical gardens at Kew, England. There is a clinic (https://www.visittci.com/kew-clinic), a *Post Office*, and a public phone on *Forbes Street* in the heart of Kew. Between Bellefield Landing and Kew you will find the *Cosmic Farm* where North Caicos farmers grow fresh fruits, vegetables, and herbs and welcome all visitors. Another mile up the *Cosmic Farm Road* are the ruins of Wade's Green. As the road ends you will find a sign with a map and instructions on how to proceed by foot. Bring a good pair of shoes as the walk from the road to the ruins can be rough. A team of archaeologists from *UCLA* excavated the ruins in 1989, and now visitors can see some of the finest Loyalist ruins in the Turks and Caicos Islands including a courtyard and jail. A small general store is on the left as you approach the Wade's Green ruins. Stop in for a cold drink and meet Cecelia, who sells her own wonderful basketwork. If you feel adventurous, spend the night in Kew as their only tourist and don't miss eating at *Ma Sue's* where Susan Butterfield will serve you up some truly authentic North Caicos fare, as well as sell you groceries, fruit, veggies, and frozen goods. At the other end of Kew, on the road from Whitby, you'll find *Forbes' Variety Store* where owner Elizabeth Forbes sells a wide range of household and auto supplies. If you wish to purchase fish and veggies in season, try Farmer John at 946-7381.

Further east along the main road, Bottle Creek offers up its own Loyalist ruins at the *Belvedere Plantation*. Bottle Creek is a small fishing community that borders *Bottle Creek* on the *King's Highway*. The creek is protected from the *North Atlantic Ocean* swells by the Bay Islands and their fringing Elkhorn reefs. In case of emergency there is a small medical facility by the high school in the heart of Bottle Creek at High Rock, just up from the government dock, or you can call *Government Nurse* on VHF ch. 16. At the airport north of Bottle Creek you will find some pretty good food at the *Super D Café*. Along *Creek Road*, the lower road in Bottle Creek, are several old, historic houses, many of them still inhabited. If you need fresh fish and veggies in season contact Peter the Haitian at 946-7303. If you want a loaf of fresh bread try Iona Gardiner (who also offers some very nice basketry) at the *Aquatic Restaurant,* on *Kings Road,* at 946-7272.

You can also get some fine native cuisine at *Titter's Restaurant* ran by "Titters" whose pea soup and steamed conch is to die for. *Titter's* is right next to the airport. If you're into dominos you'll want to visit the *Two Son's Restaurant*. Another good eating establishment is *Wendy's Restaurant*, no relation to the chain though. If you plan to stay overnight try *Gordon Black's Guest House*. For groceries try *Speed's Grocery* or *My Dee's Variety Store*. For those in search of cool libation, try *Ellie Smith's*, *Albert Grey's*, *Dar Williams'*, and *Nash's Bar and Pool Hall*. South of Bottle Creek, near Ready Money, stand the tallest pine forests in the Turks and Caicos Islands. Off the eastern shore of North Caicos, the Bay Islands are a national park boasting miles of pristine beaches. Iguanas on the nearby East Bays Cays are an outstanding example of the natural diversity of this green island. Towards the mouth of Bottle Creek sits the small village of Major's Hill, where everyone is named Gardiner. Look for big changes in the Bottle Creek area over the next few years. I've seen the plans for a dredged channel, 12' deep, into Bottle Creek that will lead to a large upscale marina and resort/condo complex called *Mare Bella*. As of this writing financing has been arranged, but construction has not begun.

Divers will want to note that diving along the north shore of North Caicos, as in the other islands, takes the form of spur and groove formations that drop in a mini-wall from 30-70 feet. This is the same barrier reef that stretches across the entire northern boundary of the Caicos Islands, and the diving is similar to that found on the north shore of Providenciales. This area sees far fewer divers than the sites at Provo or West Caicos, with a subsequent increase in marine life. Expect an excellent fish population with the occasional larger visitor.

Middle Caicos

Middle Caicos, often called Grande Caicos, is the largest cay in the Turks and Caicos Island group and the least exposed to tourists of all the inhabited cays. Middle Caicos can boast the most dramatic shoreline of any of the Caicos group with towering limestone cliffs along its windward shore, only broken by a few small beaches with gentle rolling hills in the background.

You can now drive or bike from Middle Caicos to North Caicos on the only causeway in the Turks and Caicos southwest of Mudjin Harbour as shown on Chart TCI-C17.

Navigational Information

A vessel with a draft of 6' or less can work its way through the offshore barrier reef at *Ferguson Cut* (see Chart TCI-C17) to anchor off the northern shore in an emergency. The area is littered with shallow coral heads and shoals, so good light is necessary. The anchorage would be a lee at best and only in south to southwest winds. There are also cuts northwest of Gambol Point (*Gamble Cut*) and just off the northeastern tip of the island (*Big Cut*). For the most part these cuts are usable and should only be attempted in an emergency and preferably if you can get some local assistance by VHF. Vessels heading east or west in the vicinity of Middle Caicos must give the northeastern tip of Middle Caicos just east of Gambol Point a wide berth of three miles or more. The water is shallow, about 20'-35', northeastward from Middle Caicos in this vicinity (see Chart TCI-C17).

What You Will Find Ashore

There are only three villages on the island, home to about 270 people and recently linked with a new paved road. In a recent nationwide cooperative effort, pastel colored paints have been provided to the island's homeowners to paint all the inhabited homes on Middle Caicos. Daily air service and weekend ferry service to North Caicos are the only links to the other populated islands in the Turks and Caicos Islands. Between North Caicos and Middle Caicos is an area that is known as the "*Crossing Over Place.*" Here you'll find a trail where, at low tide, one can walk from North Caicos to Middle Caicos just as the residents have been doing for centuries. The trail begins just west of the *Blue Horizon Resort* (http://bhresort.com/) and meanders along the bluffs along the northwestern shore of Middle Caicos. If you don't feel like walking across, a ferry at Pine Barrel Landing provides service between Middle and North Caicos on Fridays, Saturdays, and Sundays.

Middle Caicos is a spelunker's delight where the 12,000 year old *Village Cave* or *Conch Bar Caves* (a national park, http://www.islandlifeandtimes.com/places/conch-bar-caves/) offer over 15 miles of above sea level caves. For a local guide, try Herbert Niat; his intimate knowledge of these caves is worth the trouble of seeking him out. Ask him to take you to *Indian Cave* at King Hill where you will see an impressive 60' high cathedral ceiling. Here you'll find roots spiraling down from the ceiling to the rich soil of the floor between massive limestone arches. Artifacts found in these caves by a team from the University of Indiana headed by Sean Sullivan prove that Middle Caicos had an estimated 4,000 Lucayan Indians that thrived in pre-Columbian times. There is also evidence of a Lucayan ceremonial and trading center. Researchers have discovered over 38 Lucayan sites on Middle Caicos alone. And in 1977-1978, archaeologists unearthed a rare Lucayan ball court near Armstrong Pond. Ball courts have been found in Puerto Rico and points farther south, but never this far north. For great description of the ball game and how it was played by the ancient Lucayans, read the first chapter of James Michener's *Caribbean*.

The island's Northwest Point is a combination of beautiful inlets, marshes, mangroves and inland ponds that serves as a haven for bird life. Conch Bar is the largest of the three settlements on Middle

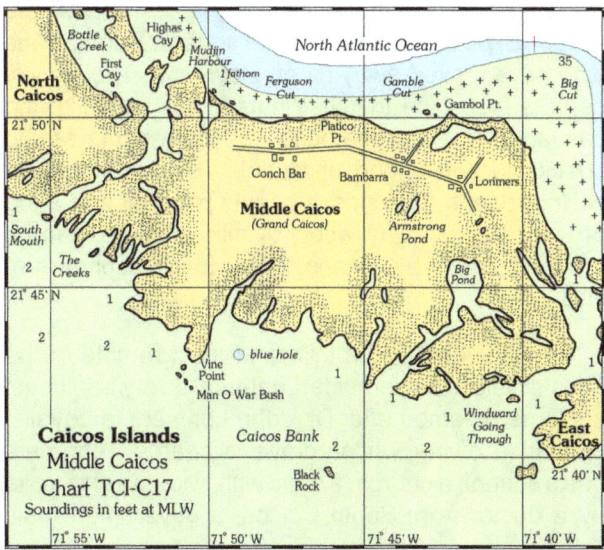

Caicos and is home to the island's only airstrip. Both *Taylor's Guest House* and *Arthur's Guest House* offer fine accommodations for the weary visitor. Nearby Mudjian Harbour, a corruption of the name Bermudian Harbour, offers a beautiful half-moon beach set against a backdrop of breathtaking limestone cliffs and is one of the most photographed sites in the Turks and Caicos Islands. The nearby *Blue Horizon Resort* offers five fully equipped villas overlooking this scenic panorama. Future plans call for condo building sites and an enlarged resort. For good local food try *Carey's Restaurant* or *T&J Boutique*, which doubles as a gift shop.

East of Conch Bar, just a scant distance from the northern reef-fringed shore, sits Bambarra, a small community with a very unique history. In 1841, the Spanish slaver *Esperanza* wrecked on the reef at Breezy Point. The surviving freed slaves settled in the Caicos Islands, while some of the survivors traveled to Grand Turk for employment.

The following year another Spanish slaver, the *Gambia,* with a hold full of slaves from Bambarra in Africa, wrecked in The Bahamas. The survivors were sent to Middle Caicos, where they founded the settlement of Bambarra situated about five miles east of Conch Bar. The name refers to the Bambarra people who lived on the shores of the *Niger River* in West Africa. From offshore, Bambarra is barely visible, some of its buildings dotting the high ridge behind some casuarinas. The only store is Emmanuel Hall's well-stocked little grocery store.

Bambarra is home to the *Middle Caicos Expo*, an annual event held in mid to late August that some say is the best party in the Turks and Caicos. The *Middle Caicos Expo* is a homecoming of sorts for Bambarrans who have moved away for employment. The activity centers along the thatched huts in the shade of the casuarina trees on the beach where vendors set up shacks to serve food and drink. Events include a sailing regatta, dominos, a beauty pageant and a tug of war. Pelican Cay, about ½ mile offshore, can be reached at LW by a sand "road" that disappears at HW.

Further east is the third and most remote of the Middle Caicos settlements, Lorimers, a very traditional settlement named after Dr. John Lorimers, a Loyalist plantation owner whose grave is nearby. Lorimers has a school, a church, a clinic with twice-weekly visits by a doctor from South Caicos, a government built water tank and two wells, *Big Well* and *Dark Night Well*. There are no stores here but residents may have an item that you are in need of, ask around. The creeks to the east of Lorimers offer some excellent bonefishing and exploring possibilities.

Divers will want to explore the blue hole near the south shore of middle Caicos just northeast of Man O War Bush as shown on Chart TCI-C16. This dive site is best visited from Leeward Going Through by small boat or from one of the anchorages in the area of Fort George Cay. The hole is about 400 yards in diameter and over 200' deep and is surrounded by shallow banks rich in sea life, including sharks and rays.

East Caicos

Waypoints
Jacksonville Cut - ¼ nm N of:
21° 47.00' N, 71° 35.90' W

East Caicos holds the distinction of being the largest uninhabited island in the Turks and Caicos Islands. Like West Caicos, East Caicos is now an uninhabited paradise, though there was once a considerable bit of industry here. The ancient Lucayans once settled here and there are several caves on the island adorned with Lucayan artwork. Near Jacksonville

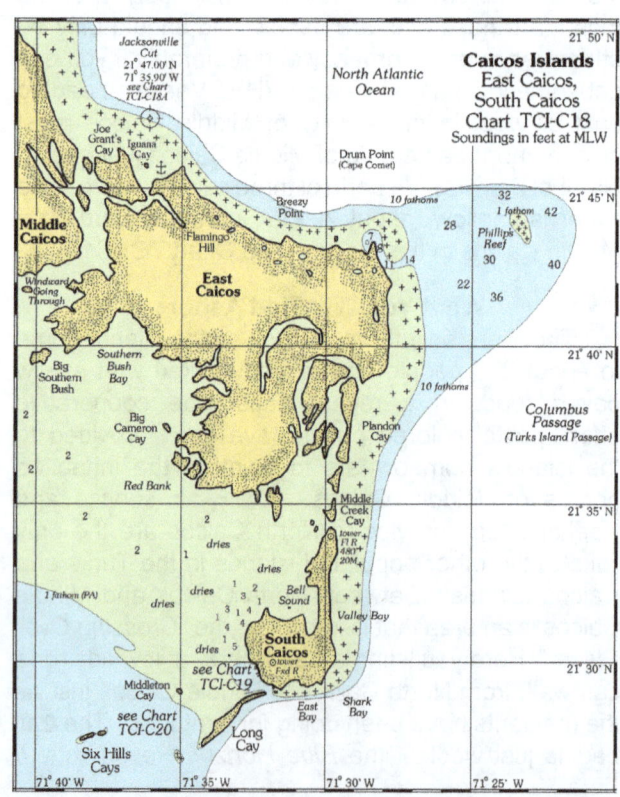

there are several caves where skeletons have been found. In a cave known as "New No. 1," there are prehistoric petroglyphs on the walls. Loyalists settled here in 1791, but as elsewhere, didn't last more than a few decades.

The sisal industry flourished following the Loyalists, finally collapsing in the late 1820s. In the 1960s, a newspaper Tycoon rebuilt the ruins of the old Jacksonville Plantation on the northern tip of the island where railroad tracks stand in silent testament to a former life. Jacksonville was once the home of the *East Caicos Sisal Company* and the *J. N. Reynolds Cattle Farm*. Today the most noteworthy inhabitants are the feral cows and donkeys that still roam this island's 18-square miles, descendants of the animals used by the early farmers. Nearby Iguana Cay boasts, as you have probably guessed by now, a large colony of iguanas. Due to the shallow waters and even shallower reefs, East Caicos is rarely visited, except by small boat or dinghy.

Navigational Information

A vessel with a draft of less than 6' can work its way through *Jacksonville Cut* to anchor between Iguana Cay and East Caicos in *Jackson Cut Bay* as shown on Chart TCI-C18A. A waypoint at 21° 47.00'N, 71° 35.90'W places you approximately ¼ mile north of the cut as shown on Chart TCI-C18. After you work your way through the break in the reef you will then have to pick your way through a minefield of shallow coral heads until you can anchor in the deeper water between Iguana Cay and the mainland of East Caicos. This anchorage is great in winds from east through south to west though a bit of swell works through from the open Atlantic in moderate and stronger winds. Shallow draft boats can work their way over a shoal (1' at MLW) to anchor in 6' between East Caicos and Joe Grant's Cay as shown on the chart.

Iguana Cay was the site of Lucayan settlement over 600 years ago. Researchers recently found the

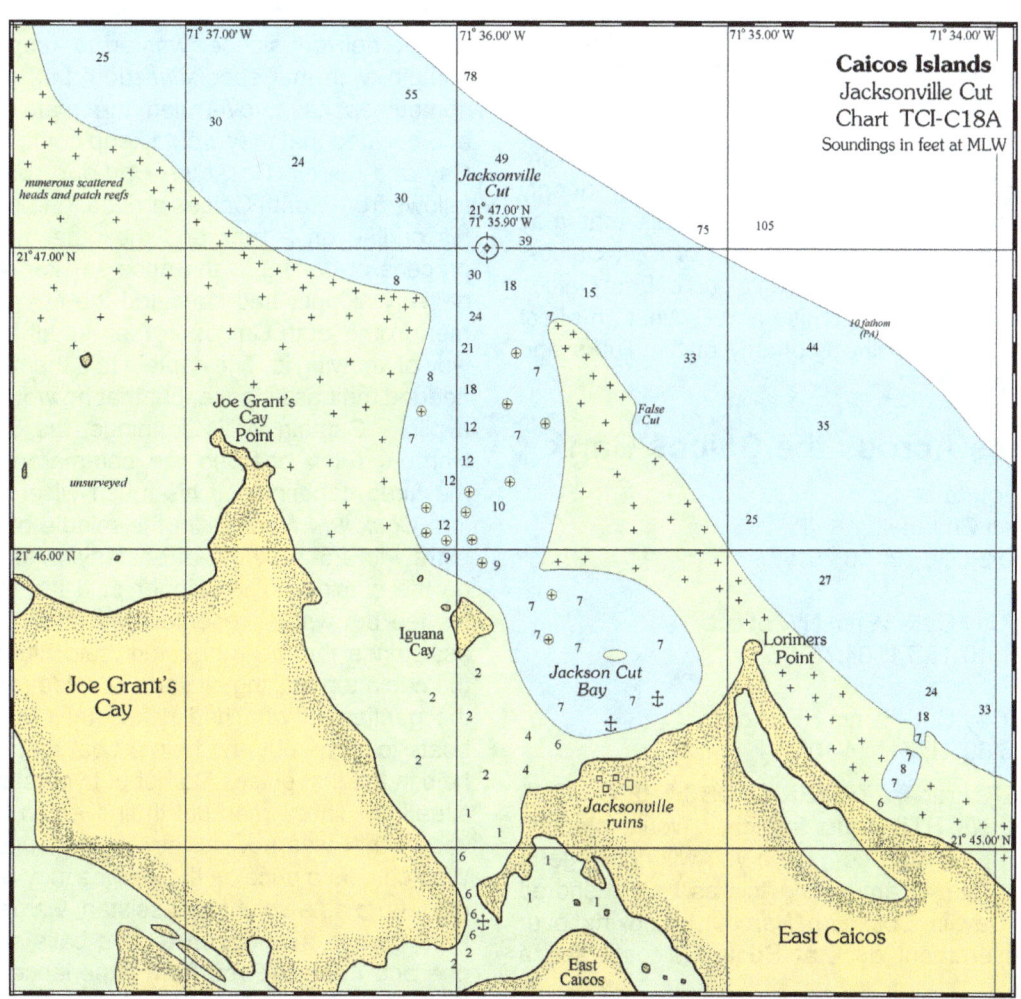

1841 wreck of an old slave ship, a 100' brigantine called the *Trouvadore*, in the waters of *Jacksonville Cut*. This shipwreck holds particular significance to the Turks and Caicos Islanders, many of whom can trace their roots to the surviving slaves (there was only one casualty, a woman who was shot on the beach after the shipwreck).

What You Will Find Ashore

Though swamps and mangroves inundate much of the island, you can find the highest point of the entire Turks and Caicos Islands here on East Caicos: *Flamingo Hill*, which rises to a height of 230' and overlooks the deadly *Phillip's Reef*. *Phillip's Reef* and nearby Haulover Point have been the home of numerous wrecks over the years. When transiting the area north and east of East Caicos, mariners are advised to pass to the east of *Phillip's Reef*. It is possible to pass inshore of *Phillips Reef* in water from 22'-30' deep, but it is so much safer to pass east of *Phillip's Reef*, even though you'll travel a few more miles.

There is a splendid 17 mile beach on the north coast of the island that is usually only used by sea turtles to lay their eggs because of the large mosquito population.

In the late 1990s, feasibility studies were completed, and developers are currently deeply involved in the decision-making process that may eventually lead to the re-settlement of East Caicos. Plans are said to include making a part of East Caicos into "the world's largest cruise port." What an effect that would have on the economy of the Turks and Caicos Islands!

Routes Across the Caicos Bank

Waypoints
Starfish Channel:
21° 30.25' N, 72° 06.75' W

Long Cay Cut - ½ nm NW of cut:
21° 27.40' N, 71° 34.75' W

Long Cay Cut - ½ nm SE of cut:
21° 26.60' N, 71° 34.10' W

NEVER, I repeat, **NEVER CROSS THE** *CAICOS BANK* **AT NIGHT!** I just thought I would mention that right at the start so maybe you will not forget it and tempt fate. I am writing this as I sit anchored off Long Cay in *Cockburn Harbour*. Looking over at the government dock at South Caicos I see a 42' catamaran that attempted to negotiate the area between Six Hills Cays and Long Cay last night in a nice east wind of 25 knots on the nose, no moon, and only a spotlight to locate the scattered heads and reefs that you often find on the *Caicos Bank*. Please note that on a moonless night you cannot pick out the reefs with a spotlight unless they are breaking and they probably won't be doing that. The cat, with a delivery crew aboard, promptly ran aground on one of the several reefs in the area and the Captain put out a MAYDAY distress call on VHF. ch.16; they immediately received word from South Caicos that help was on the way.

The folks at South Caicos are seamen; they make their living from the sea and they know what it is like to be in trouble at sea. Soon two small boats set out to render assistance in the rapidly deteriorating weather. Before they could arrive at the stricken vessel the captain was able to get his boat off the reef and the mate suggested that they anchor where they were in 15' of water. The mate also suggested this before they ran aground. He knew there were reefs around but the delivery skipper wanted to keep going. The captain, with that special wisdom that only captains sometimes have, overruled the mate's suggestion and decided that they would keep going on past Long Cay and up into *Cockburn Harbour*. Meanwhile the fellows from South Caicos arrived, one had damaged his engine on a rock and the other his hull in the process of getting to the once-stricken vessel. The delivery skipper had canceled the MAYDAY but the men from South Caicos in their small boats had no way of knowing it. The captain told them he no longer needed their assistance, but that he would like to hire a pilot. Captain Willis Jennings, the South Caicos Harbour Pilot, boarded the catamaran and guided the hired captain, and his much wiser mate, safely into *Cockburn Harbour* in the middle of a moonless night with 25-30 knots of easterly wind and 8' seas on the outside. The skipper paid the Harbour Pilot his fee but when presented with a bill for the other assistance that he requested, said hired skipper hit the cabin top making all sorts of snide remarks about the gentlemen who had risked their lives and their boats to come out and help a boat that did not need help in the first place. Do not put yourself in a similar situation. Those men put their lives on the line for a vessel that was not in distress, only uncomfortable. Who can put a price on the service they rendered? In my tenure as a volunteer assistant warden at Exuma Park I went on a dozen rescue calls similar to this one and I can tell you from experience that you do it because you have to, because somebody has to help and you are the only one there to do it. Were the warden and I to put a price on the services we rendered, I am sure it would seem staggering to the average boater, but then again they weren't out there in the wind and the seas. I know a certain salvager in The Bahamas who would not have stirred from his bed without being guaranteed twice what the good men of South Caicos asked for. Do not let this happen to you. **DO NOT CROSS THE CAICOS BANK AT NIGHT!** There, now that I'm finished getting up on my soapbox, let us continue.

I've always considered local knowledge the best knowledge when it comes to navigating any waters anywhere, and the *Caicos Bank* is no exception. The local knowledge here is that when crossing the *Caicos Bank*, if you can see land to the north, you are too far north towards the shallower water - good advice when crossing from Provo to South Caicos, Long Cay, Six Hills Cays, or the Ambergris Cays. There are several routes to choose from depending on your draft as shown back on Chart TCI-C1. As I just mentioned, and probably cannot repeat often enough, none of these routes should be attempted at night as you may come across the stray coral head or small patch reef anywhere on the *Caicos Bank*. If you see any dark patches of water, by all means steer around them. Even in areas on the *Caicos Bank* where the heads and patch reefs are particularly thick you can always find deeper water between them and plenty of room to steer around them. One pleasant sight that you'll find on the *Caicos Bank* is the phenomenon of the *Emerald Cloud*. On certain days when the sun and the clouds are right the bottoms of the clouds take on a lovely green hue. What happens is that the green water of the bank is reflected off the underside of the cloud giving its emerald appearance.

Navigational Information

From the waypoint at *Sapodilla Bay*, a heading of 122° for 43.1 nautical miles will bring you to a waypoint at 21° 27.40'N, 71° 34.75'W, approximately ½ mile inside *Long Cay Cut* and just west of the southern end of Long Cay as shown on Chart TCI-C20. In the first edition of this guide I mentioned that this route across the *Caicos Bank* could accommodate drafts of less than 7' at MLW and drafts of up to 8½' with the tide and was the easiest and preferred route across the bank. Although still easy, areas of the route have shallowed to the point that the controlling depth as shown on Chart TCI-C1 is a bit over 5' at MLW and 6½' with the tide, which limits the use of this route to fewer vessels. The shallower areas are on the northern side of this route between 72° 07' W and 72° 00' W, so if you find the water getting progressively thinner, try heading a bit south of the course-line. You will still have to steer through some scattered heads in the vicinity of 72° 05'W through 71° 55'W, but once east of this area you will find the heads more scattered. Depending on the wind direction, you can anchor north or south of the Six Hills Cays. This pair of cays with a small rock between them is easily identified, the six hills, three hills on each cay. Here you'll find good snorkeling on the reefs on the southern side of the cays but getting the hook to set here can sometimes be a pain. There are several areas of rock and grass but if you look around a bit you'll find a good sandy spot in which to drop your hook.

You can anchor in the lee of the southern tip of Long Cay in easterly winds, but keep a good eye out for the scattered heads and patch reefs in the area, as shown on the chart. If you have enough time you can head out *Long Cay Cut* into the deeper water of the *Turks Island Passage* and head northeast to enter into protected *Cockburn Harbour* at South Caicos (see next section *South Caicos*). When heading out through *Long Cay Cut*, watch out for the rocks south of Long Cay and the large breaking reef lying southwest of the cay as shown on Chart TCI-C20. Skippers with shallow drafts or those who love a challenge can pass north of *Middleton Bar* and then parallel it on its north shore to work in along the northwestern tip of Long Cay into *Cockburn Harbour*. I do not recommend this route unless: A) you absolutely have to be in South Caicos and conditions do not allow an outside transit of Long Cay; B) you have a draft of less than 5' and

NEVER cross the Caicos Bank at night

you are attempting to round or cross the bar at high tide; and C) you are simply adventurous and like a challenge. If you are attempting to round *Middleton Bar*, a waypoint at 21° 30.90'N, 71° 36.10'W will place you approximately ¼ mile northwest of the shallow northwestern end of the bar. From this position head generally southeast keeping in the deeper water on the northern side of the bar until you begin to find the deeper water closer in towards Long Cay. If you headed south from *Leeward Going Through* across *Boy Stubbs Shoal* and enjoyed that passage, you'll love this one. You would not be able to guess by looking at the island, but Middleton Cay was once home to Lucayan Indians. Recent digs have unearthed a Lucayan site on this tiny cay.

Vessels heading to the Ambergris Cays from *Sapodilla Bay* (as shown on Chart TCI-C1) can steer 134° for 43.8 miles from the *Sapodilla Bay* waypoint to a waypoint at 21° 19.75'N, 71° 39.75'W. This waypoint places you approximately 1 mile northwest of the anchorage between Little Ambergris and Big Ambergris as shown on Chart TCI-C21. Of course, if you are heading from Big Ambergris to *Sapodilla Bay* you will steer 314° for 43.8 miles to reach the waypoint south of the *Sapodilla Bay* anchorage. This route takes you through the *Pearl Channel*, which lies between two relatively shallow banks with about 6' at MLW.

The more traditional routes across the *Caicos Bank* make use of the *Starfish Channel*, which lies south of the major area of shallows on the bank. From *Sapodilla Bay* take up a course of 154° for 17.1 nautical miles to a waypoint in *Starfish Channel* at 21° 30.25'N, 72° 06.75'W. If bound for Long Cay from *Starfish Channel*, take up a course of 104° for 30 nautical miles, which will bring you to the anchorage off the southwestern tip of Long Cay. A note of caution on this route; take care not to run up on the Six Hills Cays, you can pass them on either their north side or their south side, but you cannot go straight through them. Your course north or south of the Six Hills Cays will depend on whether you are heading for the waypoint at the anchorage off the southwestern tip of Long Cay, or if you are heading for the deep-water waypoint at *Long Cay Cut*.

From the waypoint at *Starfish Channel* a course of 122° for 28. 2 miles will bring you to the anchorage between Big Ambergris Cay and Little Ambergris Cay. If you're at French Cay and wish to head to Ambergris Cay, this is also a good route to take. One can also head east of French Cay, past the shallow reefs to work your way up onto the banks about 4-5 miles east/southeast of French Cay where you can take up a course to the Ambergris anchorage. There will be several areas of heads lying just to the east of French Cay that you will have to dodge.

Vessels heading toward Long Cay and the route across the *Caicos Bank* towards *Sapodilla Bay* and Providenciales can head to a waypoint at 21° 26.60'N, 71° 34.10'W placing you ½ mile southeast of *Long Cay Cut*. Pass between the southern tip of Long Cay (watch out for the rocks off its southern tip) and the reef lying just southwest of Long Cay as shown on Chart TCI-C20. Work your way up inside of Long Cay, as shown on the chart, to take up your course of 302° to *Sapodilla Bay*.

South Caicos

Waypoints
Cockburn Harbour - ¼ nm SE of:
21° 28.70' N, 71° 31.70' W

South Caicos, or Big South as some of its residents describe their island, is relatively small, only 8½ square miles, but it is quite densely populated by Turks and Caicos Islands standards. Most of the island's 1,200 inhabitants live in Cockburn Harbour, which should not be confused with Cockburn Town on Grand Turk. Cockburn Harbour, or East Harbour as it is sometimes called, dates to Bermudian Salt Raker days. The salt pans north and east of the town now lie abandoned since the failure of the salt industry in the 1960s. South Caicos is home to what is known as the *Boiling Hole*, a natural ocean hole where the water that boils out contains a high degree of salinity, making it perfect for salt production. The Boiling Hole fed the salt pans that once made South Caicos the Turks and Caicos' largest producer of salt. Today most of her people rely on the sea for their livelihood and South Caicos exports large numbers of conch and lobster to the United States and France through her two fish processing plants. Some sport-fishermen call South Caicos the big fish capital of the Turks and Caicos, with the larger pelagics often seen here in great numbers. A vertical wall wraps around the southern edge of South Caicos, then extends the length of Long Cay and is often reputed to have the finest diving in the Turks and Caicos. On the northern tip of the island is the 480' tall red and white antenna of the old *U.S. Coast Guard Loran Station, NMA-5*, that is now a private station that transmits in Spanish at 50,000 watts, a great landmark that flashes red

The Caicos Islands

at night. Don't confuse it with the much shorter (260') red and white *Cable and Wireless* tower at the southern end of the island at Cockburn Harbour that has a fixed red light at its top.

Navigational Information

Cockburn Harbour, one of the best natural harbors in the Turks and Caicos Islands, is a working harbor with a regular fleet of fishing boats and trading vessels bound to and from Haiti and the Dominican Republic. It's not unusual to walk down the streets of town and hear Creole on one corner and Spanish on the next. The entrance to the harbor is lighted and easy to enter, even at night. If approaching *Cockburn Harbour* from the north, stand off South Caicos at least a mile or more to avoid the fringing reefs. The entrance to *Cockburn Harbour* will lie about a mile or so south of the long unfinished hotel on the southeastern shore of South Caicos. A waypoint at 21° 28.70'N, 71° 31.70'W, will place you approximately ¼ mile southeast of the entrance channel between Long Cay and Dove Cay as shown on Chart TCI-C19. A good landmark is the huge green house with the pointed roof on the hill and the conspicuous white concrete light tower. The light tower shows a fixed white light at 90' above sea level from 90°-180°.

Cockburn Harbour has received a bad rap as having poor holding but those that reported bad holding have simply been anchoring in the wrong spots. I have ridden out fronts with prolonged winds of over 30 knots here without a problem. The holding, if your anchor is set well, is good throughout with the exception of a few places. At the eastern end of the harbor near Dove Cay, and close in along the southern shore of South Caicos, there are several areas of what the locals call "slate," hard, crusty, scoured sand that is difficult to get an anchor to set in.

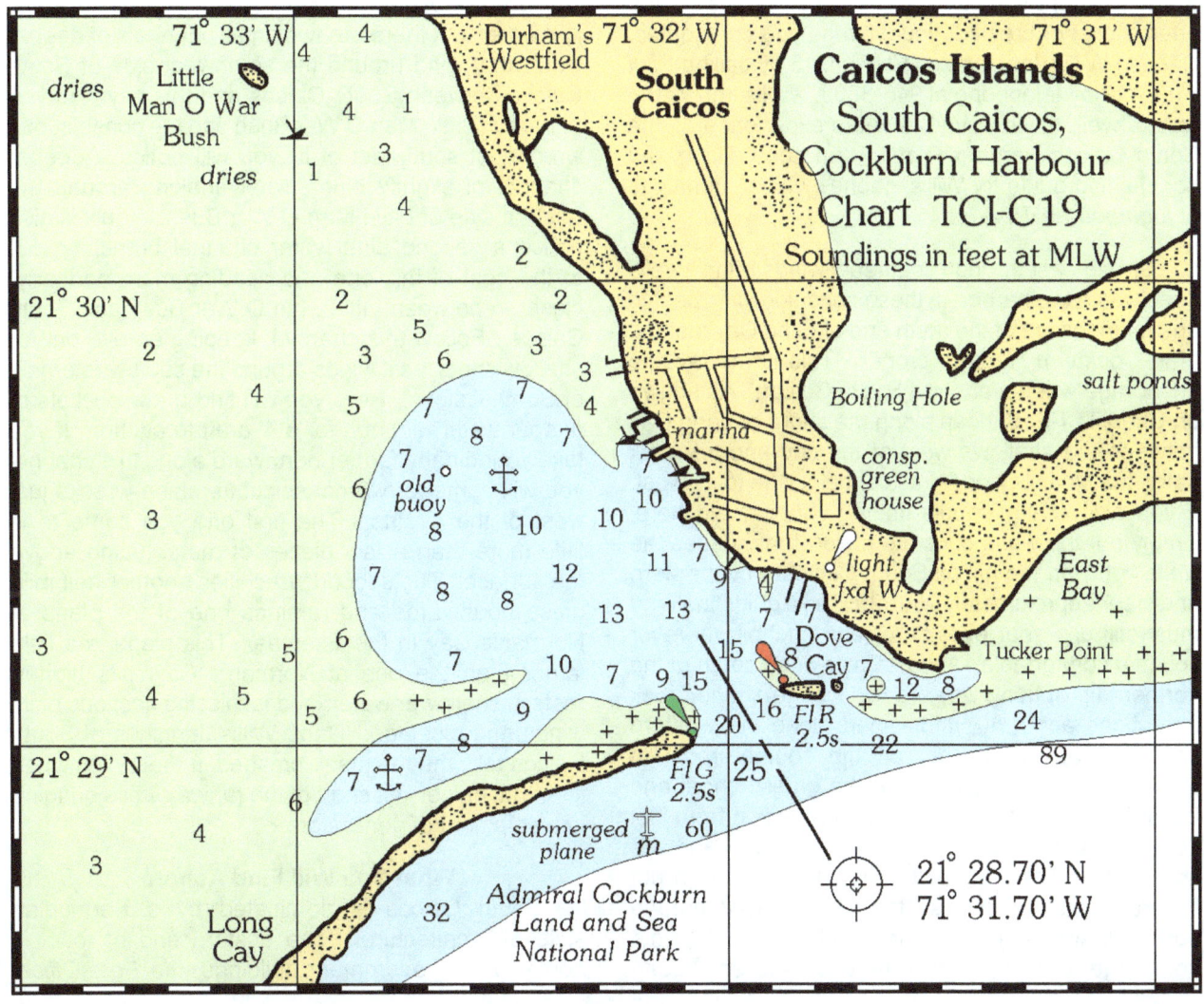

The best holding is at the western end of the harbor, between the remains of an old buoy and the shore. You will notice that this is where the locals anchor their boats, even during hurricanes. I am told that the old buoy drifted into *Cockburn Harbour* from Puerto Rico during *Hurricane David* back in the 1970s and has been in its present position ever since.

Close in to the South Caicos shoreline you must avoid several submerged railways west of *Sea View Marina* between the marina and the wooden dock with the small wooden building on the end. *Cockburn Harbour* offers excellent protection, even in strong winds, as the banks to the west and northwest dry in places at low water. However, if I knew a strong front was heading my way with westerly winds of 40 knots or more, and if I had the time, I would try to get over to Grand Turk to tuck into *North Creek* for the best protection and the most comfort. In periods of light or no wind, you might need to set a bridle to keep from rolling as there is a little current in the harbor. If you need a pilot or crew for your voyage you can contact Captain Willis Jennings on VHF ch. 16 by calling *Pilot House* or by telephone at 946-3308. Willis knows the waters well, having over 20 years experience as the South Caicos Harbour Pilot. For a good diving and bonefishing guide try Willis' nephew Gilbert Jennings at *Lightbourne Taxi.*

Strong east through southeast winds bring swells directly into the harbor; in these conditions it is best to anchor in the lee of the north end of Long Cay instead of in *Cockburn Harbour* proper. This is my favorite anchorage whenever I visit South Caicos. As shown on Chart TCI-C19, head along the shore of Long Cay between the shallows west of the cay and the dark patch that is a rock and grass shoal a little to its west. If you are having trouble finding your way in here, simply put the white concrete tower (that houses the white light) on the hill on South Caicos on your stern and steer approximately 250°-255° as a guideline (you must still use your eyes here) and anchor wherever you feel comfortable. About ½ mile or so south of the northern tip of Long Cay are two wedge-shaped rock formations about 50 yards apart along the western shore. I usually anchor off the southernmost of these, about halfway between the grassy shoal and Long Cay. This spot offers great protection from just north of east through south to southwest, and the holding is excellent in soft sand. I have ridden out several fronts here with sustained southwest through northwest winds of 30-40 knots and my one CQR did not budge; yes, the holding here is excellent. *Long Bar* and *Middleton Bar* break the larger seas and all you wind up with off Long Cay is a 2'-3' chop. When the wind goes into the northwest the best spot is at the far western end of *Cockburn Harbour*, where you can find good protection in the lee of Man O War Bush and the large bank area surrounding it that dries at low water. You'll get some chop in a strong westerly here, but nothing dangerous. The *School for Field Studies* (http://www.fieldstudies.org/tci) at South Caicos wishes to remind boaters to please not anchor in the large turtle grass beds in the area west of Long Cay; these are study sites for their students. There is plenty of good clean sand to drop the hook in, so please avoid the large turtle grass beds.

Vessels drawing less than 4' can find a nice alternative anchorage west of *Cockburn Harbour*, but for safety's sake you should check out the approach by dinghy beforehand. Just before high tide head towards Little Man O War Bush, keeping it just off your port bow. Most of the water around this cay dries at low water, but there are two small channels of deeper water that wind around the southwest side of South Caicos between South Caicos and this cay. As you approach Little Man O War Bush and the conspicuous wreck just southeast of it, you will notice a deeper channel of slightly bluer water snaking around the eastern side of Little Man O War Bush. You will also notice a second blue water channel branching out to the right of this one and heading more northerly, closer in between Little Man O War Bush and South Caicos. Follow this channel, keeping an eye out for shallow spots, as it winds around the southwestern tip of South Caicos. Here you will find a few pockets of deeper water, enough for a 4' draft to anchor. If you take your dinghy further northward along this channel you will come to two conspicuous plane wrecks just west of the airstrip. The first one you come to is little more than a few pieces of metal jutting above the surface. The second wreck lies another half mile or so northwards and reminds one of the plane at Norman's Cay in the Exumas. This plane is a little larger than the one at Norman's Cay, sits higher, rests in shallower water, and is missing sections of its wings and fuselage. Capt. Willis Jennings of South Caicos tells me the plane crashed in the 1970s when it ran out of fuel just short of the runway while bringing in a shipment of generators.

What You Will Find Ashore

South Caicos is dominated by a Bermudian style of architecture. The eastern end of town is home to the government buildings, the *Post Office*,

Courthouse, government clinic, and the water and fisheries departments. High on a hill to the east of these buildings is the *Residency*, an 18th century structure that was the district commissioner's home and is now *Mae's Bed and Breakfast*. You can't miss *Mae's*. It's the huge green house with the pointed roof that was your landfall as you approached *Cockburn Harbour*. Call first if you wish to dine here. Just to the east is a cemetery with several old gravestones. Throughout town you'll see many wooden jetties, warehouses, and churches that date back over 200 years. Along the eastern shore of South Caicos northeast of *Mae's* are the unfinished remains of a huge hotel complex sitting on the ridge above the beautiful beach at *East Bay* where you'll find good beachcombing after a northeast through southeast blow. The Norwegian investors backed out of this hotel project around 1988; today it stands unfinished, but it remains a great landmark. There is a trail from *Mae's* leading to the beach.

On the northern shore of *Cockburn Harbour* you will see a large concrete dock with several conspicuous storage tanks. This is the *Sea View Marina* where owner Captain Lewis Cox and his son Norman are your hosts. You can get fuel right at the dock, or, if you draw too much to come alongside (7' at low water), either Lewis or Norman will be glad to meet you at the government dock with their 2,500-gallon fuel truck. The marina offers free overnight dockage, yes, that's right, free overnight dockage with or without fuel purchase, but the dock can only handle up to three boats - weather permitting. When was the last time you heard of a marina offering free dockage? Thirty-amp 110v power is available and fresh water can be trucked in with a 55-gallon minimum. If you need just a few gallons, Norman says he can help you right from his tank.

You can also arrange for fuel from *Pinnacle Fuel Suppliers* (649-946-3283), and *Charlie Alpha (VHF ch. 16)*, Captain Bruce Lightbourne and his *ESSO* fuel truck for delivery to the government dock. *Charlie Alpha* will also deliver groceries and fuel to your boat if you are at anchor.

Sea View Marina can also hold your mail for you, arrange a *FedEx* or *UPS* package delivery through Provo, supply a diesel or outboard mechanic, arrange a propane tank fill, and even rent you a car. There's little that Lewis and Norman can't do for visiting boaters. Their very well-stocked *Sea View Market* is the best on the island with fresh fruits and veggies, frozen meats, ice cream, all sorts of dry goods, some small boating supplies, and a phone just outside the front door. Next door, their *Café Columbus* is currently closed and they don't know when they will re-open it. For more info call *Sea View Marina* on VHF ch. 16.

For a taxi you can use ch. 16 to raise *Glinton's Taxi*; owner Bertram Glinton will be happy to take you all over the island at a very reasonable price. For an interesting history lesson, ask Bertram about his years in salt production. You can also try *Lightbourne Taxi*, *Hillside Taxi*, or *Wee 10 Base*. Garbage can be placed in the dumpsters on the street in front of the *Sea View Marina* or by the fish factory docks. Across the street from the *Sea View Marina* is *Anita's Bakery* at *Anita's on the Bay* where owner Anita Clarke bakes wonderful fresh bread; she can even whip up something for you to eat in a pinch.

If you need Internet access there is a small computer shop near the end of the town dock.

You will notice that almost everyone in South Caicos has a smile and a hello for you. This community is as far from Provo in distance as it is in atmosphere. I cannot say enough about the wonderful people that are South Caicos' true treasure. This is my favorite island in the entire Turks and Caicos archipelago. I once found myself in dire straits in my data acquisition vessel when my automatic bilge pump burned out and my sixteen-footer was swamped at dawn after all-night 40-knot squalls. I received more than enough help from the good people of South Caicos and none wanted anything in return. All they wanted was the chance to help somebody. They informed me that, after all, that's what we are all here for, to help each other. South Caicos and her people will always hold a dear spot in my heart, especially my good friends Capt. Willis Jennings and Marvin. By the way Marvin, if you're reading this, I still have those plugs and they're still working fine. Oh, and hello to you too, Willis!

As you walk around town it's not unusual to see donkeys, cows, or dogs competing for the road with you and the occasional car or motorcycle. As for bars, *Miss Trudy's Jetaway Bar* is the place for nightlife in South Caicos. For good native food *Muriel's* is the best and she is just east of the *Immigration* office and government dock. Another stop is *Carver's Restaurant* behind *Bayside Auto Parts* across from the *Wee 10 Market* also just east of the *Sea View*

Marina. You can also try the *Eastern Inn* for good takeaway food. *First Caribbean Bank* has an office in town, though they are only open on Wednesdays from 0900 till 1300. Next to the bank is *Myrna Lee's Restaurant*. For hardware or lumber try the new *G & H Hardware and Lumber Co*. On the airport road at the salt pans is the *Pond View Restaurant*, a good choice for lunch or dinner. Other options are *Ocean Haven*, *Love's* on the *Airport Road*, and *Miss May's Bed and Breakfast*.

High on a hill above the harbor is the *Admiral's Arm Inn*, a charming and historical location that was the first hotel built in the Turks and Caicos Islands. Until about 35 years ago, the *Inn* was being used to process cotton. With the disappearance of the owner, Diane, her brother could not keep the inn going, and despite his best efforts, the inn and its garden became a pasture for goats and donkeys. Today the inn serves as housing for students in the *School for Field Studies Program* and it's still worth a visit. The large pink two-story building next door is the *Club Caribe Harbour and Beach Resort* (http://www.fortmyers.com/turks/clcarib.html), the only hotel on the island. The *Club Caribe Sunset Bar and Restaurant* has large glass windows with a stunning view of the rocky cliffs and turquoise waters of the harbor below.

Club Caribe has the only dive operation on the island and it is here that you can get all your diving questions about South Caicos answered. The diving off South Caicos includes wall dives as well as some beautiful shallow water reefs and coral gardens teeming with marine life.

Just off Long Cay, as shown on Chart TCI-C19, is a dive site known as the *Plane Wreck,* a *Convair* 340 lying in about 60' of water. The wreck is situated approximately 300 yards off the cay, actually just opposite the first rock formation on the shoreline south of the entrance to *Cockburn Harbour,* and is marked by a buoy. Please don't tie your big boat to this buoy, it only strong enough for small boats and dinghies.

Another interesting site is the *Eagle's Nest*, named for the community of stingrays that lives amidst its unusual seascape of sand channels and ledges. Ask about the shallow water dive sites such as *Lion's Head Rock, Boulder Ground,* and the *Admiral's Aquarium*. As I mentioned earlier, ask for Gilbert Jennings at *Lightbourne Taxi* for a knowledgeable diving guide.

Just west of the *Sea View Marina* are several concrete and rip-rap jetties for small boats to tie to; this is where you'll want to tie up your dinghy, but be sure to use a stern anchor to keep your bow off the concrete wall in the surge. At the head of the docks is one of the two fish factories in town. The second, just to the west, lies at the head of the wooden dock with the small wooden building on the end. Just up the hill from the fish factories is the *Cham B Grocery Store* and around the corner is *Hillside Grocery*.

In late May, South Caicos is host to one heck of a big party, the annual *South Caicos Regatta*. People from all over the Turks and Caicos Islands flock to Cockburn Harbour for this colorful, energetic festival. The excitement builds during the Saturday morning sloop races and climaxes Saturday afternoon and night with music, dancing, donkey races, and maypole dancing. If you are in the area do not miss this event.

The Southern Cays

Waypoints
Fish Cays - ¾ nm N of:
21° 23.50' N, 71° 37.25' W

West Sand Spit - 2 nm SW of:
21° 20.50' N, 72° 10.05' W

Big Ambergris Cay - 1 nm NW of anchorage:
 21° 19.75' N, 71° 39.75' W

The Southern Cays is the name given to the numerous small islands that lie on the Caicos Bank to the south of Six Hills Cays and Long Cay, stretching about 20 miles south and southwest of Cockburn Harbour on South Caicos. There are three groups, the Fish Cays, the Ambergris Cays, and the Seal Cays. With the exception of the Ambergris Cays these cays are rarely visited except by local fishermen and divers.

Navigational Information
The Fish Cays are small, rocky, and offer little to passing yachtsmen. The largest of the three is worthy of a dinghy trip if you are interested in cactus and lizards, and there is a beautiful Elkhorn coral reef off this cay's northwest shore. You can actually anchor on the western side of this cay in settled weather or prevailing winds, but you'll have to thread your way through some coral heads and small reefs. The cay is covered in prickly pear cactus and is a nesting site for Sooty Terns in the summer months. There are three small beaches on the western shore and

several shallow reefs that are excellent for snorkelers and fishermen. If passing through from *Sapodilla Bay* to the *Turks Island Passage*, a waypoint at 21° 23.50'N, 71° 37.25'W, will place you approximately ¾ mile north of the Fish Cays in good water as shown on Chart TCI-C21. From here you can head straight to the Turks Islands or the Dominican Republic.

Between the Fish Cays and the Ambergris Cays are numerous coral reefs and heads, some lying just inches below the water's surface; the water in between them, though 25'-35' deep in places, is affected by strong and sometimes confused tidal currents. If you are headed west onto the *Caicos Bank* and wish to anchor south of the Fish Cays between the Ambergris Cays, the best idea is to do what the locals do. Head west on the bank until Little Ambergris is abeam and then head south. This will get you past the majority of the shallow reefs that lie between the Fish Cays and Big Ambergris Cay. This area is a cartographer's nightmare. There is absolutely no way that I could show each and every reef in this area on Chart TCI-C21 at that scale. A word to the wise usually being sufficient, I would suggest you avoid this area unless you can read the water well and don't mind a little white knuckle maneuvering. It is possible to leave the anchorage between Little and Big Ambergris and work your way through these reefs to gain the deeper water of the *Turks Island Passage*, but it might be prudent to avoid them altogether. The choice is yours; I can only advise.

A waypoint at 21° 19.75'N, 71° 39.75'W, will place you approximately one mile northwest of the anchorage that lies between Big Ambergris and Little Ambergris Cay. Watch for scattered heads and shallow patch reefs in this area. The anchorage has great holding, but the shallows stretch out a good bit off the shore of both cays. A 5' draft can usually get within ½ mile of Big Ambergris Cay for good protection from east and southeast winds just off the house and small dock. If you anchor just north of the buildings on Big Ambergris, you can tuck in a little closer but there are a few more shallow reefs to avoid. If you head north from here to round the Fish Cays, once again it is best to do it just like the locals do. Put the eastern end of Little Ambergris on your stern as you head north to avoid the majority of the shallow reefs between the Fish Cays and Big Ambergris Cay.

What You Will Find Ashore

The Ambergris Cays, Big Ambergris (East Ambergris) and Little Ambergris (West Ambergris) are named after the wax-like substance that is

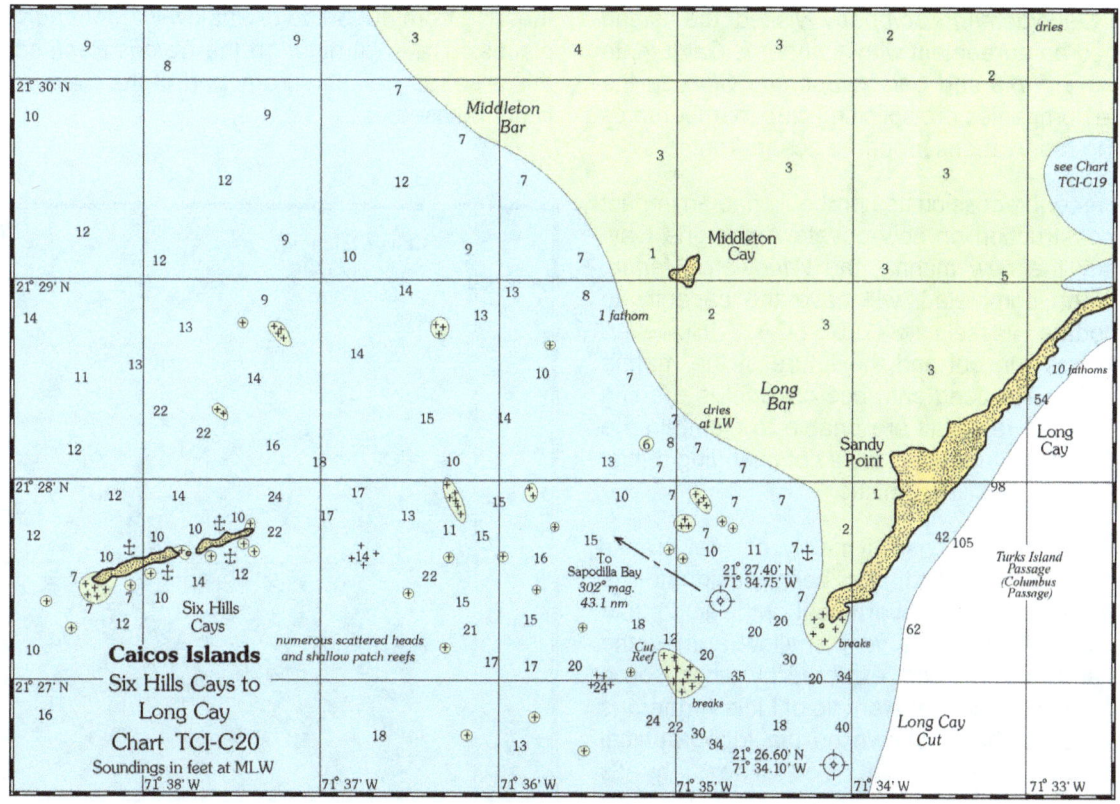

excreted by the humpback whales that pass through the Turks Island Passage and often found on the windward shore of Big Ambergris. Big Ambergris and Little Ambergris are as distinctly different as night and day. The easternmost cay, Big Ambergris, is slightly hilly (max. elevation 96') while its neighbor one mile to the west, Little Ambergris, is larger in area but quite lower in elevation. There are some ruins of pasture walls and a couple of buildings on the southern end of the Big Ambergris, remnants of earlier inhabitants of the cay. John Lightbourne purchased Big Ambergris Cay from The Bahamas in 1811 and sold it in 1837 for 6,000 bushels of salt. The island was used for the growing of sisal until the late 1800s. Following the taking of the first whale in the Turks and Caicos Islands on Feb. 4, 1846, a whaling lookout post was established on Big Ambergris Cay. Later on the island was used as a sisal plantation. Today you'll find a colony of rock iguanas inhabiting the cay along with a lot of Turk's Head Cactus. On the eastern shore is a beautiful beach in Long Cay that is excellent for beachcombing. Grab a comb and have at it!

Big plans are in the works for Big Ambergris Cay. In 1995, the cay was purchased by a group of investors who had a goal or establishing a marina and resort on the island. This did not work out for one reason or another, but in 2002 the *Dolan, Pollak, and Schram Development Company* visited the island and signed an agreement with *Ambergris Cay Ltd.* to develop the *Turks and Caicos Sporting Club* on the cay. The companies are soliciting club memberships and taking reservations for prime ocean-front lots.

The recent recession has probably had an impact on the construction on now-private Ambergris Cay, particularly the new marina, the *Windward Marina*, which, when completed, will have the capacity to accommodate vessels to 200' LOA. However, financing has run out and the future of the marina is uncertain. The long entrance channel is eroding quickly and the few staff are unable to maintain the facilities. But the future has a way of changing things so the owners are still optimistic.

Little Ambergris consists mainly of tidal creeks and mangrove flats and has been designated a *Nature Reserve* by the Government of the Turks and Caicos. The shoreline is very shallow around the entire island and it is best explored by dinghy on a rising tide. Off the northeastern tip of Little Ambergris Cay is an area that is shown on the topographical maps as the Conch Ground. You'll know why it's called that when you investigate pile after pile of conch shells that are probably hundreds of years old. These piles are much taller than I am and there must be at least two dozen of them along the eastern shore of Little Ambergris; it is quite a sight. The surrounding dune and rock structure support a large colony of rock iguanas. Hawksbill and green turtles use the western shore of Little Ambergris Cay for nesting sites during the spring and early summer months; please do not disturb any turtles you may see there and don't dig in the sand for their nests. These cays are often used as a stopover before heading to Luperón, which isn't a bad idea, the reef snorkeling, at its worst, is fantastic.

South of the Ambergris Cays the banks are studded with numerous coral heads that reach up from 20' depths to break the surface. Just south of Big Ambergris Cay lies Bush Cay (as shown on Chart TCI-C1), a protected sanctuary (visits ashore require a permit from the *DECR*) and this tiny tree covered island has a navigational light tower. The Seal Cays, another protected sanctuary, are named after the now extinct West Indian monk seal and primarily used as fishing ground by Caicos fishermen along the area surrounding White Cay. These cays lie south and southwest of the Ambergris Cays and stretch for 10 miles between Bush Cay and White Cay. The waters surrounding these cays are strewn with shallow reefs that rise from 40'-60' to dry at low water in numerous places. Travel at night on the *Caicos Bank* south of this area, as well as on any part of the *Caicos Bank*, is not advised.

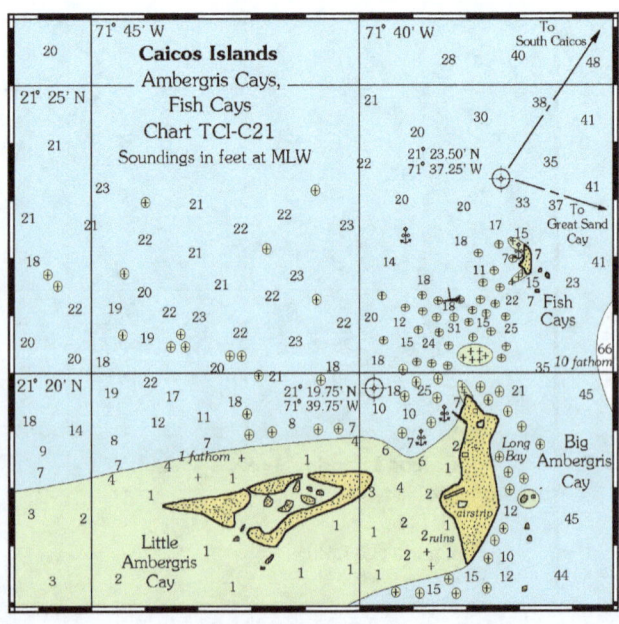

The Turks Islands

Ports of Entry:
Grand Turk (*South Base*)
Fuel: Grand Turk
Haul-Out: None
Diesel Repairs: Grand Turk, Salt Cay
Outboard Repairs: Grand Turk
Propane: Grand Turk

Provisions: Grand Turk
Important Lights:
Grand Turk Lighthouse: Fl W ev 7.5 sec
Salt Cay, Northwest Point: Gp Fl (4) W ev 20 sec
Great Sand Cay: Fl W ev 2 sec

To the east of the deep *Turks Island Passage*, sometimes called the *Columbus Passage*, lies the *Turks Bank* and the Turks Islands themselves, once

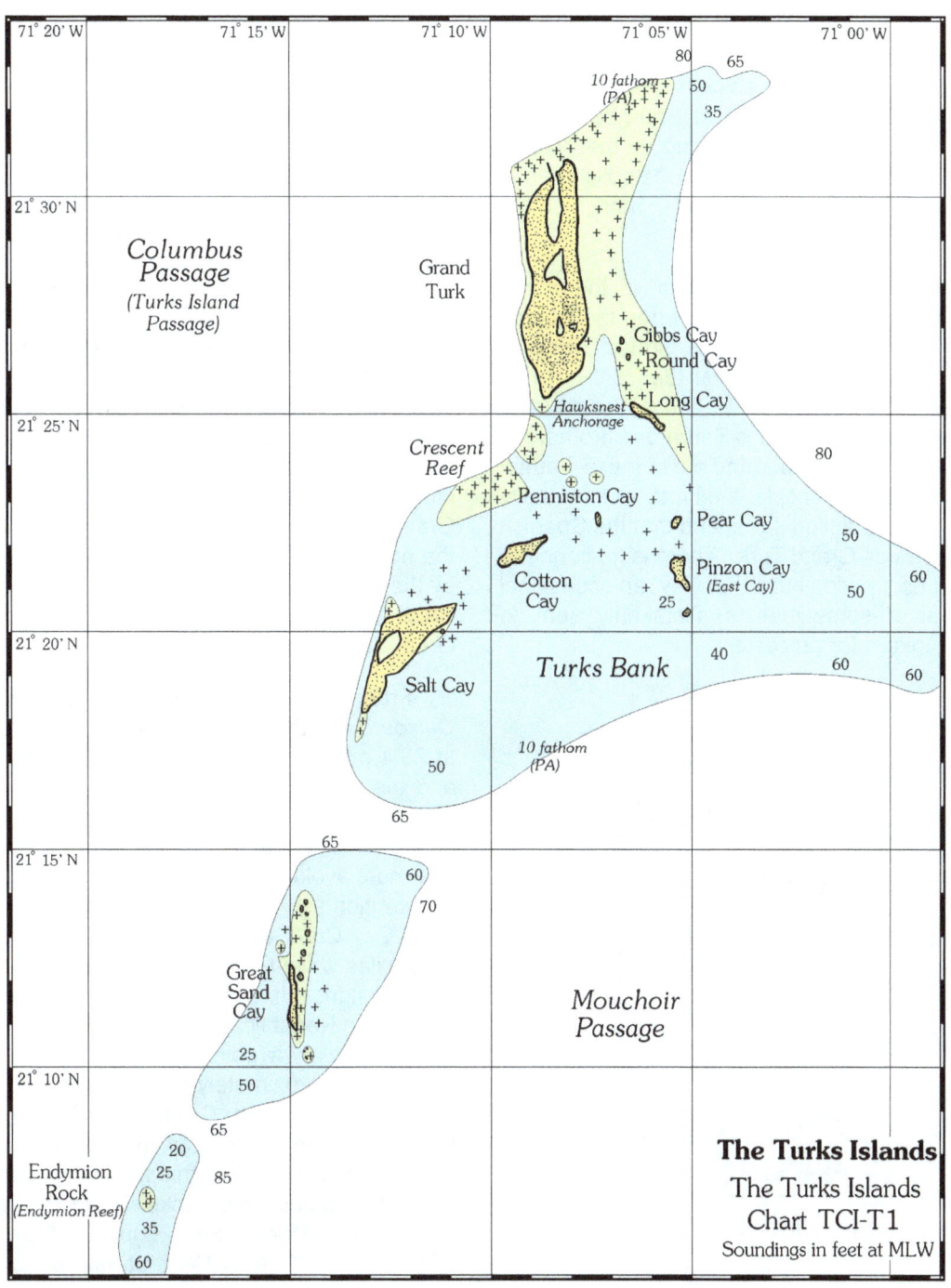

called the "Salt Islands." Here you will find the capital of the Turks and Caicos on Grand Turk, the largest of the Turks Islands and one of only two inhabited islands in the group. The *Turks Bank* is some 36 miles long and varies in width from three to fifteen miles. The sandy bottom is littered with coral heads and patch reefs making for some excellent diving opportunities. The name of the group is said to come from Sir William Phipps, who named them after the native Turks Cap or Turks Head Cactus (*Melocactus intortus*) in 1687. Phipps and his men were in the area recovering 26 tons of gold and silver from a wrecked Spanish galleon when he noticed the cactus that reminded him of a Turkish fez. Sadly so many of these turk's cap cacti have been dug up that except for the few in private gardens and establishments, they are only found growing in the more remote sections of the island group.

Another opinion as to the origin of the name suggests that it comes from a time when the islands were used as hideouts for various pirates, some of whom were said to be of Turkish descent. It has been suggested that in the 16th and 17th centuries, under the leadership of the two Barbarosa brothers, a band of Barbary pirates operated out of these waters. Originating in Constantinople, the brothers eventually settled on an uninhabited salt island that the Spanish later referred to as Grand Turk. There is no concrete proof of that occupation but either way, an occasional letter or parcel sometimes is mistakenly sent to Istanbul or Ankara for processing.

Turks Head Cactus

Approaches

The *Turks Island Passage* is a 25 mile wide, 7,000' deep trench connecting the Caribbean and the southwest north Atlantic and separating the Turks Islands from the Caicos Islands. The tidal current in the Turks Island passage is often fickle; usually it flows northward through the passage at ½-1 knot, but at other times, depending on the wind strength and direction, its speed increases and its direction may vary from north/northwest to northeast. During the months of January through March, an estimated 3,000 humpback whales traverse the *Turks Island Passage* to their winter breeding grounds that stretch from the *Silver Banks* to Samaná in the DR. Use caution when around these magnificent creatures and please don't harass them.

From the waypoint at the mouth of Cockburn Harbour on South Caicos, the *Front Street* anchorage at Grand Turk bears 101° at 21.1 miles, *South Dock* bears 107° at 21.2 miles, and the western entrance to *Big Cut* bears 110° at 21.3 nautical miles distant. From South Caicos the waypoint for entry into the protected anchorage at *North Creek* on Grand Turk bears 93° at a distance of 21.8 miles, but don't simply plug in that waypoint and go. As you approach Grand Turk you must take care to avoid the reef off the northwestern point of Grand Turk that is marked by the steel remains of an old ship. Also from South Caicos, Salt Cay bears 126° at 19.3 miles, while Great Sand Cay bears 148° at 22.7 miles distant.

From *Long Cay Cut* on the western edge of the *Caicos Bank* the *Front Street* anchorage bears 95° at 23.4 miles, *South Dock* bears 101° at 23.3 miles, and the western entrance to *Big Cut* bears 104° at 23.3 miles. The entrance waypoint for *North Creek* bears 88° at a distance of 24.3 miles. Once again, you must avoid the northwest reef off Grand Turk so use caution as you approach Grand Turk. Also from Long Cay Cut, Salt Cay bears 118° at a distance of 20.6 miles while Great Sand Cay bears 140° at 22.9 miles distant. If approaching from Luperón in the Dominican Republic, a course of 176° for 77 miles will bring you to a waypoint at 21° 10.80'N, 71° 15.50'W, which lies approximately ¾ mile southwest of the reef at the southern end of Great Sand Cay. From Puerto Plata, a course of 167° for 86 miles will bring you to the same position. Near this waypoint be sure to keep west of the small trio of rocks shown on Chart TCI-T6 as the Three Marys. From Luperón, the waypoint at 21° 17.60'N, 71° 14.10'W that lies approximately ¾

The Turks Islands

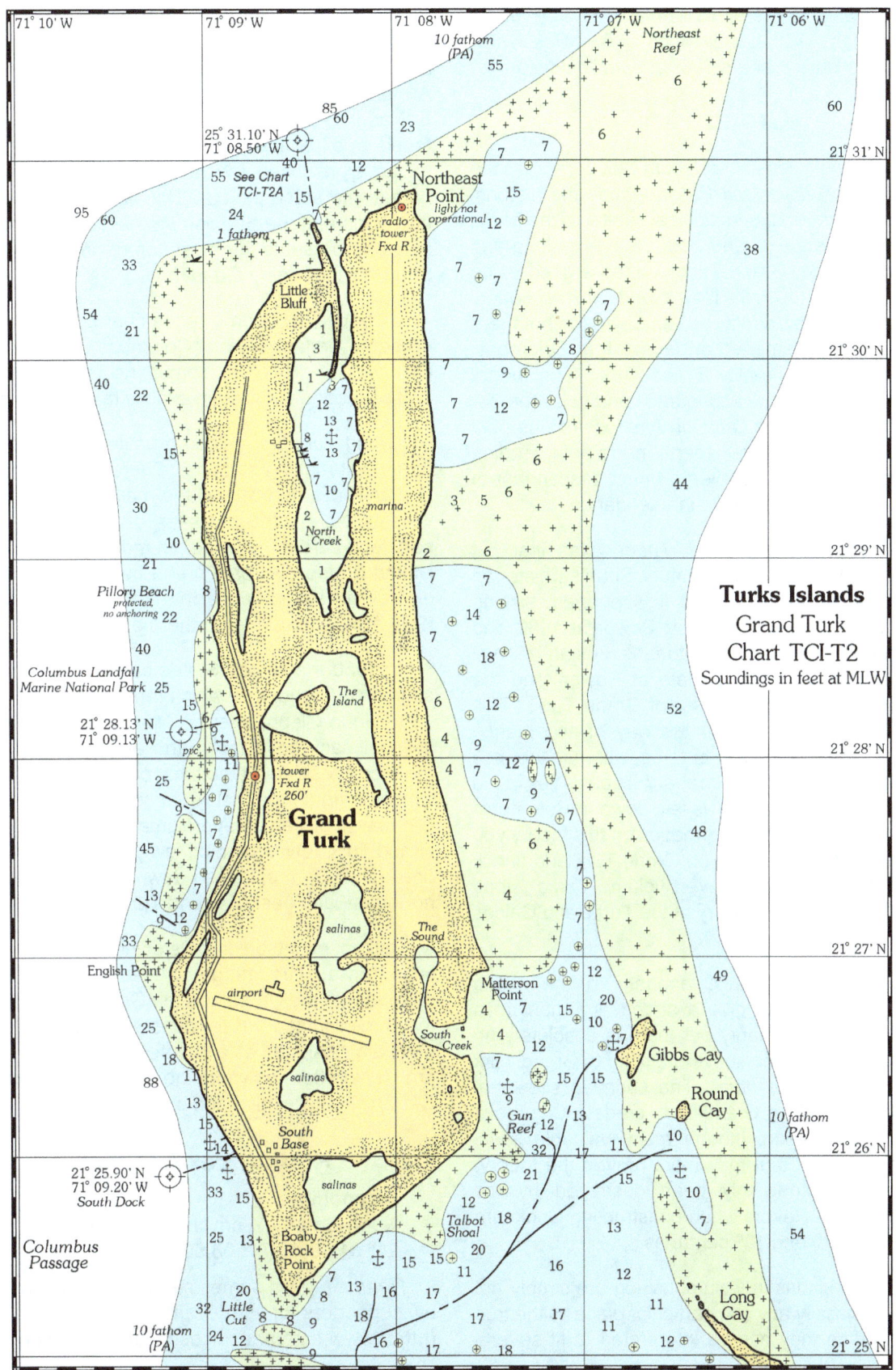

mile southwest of the reef south of Salt Cay, bears approximately 178° at a distance of 83 miles while from Puerto Plata it bears 170° at 92 miles distant.

Grand Turk

Twenty-two miles east of South Caicos, across the 7,000' deep *Turks Island Passage*, lies the historic, commercial, cultural, and political capital of the Turks and Caicos islands, Grand Turk. Six miles long and three miles wide, Grand Turk is often argued to be Columbus' first stop in the New World. Most accounts put Columbus' first landfall at San Salvador, but there is a growing movement that believe that Columbus' Guanahani was in reality Grand Turk. The theory has been getting some acceptance and in December of 1989 a *Grand Turk Landfall Symposium* was held in Grand Turk. Several experts in the field, leading Spanish historians, and even a direct descendant of Christopher Columbus were in attendance.

The *Grand Turk Landfall Theory* was first put forward by the nineteenth century Spanish historian Fernández de Navarrete and is supported, among others, by the works of Robert Power in 1982 and local Turks and Caicos historians Josiah Marvel of Providenciales, an associate of Power, and the late Herbert E. "Bertie" Sadler of Grand Turk. This theory has gained much in the way of acceptance in the last two decades but, as with all theories concerning Columbus' *Guanahani*, its basis lies in the descriptions of the islands as laid down in Columbus' log, the *Diario* (for more information on this theory you can visit the *Public Library* on Grand Turk and check out Herbert E. Sadler's seven volume *Turks Island Landfall* series on the history of the Turks and Caicos Islands).

The descriptions of *Guanahani* in the *Diario* can be interpreted to give a strong argument to a Grant Turk landfall theory but there is absolutely no physical evidence whatsoever pointing to Grand Turk as a possible *Guanahani*. The Lucayan sites that have been found on Grand Turk predate Columbus by almost 500 years though many valuable sites, including the one that may have proven the theory, could have unknowingly been destroyed by the Bermudian Salt Rakers when constructing Cockburn Town in the 17th and 18th centuries.

The descriptions in Columbus' log are simply not enough to classify any one particular place as the true *Guanahani* as they can be interpreted to fit several locations. Most experts point to San Salvador in the Bahamas as being Columbus' *Guanahani* and they are supported by some strong physical evidence. Archaeologists have dated Lucayan sites on San Salvador to the end of the 15th century and have also found small beads and brass bells that were similar to the types used by the Spanish for trading that date to the same period. This firmly establishes the Lucayans and the Spanish on the island at the same time and presents the most compelling argument for San Salvador being *Guanahani*.

However until some researcher somewhere digs up some artifact saying "Columbus arrived here on October 12, 1492," or something to that effect, all these theories will remain exactly that - just theories.

Grand Turk first gained prominence in the 1600s for its salt-making stations. There was a time when Grand Turk's harbor was the main shelter for British vessels out on the business of the empire in this particular part of the world. In more recent times, the United States Air Force had a base on the southern end of the island, while the U.S. Navy had a base (Pan Am Base) at the northern end.

In 1950 the United States built a missile tracking station on Grand Turk which remained until 1981. In 1962, John Glenn, after his famous space flight, first set foot back on planet Earth at Grand Turk. LBJ, the Vice President at the time, came to Grand Turk to welcome home the first American to orbit our planet. Glenn was picked up approximately 160 miles east of Grand Turk. Over the next few years five Gemini and one Apollo craft splashed down in the waters north, northeast, and east of Grand Turk.

Sailors might be interested in this bit of Turks Island trivia. The first great American Merchantman to trade with the Orient was the *Grand Turk*. The 300-ton three-masted vessel boasted 22 guns and was originally designed as a privateer. The *Grand Turk* is probably better known as the ship seen on bottles of *Old Spice* after-shave and cologne.

North Creek Anchorage

Waypoints
North Creek - ¼ nm N of entrance:
21° 31.10' N, 71° 08.50' W

North Creek is sometimes called *Columbus Lake* by supporters of the *Grand Turk Landfall Theory* (http://www.turksandcaicos.tc/landfall/descript.htm).

The Turks Islands

Entrance Channel to the anchorage in *North Creek*
Photo by Author

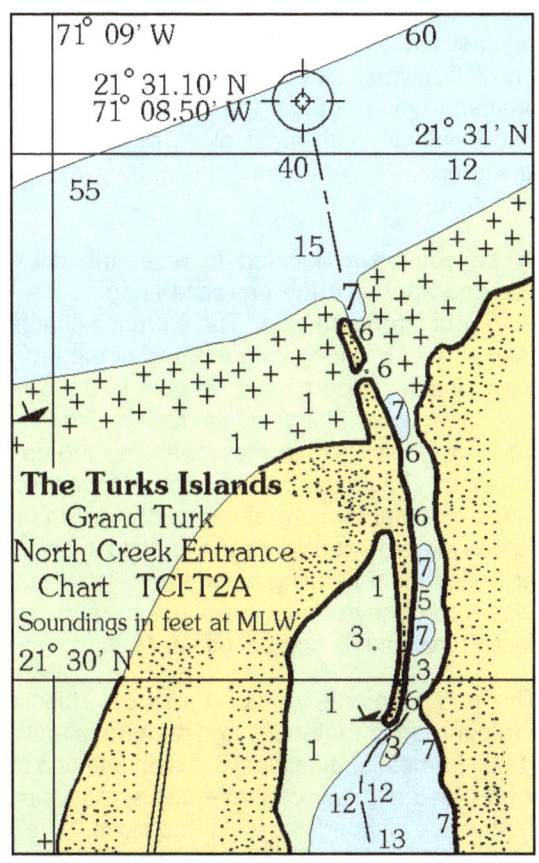

Lighthouse Park at *North Creek*

If at all possible, I suggest that everyone who visits Grand Turk, if your draft allows, should anchor in this well-protected harbor to explore this marvelous island. Here boats with drafts of 5½' will find excellent holding in 10'-15' of water with protection from every direction and only a relatively few bugs on calm nights. Have I convinced you yet? Sounds too good to be true, right? It almost is.

Due to storms over the last several years, the depths in the channel have changed. When this guide was first published you could take a draft of 6½' into this anchorage, today, the entrance channel limits entry to vessels of 5½' at high water.

The hardest part about gaining access to this anchorage is finding a weather window to permit entry at certain times of the year, primarily the winter months. The entrance channel is easily blocked by northerly swells that tend to break all the way across the narrow mouth, making the channel impassable. Now just because you have light east or southeast winds as you approach Grand Turk, do not assume you can easily enter the channel. Swells from frontal passages that did not make it as far south as the Turks and Caicos Islands or from large storms to the north can easily build and spend themselves along the northern shore of Grand Turk. One day I approached the entrance with a long, lazy 8' northerly swell running in calm wind conditions and could not even get close to the cut. That lazy swell had been transformed into huge crashing breakers along the entire northern shore of Grand Turk. On another occasion I had a light east/southeast breeze of less than 10 knots and a 4'-6' northeasterly swell and had no problem entering. Sometimes you just have to get close enough to take a good long look at the cut before deciding to proceed. Or you can call *Flamingo Cove* or *MPL* on VHF ch. 16 and perhaps if they have seen the cut that day they can tell you whether the cut is passable; they can also arrange a pilot for a fee. Some yachtsmen enter *North Creek* under the mistaken impression that they can clear *Customs* and *Immigration* once inside. If you need to clear in at Grand Turk you must do so at the new freighter dock on the southwestern side of the island at *South Base*.

Navigational Information

When approaching the northern shore of Grand Turk from the west or the north your landmarks will be the large red and white checkerboard water tower, the old and unused lighthouse on Northeast Point, and the radio antenna that shows a fixed red light at night.

As you approach the northern shore from the west, the actual entrance will be hard to discern against the background of the shoreline, but it will appear to lie below the white-roofed building that sits about ¼ mile south of the water tower. A waypoint at 21° 31.10'N, 71° 08.50'W, will place you approximately ½ mile north of the narrow entrance channel and the jetty as shown on Chart TCI-T2 and on the blow-up, Chart TCI-T2A. At the time of this writing there were two white PVC stakes near the end of the jetty that lies on the western side of the entrance channel. Captain Bob Gascoine set these PVC stakes up as a range to help you line up your entry. This may change at any time, so use caution.

In normal conditions the swells will break across the reefs to the east and the west of the channel with lighter action actually in the channel itself. The prudent mariner will likely pass by the entrance once or twice at a close but safe distance to get a good feel for the way the channel lies. The channel is the only entrance to the lake inside and all the water goes in and out of this one channel with the tide, so expect a lot of current. You'll have better steerage if you go against the tidal flow but I have done both and had no difficulties. However, if it is your first time, I recommend going against the flow, or if possible to time your entry for high water, slack, or just as the tide begins to ebb. Never attempt this entry with the sun directly in your eyes.

When you have decided to enter the channel, line up and approach the entrance keeping the jetty close to your starboard side. The entrance channel is narrow, about 75' wide along the end of the jetty but it widens inside. You should be able to discern the deeper, bluer water alongside the jetty and the yellow and brown of the shallow rocky water to the east of the channel. The reefs to the east and west of the entrance channel stretch farther northward than the end of the jetty so keep your eyes open to avoid them. Enter the channel keeping close to the jetty, but not too close; you'll have 6' just inside the entrance and 8' in places through this first section at MLW.

The jetty is made up of large rocks, blocks of concrete, dredged materials, and numerous rusty car and truck frames, engine blocks, axles, and one small front-end loader. Any of these can easily damage the inattentive skipper's vessel if too close. The jetty has a small break in it as it reaches the shore, so don't confuse this with the channel you are in. The break is shallow and has the top of a large rock in the center of it at high water. Both sides of the channel shallow slightly at this break so keep to the center of the visible channel if at all possible and you'll have 5' at MLW. Proceed along the entrance channel paralleling the jetty and as you pass between the jetty and the shoreline to the east the channel will widen a bit. Favor the jetty side as the eastern shore is very shallow and the channel still follows close to the jetty.

As the anchorage comes into view you will notice that the jetty has a large rusty crane on it as well as a barge at its southern end that also has a crane on it. Between these two cranes you will find the shallowest spots in the entrance channel. The bottom through here is sand and the current has built up over a dozen or so shallow sand mounds (easily seen in good light) that lie perpendicular to your course and stretching from the jetty to the shallows of the eastern shore. These sand mounds, one or two of which only have about 3'-3½' of water over them at MLW, are not very wide and if you bump you will likely be able to power over them. Sometimes there are shallower spots on one side or the other of these mounds so you might be able to zigzag your way through. Depths between these mounds are generally 6'-7' at MLW. As I mentioned earlier, 5½' can enter here but if you don't choose a good tide to enter on you might have to power your way over these humps. I believe that in an emergency, a 6' draft could enter here on an extremely high tide if the skipper didn't mind powering over these humps. The only problem would be that this same skipper would then need another extremely high tide to get back out.

As you approach the end of the jetty by the remains of the huge barge and crane, don't get careless, you have one or two more obstacles to avoid. At the eastern end of the entrance channel, across from the end of the jetty, lies a huge piece of steel bar that once marked the eastern end of the entrance channel. Instead of being exactly vertical, this bar leans over and is awash at high water and only about 6" of it juts above the surface at low tide. This steel bar could do a lot of damage to your boat, so keep an eye out for it and don't stray too close to it. Just as you reach the end of the entrance channel at the barge you will come upon a grassy shoal that is not shown on other charts of the area. The reason for this is that it has just appeared over the last few years. The shoal, easily seen in good light, only has 3' of water over it in most places. If you have a high tide you can pass it on either side, but if the tide is low you can only pass between the shoal and the end of the jetty in 5'-6' at MLW close in to the jetty.

Once around the grassy shoal area you will be in 8'-15' of water and you can anchor wherever your draft allows and you feel comfortable. The anchorage shallows west and northwest of the end of the jetty and south of the *Flamingo Cove Marina* dock on the eastern shore of the lake. You'll see several boats moored around the periphery of the anchorage and if you wish to explore the edges of *North Creek*, keep on the lookout for bits of floating line; these are mooring lines that no longer have floats on them. The *Flamingo Cove Marina* has been severely damaged by storms but is still functional and willing to do whatever is necessary to welcome visitors. The marina can accept vessels to 40' LOA with 5' at MLW. Transportation to town can be arranged.

About midway down the western shore is a government dock at North Wells where the police boat is kept. You are not allowed to tie to this dock, but you can dinghy in to the beach just north of the dock to leave your dinghy while you walk or hitchhike the mile or so into town. About 150 yards south/southeast of the police dock is a submerged wreck in 7' of water, so keep an eye out for it if you are in that vicinity. There is also a floating line next to the wreck with no float attached; you'll want to avoid it and keep that poly line out of your prop.

What You Will Find Ashore

If you take the road along the eastern shore of *North Creek* you will come to the ruins of the old U.S. Navy base and the *Grand Turk Lighthouse*. In the mid-19th century, at the height of the industrial revolution, this entire lighthouse was cast in iron in England and then shipped to Grand Turk. The light was reassembled on a bluff overlooking *Northeast Reef* in 1852-1854 and is credited with helping to sustain the lucrative salt industry in the Turks salt islands as well as saving countless ships. Today this one hundred and fifty-year-old lighthouse, the Silent Sentinel, awaits restoration. To get there by car, follow *Lighthouse Road* past the *Coral Reef Club* with its palm-tree shaded, hillside units, restaurant, swimming pool, and tennis court. Drive up The Ridge, Grand Turk's better residential area, past the entrance to *Flamingo Cove Marina* and you will come to the entrance of the abandoned U.S. base. Here you can take the dirt road to the left of the fence to reach the lighthouse. Watch out for the feral donkeys as you approach the old base.

Divers on the nearby *Northeast Reef* might find the huge sections of railway that a sinking ship jettisoned on the reef in 1912.

High on the ridge at the southeastern end of *North Creek* is the red roofed *Island House*, a Mediterranean style villa featuring air-conditioned units with a swimming pool and a great view of the anchorage. Just south of the *Island House* is a *Texaco* gas station where you can jerry jug fuel to your dinghy on the shore below it. The nearby *Arches of Grand Turk* is newly constructed and features four 2-story townhouses that are perfect for those looking for quiet accommodations.

Just west of the northwestern shore of *North Creek*, Brian Riggs and other researchers found a Lucayan Indian site that was carbon-dated to 700 A.D., predating a site in Inagua that was estimated to be from around 900 A.D. A local dive instructor, Captain Bob Gascoine, who lived aboard his *Aquanaut* in the upper reaches of *North Creek*, found an ancient Lucayan paddle preserved under layers of mangrove leaves in the northwestern corner of *North Creek*. The paddle was dated to around 1100 A.D.; although off the island now for scientific evaluation and restoration, the paddle will soon be on exhibit at the *National Museum* in Grand Turk. This leaves Captain Bob once again up *North Creek* without a paddle (with apologies to Piers Xanthony).

A note for birdwatchers, there is a large flock of pink flamingos that are often seen in the area of the shallows around the entrance to *North Creek*.

Front Street Anchorage

Cockburn Town, and South Base
Waypoints
Front Street anchorage - ¼ nm W of reef:
21° 28.13' N, 71° 09.13' W

South Dock - ¼ nm WSW of end of dock:
21° 25.90' N, 71° 09.20' W

The western shore of Grand Turk offers a fair lee anchorage just below the large *Cable and Wireless* tower. There are several breaks in the reef here and vessels with drafts to 8' can enter and anchor just off the heart of *Front Street*. The western shore of Grand Turk is a national park and vessels over 60' LOA are not allowed to anchor here except in two designated areas near the freighter dock by *South Base* as shown on Chart TCI-T2. The western shore of Grand Turk is only tenable in winds from northeast to southeast. If a front threatens it is time to move around to the north side to enter *North Creek* or head south to anchor off the southeastern shore of Grand Turk at *Hawksnest Anchorage*, or in the lee of the island at *South Creek*.

The anchorages along the western shore of Grand Turk near *Front Street* can be quite surgy at times and that is one reason I recommend the *North Creek* anchorage so strongly. Another reason is the number of shallow bars and rocky shoals that lie between the reef and the shore. I much prefer to anchor in *North Creek* if at all possible.

Navigational Information
A waypoint at 21° 28.13' N, 71° 09.13' W, will place you approximately ¼ mile west of the break in the reef at the *Front Street* anchorage (sometimes shown as the *Turk's Head Anchorage*). There are actually three breaks through the reef here. The waypoint will place you just off the northernmost one, the widest of the three. None of these reef entrances should be attempted early in the morning with the sun right in your eyes; good visibility is necessary anytime you attempt to pass through any break in any reef anywhere. The northernmost cut, the one most boaters use, is marked on its southern side by a white PVC marker at the time of this writing. If the marker is still there when you are, keep it to starboard when passing through this wide cut.

If in doubt as to which side to take it on, check it out first by dinghy or call *MPL* on VHF ch. 16 or any of the dive shops on VHF ch. 68 for the latest in local knowledge. The cut itself has a minimum depth of 6' at MLW and is easily seen in good light. Any of these three cuts can be used to gain entry to the anchorage area inside the reef, but be warned that there are several shoals and rocky bars between the reef and the shoreline that you must avoid if you attempt to maneuver north or south along the shoreline.

About ½ mile north of the waypoint for the *Front Street* anchorage there used to be a nice anchorage just off *Pillory Beach*. The entrance is through a wide gap in the reef that is easily seen in good light and the holding good just off the resort. The Grant Turk landfall theory recognizes this as the place where Columbus first set foot in the New World and the area is now protected and no anchoring is permitted.

What You Will Find Ashore

If you have anchored near the dock, you can land your dinghy on the beach by the dock. If you need a SCUBA tank filled, any dive shop can handle that for you (several dive shops are located near the beach south of the anchorage). There is Wi-Fi available if you have a good antenna.

Since 1766, the seat of Government for the Turks and Caicos Islands has been located in Cockburn Town on the western shore of Grand Turk. Although its legal name is Cockburn Town, everyone usually just says Grand Turk when referring to the island or the town. Cockburn Town, pronounced Co'burn Town, was first established by Bermudian Salt Rakers and the architecture hints of that heritage as well as others that influenced this British colony over the last 330-odd years. The houses on Grand Turk all reflect a lovely Old World charm; Duke and Front Streets are lined with historic 18th and 19th century landmarks that reflect the Bermudian architecture style of the salt era. The sidewalks of Cockburn Town are paved with cobblestones and the streetlamps are restored antiques, suitable for display in other places, but hard at work here.

The town itself is well suited for a walking or bicycling tour (it's not unusual to find people bicycling around town going about their everyday business), and almost every building has a walled courtyard meant to keep wandering donkeys from munching on the foliage. Today the occasional donkey is a rarity. Most of the 100 plus donkeys were moved to the northeast end of the island in 1995 and some were spayed and neutered to control their rate of growth. These donkeys are the descendants of those that the Bermudian Salt Rakers brought with them to haul the salt carts around the island. At one time there were over 800 donkeys roaming the streets of Grand Turk. Some folks will gladly tell you tales about the infamous Buster. It seems that Buster had a reputation for having an aggressive sexual drive and was known to bite women on the rear. To be perfectly honest, Buster would bite just about anybody. Buster got to be such a pain (no pun intended), that he had to be put to sleep.

If you need medical assistance the *Grand Turk Hospital*, north of the *Front Street* anchorage, is open 24/7 and can be reached by phone at 649-946-2040, 649-943-1212, and 649-946-2333 (in an emergency). Also in Cockburn Town is the *Downtown Clinic* (649-946-2328) open from 0800-1230 and 1400-1630.

There are several couriers located on Grand Turk. *FedEx* has an office here (at *Harbour House* on *Front Street*) and can be reached at 649-946-2542. *DHL* can be reached at 649-946-4352 and has daily service from Provo. *UPS* only has an incoming package service (*Cee's Warehouse Groceries*).

There are two banks on Grand Turk; *First Caribbean International Bank* (https://www.cibc.com/fcib/) and *Scotia Bank*. Both are on *Front Street* and both have ATM's.

For provisions your choices are *Cee's Warehouse Groceries and Sundries*, *Dot's Food Fair* and *D&G Wholesale*, all on *Pont St.* with the *7/11 Grocery* just around the corner. On *Frith St.* you will find *Sarah's Shopping Centre* and *Sunset Pharmacy* while on West Road you'll find *Robinson's Foods*.

Front Street is the heart and soul of Cockburn Town, with several government offices and many businesses located along this seaside promenade. You may see a lot of folks riding bicycles, but not on narrow, one way, *Front Street*. The southern end of *Front Street* effectively starts at the southern end of *Pond Street* (and is called *Duke Street* at this point). Just southeast of the end is the *Building Materials* store, a large hardware store that also rents cars. Here you'll also find *K's Drugs* for over the counter medications. A block south of *Building Materials* is the *Diplomat Café*, home to fine native cuisine and a popular spot. As you proceed up *Duke Street* the first place you will come Cecil Ingram's *Sea Eye Diving* (ci@tciway.tc) is one of only three dive operations on the island and is wholly Turks and Caicos owned and operated.

As you proceed north you will notice a few private residences mixed in with the businesses along the Grand Turk waterfront. Next you'll come to *Captain Kirk's Guesthouse* (No relation to Captain James T. Kirk of the Starship *Enterprise*) and *MPL*, the local *Yamaha* distributor, *Carolina Skiff* dealer, and the only outlet for marine supplies on Grand Turk. If you need a diesel or outboard mechanic call *MPL* on VHF ch. 16 and ask for Kirk. Kirk and his wife Leah also run *Flamingo Cove Marina* on *North Creek*. Next door is the *Osprey Beach Hotel* (http://www.ospreybeachhotel.com/) offering the *Courtyard Café* where you can dine on excellent home cooking in the cool shade of their courtyard. On Wednesdays and Sundays, owner Jenny Smith offers a barbecue with live entertainment. Next door is *Oasis Divers* where owners Everett Freites and Dale Barker love to pamper their guests on dives around Grand Turk and Salt Cay. Nearby is the famous *Salt Raker's Inn*, the 150 year old ho me of a Bermudian shipwright that is now a 12-room hotel with restaurant (http://www.saltrakerinn.com/).

Your next stop is the recently restored *Turk's Head Inne* (http://www.turksheadinne.com/), originally built in 1840. All seven of the hotel's rooms are individually furnished with genuine antiques in keeping with the hotel's unique history as the original home of the island's salt overseer, then serving as the British governor's guesthouse and also as the American Consulate. Many of the rooms have a private balcony with a sea view or a private garden patio as well as air-conditioning and cable TV. Guests of the hotel also have access to the governor's private golf course. The restaurant is highly rated by islanders and visitors alike, and serves up some of the best in international and local cuisine served in elegant surroundings. You'll want to try the *Turks Head Inne Bar & Restaurant* for a meal in the beautiful shaded garden that surrounds the hotel, an excellent spot to beat the heat with an ice cold drink, or dine indoors on their upstairs deck. Just north of the inn is *X's Place*, a unique art gallery with antiques and crafts available. Next door is *Sadler's Seaview Apartments* offering beautiful ocean views in a private garden setting.

At this point *Duke Street* curves to the sea and actually becomes *Front Street*; the seawall is all that separates you from the *Turks Island Passage*. On your right is the huge *Lime* (formerly *Cable and Wireless*) complex and to your left is the anchorage just off the town. The 260' tower is topped with a fixed red light at night. Here you can purchase phone cards, place a call, and even send or receive a fax.

Northward you'll come to the *Arawak House* and the *Public Treasury* where you can purchase Turks and Caicos commemorative coin sets. Next door is the *Shell Shack* where owner Doug Gordon makes some of the most unique shell jewelry you'll find anywhere, you must check out the *Shell Shack*. Next door, the *Beachcomber Guest House* (http://www.saltcay.org/beachcomber/), is a charming bed and breakfast inn right on *Front Street*.

Next you will come to the government complex on *Front Street*. Here, in the center of the historic district, is the hub of some of the Turks and Caicos government though most offices have moved to the *South Base* complex. The bright blue West Indian flavored *Post Office*, the Bermudian accented *Legislative Council*, and several other government offices still open for business here every day. In 1989, these buildings were renovated, a new brick forecourt was laid, and numerous trees and shrubs were planted along *Front Street*. Just behind the post office on *Pond Street*, the road that parallels *Front Street* and the town salinas, is the new Courthouse where you are welcome to sit in on court hearings as long as you are properly dressed (ladies no slacks, men no shorts, and no T-shirts on either of you).

Outside the government compound you will see some ceremonial cannons and the Turks and Caicos national flag. The flag consists of the Union Jack on a blue background along with the Turks and Caicos coat of arms depicting a flamingo, pelican, queen conch, turk's cap cactus, and a spiny lobster. A predecessor to the current flag showed the emblem of salt and sailing ships that was the official flag of the Turks and Caicos Islands during the salt days. One of the salt stacks on the emblem had an entrance resembling the entrance to an Eskimo igloo. The flag maker commissioned for this job mistakenly thought the Turks and Caicos Islands were near the North Pole.

Further down *Front Street* you'll pass *St. Mary's Anglican Church* and its memorial to the Turks and Caicos islanders who died in World Wars I and II. The other Anglican Church on the island is *St. Thomas* situated next to the Anglican cemetery. If you head east on *Moxey Street* by the Courthouse you will cross the pond and the pink building on your right will be *City Market*, a pretty nice little grocery store. A note about shopping in Grand Turk. The plane comes in on Wednesdays and the fresh fruits, veggies, and meats that arrive then will show up on the shelves that afternoon and there are usually some left the next day also. In other words, Tuesday is not the day to shop for fresh goodies on Grand Turk. Passing *City Market*, take your second right at the two story yellow building on *Frith Street* and *Sarah's Shopping Center* will be on your right. *Sarah's* has fresh veggies, fruits, milk, ice cream, and frozen meats as well as some bulk goods. Grocery shopping on Grand Turk involves going to each of these stores as no one particular store is likely to have it all. If you head north on *Pond Street* from the courthouse and take the next right at Church Folly you will come to *Missick's Bakery*, *Neville's Auto Parts*, and the *Philatelic Bureau*. The Turks and Caicos Islands are known far and wide to stamp enthusiasts for their colorful postage stamps and a visit to the *Philatelic Bureau* is a must for anyone with an interest in the Turks and Caicos series of postage stamps.

Back on *Front Street*, your next stop on your northward journey is the *Victoria Public Library*. Here you can check out a book for a small deposit and they have quite a selection of reading material as well as reference books. If you have any books that you would care to donate, by all means please do. The nearby *Library Tennis Court* hosts several concerts and variety shows each year. You will now come to the intersection of *Front Street* and *Prison Folly*, the wide road that takes you one block east to the old prison and a new modern office development.

Next is the *Harbour House* where you will find the local *FedEx* office. Garbage is a problem on Grand Turk. There used to be several dumpsters scattered about the island but they have all rusted. Today all garbage pickup is done on a door to door basis, though you might see the odd can bolted to a power pole but they won't hold much. For boaters, it has been suggested that you take your bagged garbage to a wooden walled outdoor receptacle next to *Scotia Bank*. This is where everybody in the *Harbour House* leaves their garbage and it must make do for the occasional cruiser too. Behind the Harbour House on *Pond Street* is *Caribe West Discount Liquors*, a *FedEx* office, and *Cee's Warehouse Groceries*. *Cee's* is a great place to stop to pick up bulk goods with excellent prices on cases of sodas. *Cee's* is also the island's *UPS* agent (incoming packages only).

After *Harbour House* the one-way section of *Front Street* ends at the *Odd Fellow's Lodge*, a two-story building with a large eye painted on one side. The *Lodge* is one of Grand Turks several *Masonic Lodges* and it is said that the proclamation of the emancipation of slavery was read from the veranda of this building on August 1, 1838. Northward from here is the old *Customs Shed* which houses the *Turks and Caicos Islands Tourist Board* so if you need tourist related information, this will be a handy place to stop.

A great place to eat is next, the *Poop Deck*, a great local hangout serving some of the best native cuisine at affordable prices with an ever-changing daily special. Across the street is *TIMCO, Turks Islands Importers*, where you can get some fresh and frozen foods, as well as cases of sodas, and alcoholic beverages. Next door is *A-1 Business Machines*, a *Canon* dealer where you can pick up computer and office supplies and have minor repairs made.

I'm sorry to report that Peanut's Butterfields has passed away and her well known *Pepper Pot Snack Shop* has closed, so you'll have to go elsewhere for *Dragon Stout* and *rhythm pills*. East of Peanut's old place on *Pond Street* is *Dot's Food Fair, Dot's Liquor Store,* and *Dot's Gift Shop*. *Dot's Food Fair* is a very well stocked grocery and dry goods store with fresh produce, canned goods, ice cream, fresh meats, non-prescription drugs, and a selection of beers. *Dot's Boutique and General Merchandise* on *Pond Street* carries clothes, household furnishings, office supplies and books.

Heading north from *Pond Street* you'll come to Mitch Rolling's *Blue Water Divers* (mrolling@tciway.tc). Mitch also owns the *Eagle Ray Recording Studio* that he built in the basement of his home. Mitch, who is known as the singing divemaster, and his friend Dave, another singing divemaster, have released an album entitled *Grand Turk Blues*. Mitch performs at the nearby *Osprey Beach Hotel* during their Wednesday and Sunday night barbecues.

Next to *Blue Water Divers* is the *Guinep House*, one of the oldest stone buildings on the island and named after the large tree in the front yard. *The Guinep House*, situated on *Front Street* directly facing the sea and the *Columbus National Marine Park*, is the home of the *Turks and Caicos National Museum* (http://tcmuseum.org/) and was constructed of ship's timbers in Bermudian seafarer's tradition. The building itself is fully air-conditioned and on those hot afternoons it's a perfect place to escape to and cool down. But relief from the climate is not the only reason one should pay a visit to the museum. The *Turks and Caicos National Museum*, opened in 1991, has recorded in its archives and displays, the cultural history of the Turks and Caicos Islands, their discovery, the impact of the early European settlers, and the role that the islands played in the great 20th century space race. Tools and pottery that date back to Lucayan times will give you an idea of how these peaceful people lived. The museum proudly displays an extremely well presented marine reef replica with many interesting facts on reefs and reef fish. But the museum's centerpiece is its fascinating collection of artifacts from the *Molasses Reef Wreck*, the oldest shipwreck in the Americas and the first shipwreck site in the Caribbean to be scientifically excavated.

Measuring just 19 meters long, the caravel, having safely crossed the treacherous Atlantic, ran aground on the reef and sank in about 15'-20' of water, laying undiscovered for some 400 years until it was found by treasure divers in 1976. An unscrupulous salvager tried to gain financially from the excavation by claiming the ship was the *Pinta*, one of Columbus' original three ships. The claim was soon proven to be false and the government of the Turks and Caicos Islands took over the salvage and identification process. A government permit was issued to the *Institute of Nautical Archaeology* at *Texas A&M's National Museum* under the direction of Dr. Donald H. Keith. Irate treasure hunters then tried to dynamite the site but their efforts resulted in minimal damage.

Dating of Lucayan pottery pieces found on the site placed the ship on the reef prior to 1513 (remember, all the Lucayans were forcibly removed from the Turks and Caicos islands by 1513) and researchers speculated that the ship was a slaver en route to Hispaniola. The ship was armed with state-of-the-art weapons of the period, and the *National Museum* can boast to having the largest selection of 16th century wrought iron, breech-loading cannons in the world. Following the salvage, cataloguing and preservation of the 2,000-plus artifacts comprising selections of arms, tools, personal effects and pottery, the artifacts were returned to Grand Turk, where they are now exhibited at the museum with the ship's huge anchor hanging from the wall as the centerpiece of the exhibit.

The Turks and Caicos National Museum has a new newsletter, the *Astrolabe*, and plans are afoot to build a complementary museum in Provo, not a duplicate, but one with different offerings oriented to the Caicos group of islands. Definitely stop in and visit the museum's Director Barry Dressel and Manager Brian Riggs and visit the gift shop, with its locally made crafts and selection of Caribbean books located on the second floor.

North of the museum, shoppers might want to visit one of the last fish processing plants in the Turks and Caicos Islands, the *Sea View Fish Market*. Owner Jonathon Missick has been fishing these waters since he was nine years old. Jonathon is an excellent source of fishing tales if you can find the time to listen. He can tell you how the fishing was big on Grand Turk before the "old people died away." Next door is Captain Sam Seymour's tiny but well stocked *Pilot House Store*.

If you head east from here you will come to *Pond Road*. Take a left on *Pond Road*, which now becomes *Hospital Road*, and you'll find *The Regal Begal* a few blocks north. This is probably the best place on the island for local dishes johnnycake, boiled fish, peas and rice, and anything made with conch.

Just north of the *Front Street* area on the western shore of Grand Turk is the *Bohio Dive Resort* (the old *Guanahani Beach Resort*) on *Pillory Beach; www.BohioResort.com*), thought by some to be the first place Columbus set foot in the New World. The resort has *Guanahani Restaurant* and the *Ike & Donkey Beach Bar*.

If you were to drive south from *Front Street* towards the southern end of the island you will pass the airport and soon come to *Government House*, the governor's residence that is called simply *Waterloo*. *Waterloo* was built in 1815 (the same year as the *Battle of Waterloo*) and is not open to the public except by special invitation. The cabinet, the *Executive Council*, meets every week at the governor's office, a small modern single-story building with its own entrance marked *Governor's Office*. Just past the white wall that surrounds *Waterloo* and the governor's private golf course is the entrance to *Governor's Beach*, a beautiful sandy beach with a backdrop of shady casuarinas. As of winter 2002, a 72-room hotel/resort complex is still planned for construction on *Governor's Beach*. The plantation styled edifice is to have elements of Bermudian and Grand Turk architecture to retain the quaint character of Grand Turk while it caters to the upscale tourist clientele.

Navigational Information

A little further south is the entrance to *South Dock* and the huge *South Base* government complex which houses *Immigration*, *Customs*, and several other prime governmental agencies. Your first sight of Grand Turk when approaching from South Caicos or points south will probably be the huge white bulbous *FAA* antenna that at first glance resembles a water tank high on the hill above *South Base*. The large *FAA* antenna there has a fixed red light at its top. The new concrete *South Dock,* just south of the older steel dock, is the place you'll need to tie up to clear in at Grand Turk. If you need fuel call *Texaco I* on VHF ch. 16 and they will deliver fuel to the dock for you.

A waypoint at 21° 25.90'N, 71° 09.20'W will place you approximately ¼ mile west/southwest of the new *South Dock*. If your intent is to clear in call *Grand Turk*

Harbourmaster on VHF ch. 16 for instructions. If you only need fuel and have already cleared in elsewhere call *Texaco 1* for instructions. Vessels over 60' are allowed to anchor in the vicinity of the dock between latitude 21°.26.12' N and 25°25.85' N. The dock itself is designed for vessels to 275' with drafts of 12' at the bow and 15' at the stern.

What You Will Find Ashore

South Base today is the *Carnival Cruise Ship Port* and center for a burgeoning tourist industry. Just to the east of *South Base*, along the road that leads southward around the complex, is a remarkable sight, especially for sailors who use wind generators aboard. Here is a 75' tall, red and white striped wind powered generator that was built with a grant from the Canadian government. The 5 kilowatt AC generator is a vertical tower with two blades that resemble an eggbeater. The top is buoyed by wires and the whole contraption revolves with an incredible amount of noise (and I thought my old *Windbugger* was noisy!). It takes 17 knots of wind for the unit to create enough power to be efficient; less than 17 knots and the unit is not even turned on.

Just south of *South Base* is the *Arawak Inn and Beach Club* located at one of Grand Turk's best beach diving locations on a secluded stretch of white sandy beach on the southwest side of Grand Turk. The *Inn* features 14 air-conditioned units right on the beach, cable TV, a fresh water pool, a beach bar and restaurant, horseback riding, and a daily shuttle service into Cockburn Town. Wade into the water and out a few hundred yards and you can dive on the pristine Grand Turk Wall that hosts a magnificent array of marine life.

Divers will also want to check out the old South Dock and the area called *The Pits*. The old steel *South Dock* was constructed in the mid-1950s to service the island's shipping and the U.S. missile tracking station on Grand Turk. Over the years, *South Base* garbage, cargo, and all manner of flotsam and jetsam associated with the exchange of freight have settled in the surrounding waters. A variety of marine creatures have taken to calling this garbage dump home and can be viewed and photographed in their natural environment. Please exercise caution as some of the debris, such as monofilament fishing line left by careless fishermen, may entangle and trap the unwary diver.

Grand Turk celebrates a couple of unique holidays such as the *McCartney Day* celebrations on June 5th. James Alexander George Smith (JAGS) McCartney inspired Turks and Caicos Islanders to be proud of their heritage. McCartney witnessed a certain pride that Jamaicans had in their roots and endeavored to bring the same pride to his people in the Turks and Caicos Islands. The *Grand Turks Cactus Festival* has replaced the yearly carnival as one of the most popular events of the year. The *Cactus Festival* features sports, dancing, art, and costume contests as well as an island beauty pageant.

Hawksnest Anchorage

Waypoints
Big Cut - ¼ nm NW of:
21° 24.60' N, 71° 09.25' W

Along the southeastern shoreline of Grand Turk is the historic *Hawksnest Anchorage* as shown on Chart TCI-T2, a good shelter from westerly winds. Hawksnest Anchorage offers good protection in winds from west/southwest through northwest to north, while safe anchorage can also be found in the lee of Gibbs Cay in northeast through southeast winds. Vessels can also seek shelter from westerly winds further north along the eastern shore of Grand Turk past the entrance to *South Creek*, as shown on Chart TCI-T2. Although these anchorages can get very surgy at times, the holding is good. Entrance to these anchorages is through one of several cuts through the reef south of Grand Turk.

Navigational Information

Hawksnest Anchorage, once called *Reef Harbour*, for all practical purposes lies off the southeastern shore of Grand Turk, but, is sometimes shown on some older charts as lying between Grand Turk and Cotton Cay, protected by a reef to the west, and Long Cay and a reef to the east. *Turks Island Landfall* theorists claim that this is the anchorage that Columbus claimed would hold "all the ships in Christendom." Entrance for larger vessels of 10' draft is south of the reef between Salt Cay and Cotton Cay from the west and south of Pinzon Cay (once called Breeches Island and sometimes still referred to as East Cay) in the east. The U.S. Navy surveyed *Hawksnest Anchorage* during World War II with an eye to establishing an anti-submarine tracking base for *Catalina Flying Boats*, but nothing came of it.

Today, entrance to the *Hawksnest Anchorage* for the average cruising boat is through one of several

A Cruising Guide to the Turks and Caicos Islands

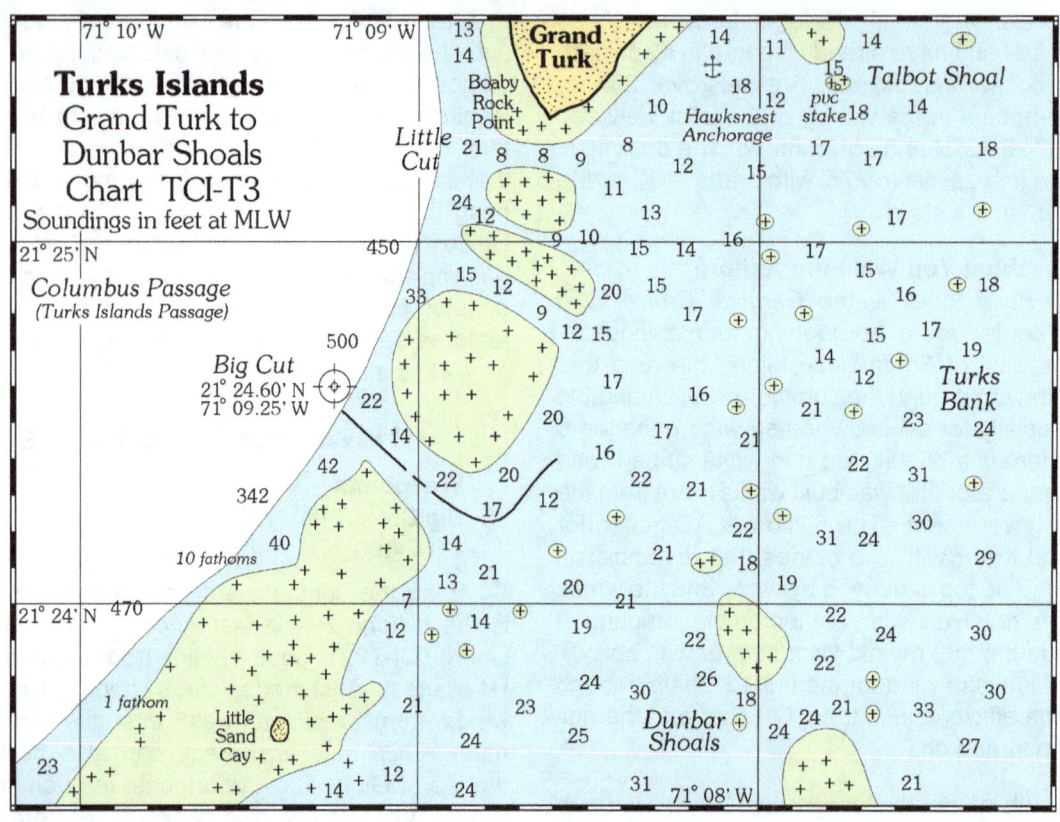

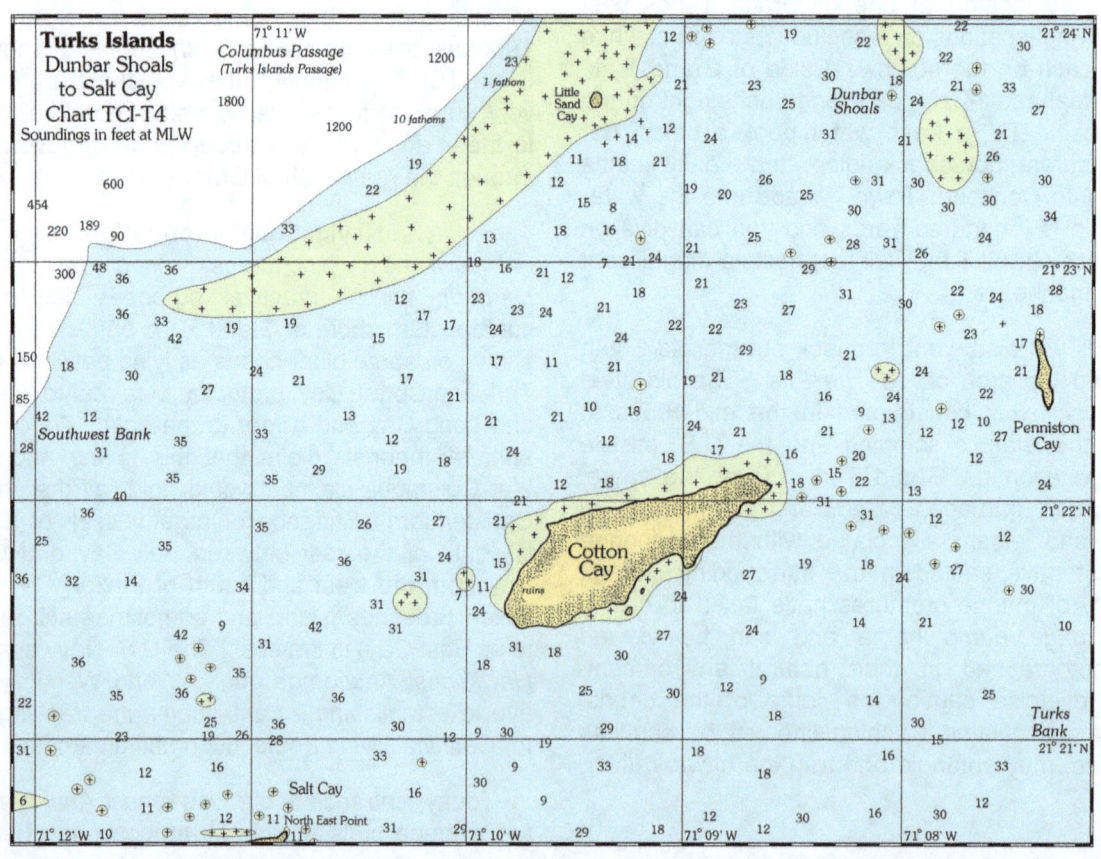

breaks in the reef south of Grand Turk. Just south of Boaby Rock Point on Grand Turk is *Little Cut*, sometimes called *Small Cut* on some charts. As well as being shallower and narrower than *Big Cut*, *Little Cut* is often hard to pick out, which is why I recommend *Big Cut* for someone not familiar with these waters. A waypoint at 21° 24.60'N, 71° 09.25'W, will place you approximately ¼ mile northwest of *Big Cut* (sometimes shown as *Great Cut*) as shown on Chart TCI-T3.

From this waypoint look southeast and you will see three cays about a mile or two distant. Line up with the center of the southernmost cay and head in on it on an approximate heading of 135°. Once again, I must advise that this heading is just for orientation; you must use your eyes to pilot through the reef here. The reef to the south, on your starboard side as you head southeast, is the shallowest and the easiest to see.

Once inside, begin to steer north/northeast to anchor in Hawksnest Anchorage proper in northwest and northerly winds, taking care to avoid the eastern side of the reefs you just passed through. If the winds are southwest to west, continue northeast around *Talbot Shoal* and *Gun Reef* to anchor in the lee of Grand Turk just south of the entrance to *South Creek* (where Lucayan Indians once kept their canoes) as shown on Chart TCI-T2. As you pass *Talbot Shoal* keep an eye out for the buoy that marks the very shallow reef of its southern tip. You can actually pass between this reef and *Talbot Shoal* but it is so much easier and safer just to round the buoy in deeper water and be done with it. Bear in mind that the buoy may be long gone by the time you cruise these waters; use extreme caution through here.

The only problem with the anchorage south of *South Creek*, other than the surge, is that you are right in the flight path to the airstrip and you will be buzzed all day long by plane after plane, including a few large jets. The well-lit building with the huge fence west of the mouth of *South Creek* is the new prison. If you seek a lee in moderate northeast to southeast winds you can anchor in the lee of Gibbs Cay with good protection but watch out for a few scattered heads in the vicinity. A word of warning: these anchorages along the southeastern shore of Grand Turk can get quite rolly when there is no wind to keep you perpendicular to the ever-present surge.

What You Will Find Ashore

The small islands of Gibbs Cay and Round Cay were once called *The Twins* and later *The Sisters* on a French chart that dates to the mid-18th century and are today protected under the national park ordinance as a bird sanctuary. During the early summer months, sooty and Noddy Terns nest here and raise their young. These islands once played a small part in the defense of Grand Turk. At the summit of Gibbs Cay you will find the ruins of a lookout post which, with the canon placement on Gun Hill on the mainland of Grand Turk, served as a line of defense for Grand Turk. Gibbs Cay was the location of a French gun emplacement in 1780 called Ft. Castries and was later used as a fort by Turks islanders in fear of a French invasion of Hispaniola in 1791. The offshore Elkhorn coral reefs offer some excellent shallow water snorkeling and even some small tunnels as well as some very friendly sting rays.

Long Cay, once called Pelican Island, lies about 1½ miles southeast of Grand Turk, as shown on Chart TCI-T2. This uninhabited island is a sanctuary for the Turks and Caicos rock iguana, the same creature that is also found on Little Water Cay northeast of Provo at Leeward Going Through. Visitors to this 1½ mile long narrow cay must apply for a permit from the *DECR*, in Grand Turk. A little further south is Pear Cay, once called Bird Island, whose rocky shoreline has little to offer save for some excellent snorkeling and diving on the reefs off its western shore. In settled weather you can anchor in the small reef-encircled harbor between Long Cay and Round Cay, but you may need to set a bridle to keep from rolling with the surge.

At 65' in elevation, Martin Alonzo Pinzon Cay, usually just called Pinzon Cay and formerly known as East Cay, is the highest of the Turks Island group. The island is named after the pilot of the *Pinta* on Columbus' first voyage to the New World. The only inhabitants of this cay were those who manned a lookout post here and treasure hunters that based here in 1970 while searching for treasure on the *Silver Banks*. The ruins of their base camp are still visible on the southwestern shore of the island. There is somewhat of a surgy lee anchorage along the northwestern shore. There is a small blow hole on the eastern side surrounded by several small rocky pools that are perfect for bathing. Pinzon Cay is home to a magnificent growth of the native Turk's Head Cactus, one of the only remaining places in the islands where they are still found in the wild.

Cotton Cay, as shown on Chart TCI-T4, is the largest and lushest of the uninhabited Turks Islands. The island is privately owned, but access is allowed as of this writing. The cay was once owned by the Harriot Family of Salt Cay fame and as such was used as a retreat and for cattle grazing. Ashore you will find the ruins of their support buildings and many pasture walls. A beautiful subterranean grotto leads to a rock enclosed cove near the ruins of the old house on the western shore of the island. Recently two Lucayan sites were found on Cotton Cay as well as two sites on nearby Long Cay. Just to the east of Cotton Cay lies Penniston Cay, whose rocky shores offer little to the cruising skipper. Tropic Birds frequent the southern shore in spring and early summer.

Salt Cay

Waypoints
Salt Cay - ¼ nm W of Deane's Dock:
21° 19.90' N, 71° 13.25' W

Salt Cay - ¾ SW of S end:
21° 17.60' N, 71° 14.10' W

Seven miles southeast of Grand Turk lies what some tourist brochures refer to as "the land that time forgot." Salt Cay was originally called *Caiceman* or *Canamani* by the ancient Lucayans and later known as *Petite Saline* by the French. Little on the cay has changed since 1900 when the salt industry flourished. The large inland salt pond that still dominates Salt Cay's land area was the attraction and the focus for commerce on Salt Cay for hundreds of years from the time of the Lucayan traders, to the Bermudian Salt Rakers who first arrived in 1645, to even more modern times when Salt Cay was still a busy port well into the 1960s. The skeletons of old windmills that pumped brine into the flats still stand in the salt ponds while nearby giant salt piles sit unused and untouched for years. In 1845, Salt Cay was the home of the *Turks Island Whaling Company*. The remains of the *Taylor House*, the old whale watching outpost, still sits on the highest spot on Salt Cay on Taylor Hill along the eastern shore, and is easily seen from anywhere on the cay.

Captured whales were taken ashore at *Whale House Bay* on the eastern shore for processing of their meat, oil, and ambergris of which a 150-lb. chunk sold for $20,000 in New York in 1955. But that was then and this is now; and nowadays an estimated 3,000 humpback whales pass by unmolested between January and March on their way to their winter breeding grounds on the *Mouchoir* and *Silver Banks* that lie east and southeast of the Turks Islands, and the humpbacks are still bringing money into Salt Cay every season. The *Windmills Hotel* (http://www.kim-carpenter-assoc.com/Windmills-Plantation/) has become a favorite of whale watchers due to Salt Cay's prime location at the eastern edge of the *Columbus Passage*. If you don't wish to bring your boat to Salt Cay, you can leave your boat in the *North Creek* anchorage at Grand Turk and take the weekly ferry to Salt Cay (please check the schedule days on their web site at: https://www.visittci.com/salt-cay-community-ferry).

Recently some local residents and a couple of American investors began an attempt to resume salt production on Salt Cay. A company called *Sun Crystals Trading Company* has leased 250 acres of Salt Cay and plans to employ modern technology in the salt production process, while employing 40 local residents. Four salinas and most of the windmills will remain as mementos of the past. Donkeys, vital to salt production in the early years on Salt Cay, will not be used - to avoid contamination. The finer grades of salt produced is intended for use in water treatment and cattle feed, while the lower grades of salt will be used for snow and ice removal in northern climes.

Today a few dozen cars wander the roads, and the streets are used as much by cows and donkeys as people (it wasn't until 1989 that a fence was built around the airport to keep donkeys off the runway).

Unfortunately, the recent government allowed an Eastern European developer to secure large parcels of Salt Cay. The project is now on hold thanks to the intersession of the current Governor, Gordon Wetherell. Governor Wetherell has ordered that no further work is permitted on Salt Cay until a current set of criminal investigations has been completed against the owner. It is said that the owner has already made a deal with a resort company based in the Far East.

Beautiful beaches border much of the Salt Cay shoreline, while herons and other birds feed in the salinas and in the marshlands to the south. The distinctively Bermudian style homes, all with dusty but neatly swept dirt yards, set a unique tone and style. Salt Cay is a vestige of the old Turks and Caicos, a window to a simpler and slower time. It has been said that Salt Cay is "...what the Caribbean used to be." Salt Cay, often regarded as a living museum of industrial archaeology of the Salt Raker era, has been designated a *UNESCO World Heritage Site* to preserve the history and culture of this tiny island. This ensures that all future development on Salt Cay must be in absolute harmony with its historic past.

You will probably notice that the island is primarily inhabited by the very old and the very young; those in the middle, for the most part, are off on the other islands seeking their fortunes. The 200 or so residents that remain are all very friendly and quick with a bit of conversation for the passing stranger. The sign at the airport says it all: *Bon Voyage! Return by any means!* Salt Cay is one of those islands that, no matter how long you stay, you find that you really did not stay long enough. I am certainly guilty of that.

Navigational Information

A waypoint at 21° 19.90'N, 71° 13.25'W, will place you approximately ¼ mile west of *Deane's Dock* as shown on Chart TCI-T5. If approaching from the south or east your first sight will probably be of the huge *White House* that absolutely dominates the Salt Cay shoreline. The holding along the eastern shore of Salt Cay can only be rated as poor to fair with a light layer of sand mixed with rocks and other rubble over a rock bottom. You can anchor anywhere along Salt Cay's western shore between *Deane's Dock* and the *White House*; the holding is about the same. The entire western shore of Salt Cay is quite rocky as you get closer in to shore. The southern third of the western shore has a few more sandy patches to set your anchor in but I never feel comfortable anchoring off Salt Cay's western shore.

My favorite anchorage, and one that is rarely taken advantage of by visiting cruisers, is in *North Bay* just off beautiful North Beach on the northern shore of Salt Cay. The entrance is gained by going north of the reef at North West Point and working your way in towards the beach, dodging the few coral heads and small patch reefs that are easily seen in good light. Don't try this route early in the morning with the sun in your eyes. The holding is good in sand, but the anchorage is only good in southeast to southwest winds and a little surge might work its way in during periods of stronger winds. This anchorage is not recommended with winds from west through north to east or with the threat of a windshift to those directions during the night, as you won't find your way out in the dark.

Deane's Dock is well protected but open to the southwest. The entrance is over a rocky bottom with only 4' at low water at the entrance, with anywhere between 2'-4' at MLW along the walls where you could tie up once you get around the shallow spot in the center. If you should tie up inside during a frontal passage, expect a strong surge to move you about quite a bit. For information on how to enter the dock call *Salt Cay Divers* on VHF ch. 16. If you need gas, diesel, or groceries, you can get all three at Nathan Smith's place just southeast of *Deane's Dock* by the large fuel tanks. If you need a diesel mechanic ask for Perry Tolbert. If you require medical assistance not of a severe nature, you can visit the Salt Cay clinic located by the school. They are open every weekday morning and are staffed by a resident nurse.

What You Will Find Ashore

The anchorage on Salt Cay's western shore is just off the only settlement on Salt Cay, Balfour Town. Balfour Town is divided into two sections, the north side and the south side. On the north side you can find Leon Wilson's *One Down One to Go Restaurant*, also known as the *Big W*. Leon, former chairman of the *Turks and Caicos Tourist Board* and the unofficial "Ambassador of Good Will" for Salt Cay, serves great chicken, conch, and hamburgers. In town you'll also find the government clinic, well-staffed by Muriel and her assistant Coralene, with a government doctor visiting about every three weeks. Right in the middle of Balfour Town is Irene Been-Legget's *Halfway House*. The tourist brochures boast that Irene's hospitality and excellent cooking has convinced more than one of her guests to retire to Salt Cay. The *Mt. Pleasant Guest House* is also a good stop for cold refreshments in their bar or patio restaurant.

One of the hottest eateries on the island is the *Green Flash Cafe* (greenflashwhales@gmail.com) near the dock. Check out their weekly *Wednesday Wing Night* and sign up for a Glow Worm night or a whale watching trip. The *Island Thyme Bistro and Internet Cafe* (http://www.islandthyme.tc/) offers good food as well as internet access. The *Coral Reef Cafe* located at the *Salt Cay Divers Shop* has free Wi-Fi. The *Smuggler's Tavern* at *Pirate's Hideaway by the Sea* (http://www.saltcay.tc/) offers some unique twists on native dishes, while *Pat's* serves up more traditional fare for breakfast, lunch, and dinner in a garden setting. If you need some groceries you can try *H&P Mercantile*, *Ship to Shore Groceries*, *Smith's*, *Pat's*, or *Nettie's Groceries*.

On the western shore of Salt Cay you will find the impressive *White House*, the ancestral home

A Cruising Guide to the Turks and Caicos Islands

Turks Islands
Salt Cay
Chart TCI-T5
Soundings in feet at MLW

of the Harriots, Bermudian salt merchants. When the hurricane of September 1813 destroyed the old Harriot home with a 15' tidal surge, the Harriot clan decided to build a structure that would withstand whatever nature threw its way. The two-story house, the oldest standing building on the cay, was constructed between 1834 and 1840. The house was built of stone with the seaward edge in the shape of a ship's prow to protect it from heavy waves on the side-walls and possible flooding. The entire first floor was used for salt storage and even today, salt can still be seen in the interior of the first floor.

The pointed roof was fashioned by shipwrights with massive wooden beams reinforced with stout knees. She appears able to withstand quite a lot of torture and has over the last 150 years. In 1940 and 1941, *Paramount Pictures* filmed *Bahama Passage* starring Madeleine Carroll and Sterling Hayden on Salt Cay with the *White House* starring in several scenes. Also in town you can find the *Brown House*, an old wooden hotel. *The Brown House* has a beautiful veranda and currently has caretakers who rent out smaller, private homes nearby.

Salt Cay's *North Beach* is one of the most beautiful beaches in the entire Turks and Caicos archipelago. The *Windmills Plantation*, a small but luxurious resort and now a growing condo concern, sits on the beach, just a short walk from the airport. Good food and accommodations can also be found at Bryan Sheedy's *Mt. Pleasant Guest House* (more about Bryan in a moment), and at the *Castaway's Beach House* with a half-dozen getaway cottages right on the beach.

Salt Cay is an almost virgin diving area. The island is blessed with a wall drop-off running the length of its western shore. Local residents Ollie Been and Debbie Manos run the very relaxed *Salt Cay Divers* (http://ww.saltcaydivers.tc/) and they will be happy to be your guides to Salt Cay's wealth of dive sites, including the much acclaimed wreck of the *H.M.S. Endymion*. Lying about 15 miles southwest of Salt Cay near Endymion Rock as shown on Chart TCI-T1 and Chart TCI-T7, the *H.M.S. Endymion*, a 140', wooden-hulled British Man-of-War lies in only 25' of water near Endymion Rock, sometimes called *Endymion Reef*. She was carrying reinforcements to the islands during a war with France when she went down in 1790 after hitting the reef and was only recently discovered. Divers can explore her 18 nine-foot long cannons, her four 15' anchors, her huge bronze keel bolts that can testify as to the size of the warship, and all sorts of other debris lying scattered about the nearby and for seabed. Needless to say, settled weather is necessary to visit this site.

Military personnel from the bases on Grand Turk used to dive on the wreck site in the 1950s, but over the next few decades it was all but forgotten. Bryan Sheedy, an American who owns and operates the *Mount Pleasant Guest House* (http://www.mountpleasantguesthouse.com/) on Salt Cay, rediscovered the wreck in 1991. The *Mount Pleasant Guest House* was built in 1830 and is simply chock full of fine furniture, pewter artifacts, original paintings, and bicycles that you can rent to tour the island. The *Mt. Pleasant Guest House* also offers horseback riding. Bryan, a rodeo rider in his youth, used to run *Porpoise Divers* before turning over the operation to Ollie and Debbie, who renamed it *Salt Cay Divers*.

The eastern shore of Salt Cay is very rocky and is best explored by dinghy on a calm day. In the salinas along the eastern shore are two blue holes lying almost side by side. The blue holes are only about 20'-30' in diameter and who knows how deep.

One diver has reportedly entered the holes to a depth of 250' without seeing bottom.

On *Southwest Beach* the *Sunset Reef* has two air-conditioned units with TV, CD, complimentary bicycles, whale watching deck, and golf cart rentals available.

Those skippers bound for the Dominican Republic can head south of Salt Cay to a waypoint at 21° 17.60 N, 71° 14.10'W, approximately ¾ mile southwest of the reef south of Salt Cay. From this position you can take up a course of 178° for the 83-mile run to Luperón or a course of 170° for approximately 92 miles to Puerto Plata. This route will carry you over part of the *Turks Bank* that lies east of Great Sand Cay; you should have water at or near 10 fathoms in its vicinity. If you begin to get into water much less than this you have perhaps drifted to far to the west, nearer the eastern shore of Great Sand Cay. If this happens simply head a little more east until in deeper water.

Great Sand Cay

Waypoints
West Bay - ½ nm W of anchorage:
21° 11.65' N, 71° 15.50' W

Great Sand Cay - ¾ nm SW of S end:
21° 10.80' N, 71° 15.50' W

Great Sand Cay, commonly called Big Sand Cay (it seems as if nobody calls it Great Sand Cay anymore even though that is its name) and shown on some older charts as Seal Cay, was once a habitat for the West Indian monk seal and the manatee, the former hunted to extinction and the latter well on its way. Legend has it that Spanish treasure is buried on the cay and it is claimed that a British captain named Delaney recovered $130,000 in pirate treasure from a cave on Great Sand Cay in 1850.

Great Sand Cay is a desert paradise. Iguanas and curly-tailed lizards roam the prickly pear cactus decorated landscape. Twice a year green and hawksbill turtles nest on the beautiful western beach south of the light and nurse sharks gather in the shallow lagoon during their mating season. On the eastern shore of the island a great stone arch called *The Looking Glass*, carved from the limestone by the flow of the ocean's waters, stands in mute testimony to the sea's power. The dangerous reefs southwest of Sand Cay took their toll on so many passing ships that a light was finally established on the cay in 1848. Nonetheless ships still continued to pile up on nearby *Endymion Reef*. The eastern shore offers excellent beachcombing; there is all manner of flotsam and jetsam that has washed ashore on the cay from the open Atlantic. As with so many of the land parks in the island chain, visitors are supposed to have a permit from the *DECR* in Grand Turk to walk ashore.

Navigational Information

If heading south from Salt Cay, be sure to keep west a bit to avoid the reefs north of Great Sand Cay as shown on Chart TCI-T6. The large light tower (Fl W ev 2 sec, 85' 10M, usually not working) on Beacon Hill just north of the beach is easily seen from seaward and makes a great landmark from any direction. A waypoint 21° 11.65'N, 71° 15.50'W, will place you approximately ½ mile west of the anchorage off the beach in *West Bay*, as shown on Chart TCI-T6. From this waypoint, head in towards the beach and anchor wherever your draft allows. This is a great anchorage in winds from northeast to southeast, though some surge can make it quite rolly at times. The holding is good in sand and there are plenty of reefs, heads, and ledges to snorkel north and east of Big Sand Cay.

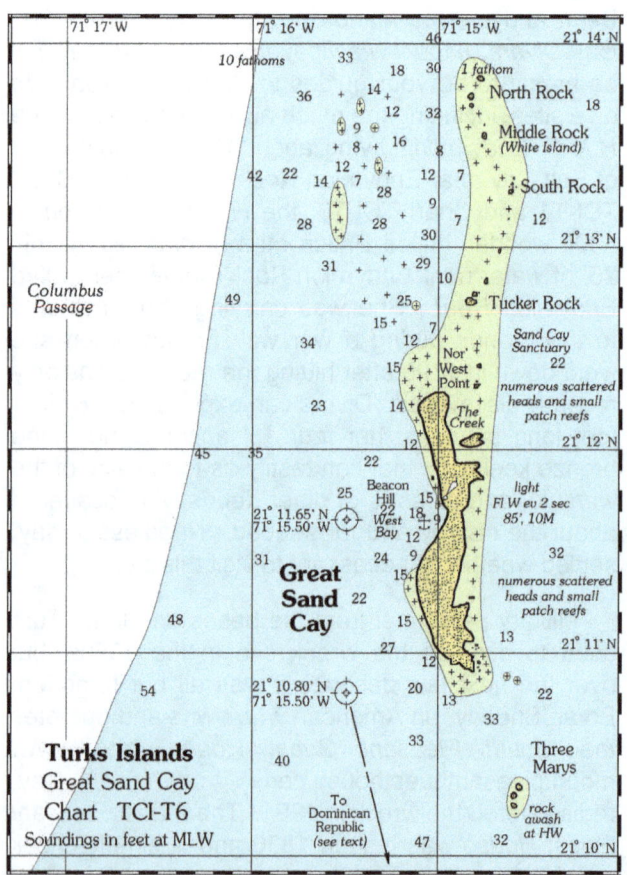

Those skippers bound for the Dominican Republic can head south of Great Sand Cay to a waypoint at 21° 10.80'N, 71° 15.50'W, approximately ¾ mile southwest of the reef at the southern end of Great Sand Cay. From this position you can take up a course of 176° for the 77-mile run to Luperón or a course of 167° for approximately 86 miles to Puerto Plata. Be sure to keep the small trio of rocks shown on Chart TCI-T6 as the Three Marys well to port when heading southeastward towards the DR. Also, don't stray near the vicinity of the *Endymion Reef* (or Endymion Rock as it is sometimes shown) as shown on Chart TCI-T1. The water over the reef is between 4' and 8' in places. It's best to give it a wide berth to the west or pass between it and Great Sand Cay.

The Dominican Republic

The Dominican Republic

Ports of Entry:
Barahona, Manzanillo, Luperón, Cofresi (*Ocean World Marina*), Puerto Plata, Samaná, *Puerto Bahia Marina*, Salinas, Santo Domingo, Boca Chica, Casa de Campo
Fuel: Luperón, Cofresi, Puerto Plata, Samaná, La Romana, Boca Chica, Casa de Campo, Cap Cana
Haul-Out: Luperón, Boca Chica, Haina
Diesel Repairs: Luperón, Cofresi, Puerto Plata, Boca Chica, Cap Cana, Casa de Campo
Outboard Repairs: Luperón, Cofresi, Puerto Plata, Boca Chica, Cap Cana, Casa de Campo
Propane: Luperón, Cofresi, Puerto Plata, Samaná, Boca Chica, Cap Cana, Casa de Campo
Provisions: Luperón, Cofresi, Puerto Plata, Samaná, Boca Chica, Cap Cana, Casa de Campo, Santiago, Santo Domingo
Important Lights:
Luperón-head of dock: Gp. Fl R ev 10s
Ocean World Marina Sea Buoy: Fl W
Puerto Plata Sea Buoy: Fl R
Punta Fortaleza: Fl W ev 6 sec
Puerto Plata Range: Fl R
Cayo Vigia: Fl R

This section is not intended to be a cruising guide to the Dominican Republic - far from it. Rather, I offer the three most popular destinations that cruisers visit before or after their Turks and Caicos cruise. First we will discuss Luperón, by far the most popular stopover in the Dominican Republic, and arguably the best hurricane hole in the Caribbean. Next we'll visit the relatively new *Ocean World Marina* complex at Cofresi. And finally we will cover Puerto Plata, the commercial center of the northern coast of the Dominican Republic (usually just called the DR). I urge all mariners plying these waters to carry adequate charts of the Dominican Republic aboard. As for routing information along the northern coast of the DR between Luperón and Samaná, I will not even attempt to offer any suggestions for this route save to say that I suggest you get a copy of Bruce Van Sant's *The Gentleman's Guide To Passages South* and follow the advice contained therein.

Located on the northern edge of the Caribbean Sea, the Dominican Republic (*Republica Dominicana*) occupies the eastern two-thirds of the island of Hispaniola, the second largest island of the Antilles. Although it shares a border with Haiti, the two vastly different countries and cultures have little in common. While the inhabitants of Haiti have French and African cultural roots, the population of the Dominican Republic has a mixture of African, Amerindian, and Caucasian roots, and the culture and language is Hispanic. Economically the DR is far more developed than Haiti, with a much higher standard of living and quite free of the unrest that plagues Haiti. The principal religion is Roman Catholic and the Church is very influential on several issues such as education, divorce, and birth control; but its overall influence has diminished over the years.

The Dominican Republic has three major metropolitan areas. Santo Domingo, with a population of over two million, is the capital and lies on the southern coast. On the northern coast lies Puerto Plata, one of the DR's main tourist draws, with some 60,000 year-round residents. Santiago, located in the central highlands, is the country's leading industrial center, with a population of over 250,000. Sosúa, near Puerto Plata, and La Romana and Punta Cana, at the eastern end of the island, all have growing resort populations. The rest of the DR's seven-million-plus population lives in or around a dozen or so smaller towns and villages.

The economy of the DR is dominated by agriculture, with 56% of the country used for crops or pasture. Small farmers produce staple foods such as plantains, beans, and sweet potatoes. Agricultural products account for two thirds of export earnings. The rest comes largely from minerals, like bauxite, nickel, and gold. The DR is among the top ten gold producing countries of the world and has the largest single gold mine in the Western Hemisphere. The income from the export of these metals is about equal to the amount spent on imported petroleum. Most of the remaining imports are manufactured goods such as machinery, chemicals, and foodstuffs. In recent years the government has made great efforts to improve the economy by stimulating the tourist industry and today more than 500,000 tourists visit the country each year to enjoy the climate and the beautiful beaches. The DR has a little bit of everything for everyone. Its main cities offer all kinds of attractions, from its breathtaking landscapes and pristine beaches, to its modern shopping malls and exciting nightlife. But by far, the most attractive feature of the DR is the friendliness of its people.

The Dominican Republic

Since the Dominican Republic is located just south of the *Tropic of Cancer*, the temperature varies little from season to season. Average temperatures range from 80°-95° F during the day to the low 70's at night. Although the DR is in the tropics, the trade winds, the surrounding ocean, and high elevations combine in some areas to produce a climate that is far from typical of the tropics. In fact, frost is common on the highest peaks of the *Cordillera Central*. In most areas, however, temperatures are moderately high and vary little from season to season. Rainfall is normally greatest on the mountain slopes over which the easterly trade winds blow and decreases on the opposite slopes and in the major valleys. Annual precipitation averages about 60 inches, but the mountainous areas receive considerably more moisture. The rainy season is from June to November.

Citizens of the United States and Canada may enter the DR with a passport, no Visa is required. Minors may enter with only an original birth certificate. Cuban residents of the United States may enter with their U.S. residency card and additional official photo-bearing document. American and Canadian visitors are required to purchase a tourist card for US$10 upon entry. If you're heading to the DR from the Turks and Caicos or the Bahamas, remember to get a departure clearance when leaving those waters. Visitors leaving by air are required to pay a US$27 departure tax. Personal electronics are admitted into the Dominican Republic, although professional video equipment, television cameras, and other related items may need special clearance. Guns will need to be checked in when entering. For more detailed info on clearing in or out of the DR, see the section on *Customs and Immigration* in the chapter *The Basics*.

After clearing into the DR you will probably want to exchange your dollars for pesos. Don't change more money than you plan to spend. Only 30% of Dominican currency exchanged by visitors can be changed back into dollars upon departure (a tip - save your currency exchange receipts). Although it's extremely tempting, one should avoid changing money on the black market. Absolutely no more than US$5,000 may be taken out of the country when you leave. Arrests have been made for even small currency-law violations. Foreign currency can be changed into Dominican pesos at *Banco de Reservas* booths at the airports, major hotels, or at commercial banks. Banking hours are 0830 to 1500, Monday through Friday. Airport booths remain open to service all incoming flights, up to 24 hours if necessary. Traveler's checks and major credit cards are widely accepted. Cash advances are available at some commercial banks. When tipping, a 10% gratuity (as well as an 8% sales tax) is often included in the bill. Please note that the practice of tipping taxi drivers is not the custom in the DR but it is widely practiced, and just as widely appreciated. As for provisioning, you'll want to check out the excellent deals on wine, rum, cigars, and *El Presidente* beer. Bear in mind that the DR practices the Latin tradition of the siesta. Many shops close for long lunches from 12:30 P.M. to 2:30 P.M. However, major shopping centers, supermarkets, and stores frequented by visitors usually remain open from 9 A.M. to 7 P.M. In the DR you'll find *Atlantic Standard Time* in effect year round, so the time here is one hour ahead of *Eastern Standard Time* in the Fall and Winter and the same as *Eastern Daylight Time* in the Spring and Summer. Electricity is 110 volt, 60 cycle.

Baseball is a passion in the DR; there are more baseball players from the Dominican Republic playing in the North American major leagues than from any other Caribbean nation. Most major league clubs maintain small baseball camps in the Dominican Republic, and the DR's professional winter league draws many U.S. players.

The famous *Merengue Festival* is a lively celebration of the country's national music, with *Merengue* bands performing at most major hotels and along the Santo Domingo Malecón. This huge party takes place from the last week in July through the first week of August. The term *Merengue* refers both to the music and the dance, which evolved in the Dominican countryside among the happy people of a divided island. The history of the *Merengue* is woven into the fabric of Dominican history itself. This Afro-Caribbean dance became part of country life and is still danced today around the squares of small villages, next to bonfires on secluded beaches, in ballrooms, and in nightclubs throughout the world. In the traditional countryside settings, the music is provided by a *Perico Ripiao*, a small band made up of an accordion, a drum, a guiro and a box bass. Puerto Plata's *Merengue Festival* is held during the second week of October. Christmas celebrations begin in early December and end on *Epiphany Day*, Jan. 6..

Americans needing the assistance of the *U.S. Embassy* in Santo Domingo can telephone 809-541-2171, or fax the embassy at 809-686-7437 (http://santodomingo.usembassy.gov/). In Santo Domingo the embassy sits at the corner of *Calle Cesar Nicolas Penson* and *Calle Leopoldo Navarro*.

The Dominican Republic postal service boasts over 190 branches and is the least expensive (although slowest) way of sending and receiving international mail. The postal service also has a higher priced express mail service similar to the *U.S.P.S. Priority Mail*. Private couriers include *DHL*, *FedEx*, *UPS*, and several local P.O. Box courier services such as *Express Parcel Service*. There are 120 AM radio stations on the island, 6 HF stations, and 18 television stations scattered about. Amateur radio operators can get a 30-day reciprocal (HI) for no charge upon clearing in.

Divers will be happy to know that the waters surrounding the island of Hispaniola hold some 400 shipwrecks that have produced many valuable artifacts over the years. The DR is great place for beginner divers as well as for serious underwater explorers. Although the North coast near Puerto Plata and Sosua might prove disappointing for the experienced diver due to the extensive damage the reefs there have suffered, the southern shore and the eastern side of the island offers dive sites to satisfy the most demanding diver. *La Caleta Underwater Park* is located just a short boat ride from Boca Chica and there divers will enjoy good viz and a fertile underwater life. Divers may also visit the wreck of the *Hickory*, an old treasure hunting ship. Isla Catalina is a good spot for wall diving and large fish. Isla Saona is also a great spot for the larger marine creatures. As tourism develops on the island, diving in the Dominican Republic might soon become very popular and the dive sites more crowded.

Places of Interest

Visitors will probably want to visit some of the better known historical sites in the DR. In Santo Domingo you can check out *Columbus' Castle* (*Alcazar*), the *St. Francis Monastery*, the *Cathedral of Santo Domingo*, the *Museum of Royal Houses*, *Columbus Square*, the *Ozama Fortress*, *El Faro a Colón* (the *Columbus Lighthouse*), and the first street ever built in the new world, Calle Las Damas. The *Autonomous University of Santo Domingo* (*UASD*), is the oldest university in the Americas dating back to 1538. In Puerto Plata, *Fort San Felipe* bears witness to Nicolás de Ovando's founding of that city in 1502.

There are 16 national parks, 9 natural monuments, and 7 reserves in the Dominican Republic, all under the control of the *Dirección Nacional de Parques*. Among the most popular is *Bermudez National Park* at *Duarte Peak*. A word of warning here; the strenuous hike up and down *Duarte*, the highest mountain in the Caribbean at 10,417 feet, takes at least two days. *Los Haitises National Park*, located on the southern shore of Samaná Bay (Bahía de San Lorenzo), is a protected coastal region known for its mangrove swamps, its caves with Taino rock paintings, and strange rock formations called *mogotes* that emerge from the sea and are unmatched for their eerie beauty. The *National Park of the East*, southeast of La Romana, is of great interest to those who want to explore prehistoric caves, some of which boast pre-Columbian petroglyphs. Not far off its beautiful beaches lies Isla Saona, which has several excellent hiking trails. The *Reserva Antropológica de las Cuevas de Borbén* was extended in 1996 to protect the *El Pomier* caves, in San Cristóbal, under threat from limestone quarrying. The caves are of enormous archaeological value, with over 4,000 wall paintings and 5,000 rock drawings. Cave #1 contains 590 pictographs, making it superior to any other cave painting site in the Caribbean. Other places of interest are the *Los Tres Ojos National Park*, the *Marine Mammals Sanctuary*, the *National Botanical Garden*, and the *Parque Zoológico Nacional*. The *Reservas Científicas*, the *Scientific Reserves*, include lakes, patches of forest and the *Banco de la Plata*, the enormous *Silver Banks* where hump-backed whales migrate from the Arctic every year to mate and give birth. About 50 boats conduct trips to the *Silver Banks* out of Samaná.

The Future

Big changes are in the works for the Dominican Republic. First, design and development has begun on the *Amber Cove Cruise Center* (http://www.ambercove.com/port-information.aspx) which will accommodate up to two cruise vessels, or 10,000 people daily in the *Bay of Maimón* just west of Cofresi and Puerto Plata, and east of Luperón. There is also a new highway under construction that will service Puerto Plata, Cambioso (and its pristine beach), and what may become the Punta Alma project near Luperón. The highway will make the trip to the airport at Puerto Plata much faster. New high tension power lines are being installed to bring 24-hour per day electricity to Luperón.

A Brief History

The island that we know as Hispaniola was first inhabited by Ciboney Indians and later by Taino Indians who still occupied the island when Christopher Columbus discovered it on December 5, 1492. The native Indians had named the island *Quisqueya* but Columbus changed its name to Hispaniola (from *Isla Espanola,* the "Spanish Island"). Columbus lived here for many years prior to his death, and his remains are said to be buried in the *Cathedral of Santo Domingo* in Santo Domingo. Christopher Columbus' brother Bartholomew founded Santo Domingo in 1496, making the city the oldest permanently occupied settlement in the Americas.

At that time there were more than a million native Taino Indians on the island but within 50 years most had died of starvation, overwork in the gold mines, and epidemics of European diseases. The gold that could be obtained using the 16th century mining techniques was exhausted by 1530. Spain lost interest in Santo Domingo soon after the discoveries of Mexico and Peru. The Spaniards who remained on the island turned to cultivating sugar cane, using black slaves imported from Africa.

In 1697, Spain ceded the western third of Hispaniola to France. By the end of the 1700's, the new French possession known as St. Domingue was one of the world's richest colonies, producing vast quantities of sugar and cotton. By 1795 France had gained control of the entire island but slave uprisings in the western section in 1804 led to the creation of Haiti, the world's first black republic. In 1814 Spain regained control of the eastern part of the island, but the Dominicans declared their independence in 1821. In 1822 the Haitians invaded the Dominican Republic and ruled it by force for almost 22 years, but the Dominicans did not lie down and accept this intervention. They launched the *Trinitaria*, a secret society founded by Juan Pablo Duarte, and under the leadership of Ramon Matias Mella and Francisco del Rosario Sanchez, the Spanish-speaking inhabitants of the east rebelled against the Haitians and proclaimed their independence on February 27, 1844, calling their nation the Dominican Republic. This period of occupation is often considered the cause of an antagonism that still separates Dominicans from Haitians. One favorable consequence of Haitian rule, however, was the freeing of slaves in the DR.

Unhappily, liberation from the Haitians did little to bring peace and economic progress to the DR. During the rest of the 19th century, the Dominican Republic suffered severe economic difficulties, scores of revolutions, armed invasions from Haiti, and another period of Spanish domination from 1861 to 1865. Money was borrowed and spent recklessly by corrupt governments, and by 1916 the country was in political and economic chaos.

In 1905, the United States established partial control of the Dominican economy to protect American investors. Increasing debts and internal disorders resulted in the occupation of the DR by U.S. Marines in 1916 in order to restore order and protect the approaches to the Panama Canal. This occupation lasted for eight years, and, though there was opposition to it, the enforced political stability permitted major social and economic advances.

In 1924, the U.S. occupation ended; in 1930 there was another revolution and the DR fell into the hands of a dictator, Gen. Rafael Leonidas Trujillo Molina. For nearly 31 years, until his assassination in 1961, Trujillo headed a ruthless police state. At the cost of political freedom, the DR had another period of imposed stability that, combined with favorable sugar prices, stimulated impressive economic growth. In December 1962 the first free elections in nearly 40 years brought the leftist Juan Bosch to the presidency. His reform program led to his overthrow by the military in September 1963.

Five years of political turmoil after Trujillo's death led to another intervention by the United States. When Bosch's supporters attempted to restore him to power in 1965, civil war broke out, and U.S. troops were sent in to restore order and the status quo and ease U.S. concerns about the possibility of a Cuban-style Communist takeover. Since then the political scene has been relatively orderly, with freely elected presidents. In 1966, Joaquin Balaguer was elected president. His right wing authoritarian rule continued until the election of 1978, when Antonio Guzman defeated Balaguer in a very controversial election. Guzman was in turn defeated by Salvador Jorge Blanco in 1982. Balaguer, elderly and blind, was narrowly reelected in 1986 and 1990. In 1988 Blanco was convicted of corruption in absentia and in 1992 was sentenced to 20 years in prison.

Much wealth has been generated, but it has always been unequally distributed. The bulk of the population remains poor and undernourished. In the 1980s the low price of sugar in the world market brought on a series of economic crises. Under Salvador Jorge Blanco, who was president from 1982 to 1986, the government instituted an austerity program. Wage controls and the removal of food subsidies led to rioting in 1984. Economic difficulties persisted in the debt-ridden nation through the 1990 election, in which Balaguer defeated his long-time opponent, Juan Bosch. Austerity measures dictated by the International Monetary Fund were still in force in 1992. The 1991 deportation of illegal Haitian immigrants worsened relations with Haiti.

Medical Help

In the DR, the phone number for a medical emergency is 911, but don't count on it working all the time. Most medical centers are bi-lingual, many accept international insurance, and the costs can be 1/3 of the prices in the U.S. All the clinics are free to residents of the Dominican Republic and cruisers, but the more serious medical problems, such as those that require a visit or a stay at one of the hospitals in Puerto Plata or Santiago can cost quite a bit. Most medical insurance is accepted throughout the DR and drugs that can only be acquired by prescription in the US, are available without a prescription in the DR, and most are very inexpensive. It helps to know the Spanish translation of the drug when you head for the *pharmacia*.

There is a medical clinic in Luperón where two of the three doctors in residence speak passable English. The clinic is located at the end of *Calle Luperón*, two blocks south of *Verizon* and then three blocks southwest. While the clinic can deal with most basic health problems, for testing you will be referred to the *Laboratory Luperón*, just across from the *guagua park*. If you have your samples in before 1200 you can usually get the results by 1700. If you need a dentist try the *Medicon Dental Implant Center, Independencia No. 9*, (phone 888-848-7639, ext: 24368).

If you need medical attention in Puerto Plata visit *Centro Médico Bournigal* (809-586-2342, Fax: 809-586-6104 or email them at info@bournigal-hospital.com, http://www.centromedicobournigal.com/).

In Santiago you can find medical attention at HOMS, the *Hospital Metropolitano de Santiago, Duarte Highway* Km 2.8 (829-947-2222 Ext. 5000, Fax: 829-947-2223, or you can reach them by email at info@homshospital.com, http://www.homshospital.com/).

In Sosúa or Cabarete you can visit the *Medical Center Carretera Sosua-Cabarete* Km 1, Sosúa, 809-571-4696, or you can reach them by email at cmc.sosua@gmail.com. In Cabarete visit *Servi-Med* Dr. Gidion or Dr. Naurio Carretera, *Cabarete 25* (809-571-2903). If you need a vet in Sosúa or Cabarete, visit *Dr. Bob's*, on the main road from Sosúa to Cabarete. (24-hour phone number 809-430-5503). After *El Choco Road* you will come to a *Coastal* gas station, just past the station is the *Dr. Bob's* sign.

In Samaná, Dominican Republic, quality medical care can be found at the *Centro Medico de Especialidades Samaná* (with ambulance service), located at *Calle Coronel Andrés Díaz No.06,* phone: 809-538-3999, 809-538-3888, or fax them at 809 538-2424 (http://cmes.com.do/). The *International Medical Center* (info@internationalmedicalcenter.com) is located in the *Plaza Pueblo Principe,* Local 4, in the heart of downtown Samaná and is open 24/7 (809-552-1117, Fax: 809-538 2675). If you need a dentist in Samaná, visit Dr. Elizabeth Frias de Martinez, her clinic (*Miami Family Dental*) is located at *Calle Peter Vander Horst No.2* (809-538-3180, Cell: 809-988-1705.

In Santo Domingo, *Clinica Abreu*, (http://clinicaabreu.com.do/) at *Calle Arzobispo Portes No. 853,* has 24-hour emergency service and free treatment for foreigners (809-688-4411). the *El Hospital Docente Padre Billinil* is located on *Calle Padre Billini y Santomé, Zona Colonial*, and offers free consultations (809-333-5656, http://www.hospitalpadrebillini.gob.do/main/index.php?zone=inicio). If you need an ambulance call *Movi-Med Ambulance Evacuation Service* at 809-532-0000.

The Northern Coast

The northern coast of the Dominican Republic is popular with cruisers headed to the Caribbean, although many tend to skip it when returning. Since the officials in the Dominican Republic are a bit more open to cruising boats along this shore, the anchorages here are much more inviting as more than just an overnight stopover. We will explore the northern coast from west to east.

The Dominican Republic

Luperón

Waypoints
Luperón - 1 nm N of entrance:
19° 55.50' N, 70° 56.51' W

By far, the nearest, most popular destination when heading to the Caribbean from the Turks and Caicos, is Luperón. In years past we would have to give that honor to Puerto Plata; but since Luperón became an official port of entry, Puerto Plata's yacht traffic has dropped off considerably. Luperón was named after General Luperón, who was one of the Dominican Republic's greatest heroes. In 1879, under his leadership, the country was reorganized and set on the road to economic recovery. Luperón, which is sometimes shown as Puerto Blanco on some charts, is usually the name given to this entire area, but most insist that Puerto Blanco is the bay and Luperón is the town. Either way, it is a favorite stop for cruisers bound north or south.

This tiny harbor is one of the best hurricane holes in the Caribbean and many cruisers tend to call it home for the season staying months at a time. I know a couple who might just spend the rest of their lives there. They love the cheap rum, wine, and dining as well as the secure protection that Luperón has to offer. The people love boaters in Luperón; boaters really help the economy here and the locals appreciate it and go out of their way to be accommodating. There is a boater's net every Sunday and Wednesday on VHF. Ch.72, at 0800. Here you can pick up the latest info about what's going locally including business announcements, upcoming festivities, boat gear sales, and info on who's just arrived in the harbor. VHF ch. 68 is used for all local communications, usually only the Navy uses ch. 16.

Navigational Information

From Great Sand Cay in the Turks and Caicos Islands, the waypoint off Luperón bears approximately 176° at a distance of 77 nautical miles. If approaching from the waypoint just south of Great Sand Cay you can head directly for this waypoint with no dangers. Your first sign of impending landfall may well be while you are still 20 miles north of the Dominican Republic. Cabo Isabella is clearly seen as the highest spot around. As you approach the entrance to the bay at Luperón, keep Cabo Isabella to starboard. There are some hills to both the right and left of the entrance channel, but the very conspicuous light-colored roof of a hotel/resort complex makes another good landmark. Keep the hotel well to starboard; the entrance to Luperón lies approximately ½ - ¾ mile to the east of the hotel.

If the wind is right, usually out of the southeast, your dog may alert you to your impending landfall from many miles out to sea. Suddenly the air will be filled with the aroma of dirt, trees, animals, and smoke and you might find your dog sniffing the air trying to figure out where these new scents are coming from. If your sniffer is up to snuff you too might be sniffing the air along with your pooch. Quite a refreshing change if you've gotten used to the dry, almost desert-like islands of the Turks and Caicos.

As shown on Chart DR-1, the entrance to Luperón lies between a large shoal area on the western side of the entrance and another area to the eastern side of the entrance. Caution is called for when entering the channel to Luperón, in poor light the shoals are difficult to make out.

Approaching the entrance slowly in the morning light, you may be able to make out the shoal fairly easily, as the water may still be clear then. Later during the day, as the winds pick up (about 0900 the breeze fills in and blows all day until around sunset); it gets a little harder to discern the shoal from offshore.

From the waypoint at 19° 55.50' N, 70° 56.51' W (approximately one mile north of the entrance channel), a good course is to keep the eastern cliff close on your port bow until you can make out the buoy that now marks the shoal on your starboard side. As of this writing there are two buoys (and bear in mind that this may change at any time) and the westernmost buoy is in shallow water and should be kept WELL to starboard upon entering. Keep an eye out for the breaking shoal off the eastern shore and take the westernmost buoy to starboard upon entering. The entrance channel leading into the anchorage is often hard to make out until you get fairly close and it opens up before you.

As you approach the entrance, keep close to the eastern shoreline where the deeper water lies and keep the buoys well to starboard. Once inside you'll see *Caño Quitano* to the east, but do not enter that harbor at this time (though many cruisers leaving Luperón anchor just inside the entrance to ease a night departure).

As the entrance to the inner harbor opens up to starboard, pass roughly midway between the northern and southern shore watching out for the shoals off

A Cruising Guide to the Turks and Caicos Islands

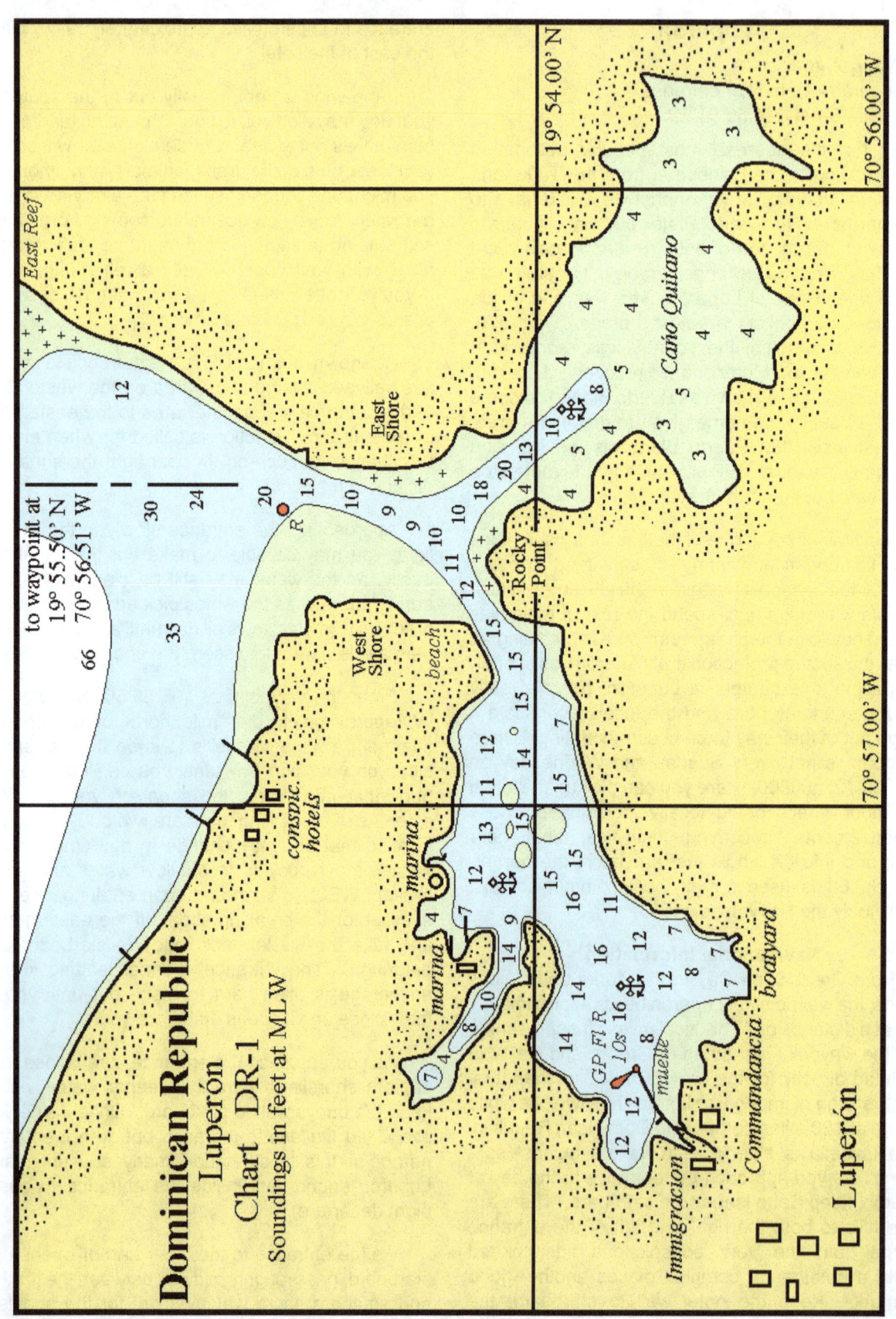

116

each one. As you enter the harbor the deeper water lies along the mangroves on the southeastern shore. If you pass along those mangroves you'll avoid the large, shallow mud shoals that plague the center of the harbor and change and grow with each passing season. The shoals rise up from 20' depths to lie about 1'-2' under the surface; use caution as lots of folks run aground here. Boats can anchor anywhere in the harbor, near the marina or by the town dock. Usually where there is a large gap with no boats you'll find a shoal so keep your eyes open. The water in the harbor is muddy brown and the visibility is nil. The bottom here is basically mud and the holding is great, but it takes a few days for your anchor to set here. Boats drag frequently as people often forget that they are anchoring in 20' of water and fail to put out enough scope. But if you do drag, unless you run into another boat or the dock, it's all mud and mangroves around you to act as a cushion. The town dock is marked with a red light (GP Fl R, ev 10 sec.) that works well although it is not visible outside the harbor.

What You Will Find Ashore

If you need to clear in, it would be convenient for the officials if you anchored near the town dock (*muelle*) at the southwestern end of the anchorage. After anchoring, hoist your "Q" flag and sometime during the day the *Commandancia's* official will come out to your boat to clear you in. This person will likely say he is with the "Navy" and may or may not have a translator with him. A lot of boats simply take their papers into town to clear in and save the *Commandante's* men a trip out (you know how impatient we cruisers can be), and I've done that myself. Sometimes it's okay, while at other times the *Commandante* may tell you to go back to your boat and wait (which has also happened to me). At the time of this writing standard procedure is to wait for the *Commandante*.

After the *Commandante* and his entourage have cleared you (*Agriculture* will be along as well: at the time of this writing there is no fee for the Navy clearance, but you will have to pay for *Agriculture*), you must now go to the *Immigration* office and all aboard must come into town to clear.

The dinghy dock is in the SW corner of the harbor at Luperón, it lies on the NW side of the *muelle*. You can also get water here and drop off garbage for a fee. Just up from the dinghy dock on the road into town is a small blue trailer, this is the *Immigracíon* office. You will have to pay a fee per person aboard, and a fee for the boat (please note that all fees are subject to change depending on time and the exchange rate of the peso versus the American dollar). The *Immigracíon* office is also where you'll find the *Ports* representative and have to pay for harbor clearance. Across the street, over the small bridge and up the hill is the *Commandancia's* office, this is where' you'll need to go to get a *despacho* when you clear out.

When clearing out you must obtain a *despacho*. On the day of your departure, one hour before you plan to leave, you must go to the *Port Authority* office to pay your bill. Take that receipt to the *Commandancia* to obtain your *despacho*. The *Commandante*, or his representative, will then come to your boat for an inspection and give you your *despacho* which is supposed to be good for 24 hours, but you may be told that you should leave within an hour. However, if you have an engine problem what can be done? Stay overnight and leave in the morning if you desire, but don't tell anybody that I suggested this. I have also left the main anchorage in Luperón and anchored overnight in *Caño Quintano*, leaving at first light the next morning.

In a small cove that lies just to starboard off the entrance channel is the *Marina Puerto Blanco*, the oldest, marina in the harbor. The marina has a small boat dock with room for about 10-15 boats and it usually stays full. The bar at the marina is a popular hangout for cruisers with Wednesday night pot lucks, daily happy hours from 1700-1900 PM, and other events during the week such as the Sunday nautical swap meet where cruisers buy and sell their no-longer-needed charts, courtesy flags, and all manner of used boat gear that's been sitting in various lockers doing nothing but taking up room. There is electricity and water dockside, but be prepared for frequent power outages. There is also a dinghy dock where you can get water for washing. Some folks will drink this water but I don't recommend it; bottled water is sold here as well as throughout town in 5 gallon bottles. You can drop off your laundry here for what is usually same-day service. The marina also has showers and car and truck rentals. You can phone the marina at 809-571-8644.

High atop a ridge across and to the east of the *Puerto Blanco Marina* is the newer *Luperón Marina and Yacht Club* with their dock and 69 steps that lead up the hill to the restaurant and bar. The restaurant has a great view and good access to any breeze that might be blowing. There is limited dockage and free internet access. The marina offers a clearance service, call ahead on VHF ch. 68 for entry instructions and to let the marina know that you need clearance. The docks have water, electricity, showers, and the marina also offers ice, a laundry service, and Wi-Fi.

A short walk north of the marinas is the *Caribbean Village Luperón*, the beachfront resort that you used as a landmark when approaching Luperón. The resort is spread over 16 lush, landscaped acres, with gorgeous views of the *Atlantic Ocean*. The large resort boasts 441 beautifully appointed air-conditioned rooms. The resort offers SCUBA lessons

Shopping in Luperón

Just watching the world go by in Luperón

Luperón Marina and Yacht Club

The Dominican Republic

in their pool, bicycles, windsurfing, snorkeling, sailing, tennis, a gym with sauna and *Jacuzzi*, aerobics, table tennis, billiards, and horseback riding on the beach. Also on-site are several boutiques, a buffet-type restaurant, a beach restaurant, and a disco. There is some nice snorkeling along the jetties by the hotel, but be forewarned: if you walk the beaches in the DR you will sometimes find vendors hawking their wares. They're usually very friendly and understand a firm no. This is not much of a problem in Luperón, as the vendors are not allowed on the beach. It tends to be more of a problem from Puerto Plata eastward.

At the southern end of the anchorage area, southeast of the government dock, is *Marina Tropical* and its haulout yard. The marina has a 30-ton lift, a *Cono-Lift*, which is basically a hydraulic trailer, limited water, showers, toilets, power (intermittent), workshops, and a bar. The yard can haul boats to 47' LOA. You can reach the marina by phone at 829-440-9926, or email them at marinatropical.dr@gmail.com.

Just inland from the *muelle* and the dinghy dock is the town of Luperón. Not much bigger than South Caicos, Luperón is quite a bit busier, and much more alive. Everywhere you go you'll find people talking, music playing, and cars and motorcycles roaring by. Many people live in homes that also house their business where they might sell fruits and veggies, rum, water, roasted chickens, or sodas. Prices are great in the DR and Luperón is no exception. You can easily find rum at $3-$4 a bottle, wine for $2-$3 a bottle, and a carton of DR produced cigarettes for half of what an equivalent brand would cost in the States (and I'm told they taste as good as US brands). You can eat out for next to nothing; a lunch in one of the more inexpensive places will run you in the neighborhood of $2-$4. I love *Laisa's* just in from *Verizon* on the same side of the street. Almost directly across from *Verizon* is a great little restaurant on the corner that serves excellent food (lunch for four costs under US$25 there).

To start our tour of Luperón, let's begin with the first stop you will have to make; you must change your American dollars into pesos. The first rule is do not change very much more money than you plan to spend. Only 30% of Dominican currency exchanged by visitors can be changed back into dollars upon departure (a tip - save your currency exchange receipts). Although it's extremely tempting, one should avoid changing money on the black market; not to worry though, there is little if any black market activity in Luperón.

The *Claró* office in Luperón, *Altagrácia* (even though many people still call it *Codatel*), is the most convenient place to exchange your dollars although there are others (*Alejandro Pharmacia* and *Alexandria's Gift Shoppe* to name just a couple). To find *Claró*, walk into town on the main road from the government dock. As you enter town it splits and *Duarte Street* forks off straight in front of you on your right hand side. Follow *Duarte Street* for two blocks and *Altagrácia* will be on your left. *Altagrácia* is also a great place to go for Internet access although most of the gringo restaurants have Wi-Fi.

Next, you'll want to know how to get around Luperón; the easiest way of course is by foot. The town lies just up from the town dock and is only about a mile long. But if you want to get anywhere else, or if you have to pick up something, you have your choice of several different modes of transportation. For those on a budget, and the adventurous, there are the *motorconchos*. These are small motorcycles that roar around town all day and most of the night. If you need a *motorconcho*, they hang out all day long at *Codatel*.

Next up in the conveyance chain are the taxis and *guaguas* (basically cars are taxis and minivans are *guaguas*). The taxis are the priciest means of transportation but they will take you wherever you wish to go. A motorconcho from town to the hotel costs 15 pesos; a taxi costs 100 pesos. As anywhere in the DR, you should negotiate for a better deal, but the taxi drivers seem to stand pretty steadfast. It would pay to rent a van with others for the most economical method. *Guagua*s can be found in town at the *guagua park*, *parquecito*, the small park at the end of town away from the town dock. If you want to get to Puerto Plata this is the way to go, but you must leave Luperón with enough time to shop at the other end.

With the exception of the *pharmacia* and the larger grocery stores, most places close from noon till two for siesta. The *guaguas* run all day but only when they're full; they are truly an experience. You're likely to find yourself stuffed into a minivan with 16 other people, a dog, a chicken, and a couple of goats. If headed to Puerto Plata, take a *guagua* to Imbert (home of the closest bank and *ATM* machine though you can draw pesos at *Codatel* on your *Visa* card) and pick up a bus there that's headed to Puerto Plata. If you need a trusted taxi driver, try *Nino's Taxi* to go to Puerto Plata or Santiago; his phone is 809-493-6950.

If headed to Santo Domingo, there is a daily bus available from Luperón, it leaves about 1330 and the trip takes about 7 hours. One final note: if you are planning on doing major provisioning, you should consider renting a van for the day; you won't be able to carry a lot on a *guagua*.

If headed to Puerto Plata, take a *guagua* to Imbert (home of the closest bank and *ATM* machine though you can draw pesos at *Codatel* on your *Visa* card) and pick up a bus there that's headed to Puerto Plata. If headed to Santo Domingo, there is a daily bus available from Luperón, it leaves about 1330 and the trip takes about 7 hours. One final note: if you are planning on doing major provisioning, you should consider renting a van for the day; you won't be able to carry a lot on a *guagua*. Call José for van rentals (see the next paragraph).

In Luperón you can rent a car or motorcycle from José Virgilio Rodriquez, known around town as José Villo (bee-yo), of *José's Adventure Tours*. José is a very enterprising young man who can get you whatever you need, diesel, water, propane, and even act as your translator. I am told that I must mention that he is very handsome (okay all you ladies, don't knock on his door all at once). You can reach José on VHF ch. 68, or you can phone him on his cell phone at 458-9506, or at his home at 571-8624, or you can fax José at 571-8082. José is a government licensed tour guide (one must attend school for this) and *José's Adventure Tours* operates all over the Dominican Republic and features trips to Santo Domingo, the waterfalls, horseback riding, and shopping expeditions to Santiago. I cannot recommend a more valuable and trusted contact for you than José in Luperón. José is also in the process of opening up a *Casa de Cambio, House of Exchange* where you can change your dollars to pesos. As you approach town from the dinghy dock, the first house on the left is José's.

For car rentals you can also try *Odalis* (Pedro Odalis Cueto) on VHF ch. 68 or phone them at 223-3580, or you can speak to José, on VHF ch. 68. Now that you have your pesos, if you're like most cruisers you're ready to search out a place to eat. The typical Dominican meal consists of a meat, rice and beans, and plantains and can be had for about 75-90 pesos at the many *comedors* around town. As you walk around town you'll find many small shops selling notions, fruits, veggies, bottled water, roasted chicken, and all manner of goods. Every street has a place to eat and half the fun is discovering the best places. *Laisa's Pico de Pollo* is one of my favorites and may become one of yours as well.

A very popular spot is *Capt. Steve's Bar*, six blocks up from the dock. The ambiance is Mexican with food to go, Wi-Fi, motorcycles for rent, horse riding excursions, and many other activities. *Wendy's Bar* and *JR's Tropical Bistro* are both on the right as you enter town from the government dock. *Wendy's* has movie nights on Mondays and Tuesdays, *Karaoke* on Fridays, and all kinds of drink specials every day of the week. Wendy's is a gathering spot for the folks involved with the weekly gringos versus locals softball game. *JR's* has movie nights on Thursdays and Fridays, with trivia night on Wednesdays, and Tuesday is taco day. *JR's* is closed on Sundays and Mondays.

La Yola has a great atmosphere, cool breezes, and a two for one happy hour. The menu has reasonable prices for lunch and dinner and offers pizza with a good variety of toppings.

Now that you've filled your cruising tummy, you'll probably want to check out the shopping. But we'll discuss shopping in Luperón in a moment. First, let's start with some basic needs. There is a medical clinic in Luperón where two of the three doctors in residence speak passable English. The clinic is located at the end of *Calle Luperón*, two blocks south of *Verizon* and then three blocks southwest. While the clinic can deal with most basic health problems, for testing you will be referred to the *Laboratory Luperón*, just across from the *guagua park*. If you have your samples in before 1200 you can usually get the results by 1700. The prices are right here. A blood and fecal test is US$10 and the office visit is free. All the clinics are free to residents of the Dominican Republic and cruisers, but the more serious medical problems, such as those that require a visit or a stay at one of the hospitals in Puerto Plata or Santiago can cost quite a bit. Most medical insurance is accepted throughout the DR and drugs that can only be acquired by prescription in the US, are available without a prescription in the DR, and most are very inexpensive. It helps to know the Spanish translation of the drug when you head for the *pharmacia*. The folks at *Farmicia Danessa*

The Dominican Republic

on *Parque Central* are very knowledgeable and even have photo developing available.

If you need marine supplies visit *Banegra's*, located at *27 de Febrero*. Their supplies are limited but they do carry basics such as charts, filters, flags, and can even arrange canvas repairs. *Flaco* can also be counted on for sail and canvas repairs, they are located on *Calle Duarte*. *Calamity Canvas* is a cruiser owned business and owner Ron can handle your canvas repairs. Ron can be reached on VHF ch. 68 or by phone at 809-523-6987.

Persio Núñez at *Núñez & Núñez* in Santiago has a nice machine shop and rebuilds gasoline as well as diesel engines. His number is 809-522-8202, or 522-2200. There is a small welding shop on the right as you approach Luperón from the town dock. If you need a good refrigeration man, look up Mariano in town. For major diesel problems Mike is your best bet, and Santiago has almost anything you need to repair your engine.

Gasoline and diesel are usually both easily available at the gas station in town, though if Luperón is out, you may have to get a taxi to El Estrecho to visit the station there. You can haul your own jerry cans, but the gas station is on the road to Imbert, all the way on the other side of town, about a mile from the dinghy dock. You'll find several Dominicans hanging around the dock that will take your cans and fill them for you, usually for about a $.25 a gallon more. These very innovative young men will bring 55-gallon drums of fuel out to your boat and siphon the diesel into your tank. ALWAYS use a *Baja Filter* to clean any fuel going into your tanks when in the Dominican Republic.

It's usually easiest to call *Papo* on VHF ch. 68 and Papo will deliver fuel, water, propane, or anything else you need to your boat, Papo will make your life at anchor much easier. Another option is to hire a *motorconcho* for a few pesos. The only problem with that is that you must hang on to the bike and the gas cans while en route. Rafael or Handy Andy (VHF ch. 68) an also deliver fuel or water to your boat, as well as clean the bottom of your vessel.

If you need propane, the propane fill station is past the cockfight arena (a busy place on a Friday afternoon), just past the gas station. You'll notice it by the conspicuous white propane tank. The normal way to get propane is hire a *motorconcho* for a few pesos. Once again, if you need propane, you can call *Papo* on VHF ch. 68 for same day service.

There are several Internet cafés in town: *Claro, Codatel* (*Calle Duarte*), *Orange, Punto Internet, Independencia, Capt. Steve's Bar, JDMax*, and *Puerto Blanco Marina*. There is *Wi-Fi* in the anchorage for US$12 per week, US$30 per month, and plans for longer periods. Test the reception where you are anchored before signing up for a plan.

Independencia has mail service, and you can have your mail sent to you care of Anna Lopez's store, *Casa Lopez*, on the corner just up from *Verizon*. Make sure it is addressed to Ana Lopez, Casa Lopez, your boat name, #36 Calle Duarte, Luperón, Dominican Republic. Ana is the *UPS* representative here and her phone number is 809-836-1042.

If you need your laundry done, there are laundry services at *Puerto Blanco Marina* and also at *Captain Steve's Bar*. Lydia also does laundry and she is located just up the street from the *Immigration* office.

Now let's talk about the shopping in Luperón. To begin with, the produce trucks that regularly run to the marina have some of the best deals. Listen for their call on VHF ch. 68. If they don't have what you want tell them and they'll bring it next time. As you walk around town you'll notice fruit and vegetable stands (and small gift shops) everywhere and everyone is willing to deal. You'll have no problem finding mangoes, avocados, cucumbers, tomatoes, yucca, plantains, potatoes, carrots, onions and large, fresh pineapples that go for about 10 pesos. Broccoli and lettuce are hard to find in Luperón. In town, the *Supermercado* will take special orders and deliver to the marina or town dock for free, and... they speak English! *La Economica*, the local veggie market, has fresh produce delivered on Tuesdays and Fridays; selections depend on the season. Near the government dock in town is the *Able Mini Market* where you can pick up food, beer, rum, and soft drinks.

Cigar smokers will want to sample the DR's great cigars. Cigarette smokers will appreciate the fact that Dominican *Marlboros* are very inexpensive; I am told that they taste the same as U.S.-manufactured *Marlboros*. *Nacionals* are another great deal. Rum is cheap in the DR, and *Brugal* is one of the better rums to be found. For cheaper wines and spirits not available in Luperón, a trip to Puerto Plata is called for, especially a visit to the rum factory. Certain items such as bacon, cheese, broccoli, lettuce, powdered drinks (not milk), butter (not canned margarine), packaged meats, deli meats, cake mixes, canned cream, and yeast are difficult to find in Luperón. A once a month trip to Puerto Plata or Santiago will be all you need to stock up on these items if you are planning to stay a while.

We've all heard about the provisioning in Puerto Plata. You can also get anything you need in Santiago, though it is a bit farther away. The *ferreterías* and *supermercados* are literally brimming with all kinds of goodies for the cruiser with big eyes and pockets full of pesos. *La Sirena* (formerly *Pola*) and *Nacionale* are the two largest stores and are stocked like *Super Walmarts* back in the states. You can have lunch there while you do your shopping; both have nice cafeterias. *Nacionale* even has a *Baskin Robbins* for those who crave their 53 flavors. One final note: it's cheaper to buy local brands whenever possible, especially locally manufactured toilet paper that goes for about a third of the cost of U.S. toilet paper. *Ochoa* is a huge hardware store in Santiago that carries almost anything you need.

If you like horseback riding you must visit *Mario's Ranch*. Mario will pick you up and take you on half day and full day horseback riding trips or you can contact José to set up a trip to Mario's.

West of Luperón, reachable by a new road, is the town of La Isabela. Here, on his second voyage to the New World in 1493, Columbus founded the first European town in the Americas with the first court and where the first Mass was said in the New World. Today, only the layout of the town is visible, but there is a small hotel by the ruins.

The *Dirección Nacional de Parques* is undertaking the restoration and excavation of La Isabela. To get to La Isabela from Puerto Plata you can either take a tour from Puerto Plata, or take a *carro público* from *Villanueva y Kundhard* in Puerto Plata to the village of La Isabela. To get to La Isabela from Luperón, either make local arrangements with a taxi, get a rental car, or travel to Puerto Plata to hook up with a tour group. Between La Isabela and Monte Cristi are the lovely beaches of Punta Rucia and Estero Honda.

Ocean World Marina

Waypoints
Marina - ½ nm NE of entrance:
19° 50.05' N, 70° 43.65' W

Approximately seven miles east of Luperón, and two miles west of Puerto Plata, is the entrance for a top notch, world class marina, *Ocean World Marina*, located at Cofresi.

Navigational Information

A waypoint at 19° 50.05' N, 70° 43.65' W, will place you approximately ½ mile northeast of the entrance channel into *Ocean World Marina* as shown on Chart DR-2 (you will see the yellow sea buoy located at 19° 50.095' N, 70° 43.535' W). The entrance channel offers no problems in normal to moderate weather however, in heavy northerly swells the entrance may break all the way across making entrance dangerous if not impossible. Once inside you will be as snug as a bug in a rug, as long as you don't mind some surge when those northerly swells are running.

From the waypoint it's a straight shot down the channel keeping between the red and green buoys. Bear in mind that the marina frequently loses buoys during winter storms so the actual configuration you see may differ from what is on the chart in this guide. You can stray south of the green buoys and still be in nearly 20' of water all the way to the breakwater, but by no means stray outside the red buoy line which mark a shallow, breaking reef (*Palometa Reef* - you'll see it to starboard upon entry). Favor the green markers upon entry.

If you need assistance in entering the marina, give *Ocean World Marina* a hail on the VHF and the Dockmaster, Randall, will talk you in.

What You Will Find Ashore

The 35-acre *Ocean World Marina* complex is truly a class establishment with a very friendly and helpful staff. The marina has 104 slips and can accommodate vessels to 250' in length with drafts of just under 12'. If you need to clear in or clear out, *Customs* is located on-site and will come out to your boat to assist you in the process. The yard has a 35-ton lift.

In 2008, the government of the Dominican Republic passed a new law concerning the boarding of foreign vessels seeking clearance. At this time that law pertains only to vessels clearing in at marinas such as *Ocean World* or *Cap Cana*. The law states that only two officials may board your boat and they are not permitted to ask for "donations." It will be wonderful when the officials in Luperón will be required to abide by such regulations.

The Dominican Republic

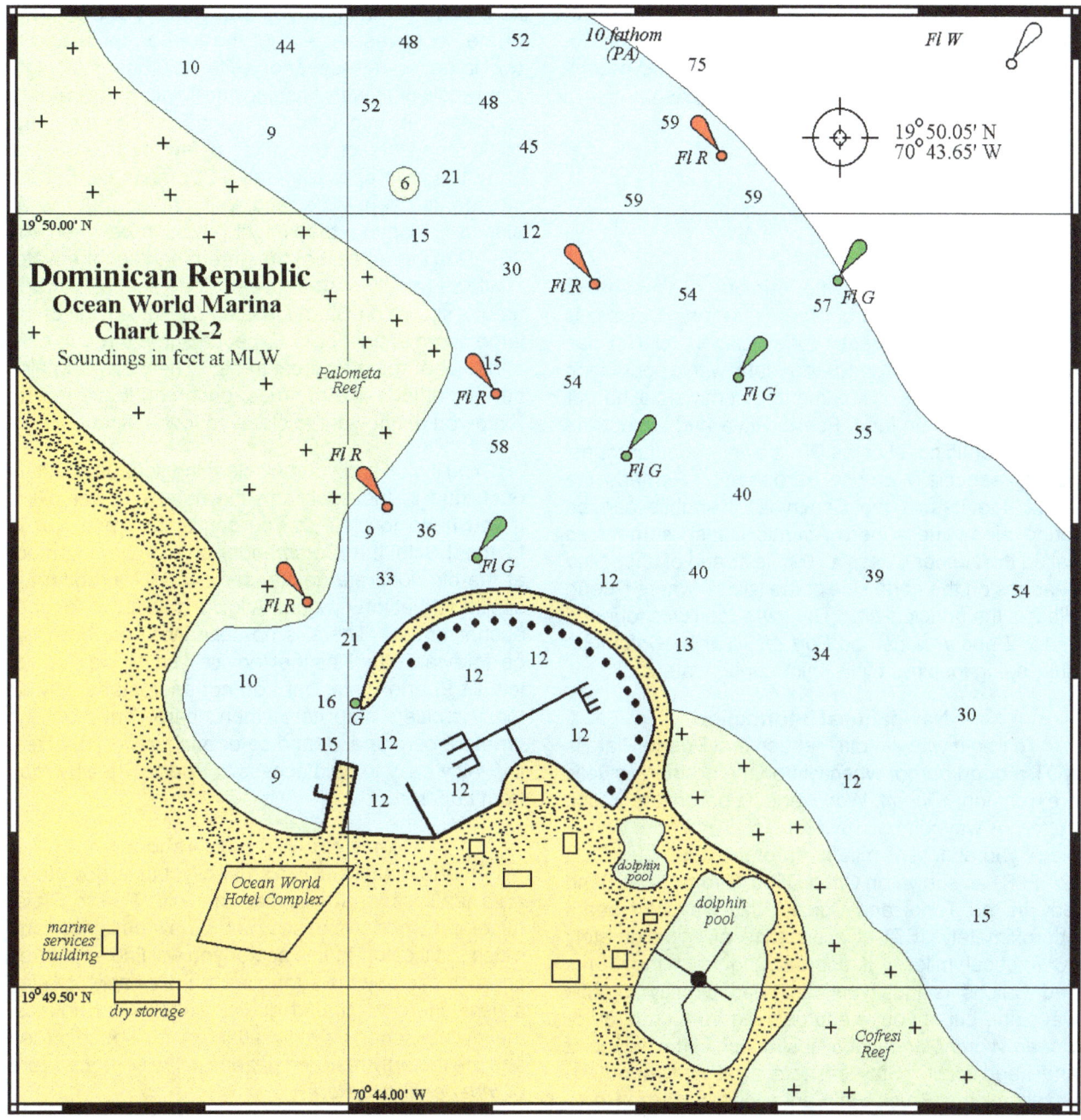

Also on-site you'll find a fuel dock, a pump-out station, quality electrical service (30-400 amp, single and three-phase), RO water at the dock, 24-hour security, personal concierge service, car rentals, mail and package delivery, weather and fax services in the marina office, the *Poseidon Restaurant*, the *Octopus Bar and Grill*, a pool with a swim-up bar, a laundry (dry-cleaning is available), Wi-Fi at your boat or internet access at the office, *Lighthouse Cocktail Lounge*, dockside telephone and cable TV, a casino, and by the time this guide is published there will also be a marine store (with fishing supplies) and a small grocery for you. There is a haul-out for small vessels and repair services as well. *Ocean World Marina* can be reached by phone at 809-970-3373, or you can contact them through their website at www.oceanworldmarina.com.

While staying at the marina you will receive complimentary admission to the *Ocean World Adventure Park* (http://www.oceanworld.net/) located next door. The park offers intimate dolphin, sea lion, and shark interaction programs; the dolphin habitat is the largest in the world with 12 million gallons of seawater in the main pool. There are several nearby restaurants to pique your culinary interests.

Puerto Plata

Waypoints
Puerto Plata - ¾ nm N of sea buoy:
19° 49.10' N, 70° 41.55' W

Puerto Plata, once the primary destination of cruisers southbound from the Turks and Caicos, is visited far less frequently today since Luperón has become a port of entry. Puerto Plata, with a population of about 60,000, is now primarily a commercial harbor and it shows. On land, Puerto Plata and almost the entire Atlantic coast of the DR is a very popular tourist haven, especially among Europeans. Perhaps the finest beaches in the Dominican Republic can be found along the superb Atlantic Coast, sometimes called the *Amber Coast*, a 75-mile strand of unspoiled beaches on the north side of the island, where Puerto Plata is the principal city. The town itself was founded in 1502 and was named *Port of Silver* by Columbus after being inspired by its shimmering waters.

Navigational Information
To begin with, let me mention that Puerto Plata is NOT a good harbor when wintertime northerly swells are running; *Ocean World* and Luperón are much better. A waypoint at 19° 49.10' N, 70° 41.55' W, will place you almost ½ mile north of the outer buoy (LR "2," Fl R) as shown on Chart DR-3. From Great Sand Cay in the Turks and Caicos, this waypoint bears approximately 167° at a distance of approximately 86 nautical miles. If approaching from the Turks and Caicos Islands you can head directly for this waypoint, but, if you're approaching from Luperón or *Ocean World Marina*, don't just punch in the waypoint and head for it. Stay offshore a bit and round the small rock that Bruce Van Sant shows as Owen Rock, keeping it well to starboard. You can pass between Owen Rock and the mainland of the DR, although there are several shallow areas of less than one fathom in depth at MLW. Also, there are numerous shallow heads and rocks that are awash at high water and lay almost a quarter mile offshore in places near the harbor entrance.

A great landmark is Mt. Torres, Loma Isabel de Torres, with its huge statue of Christ at its 2600' summit. From the waypoint, head south until you can enter between the outer buoys, red-right-returning here. In the daytime you can make out the range at the southwestern end of the harbor consisting of two large orange-capped white columns. At night this range is lit with flashing red lights that are hard to make out unless you are lined up correctly, just off to one side or the other a few degrees. The entry range is approximately 225° magnetic but the channel is deep, wide, and well-marked; but like all aids to navigation, they might not be there when you are. Don't stray east of the green markers, the water shallows rapidly in their area. The yacht anchorage area is shown on Chart DR-2 and lies just west of the large commercial dock. Expect a surge through here and a lot of roll from local traffic. The water can also be very sludge-like at times; once you leave Puerto Plata you might want to clean your waterline.

You'll also find yourself cleaning your decks quite often due to the soot from the nearby power plant. If you need to clear in you can anchor and row in to meet with the *Commandante* or you med-moor at the old concrete dock; use caution, the bottom is similar to that in Luperón. Allow a day or two for your anchor to set. There is no security at the dock, so be forewarned. I cannot advise you to visit or not to visit Puerto Plata, but I do not understand why so many cruisers stop here when nearby Luperón is a far more comfortable and safer anchorage. Besides, it is fairly easy to gain access to Puerto Plata by road from Luperón.

What You Will Find Ashore
Puerto Plata itself is a small city, but its downtown area features what is called the "old" Puerto Plata, full of old wooden houses, some new buildings, and much local color. In this sector you will find structures characterized by the strong influence of late Victorian styles. Here you'll find quaint gingerbread houses, their white fences simply aflame with bougainvillea and the recently restored gazebo in the central square of *Independence Park*.

Before we take a mini-tour of what you can expect to find in Puerto Plata, remember that if you are led into a shop by a local boy, tour guide or taxi driver, you will more than likely be paying a hidden commission on the price of your purchase, even after you have bargained the merchant down to his rock bottom price. If you want an approved guide, call the *Association of Official Tour Guides* at 586-2866. There is also a tourist train, the *Amber Tour Train* (not on rails!) that runs from *Playa Dorada Plaza* to *Fort San Felipe*, the *Amber Museum* (http://

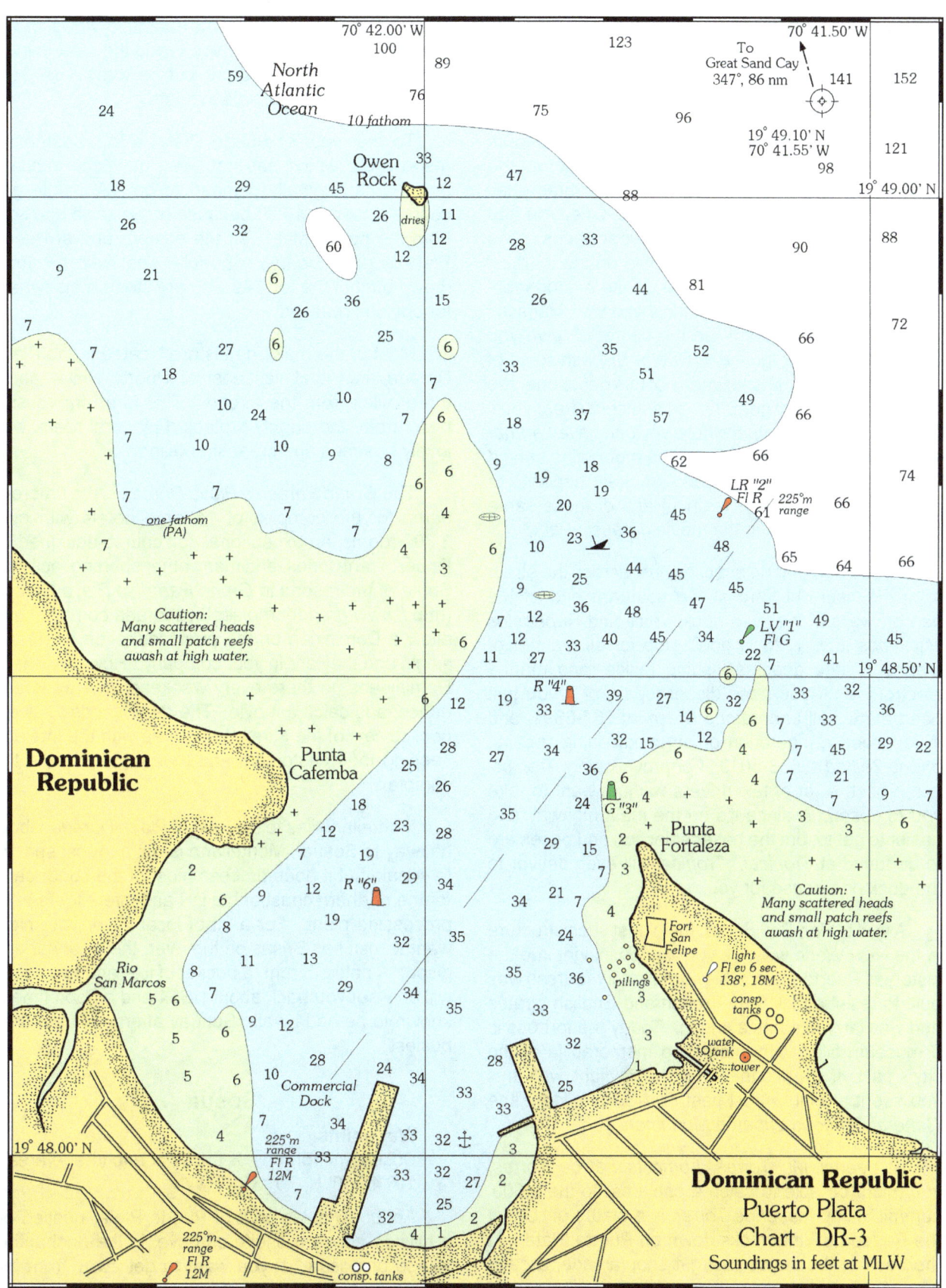

www.ambermuseum.com/), the *Rum Factory*, *Parque Central*, and several gift shops three times daily. The 2½ hour trip costs approximately US$11.50 and you can pick up tickets at the *Discount Plaza*.

By all means visit the *Rum Factory*. On their tours they used to offer all the rum you could drink (not the same today), and they used to have only three rules for those who partook of these tours. One, you had to wear a shirt. Two, you had to wear shoes. And three, you could not fall asleep while on the tour! If it's a hot day and ice cream sounds like a good idea, make your way to *Parque Central* and visit *Mariscos* for real Italian ice cream! In the center of town you can find the *Amber Museum* (*Duarte St.*) with some of the most remarkable specimens of this gemstone, the designated national gem. On an adjacent street you'll find the *House of Larimar* where you can have *Larimar* jewelry custom made on-site. The mountains behind Puerto Plata contain the world's richest deposits of amber, a fossilized tree resin. Parts of these same mountains appeared in the movie *Jurassic Park*.

If you need marine supplies, just across the street from the haul out yard at the southern end of the harbor, west of the town dock, you'll find *Repuestos Maritimos*, 586-4728, a good stop for all manner of marine related goodies, fishing tackle, and marine electronics. If you need diesel repair, or if you just need parts, call *Laboratorio Diesel* at 261-6394, and if you need refrigeration or air-conditioning repairs, phone *Zelltec* at 533-5019. For provisioning, *Tropical* is the best. A lot of taxi drivers will just want to take you to *José Luis* since it's on the main highway and easier to get to, but the better selection and prices are to be found at *Tropical*. *Tropical* will even deliver to the dock or a house for you.

A visit to *Fort San Felipe*, the oldest such structure in the New World will give you a good insight into the history of Puerto Plata. This 16th century fortress was built to resist attack from French and English pirates and was later used as a prison. Today the fortress is a museum filled with interesting memorabilia of the city's past. If you like the fort in the daylight, wait until you see it at night. Just past *Fort San Felipe* is the *General Gregorio Luperón Monument*.

At nearby *Mt. Torres, Loma Isabel de Torres*, you might be able to catch a cable car to the 2,600' summit. Atop *Isabel de Torres* is a statue of "Christ the Redeemer" that looks down on Puerto Plata. At the base of the statue is a gift shop/arcade, a café, botanical gardens, and some fantastic views of the coastline. You can even try to tackle the mountain by horseback, bicycle, and car but be forewarned: the road is next to impassable in spots.

To the west of Puerto Plata is the Costambar resort area, which has not been quite the success that it was originally planned to be. A 9-hole golf course closed in 1997, because of the noise and soot from the power plant. At the eastern end of Puerto Plata is *Long Beach*, a popular spot with the local crowd but not the tourists who are steered elsewhere for obvious reasons.

Most of the major hotels are located in the Playa Dorada area that lies east of Puerto Plata, about three miles from the airport. This is an impressive beachfront, thoroughly protected by coral reefs, with lovely beaches and great snorkeling.

The *Grand Paradise Playa Dorada* is the umbrella name for the complex of 14 large hotels with over 3,300 rooms, an exceptional golf course designed by Robert Trent Jones, and many other sporting facilities. Some of the resorts in *Grand Paradise Playa Dorada* (http://www.grandparadiseplayadorada.com/) will not allow a Dominican on the premises, even if you are single and they are in your company. However, many Dominicans go there every weekend anyway to eat, dance, and catch a movie. The resort tends to give a poor review of the surrounding area with the intent of keeping their customers and their money inside the complex.

Montellano lies to the east of *Playa Dorada*, about halfway to Sosúa. Montellano is not a tourist spot so to speak, but it does process most of the sugar cane for the northern coast of the DR and offers tours of its processing plant. For a bit of local flavor you might want to visit Las Brisas on the river, the local bar and disco. A bottle of rum, a bucket of ice, and two sodas will only set you back about US$4 and a good time is known to be had by all. Sunday afternoons are their busiest.

Sosúa

Waypoints
Sosúa anchorage - ¼ nm W of anchorage area
19° 45.60' N, 70° 31.40' W

About 16 miles east of Puerto Plata, nestled on a hillside above a sheltered cove, is the enchanting village of Sosúa. If you want to get away from the fast paced and touristy Playa Dorada, Sosúa is the place for you.

Some 600 German Jewish refugees founded Sosúa after World War II (then dictator Rafael Trujillo, hoping to gain favor with the U.S., let them in). the refugees immediately started up sausage production and a dairy. Today the town, which has a lively nightlife and an arts community, has become a center for immigrants from North America and Europe. During the Holocaust many European Jews sought refuge as a respite from the atrocities. As history's most infamous massacre was being perpetrated, a small Caribbean nation was to provide a respite from the atrocities. While the world turned its back and remained immersed in apathy, the Dominican Republic bestowed mercy on the oppressed by offering asylum. They settled on tiny Sosúa and the colony became official on January 30, 1940, when the Dominican government and a private philanthropic organization, the *Joint Distribution Committee of New York*, signed the *DORSA (Dominican Republic Settlement Association)* agreement and some 600 settlers moved in.

The atmosphere of warm hospitality found in this beautiful yet unfamiliar land was conducive to the flourishing of Jewish-owned businesses. So cordial were the locals that, over the years, the Jews assimilated their culture and co-mingled with them to create genuinely Dominican families where the Jewish traditions were still preserved and respected. What is most remarkable is the fact that after five decades, and despite the changes of government, the passing of generations and the advent of tourism, the spirit of the decree whereby the Jewish were given political asylum has remained untouched. Today, the few remaining Jews enjoy the same consideration, respect and freedom of religion as in the first days of the colony.

Navigational Information
As shown on Chart DR-4, a waypoint at 19° 45.60' N, 70° 31.40' W, will place you approximately ¼ nm W of the anchorage area outside the reef. Do not venture too close to shore as reef and rocks abound and the water shallows quickly.

The area is a national park and anchoring is not permitted. Local officials will approach your boat upon arrival and direct you to pick up a mooring.

What You Will Find Ashore
Sosúa is actually three villages straddling the bay: Los Charamicos to the south and El Batey to the north. They are not far apart and a walk through and between the two doesn't take long. Los Charamicos, where years ago the plantation workers lived, has a typical Dominican village atmosphere complete with lively restaurants and bars, street vendors, loud music, and screeching chickens.

El Batey, the part of town where the plantation owners lived, is the hub of tourist activity in Sosúa. Here you'll find upscale restaurants, bars, boutiques, and luxurious resort hotels (over 2,000 hotel rooms) and villas along with a large ex-pat community. Sosúa is popular with tourists from both North America and Europe because of its lovely beaches and dive sites. You can even take a taxi from Puerto Plata, it's only 4 miles for the airport in Puerto Plata.

If you need to exchange some money in Sosúa, your best bet is an ATM or you can visit *Western Union* (in El Batey), *Playero*, or *Caribe Express*, and *Banco Santo Cruz*.

If you need internet access, several hotels and restaurants (*Britannia, Alberto`s, Bailey`s, Cubanos* (http://sosuacigars.com/index.html), *Bar Central, Cafe Tropical* and many others) can accommodate you.

For good dining try *Bailey's*, the *Brittannia Pub and Grill* (a favorite of ex-pats, http://www.britanniapubsosua.com/), *Germania Sosúa* (for German fare, http://www.germania-sosua.com/), or the *Waterfront Restaurant* for great ocean views. *Le Papillon* (http://www.lepapillon-puertoplata.com/) offers tons of rustic and nautical ambiance as well as several aquariums. There are numerous fine restaurants in El Batey and finding the one that interests you the most is part of the fun of exploring the area.

A unique spot to visit is *Castillo Mundo King*, atop a hill with a view that is worth all the effort to get there. The castillo itself is filled with Dominican and Haitian art as well as UFO themes, an eclectic collection gathered by artist in residence Rolf Schulz (http://castillodelmundo.webs.com/).

Just east of Sosúa is Cabarete, one of the world's top windsurfing/kitesurfing spots. In the mid-1980's Cabarete was only an empty beach and a handful of old wooden houses. Then it was discovered to be the

Castillo Mundo King, Sosúa

Sosúa

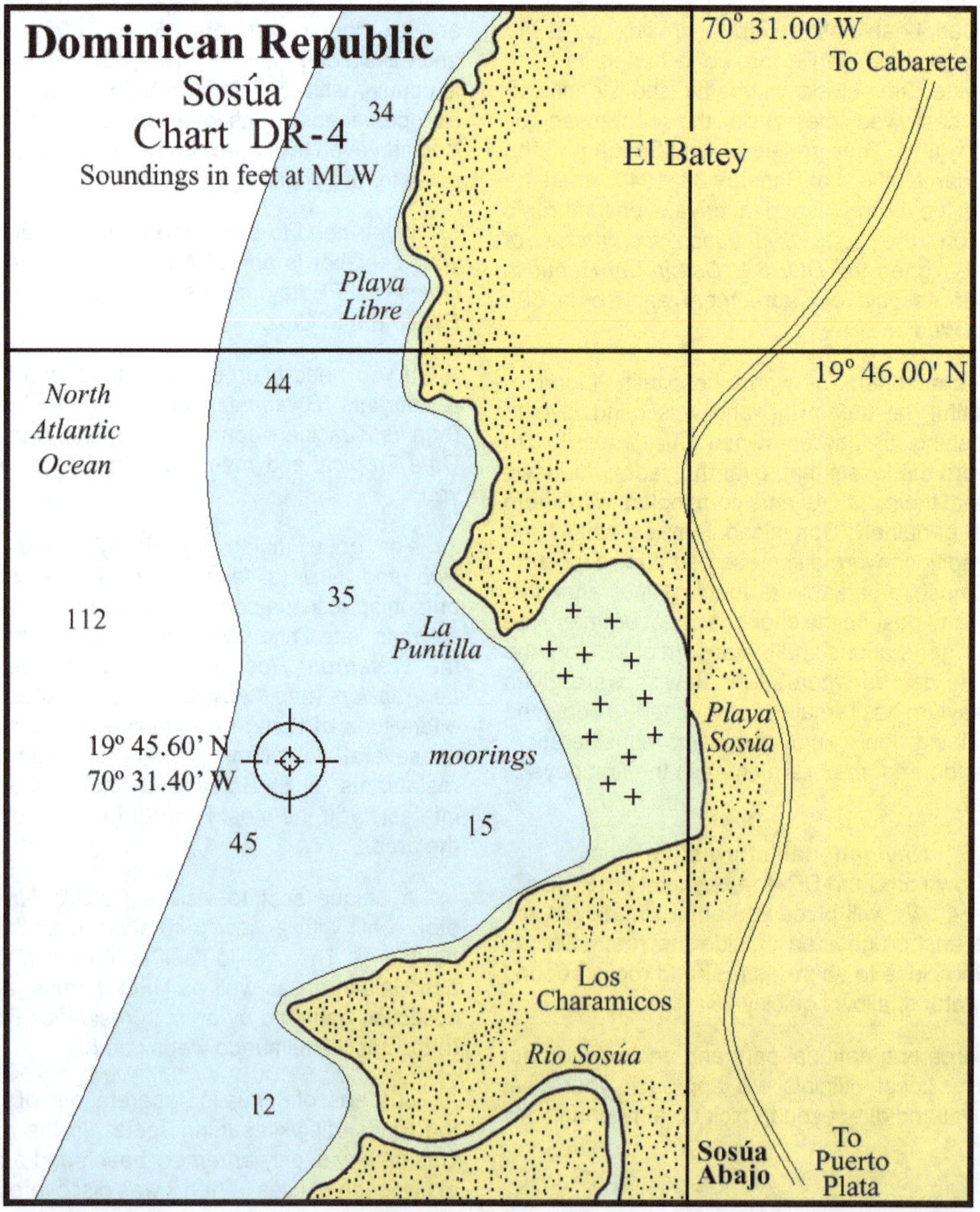

best windsurfing location in the Caribbean, and one of the best in the world. Today Cabarete hosts the annual *Windsurfing World Cup*.

For music lovers, Cabarete also hosts the *Jazz-Blues Merengue Festival*. On its mile-long main street, you will find a wide selection of windsurfing centers, hotels, restaurants, discos, and gift shops. Further east you'll find even more exotic, secluded beaches such as La Preciosa and Diamante.

Rio San Juan

Waypoints
Rio San Juan - ¼ nm W of anchorage area
19° 38.60' N, 70° 05.50' W

Rio San Juan is a good spot to overnight as you move east or west along the northern shore of the Dominican Republic. Never attempt to anchor here with winds or seas with any northerly component to them.

Navigational Information
As shown on Chart DR-5, a waypoint at 19° 38.60' N, 70° 50.50' W, will place you approximately ¼ nm W of anchorage area off the town amidst all the local fishing boats. From the way point, work your way through the shoals (never try this at night) until you can turn south to anchor. Look for a sandy spot to drop your hook. South of here are numerous sandbars that are to be avoided.

Another anchorage is to the north and does not involve threading the needle through shoals; this spot is much better if you plan to leave at night. The bottom here is hard sand and rock.

What You Will Find Ashore
Rio San Juan has numerous hotels, restaurants, and small grocery stores. *Wi-Fi* is available at most hotels; many hotels have computers you can use.

There is no shortage of quality eateries, my favorite is *Arena Y Sol*, right on the beach, featuring fresh seafood from the nearby market. *Cheo's Café* features a local flavor to their cuisine and a good bet is their huge platter of grilled seafood for two. The *Café de Paris* features international cuisine, primarily French, and fresh seafood. For Spanish flavored dining visit *Corral del Pollo* and after dinner sidle up

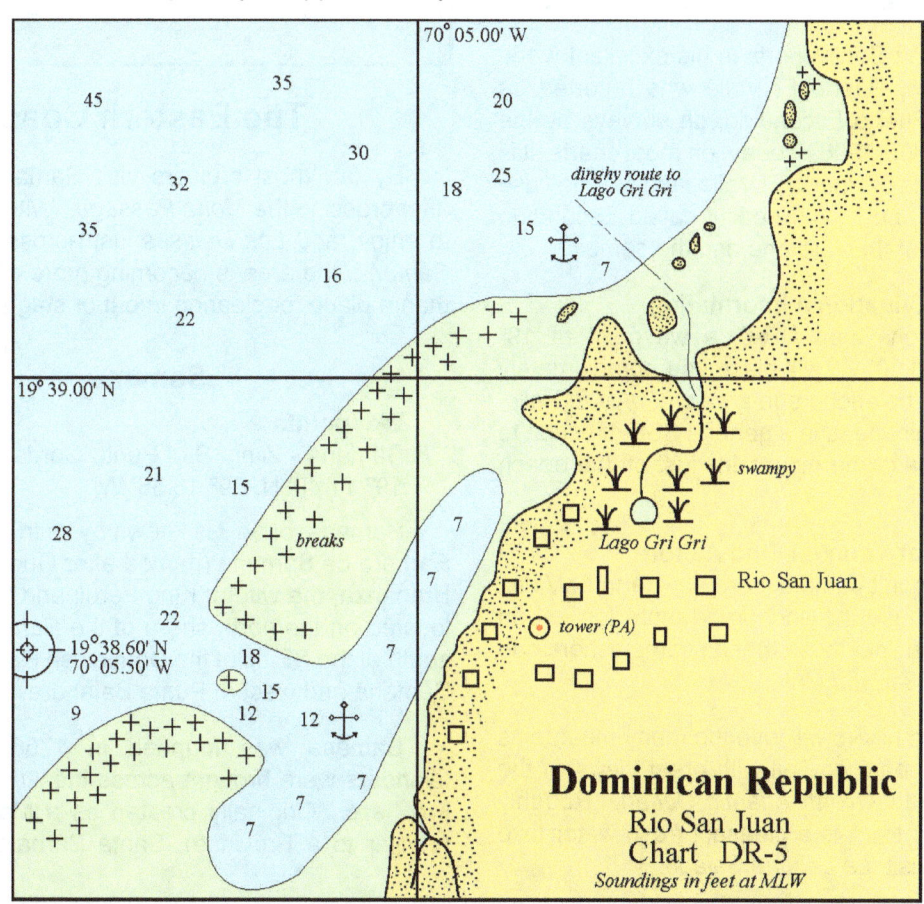

to their coffee and cigar bar. The *Villa Belia Hotel* has an excellent restaurant and nearby *La Casona* features deep-fried pizza empanadas (http://www.villabelia.com/).

Located atop beautiful cliffs along the edge of the sea near Rio San Juan, the par 72 *Playa Grande Golf Course* (http://www.playagrande.com) is the last course designed by the legendary Robert Trent Jones Sr.

Puerto El Valle

(Escondido)

Waypoints
Puerto El Valle - 1¾ nm NNW of anchorage
19° 19.00' N, 69° 20.50' W

Moving east along the northern coast of the Dominican Republic, a good stop before rounding Cabo Samaná to head to Puerto Rico or to visit Santa Bárbara de Samaná, is the anchorage at Puerto El Valle. This anchorage is best in settled weather as some swell works its way into the bay making an overnight stay uncomfortable. Never try to anchor here if seas from any northerly direction are forecast.

As Bruce Van Sant reports in his excellent work, *Passages South*, Puerto El Valle was reported as Escondido, or Puerto Escondido, on surveys by the *USS Eagle* in 1905-1906. Today, on most charts, it is shown as El Valle or Puerto El Valle, and we shall use that name here, but if you hear it called Escondido you will know that they are one and the same.

Navigational Information
As shown on Chart DR-6, a waypoint at 19° 19.00' N, 69° 20.50' W, will place you approximately 1¾ nm NNW of the anchorage area off *Playa El Valle*. From the waypoint head in a general SSE direction to anchor in the lee of the mountains just off the beach (*Playa el Valle*).

What You Will Find Ashore
Most folks don't come ashore at Puerto El Valle, cruisers tend to use the anchorage more for just an overnight layover, but those that do come ashore can enjoy *Claritzas Bar and Grill*.

Climbers and hikers will love the many mountains that are waiting on them, all with great views of the anchorage and the *North Atlantic Ocean*. Roughly two miles NE of town is a pleasant fresh-water lake that is worth a visit, *La Laguna Salada*.

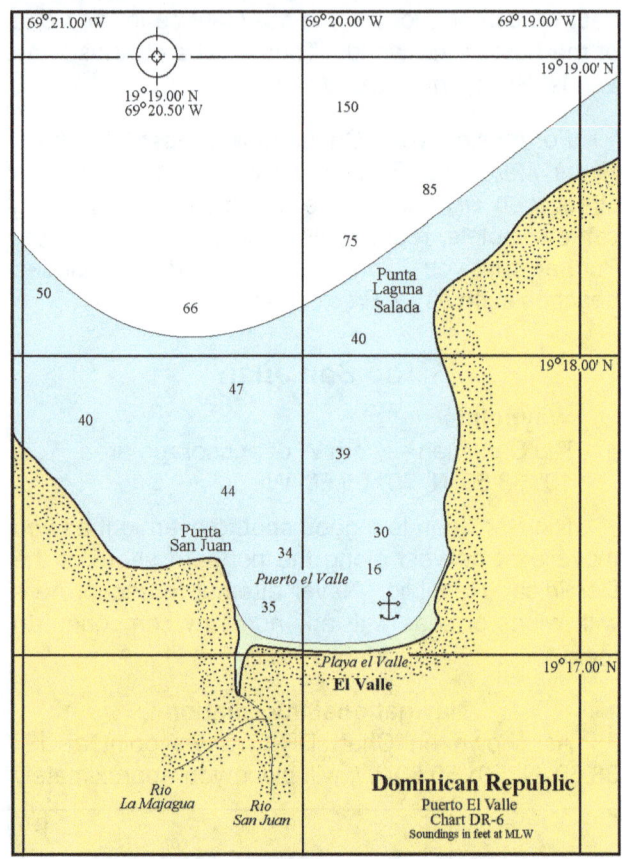

The Eastern Coast

By far, most cruisers visit Samaná before and after crossing the *Mona Passage*. With a new marina to enjoy, and *Los Haitises* just across the *Bahía de Samaná*, the area is becoming more of a destination than a place for clearing in/out or staging a crossing.

Samaná

Waypoints
Samaná - ¼ nm S of Punta Gorda
19° 11.40' N, 69° 18.85' W

Samaná, or as it is known by its true name, Santa Bárbara de Samaná (named after Queen Bárbara de Braganza, the wife of King Ferdinand VI of Spain), is located on the north shore of the *Bahía de Samaná*, south of the NE tip of the Dominican Republic at Cabo Samaná and west of Punta Balandra.

Samaná was founded in 1756 and Canary Islanders were brought across the *Atlantic Ocean* to live here. Originally created as a Maritime District (similar to a Province), Santa Bárbara de Samaná officially became a municipality and the capital of Samaná Province in 1865.

Today the culture of the people of Samaná draws much from aspects of their own ancestor's slavery as well as the imported culture of freed slaves that were brought from the U.S. during the Haitian occupation.

Samaná is served with daily bus service from Santo Domingo and Puerto Plata by two major bus lines, *Caribe Tours* (http://www.caribetours.com.do/) and *Metro*, with several smaller bus lines offering service as well.

I cannot stress enough the bad reputation that Samaná has received over the last few years. It is regarded as a good spot to have your dinghy stolen, so take the proper precautions when anchored there. If you are uncomfortable anchoring in Samaná, then head a mile or so west and stay at *Puerto Bahía Marina* (see next section).

Navigational Information

As shown on Chart DR-7, a waypoint at 19° 11.40' N, 69° 18.85' W, will place you approximately ¼ nm S of Punta Gorda in the *Bahía de Samaná*. From the waypoint, head generally NW, working your way between the mainland to the north (to starboard side as you approach) and the string of islands (Cayo Paloma and Cayo Vigia) to port (avoiding the shoals and rocks close in). You can anchor off the town or off the northern shore of Cayo Vigia. The holding is good in the main anchorage, there is little current, and moorings abound (but there is still room to anchor). It is possible to anchor in *Bahía Escondida* but it is not recommended in prevailing winds as it affords little protection

When you clear in you will likely be asked to pay US$.70 per foot anchoring fee by the Department of Ports. This is a valid charge and is actually a dock usage fee that some folks decline to pay.

What You Will Find Ashore

There are two main government docks in town where you can tie up your dinghy (out of the way of the commercial operators please) but don't tile up to the smaller cruise ship tender dock to the east.

If you need Internet access, most of the hotels and many restaurants offer free *Wi-Fi*, and there are a few small Internet *cafés* in town. If you have a good *Wi-Fi* antenna you should be able to pick up *Wi-Fi* in the anchorage. Also in town is a hardware store, an ice house, and the only watch repair service in this part of the Dominican Republic.

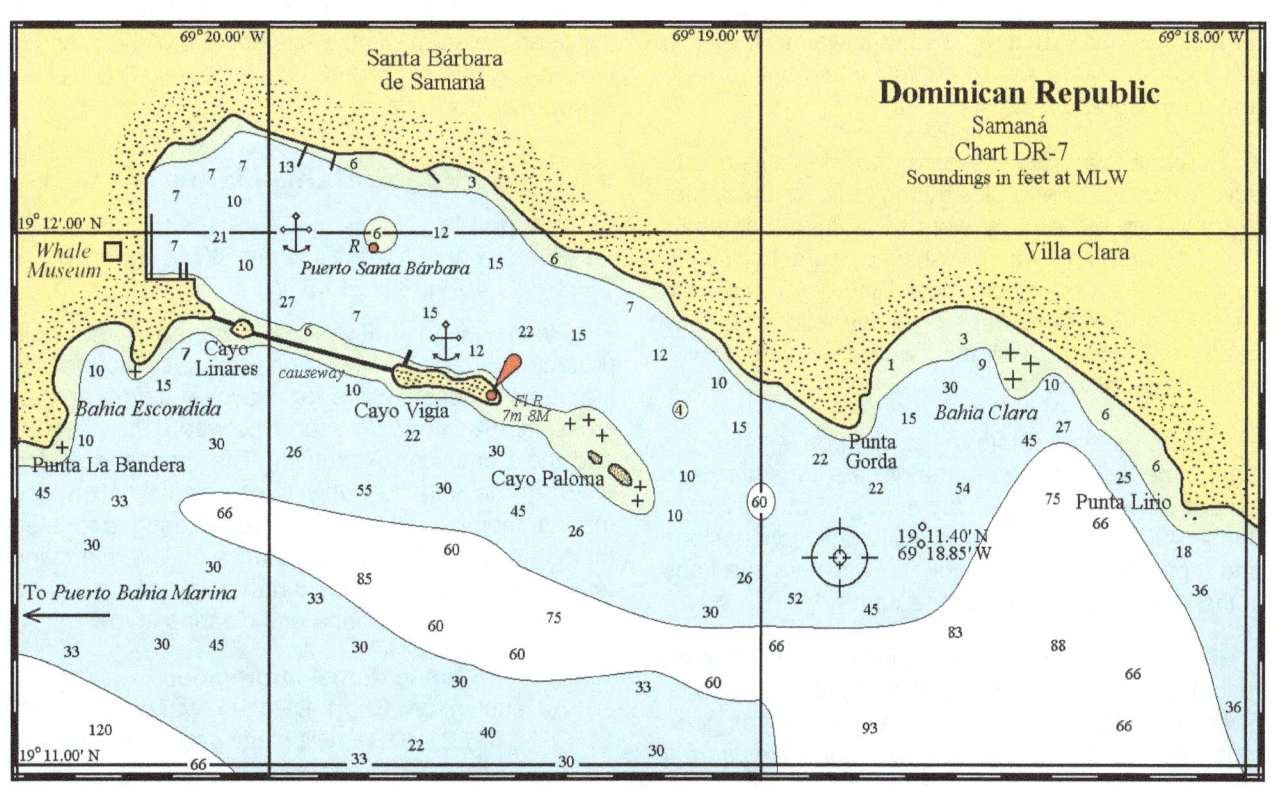

If you need groceries, the large and modern *Mimasa* supermarket is the place to go. It is located across the street from the *Scotia Bank* and is air-conditioned! Samaná also has a great farmer's market, *mercado*, in the center of town by the traffic light on the main road. This is the place for fresh produce, while at the rear of the market's central building you can pick up fresh seafood. You'll also find small butcher shops and all sorts of stalls selling everything from gifts to saddles.

If you find yourself in need of a pharmacy, visit *Pharmacy Giselle*, or the new pharmacy, *Carol Pharmacia* (http://www.farmaciacarol.com/), they deliver to *Puerto Bahía Marina*.

There are four main banks in town, *Scotia Bank*, *Banco Popular*, *Banco BHD*, and *Banco de Reserva*, and all are open Monday through Friday from 0900-1700, and on Saturdays from 0900-1200. All of the banks have ATMs that are open 24 hours (one is located just across the street from the government dock.

The most iconic sites in Samaná are *Los Puentes*, the famous *Bridges to Nowhere* that lead from the mainland to Cayo Vigia. The bridges, constructed in the 1960s, were intended to bring visitors to a casino complex that never materialized. In the 1980s, a restaurant opened for a few years but today little remains of that structure. Today however, the area is a boon for hikers and bikers with park benches and rest areas spread along its length.

Samaná is a popular spot for tourist excursions to observe humpback whales during their annual winter migration to the nearby waters. *Whale Samaná's* Kim Beddall runs whale watching tours from mid-January until late March aboard the *Pura Mia* from the dock in Samaná. For more information call Judy at 809-538-2494 or visit their website at http://www.whalesamana.com/.

On the western shore of the bay you will find the *Centro de la Naturaleza*, the *Whale Museum and Nature Center* (open Monday through Saturday from 0900-1400). Also nearby are zip line concessions and a group that will take you to swim with sea lions in the bay (http://samanazipline.com/).

If you are interested in dining in town, the following restaurants offer free *Wi-Fi* to their patrons. *Le Royal Snack* has a great view of the water as well as good food and a complete bar! *Chino Hotel & Restaurant* has been serving Chinese food in Samaná for over 30 years with over 200 menu selections. *Taberna Mediterranea* offers Spanish cuisine on the Malecón with an outdoor patio and great view of the bay. The *Restaurant La Antorcha* (http://www.antorcharestaurant.com/) boasts the largest outdoor terrace in town. *Cafesito* serves breakfast and lunch and their breakfasts are the most economical in town.

After dinner you might wish to get some ice cream and the *Bon Ice Cream Parlor & Terrace* is hoping to serve you right on the *Malecón*. *Bon Ice Cream* also has a full service bar. Nearby is *Splash*, another ice cream parlor with an outdoor terrace.

If you are ready to explore the area around town, take the *El Portillo* road heading east from Samaná and you will soon come to the town of El Limon, home to the *El Limon Waterfall (Cascada Limon)*, about 20 miles from Samaná. The waterfall sits about 900' above sea level and drops over 120' into the crystal clear waters of a swimmable pool.

For those of you who are itching to discover the waters around Samaná, a good place to start is Cayo Levantado, approximately four miles SE of Samaná, where you can anchor for the day (no overnight anchoring is permitted here), dine ashore, enjoy the beach, and shop for local crafts. The island is popular with cruise ships so don't be surprised to see one in the nearby waters. At the eastern end of the island is the *Gran Bahía Hotel* and their restaurant is not open to cruisers, guests only.

Puerto Bahía Marina

Waypoints
Puerto Bahía Marina - ¼ nm SW of entrance
19° 11.40' N, 69° 21.40' W

Lying just to the west of Samaná is the well-protected *Puerto Bahía Marina*, a full service facility that is an excellent place for a layover before or after crossing the *Mona Passage* between Puerto Rico and the Dominican Republic. The marina is a *Port of Entry*, be sure to notify the marina by VHF (the marina monitors ch. 16) before entering and alert them that you will require clearance. If I were arriving and needed to clear, I would rather do it at the marina than anchoring in Samaná and clearing in town.

Navigational Information
As shown on Chart DR-8, a waypoint at 19° 11.40' N, 69° 21.40' W, will place you approximately

The Dominican Republic

¼ nm SW of the marked entrance channel. From this waypoint head between the markers and the jetties and into the marina basin. You'll notice some current upon entering the marina, and once inside there is a bit of surge (and a 3' tidal rise and fall) so secure your vessel accordingly.

What You Will Find Ashore

Puerto Bahía Marina offers space for 107 vessels and can accommodate vessels up to 150' LOA with drafts to 10', and can supply both diesel and gasoline. The marina and resort also offers *Wi-Fi*, full electric (30, 50, 100 amp, and 3-phase, 60 cycle AC), potable water, showers and restrooms, daily weather info, marine supplies, groceries, garbage pickup, a pool, a gym, a spa and beauty salon, a children's game room, a water taxi service, free taxi rides into town, a personal concierge service, taxi and car rentals, 24-hour security, and a great gathering place for fine dining, the *Cafe del Mar*. The marina is happy to assist guests with *Customs* and *Immigration* clearance.

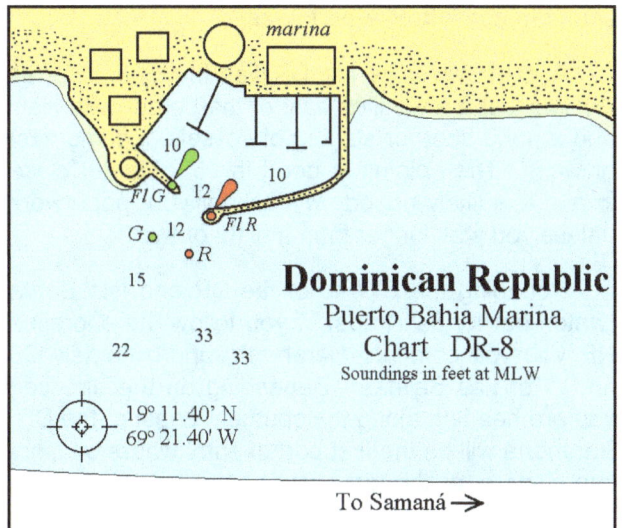

Mangrove creek, *Los Haitises*

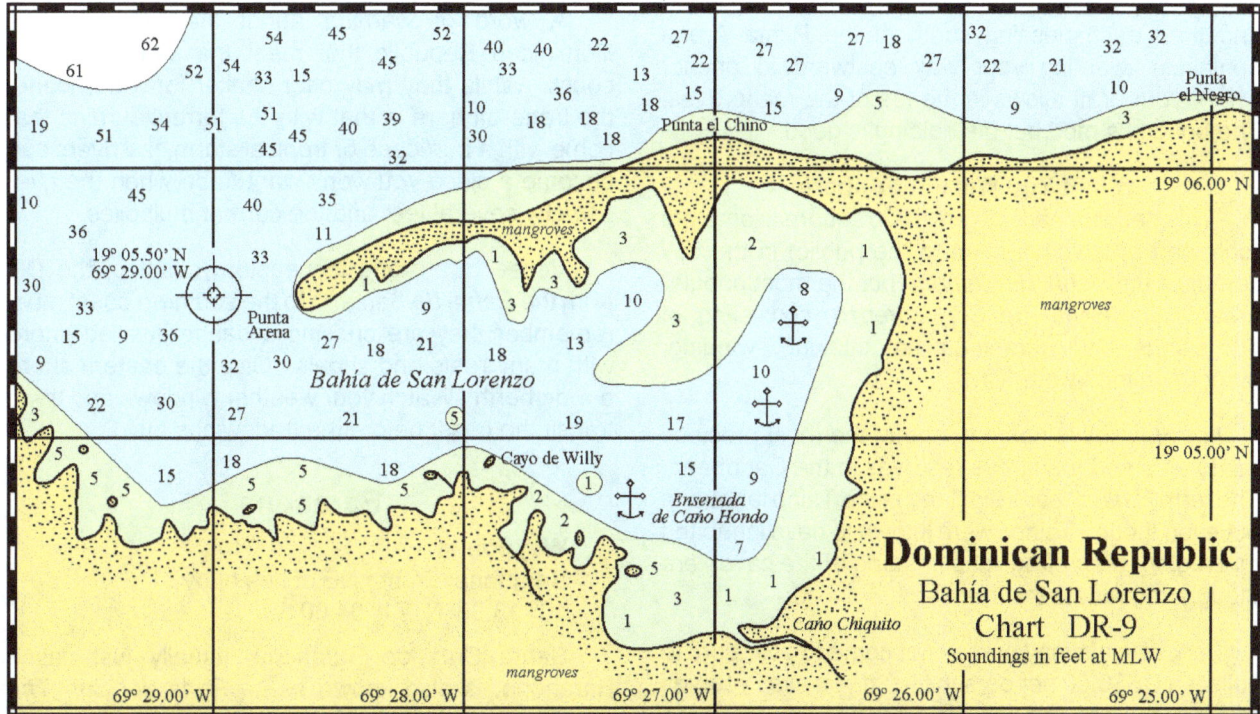

If you need local laborers, ask the dockmaster to set you up with Nelson or Pedro. For more information you can visit the marina's website at www.PuertoBahiaSamaná.com, or telephone the marina at 809-503-6363.

Between the mountains and the marina sits the *Bannister Hotel* (http://www.thebannisterhotel.com/) featuring fine suites and equally impressive service for their patrons. The hotel is named after a British captain, Jack Bannister, who fought on nearby Cayo Levantado. The hotel offers free Wi-Fi and iPod docking stations in each room.

Bahía de San Lorenzo

Waypoints
Bahía de San Lorenzo - ¼ nm W of Punta Arena
19° 05.50' N, 69° 29.00' W

The most exciting locale awaiting your exploration is along the southern shore of *Bahía de Samaná*, approximately 12 miles SW of Samaná and *Puerto Bahía Marina*, the *Bahía de San Lorenzo*, the highlight of *Parque Nacional de los Haitises*, or simply, *Los Haitises*. You can take your own boat to the park or join a tour leaving from the dock in Samaná.

Navigational Information
As shown on Chart DR-9, a waypoint at 19° 05.50' N, 69° 29.00' W, will place you approximately ¼ nm W of Punta Arena. From the waypoint, head south and then east, passing south of the Punta Arena peninsula, working your way eastward to anchor where your draft allows in the lee of the mangroves. The bottom is mud but the holding is good.

What You Will Find Ashore
This national park covers 1600 square kilometers (only part of which is open to the public) in the SW corner of the *Bahía de Samaná* but the most popular area is the *Bahía de San Lorenzo*, consisting of 58 islands and numerous breathtaking, winding, mangrove-lined waterways.

Los Haitises is home to one of the most precious rainforests and mangrove reserves in the Caribbean. The term *Haitis* means highland in the Taino language but even though Tainos were known to have inhabited this region, the petroglyphs in some of the caves are thought to predate the Tainos.

Park officials may or may not come to your boat to collect a US$3.00 per person fee. If you avail yourself of the park dock, the officials there will collect the fee from you. The mangrove creeks and rivers will soon reveal their treasures to you as you take the time to explore; up these creeks you will find everything from small restaurants and bars to pre-Columbian cave art.

The Southern Coast

Fewer cruisers visit the southern coast of the Dominican Republic, but that is changing as more and more skippers are learning of the comfortable marinas located here, all within easy traveling distance to Santo Domingo and other points of interest. Like our exploration of the north coast, we will discuss the southern coast from west to east.

At the SW tip of the DR lies the *Bahía de las Aguilas* just a few miles east of the border with Haiti and a good spot for staging of vessels heading east or west. The holding is good in 15' of water close in and it is likely nobody will ask for your paperwork unless you stay longer than a night or two.

Rounding the SW tip of the DR and Isla Beata (watch out for fish traps), if you follow the shoreline NE you will come to Barahona, approximately 30 nm W of Las Salinas. Depending on the direction you are heading along the southern coast of the DR, Barahona will be the first port of entry where cruisers can clear in, or the last port of entry for you to clear out.

A word of warning about the rivers of the Dominican Republic that meet the sea along this coast. While they may offer shelter for a hurricane, the trade-off here is that with the torrential rains that come with a hurricane or tropical storm, the rivers can become a place you won't want to be when the river rises by several feet and the current multiplies.

Vessels transiting the eastern coast of the DR from the *Bahía de Samaná* to the southern coast must remember they are cruising a dangerous lee shore with many reefs and shoals. Give the eastern shore a wide berth. Watch your weather windows and try to transit the coast before the tradewinds build.

Barahona

Waypoints
Barahona - ¼ nm NE of sea buoy
18° 13.30' N, 71° 04.00' W

Santa Cruz de Barahona, usually just called Barahona, is also known as *La Perla del Sur*, The

The Dominican Republic

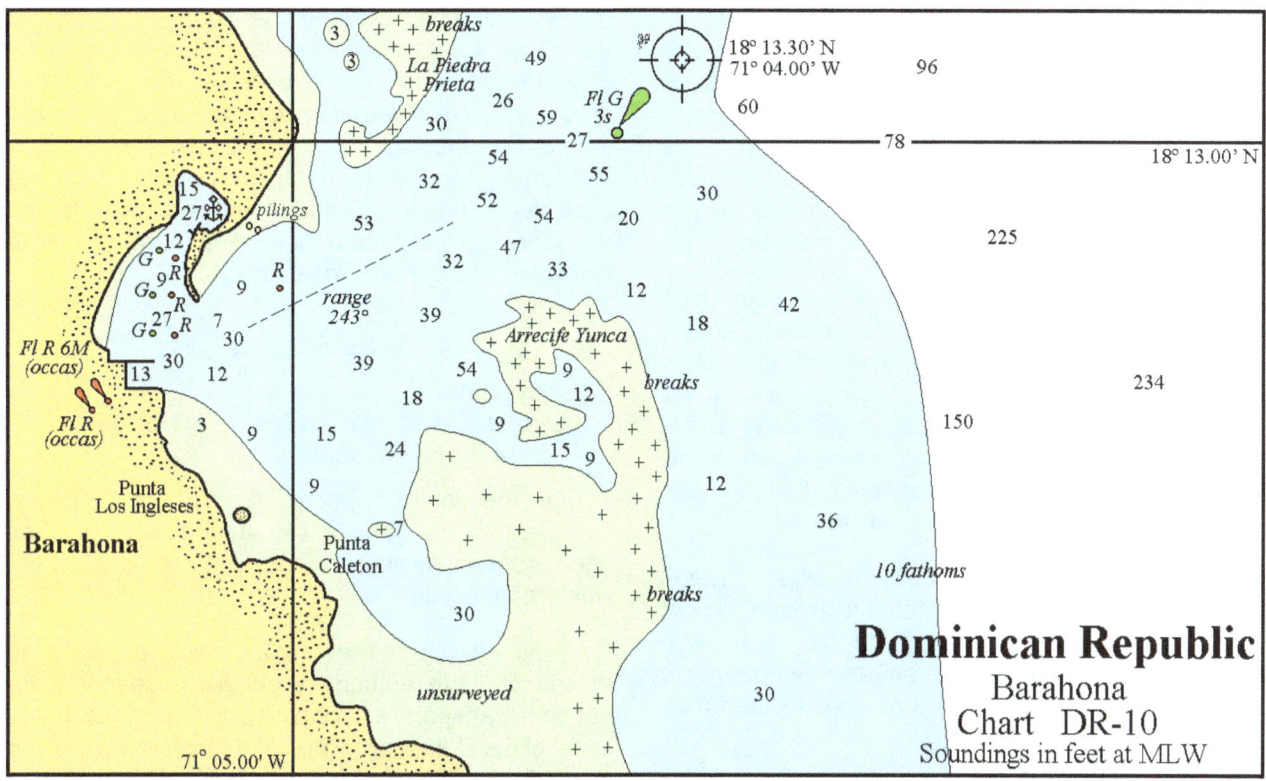

Pearl of the South. This busy port city is a favorite place to stage trips to nearby eco-tourists haunts such as the *Jaragua-Bahoruco-Enriquillo Biosphere Reserve*, a *UNESCO* site, or *Lake Enriquillo*, one of the few saltwater lakes in the world inhabited by crocodiles.

Barahona can be your first stop in the DR if approaching from the west or your last stop if you are heading west along the southern shore. An active commercial harbor, the city is renovating the waterfront area to include an open-air theater and exhibits dedicated to the golden years of the sugar industry in Barahona. If you need to get to Santo Domingo, there is a daily bus from Barahona, call *Caribe Tours* at 809-221-4422 (http://www.caribetours.com.do/).

Navigational Information

The entrance channel to Barahona lies between two reefs, *Arrecife Yunca* and *La Piedra Prieta*. As shown on Chart DR-10, a waypoint at 18° 13.30' N, 71° 04.00' W, will place you approximately ¼ nm NE of the lit (Fl G 3s) sea buoy. From the waypoint take the sea buoy to port; there is plenty of deep water around the sea buoy so you can pass it on either side.

As shown on the chart there is a lit range ashore, the bearing when entering is 243° magnetic.

There is a protected anchorage in the small cove just past the *Club Nautico* docks as shown on the chart. Just follow the buoys into the anchorage area north of the town dock; use caution in poor visibility, the markers are red and green pillar buoys and unlit. Anchor in the NE corner of the cove, the holding is fair to good in a mud bottom. On the northern shore of the cove is a power plant and it is well-lit at night. The dock on the western shore is for coal vessels so do not anchor as to block access to it.

I don't recommend it, but you can tie up to the commercial dock (*muelle*) to the south but there is a charge for this, you will have to pay for 24 hours even if you only stay a fraction of that time. One good thing about the *muelle* is that the road at the end of the dock leads directly into town.

What You Will Find Ashore

Although the harbor at Barahona is commercial, there are still some amenities here for cruisers. If you need to clear in or out of the Dominican Republic it is easy enough to do here, but be forewarned that several cruisers have complained about officials overcharging for their services. The *Marina de Guerra* has an office located at the town dock, this is where you go to get your *despacho* to continue east or to leave the country if you are heading west. *Immigration* is located a few yards away from the *Marina de Guerra* office. The officials will usually come to your boat shortly after your arrival so you shouldn't have to go into town to look them up.

You can tie your dinghy to the town dock (high dock) or you can ask to use the dock at *Club Nautico* (US$10 per day, it's easier to deal with and much safer than the town dock). If you need fuel you will have to jerry-jug it in a taxi. A good idea is to ask for Fernando at *Club Nautico*; Fernando can act as your guide, or representative in finding fuel, and can arrange any transportation you may require.

If you need Internet access there is no Wi-Fi available but there is an Internet cafe in town. There are two banks in Barahona, the largest, *Banco Popular*, has an ATM. There are also two hardware stores in town as well as two churches located near the city park (*parque central*).

Barahona is a pretty good place for provisioning. The town offers two large supermarkets, *Jacobo* on the corner of *Calle Anaconda* and *Padre Ballini* and the other one just off the park. Barahona has a large fresh produce market where you can find all manner of locally made crafts, furniture, and produce (especially the plantains and coffee that Barahona is known for). If you want a quick snack while shopping there are plenty of hot food vendors.

As you would expect in a city of this size, there are many, many places to dine, and you'll find the local favorites are often seafood and rice dishes. And if you are a coffee lover, you will enjoy stocking up with Barahona coffee, considered one of the finest gourmet coffees of the Dominican Republic.

As I mentioned earlier, Barahona is a good spot to begin your explorations of some of the local eco-tourism hotspots. If you wish to explore any of these spots you might enjoy the experience better using a local travel agent to set up your tour and take care of the transportation and security.

The most popular site is *Lake Enriquillo*, the largest lake in the DR and one of the few saltwater lakes in the world that is inhabited by crocodiles. It is the lowest point in the Caribbean, some 129' below sea level.

Another spot is along the coast southwest of Barahona, *Bahía de las Aguilas*. Here you will find crystal clear water with a backdrop of lush, green mountains. Here you will not find a hotel. Here you will not find a restaurant. You will however, probably find turtles here, in the *Jaragua-Bahoruco-Enriquillo Biosphere Reserve* (http://www.grupojaragua.org.do/reserva_english.html) one of *UNESCO's World Network of Biosphere Reserves*.

Las Salinas

Waypoints
Las Salinas - ½ nm NNW of Punta Calderas
18° 14.00' N, 70° 33.00' W

On the southern shore of *Bahía de Calderas*, Las Salinas de Bani is set amid sandy beaches and mountain views with a working salt pond on the western peninsula.

Although there are officials here to clear you in and out, the authorities generally clear you for national transport, ie: for those traveling along the coast of the Dominican Republic. Once in a while you will find an official who doesn't mind clearing you in or out for international travel, but international clearance is much easier at Barahona (warning, see previous section), approximately 28 nm to the west, or at Boca Chica to the east. There is not an *Immigration* office in Las Salinas.

Navigational Information
As shown on chart DR-11, a waypoint at 18° 14.00' N, 70° 33.00' W, will place you approximately ½ nm NNW of Punta Calderas. From the waypoint head into the bay favoring Punta Calderas and following the marked channel (some markers are missing and may or may not be replaced) to the SW portion of the bay (12' -15' of water with a sandy bottom) or further east to anchor north of the commercial docks and the road heading east to Las Calderas.

What You Will Find Ashore
Along the southwestern shore of the bay is the *Salinas Hotel and Restaurant* (*Hotel Salinas*) with about 20 privately owned slips that are often rented if empty (the large dock on the SW shore as shown on the chart). You can tie up your dinghy here if you wish to go ashore. If you need assistance, just speak to the owner, Jorge, whose English is perfect, as he is happy to help visiting cruisers. The hotel's restaurant serves breakfast, lunch, and dinner with free Wi-Fi. Jorge often lets cruisers fill up with free water at his

The Dominican Republic

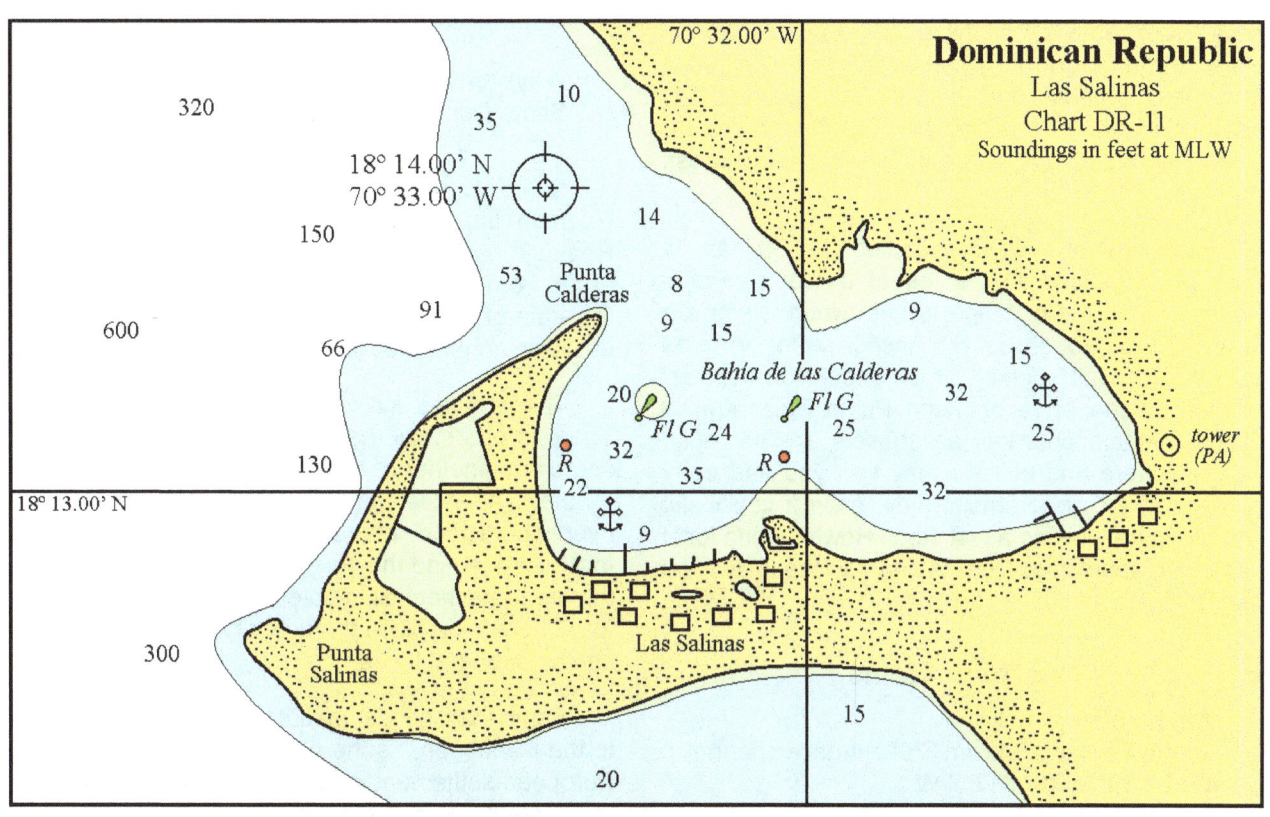

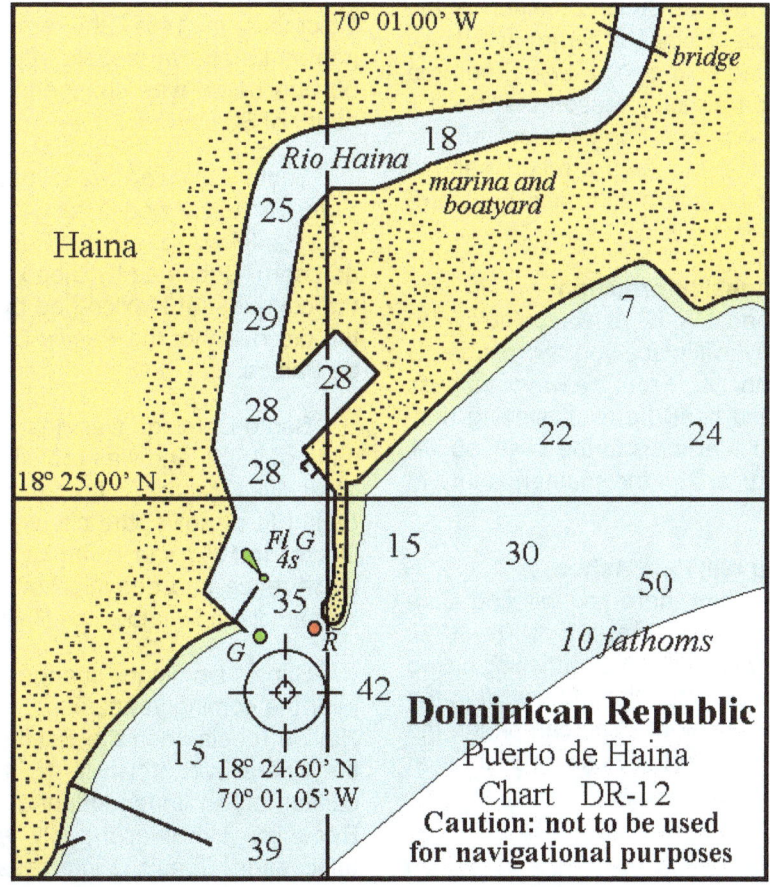

137

dock (least depth is 7.5') if you dine in the restaurant. Jorge can arrange for diesel for you or a repairman from the commercial dock at the SE corner of the bay nearer the town of Las Calderas. In town there are a few small bodegas and eateries as well as fresh produce.

Approximately 23 nm east of Las Salinas, is a small anchorage in the lee of a reef at Punta Palenque. The anchorage is best when winds are from the NE through the E. Anchor as far north as possible to avail yourself of the protection the reef affords. I cannot recommend Punta Palenque as an overnight anchorage, as cruisers are not quite welcome here and officials may visit you and deny permission for an overnight stay, even if you insist you are merely taking a rest stop. However, the local fishermen appreciate cruisers and will love to sell you part of their catch.

Puerto de Haina

Waypoints
Puerto de Haina - ¼ nm S of entrance channel
18° 24.60' N, 70° 01.05' W

Only about 7 nm SW of Santo Domingo is the entrance to Puerto de Haina, a large and busy commercial port situated on the *Rio Haina*. The area is known for crime and the only reason I mention it here is due to the marina and boatyard located just upriver. Do not consider this area a recommended anchorage, rather view it (the marina and boatyard) as an option in an emergency.

Navigational Information
As shown on Chart DR-12, a waypoint at 18° 24.60' N, 70° 01.05' W, will place you approximately ¼ nm S of entrance channel. From the waypoint pass between the jetties and head up river, staying mid-channel, and after the river turns to the east you will see the marina to starboard on the southern shore of the *Rio Haina*.

What You Will Find Ashore
As shown on the chart, here you will find *Club Nautico Haina*, on *Carretera Sánchez* at Km. 13½. The marina is popular with the local sportfishing crowd but the attraction for cruisers is their *TravelLift* in the event of an emergency haulout. You can phone the yard at 809-537-7969/3961, or you can email them at info@nauticohaina.cjb.net.

Santo Domingo

Waypoints
Santo Domingo - ¼ nm S of marked entrance
18° 27.50' N, 69° 53.50' W

Santo Domingo (actually Santo Domingo de Guzmán) the capital and largest city of the Dominican Republic, is best visited by rental car, with a tour group from any other marina, or by cruise ship from the state-of-the-art cruise terminal at Sansouci on the eastern shore of the *Rio Ozama*.

The facilities for cruisers are Spartan at best. There is one small marina along the river's eastern shore and another one to the west of Santo Domingo up the river at Haina (with a boatyard). But neither river is particularly attractive and I only mention them for those that find they are in need of the services in the area (mechanical, medical, or veterinary). By the way, there is no place to anchor here and the current can be strong at times.

Santo Domingo, sometimes called "The Gateway to the Caribbean," is the oldest continually inhabited European settlement in the New World. Founded on the eastern shore of the *Rio Ozama* by Bartholomew Columbus in 1496, the settlement was originally named La Nueva Isabela after the Queen of Spain, but the name was changed on August 5, 1498, in honor of St. Dominic.

Santo Domingo was important as a base for European expansion in the Caribbean, a starting point for expeditions to colonize Puerto Rico (led by Ponce de Leon), Cuba (led by Diego Velázquez de Cuéllar), the conquest of Mexico (led by Hernán Cortés), and the discovery of the *Pacific Ocean* by Vasco Núñez de Balboa.

Santo Domingo was destroyed by a hurricane in June of 1502, and was rebuilt on the opposite shore of the *Rio Ozama*. As the Spanish hold on Hispaniola began to dissolve, the city was captured by Francis Drake. In 1697, the Treaty of Ryswick acknowledged that France had dominion over the western third of Hispaniola, now known as Haiti.

Santo Domingo changed hands many times over the coming years, captured by the French, then Haitian rebels, then the Spanish retook the city until they were overthrown in 1821 when it became the capital of an independent nation, the Dominican Republic. However the city fell to Haitian invaders until after Spanish intercession, the city again became the capital in 1865 (although for the next 60 years it would be like a ping pong ball going back and forth between several dictators including Trujillo who renamed the city after himself. Finally, when Trujillo was assassinated in 1961, the city was once again named Santo Domingo.

Today, Santo Domingo is the cultural, financial, political, commercial and industrial center of the Dominican Republic, and is the major seaport for the nation. Santo Domingo approved legislation in 2005 to develop a huge cruise ship terminal and new marina and a decade later there is still much to be accomplished in this regard.

Navigational Information

As shown on Chart DR-13, a waypoint at 18° 27.50' N, 69° 53.50' W, will place you approximately ¼ nm S of the marked entrance channel between the jetties. From the waypoint head NE up the Rio Ozama past the cruise ship terminal staying midstream until you arrive at the marina. There is a lighted range to lead you in but it isn't really necessary for the average cruising boat as there is good water unless you get too close to the shore or jetties.

Just past the marina is a floating bridge (not shown on the chart) that blocks further inland river access to boats. There is a fair amount of current in the river, even more after strong rains.

What You Will Find Ashore

On the eastern shore of the river, north of the cruise ship terminal, lies *Rio Ozama Marina*, where all dockage is med moor with buoys for your bow (or stern) line. There are few amenities here but the owners have grand plans for the property, so who knows, maybe the future will bring about some very positive changes.

To explore Santo Domingo I suggest getting any of the better travel guides to the area, there is SO MUCH to see here starting with the *Malecón* and the *Christopher Columbus Lighthouse* (*Faro a Colón*).

If you need mechanical assistance for your boat you can call Tony Rodamentes (*Av. St. Martin*), at 809-688-2151. If you need marine supplies you can visit *Auto Marina* (*Av. Los Proceres*), 809-565-6576 (marinecenter@codetel.dom). If you require a hardware store, a good one can be found on *Av. John F. Kennedy*, the *Ferretería Americana*, and you can telephone them at 809-549-7777.

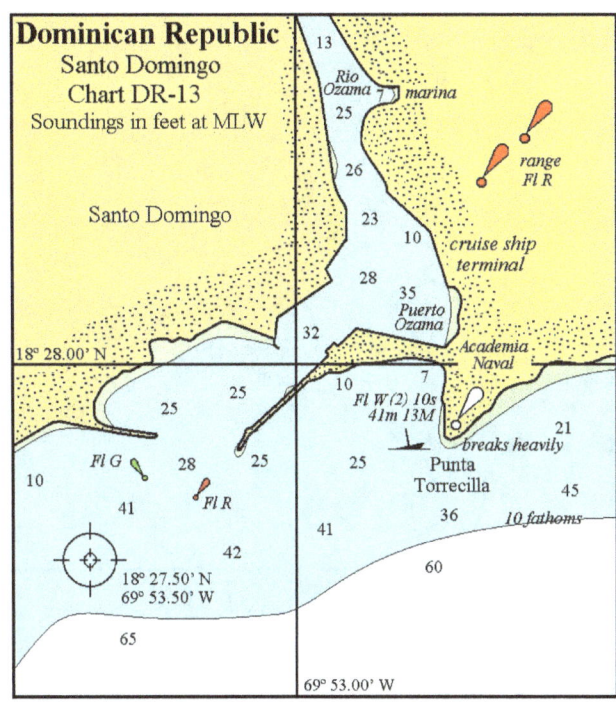

Heading east from Santo Domingo towards Boca Chica, you will find *La Caleta*, a national park lying just a few miles west of Boca Chica (see the Index Chart for the southern coast of the Dominican Republic). Once a popular stopover for cruisers, since 2013, no anchoring is permitted here to protect the reef. Although there are moorings for daytime diving use, no vessels are permitted to stay overnight.

Boca Chica

(San Andrés)

Waypoints
Boca Chica - 1¼ nm SE of entrance channel
18° 25.50' N, 69° 36.70' W

Approximately 18 nm east of Santo Domingo is the resort town of Boca Chica located in the small bay, *Bahía de Andrés*, lying NE of Cabo Caucedo. A good landmark is the conspicuous tall cranes ashore.

Boca Chica is the perfect spot on the south coast to explore Santo Domingo while enjoying a nice, comfortable marina. You can rent a car here and there is also excellent bus service with Santo Domingo.

Navigational Information

The anchorage area, the moorings, and access to the marinas are protected by a long reef and the only access is by the marked channel at the western

A Cruising Guide to the Turks and Caicos Islands

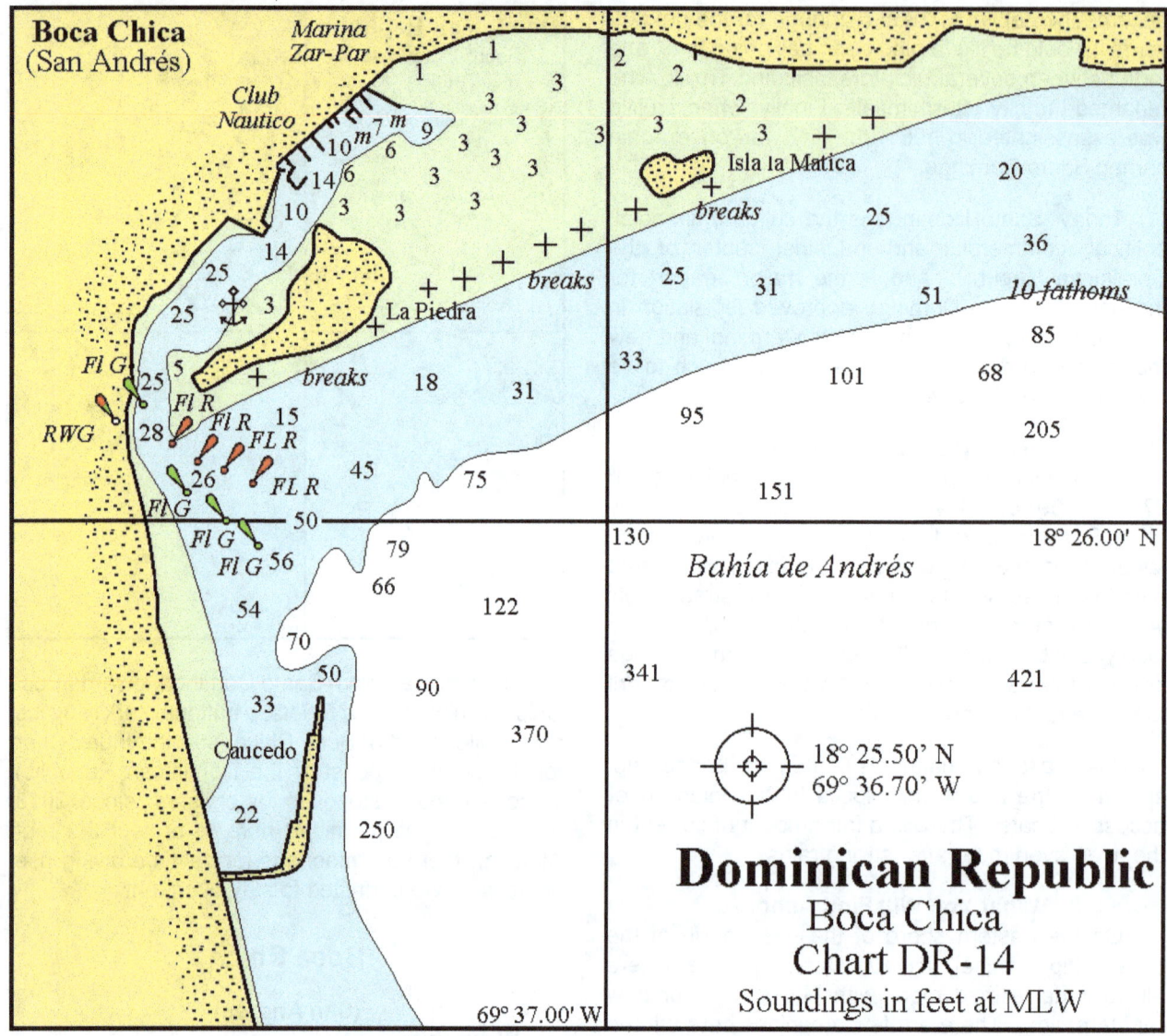

end of the shoal. If you require assistance hail *Marina Zar-Par* on VHF ch. 6 and they will send a boat to guide you (this service is not available at night).

As shown on Chart DR-14, a waypoint at 18° 25.50' N, 69° 36.70' W, will place you approximately 1¼ nm SE of the well-marked entrance channel. From the waypoint steer roughly NW (approximately 300° M) and enter the marked channel. You can avail yourself of the sectored light (*RWG*) but NEVER attempt to enter this channel at night unless you know these waters!

As you head into the well-marked channel you will pass the port area (Caucedo) well to port and avoid the end of the reef to starboard, once past the reef you can turn to starboard in the lee of La Piedra to head to the marinas. Favor the marina docks very closely as the water shoals to starboard and the channel is tight through here. The bottom here is mostly mud and sand and the controlling depth is 10' except when the wind is NE, then you can count on there be 1' less depth. If you draw more than 7' you should hail *Marina Zar-Par* on VHF ch. 6 for more information.

You can anchor in the lee of La Piedra but it is very small and space is limited. There are moorings available just off *Marina Zar-Par* but you cannot anchor further east off the public beach. If you take a mooring keep an eye on the depthsounder so that you do not run aground when the tide changes. Bear in mind that on the weekends many Dominicans come out and play in the surrounding waters and the

The Dominican Republic

area from the front of the marina to La Piedra can be VERY busy, and some even say downright unsafe. If you take a mooring all the amenities of Marina Zar-Par are yours for the use. Moorings are for use by vessels less than 50' LOA due to the shallow waters. If a mooring line is missing please contact the marina and let them know.

What You Will Find Ashore

There are two marinas here, the private *Club Nautico de Santo Domingo* and *Marina Zar-Par*, both lying on the mainland shore just next to each other.

Club Nautico de Santo Domingo, although private, has a fuel dock, transient slips, water, showers, Wi-Fi, a restaurant, a pool, and a 70 ton *Travelift* for those needing a haulout. You can phone the marina at 809-683-2582, or visit their website at http://www.clubnautico.com.do/. *Club Nautico* tells me they can handle an 8' draft with the tide.

Marina Zar-Par is a relatively new full-service marina with an *Immigration* office located above the laundromat. Although the office is officially open 24-hours a day, cruisers are only handled from 0800-1800. If you intend to clear out from here, bear in mind that you are not permitted to leave after 1800 daily, you must leave as soon as your despacho has been issued (it's best to plan an early morning departure). The fuel dock is where you will handle your clearance paperwork and if you do not take a slip you will be charged for usage of the dock. The marina also offers a clearance service if you do not wish to deal with the paperwork for a fee of US$50. This fee covers clearance handling (but not the clearance fees), usage of the dock on the day you depart, and water. If you do not wish to use the fuel dock you can anchor in the lee of La Piedra and dinghy in to handle the formalities.

The marina offers full electric (30, 50, and 100 amp service), *Wi-Fi* (with a computer in the office that you can use if you don't have one), laundry, showers, free cable TV in the *Captain's Club* (located above the laundromat), fax service, a fuel dock, and 150 slips with some that can accommodate a vessel to 100', and all with 24-hour security.

The marina also offers courtesy rides to the airport as well as the grocery store in Boca Chica just east of the marina (the grocery store will bring you back to the marina). Free cell phone usage is also supplied for guests of the marina.

The boatyard has a 70-ton *TravelLift* that can accommodate drafts to 8' and beams of 28'. The yard/marina can also help you dispose of oil and batteries. You can phone the marina at 809-523-5858, or you can visit their website at www.marinazarpar.com

If you require marine supplies visit *Centro Marino, Av. Andres #3*, or call them at 809-523-6033, or email them at centro.marino@hotmail.com. For mechanical repairs try Juan Carlos Baez at *Technical Marine*, 809-805-8125.

If you need help with electrical or electronic problems, you can contact Ian Wilson at *Wilson Marina and Villa Services* at 809-743-9503. You can also contacted *Manuel Electric*, just across from the entrance to *Club Nautico* to the west, or call them at 809-523-9769.

In town there are several banks, grocery stores, and fine eateries (with a lot of Italian restaurants) and the marinas will be happy to tell you which ones are the best at the moment. The best place for groceries is *Olé*.

East of Boca Chica

Moving east from Boca Chica there are a couple of anchorages that deserve at least a mention here although they are not high on my list of quality destinations.

Approximately 18 nm east of Boca Chica is the *Rio Macoris* and the industrial town of San Pedro de Macoris. The river should never be entered at night due to large, unlit mooring buoys that are for ships awaiting entrance to the port in town. The river entrance channel is well-marked and easy to follow, but don't venture outside the channel to the east due to shoals and foul ground. If you wish to visit San Pedro de Macoris it is best done by rental car from Boca Chica or Casa de Campo.

Approximately 17 nm further east lies Isla Catalina (see the Dominican Republic, Southern Coast Index Chart) that offers a lee from winds from north through east to southeast (although the anchorage tends to be rolly in all but the best conditions). The island is popular with cruise ships and day trippers and can be quite busy when the fleet is in. Isla Catalina is a good spot for wall diving and large fish.

Casa de Campo Marina

Waypoints
Casa de Campo Marina - ¼ nm SW of entrance
18° 23.60' N, 68° 54.40' W

Just east of Isla Catalina is the town of La Romana. While one can anchor in the river, it is not advisable due to strong currents and poor holding. Instead, head a few miles further east and get a slip at *Casa de Campo Marina* and visit La Romana by rental car or taxi (there is good shopping/provisioning in La Romana). The marina is only a few minutes away from the international airport in La Romana.

Navigational Information
As shown on Chart DR-15, a waypoint at 18° 23.60' N, 68° 54.40' W, will place you approximately ¼ nm SW of the well-marked entrance channel. From the waypoint head in a NNE direction and you will pick up the lit markers to guide you into the marina. You will notice the conspicuous red and white striped light at the end of the jetty to starboard upon entering. If you need help, hail the marina on VHF ch. 16 or 68 and they will send out a boat to guide you.

What You Will Find Ashore
Designed to become an international destination, the 370 slip *Casa de Campo Marina* is part of a much larger resort that also houses a haul-out yard, a yacht club, a sailing club, several yacht brokers, a plaza with many stores and theaters, and several fine restaurants on-site.

Some slips have finger piers while some are Med-moor, and the marina can accommodate vessels up to 250' LOA with depths ranging from 9'-15'. The tidal range is a mere 6" inside the protected harbor. The marina boasts two fueling stations (and 6 in-slip fueling points for vessels over 120"), full electric (110, 220, and 380 volt AC at 60 Hz), a laundry, cable TV, telephone, *Wi-Fi*, and golf carts for travel within the marine complex. On-site you will also find a pharmacy and bank, and of course the marina has 24-hour security. The dockmaster's office supplies mariners with daily weather reports and monitors a system of surveillance cameras to make your stay as comfortable and safe as possible.

The *IBC* boatyard has a 120-ton *Travelift*, 25 different repair services, and a chandlery. All service personnel have been fully trained and certified and undergo regular training updates. The marina can be reached by phone at 809-523-2111/2112, or by email at marinacdc@verizon.net.do.

The sailing school, located on the *Rio Chavon*, has trained some 4,000 students in the DR and Italy since 1978 and is directed by Franco Pistone.

Located on the northeastern part of the marina complex, the marina is home to the *Casa de Campo Yacht Club*. Housed in a large and impressive Colonial-designed structure, the yacht club oversees many of the marina's activities including dinners and even international regattas. Inside you will feel like you have entered an old-style yacht club that reeks of old money and a century of sailing.

The marina also boasts several prime shopping areas on-site including the unique *Coconut Mall* housing a bank, a gourmet deli, rental cars, several restaurants and three cinemas. There are numerous fine international restaurants on the marina's grounds such as *The Azimut Café, Café Juanita, The Enoteca, Il Limoncello, Peperoni, Chinois, La Casita,* and *Mistral*.

To the west is the town of La Romana and it is a long walk or a short taxi ride away from the marina. For provisioning you can't go wrong at the huge, well-stocked, *Supermercado Jumbo* (http://jumbo.com.do/ofertas.aspx). Besides the normal range of groceries the store carries a large selection of fresh produce.

Approximately 4.5 nm east of *Casa de Campo Marina* is the small anchorage at Bayahibe. Primarily a fishing village, Bayahibe has become a homeport for commercial vessels taking tourists to nearby Isla Saona to the east (generally between 0900-1100 and 1500-1800).

The town is set up to cater to the tourists and you will find several gift shops here besides the usual plethora of bars and restaurants, most on the waterfront for the view. Bayahibe is not a port of entry and if you need to clear the local officials will direct you to *Casa de Campo Marina* and La Romana for clearance. The *Dominican Republic Coast Guard*, the *Marina de Guerra*, has an office in the tan building at the end of the public beach. The anchorage is pleasant enough save for a bit of a roll. There is a small fuel dock with 4' at MLW.

Isla Saona

Waypoints
Isla Saona - ½ nm NW of anchorage
18° 12.50' N, 68° 47.00' W

The Dominican Republic

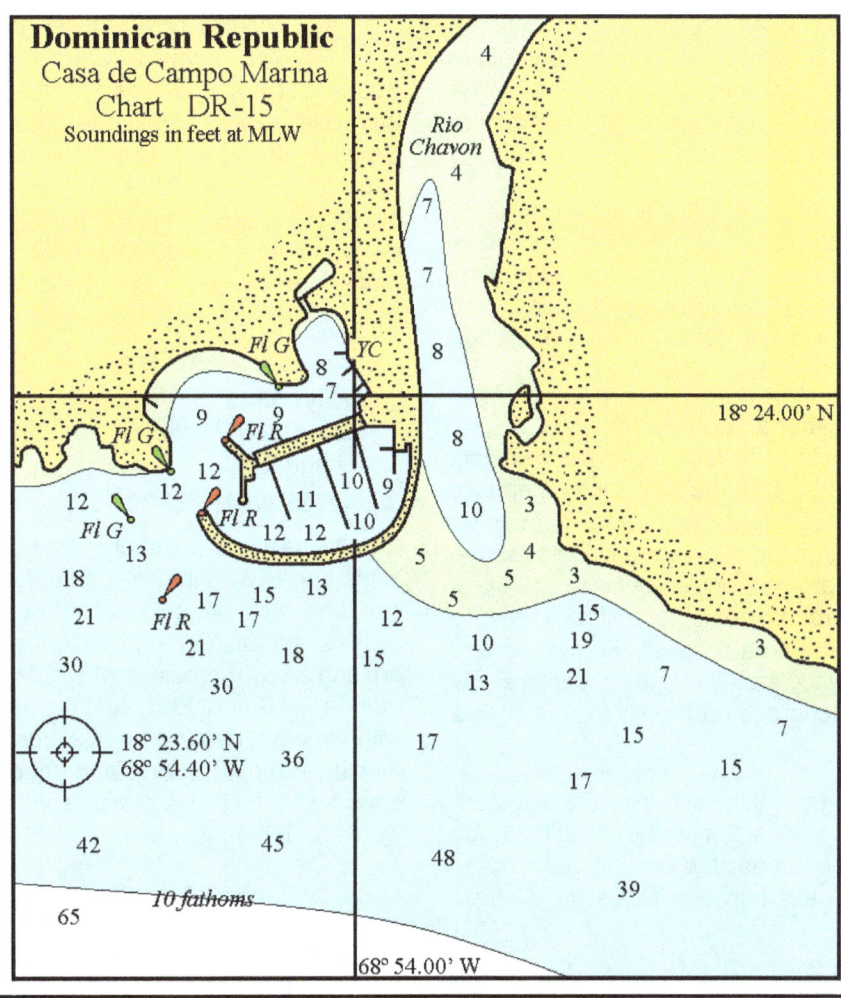

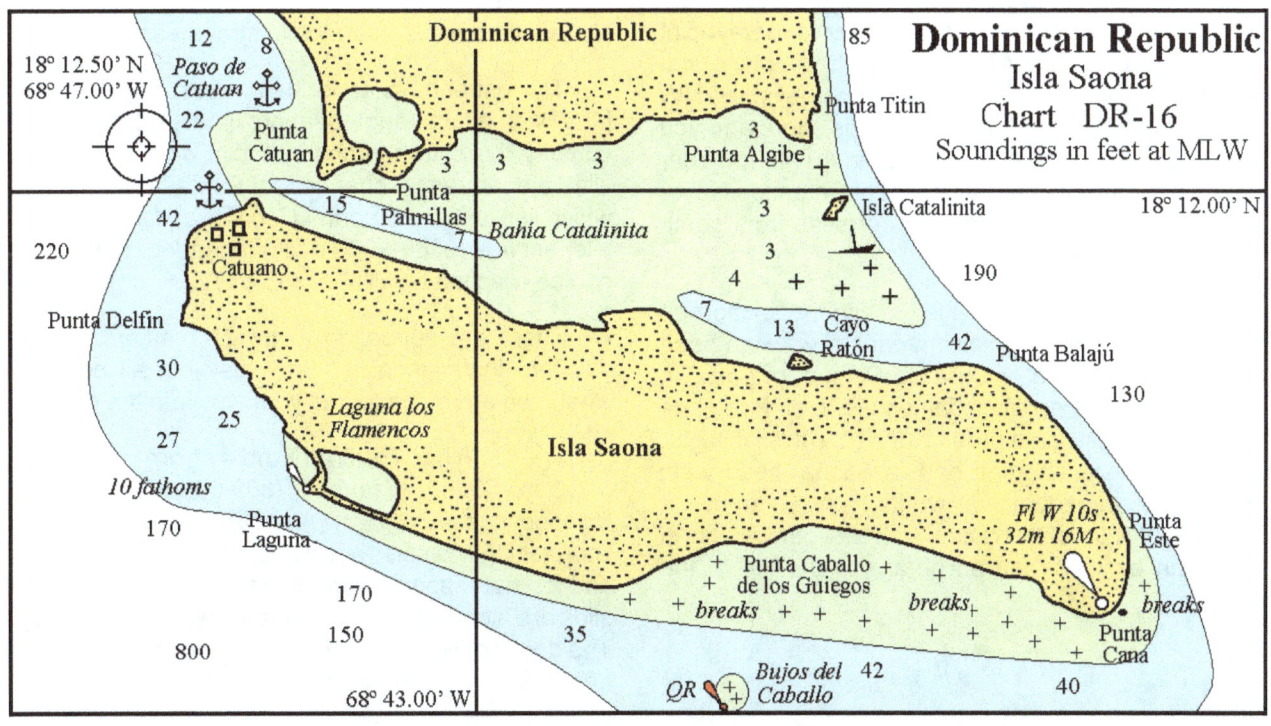

143

Isla Saona, a nature reserve, lies off the southeastern tip of the Dominican Republic and offers nothing in the way of services and amenities for the cruiser save for a good spot to drop the hook before or after crossing the *Mona Passage*.

Although Isla Saona is inhabited, many of her people cater to the tourists that arrive on daily shuttles from Bayahibe to enjoy the island's many beautiful white sand beaches. Quite a few still fish daily and don't be surprised if some come by your anchored boat to sell you some of their catch.

Navigational Information

NEVER attempt to bring your vessel between Isla Saona and the mainland of the Dominican Republic from the east, there is a huge reef system that can be treacherous. Although there is a deep water passage between the southern end of the reef and the tip of Isla Saona I do not recommend that anybody venture into these waters, the area between Isla Saona and the mainland, *Bahía Catalinita*, is best explored by dinghy from the anchorage on the NW shore of Isla Saona.

If approaching from the east, give the southern shore a wide berth, at least 2 miles, to avoid the huge reef shown on the chart as *Bujos del Caballo*. Also do not attempt to pass between *Bujos del Caballo* and Isla Saona.

As shown on Chart DR-16, as you round the western tip of Isla Saona you can make for a waypoint at 18° 12.50' N, 68° 47.00' W, which will place you approximately ½ nm NW of the anchorage on the NW shore of Isla Saona. Head in towards shore and you can anchor in good holding sand in 10'-40' of clear water just off the small settlement of Catuano. Never attempt to anchor here in winds or seas from south through west to northeast.

If the wind moves into the NE and the anchorage at Isla Saona becomes uncomfortable, you can head west to Boca Chica or Casa de Campo, or you can anchor in the *Paso de Catuan*, NW of Punta de Catuan, but use caution and don't try this at night. If leaving the anchorage off Isla Saona, head west to avoid the sandbar that works its way northwest from the NW tip of the island, to work your way north and then east into the anchorage in the lee of the mainland.

What You Will Find Ashore

There are a couple of small settlements on Isla Saona but no amenities to attract a cruiser (other than fresh seafood and good snorkeling). If you enjoy exploring by dinghy the local waters will captivate you. To the ENE lies Punta Palmillas and numerous mangrove creeks to explore. If you work your way eastward you will pick up a channel with 5'-6' of water that will take you to Cayo Raton and Isla Catalinita.

Cap Cana Marina

Waypoints
Cap Cana Marina - ½ nm SE of entrance channel
18° 29.85' N, 68° 22.00' W

On the windward shore of the Dominican Republic is the large 130-slip *Cap Cana Marina*, part of a huge condominium project that attracts upscale condo owners, sportfishermen, and cruisers prepping for, or arriving after, a crossing of the *Mona Passage*. The marina is a Port of Entry and the marina will assist you with your clearance process. Just to the north is the 34-slip *Marina Punta Cana* (http://www.puntacana.com/) which attracts mostly sportfishermen; cruisers would be better serviced at *Cap Cana Marina*.

Navigational Information

As shown on Chart DR-17, a waypoint at 18° 29.85' N, 68° 22.00' W, will place you approximately ½ nm SE of the marked entrance channel to the marina. Never attempt this entrance in strong easterly seas.

The entrance channel has a least depth of 7' at MLW with a tidal range of approximately 1.5'. Do not confuse the entrance channel for *Cap Cana Marina* with the entrance channel to *Punta Cana Marina* which lies just to the north. *Cap Cana Marina* offers a pilot service (0800-1800 daily) if needed; the marina can be reached on VHF ch. 16 or 72.

There are supposed to be 21 markers leading you into the marina but they may not all be there when you are trying to find your way into the marina.

What You Will Find Ashore

Cap Cana Marina (809-695-5539, info@marinacapcana.com) was designed for larger sportfishing vessels, not the average cruising boat, and for that reason fendering can be difficult as many slips are alongside a wall with an overhang at the top. The dockmaster, Domingo, understands cruisers and he can be a big help when you tie up.

The Dominican Republic

Cap Cana Marina has 130 slips (81 slips can handle vessels over 130' LOA), most with 40' long finger piers and full electric (110/220 volt 30 and 50 amp service along with three-phase electric to 480 volts and 100 amps). The marina can accommodate vessels to 150' LOA with a draft of 8'. Each slip has water, free Wi-Fi, and cable TV (not free). Vessels needing clearance should notify the marina by VHF (ch. 16 or 72.) prior to entry and follow their instructions. Usually the marina will direct you to the fuel dock where the officials will come aboard.

On the marina grounds you will find a dozen fine restaurants, a delicatessen, a laundry (a short golf cart ride away as are the showers), the *Sanctuary Spa* (http://sanctuarycapcana.com/), four beauty parlors, a fitness center, tennis courts, and a paddle ball and volleyball court. Nearby *Scape Park* (http://www.scapepark.com/en/) offers 74 acres of forest and 12 miles of hiking trails.

The marina maintains high quality service personnel on-site, or they can help you find an outside contractor if needed for everything from marine electronics to refrigeration, and hull painting. You can reach *Cap Cana Marina* by phone at 809-688-5587, or reach them by email at marina@capcana.com.

Situated just north of *Cap Cana Marina*, the poorly protected *Marina Punta Cana* is really not worth a stop unless by some chance *Cap Cana Marina* is full and you have no place else to go (little chance of that I believe). The entrance channel is difficult to make out but breaking seas will give you an idea where the break in the reef lies. An outer green buoy marks the channel entrance and several buoys line the entrance. The controlling depth in the entrance channel is 5' at MLW with 7' inside the marina basin (bear in mind that there is a 1.5' tidal range here). There always seems to be a swell in the marina basin and it can often be uncomfortable.

The marina offers 34 Med-moor slips, water, electricity, a fuel dock, a laundry, a swimming pool, and a nice international restaurant. You can contact the marina by phone at 809-959-2262 or by email at info@puntacana.com.

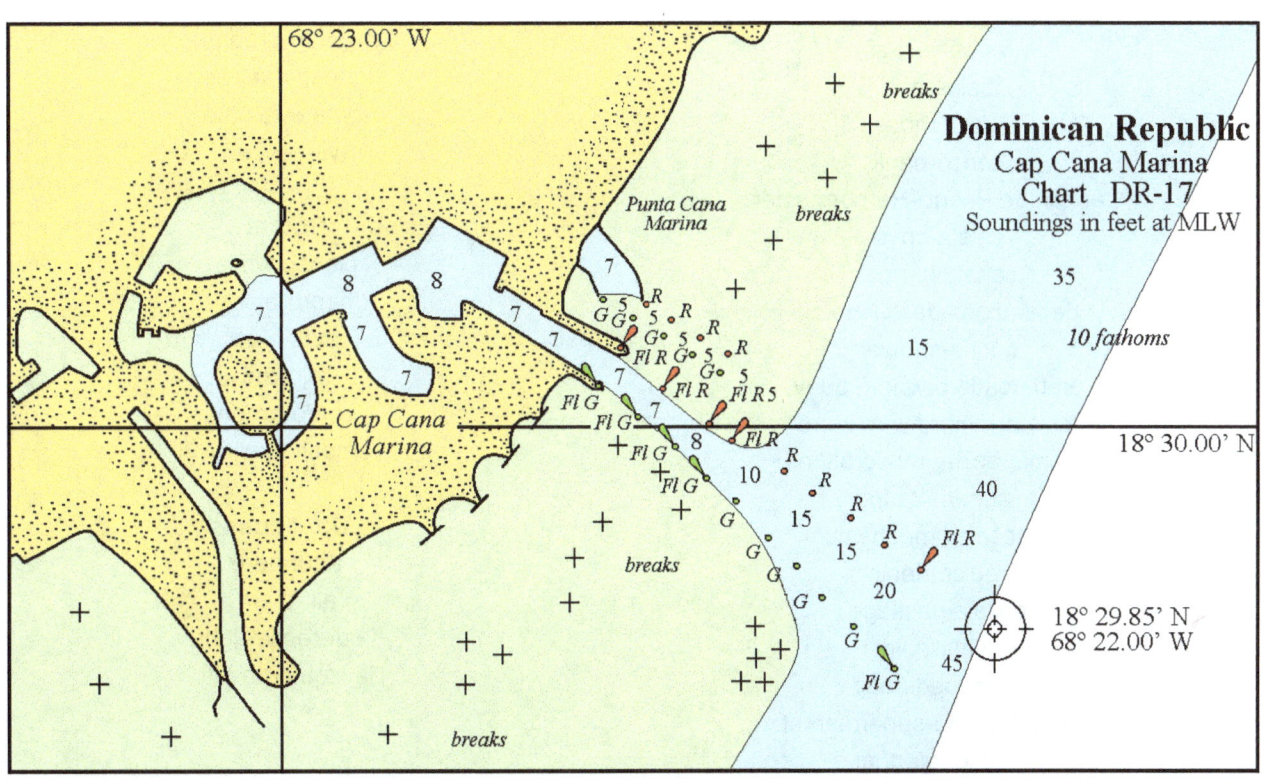

A Little Basic Spanish

(Just Enough to get you into Trouble)

While command of the Spanish language is not a prerequisite for happy cruising in the Dominican Republic, knowing a little will certainly help you get by better and everybody will love you for at least trying.

Buenos Dias. Good morning.
Buenas tardes. Good afternoon.
Buenas noches. Good night.
¿Cómo está usted? How are you?
¿Muy bien gracias, y usted? I am fine thank you, and you?
¿Como se llama? What is your name?
Me llamo es . . . My name is. . .
¿Habla usted inglés? Do you speak English?
¿Habla usted Español? Do you speak Spanish?
No muy bien. Not very well.
Muy poco. Very little.
¿Cómo se dice. . . ? How do you say. . .?
No entiendo. I don't understand.
Escríbamela, por favor. Please write it down for me.
¿Donde está el. . .? Where is . . .?
    anclaje-anchorage
    arrecife-reef
    bahia-bay
    bajo-shoal
    banco-bank
    Capitán de Puerto-Harbormaster
    caleta-cove
    canal-channel
    desembarcadero-landing
    ducha-shower
    embarcadero-wharf, quay
    ferretería-hardware store
    Immigración-Immigration
    lavandería-laundry
    mecánico-mechanic
    médico-doctor
    pasaje-passage
    punta-point
    rada-roadstead
    supermercado-supermarket
    telefono-telephone

¿Donde puedo comprar . . . ? Where can I buy...?
¿Tiene usted . . . ? Do you have. . . ?
Necesito. . . I need. . .
    agua-water
    azúcar-sugar
    café-coffee
    camarones-shrimp
    carne-meat
    cerveza-beer
    cigarillos-cigarettes
    fosforos-matches
    fuego-a light
    gasoil-diesel
    gasolina-gasoline
    huevos-eggs
    jamón-ham
    jugo-juice
    leche-milk
    limones-limes
    mantequilla-butter
    pan-bread
    patatas-potatoes
    plátanos-bananas (plantains)
    pollo-chicken
    propano-propane
    queso-cheese
    tomate-tomato
    vino-wine

Colors
blanco-white
negro-black
azul-blue
rojo-red
verde-green
amarillo-yellow

Directions
aquí-here
allí-there
la derecha-right
la izquierda-left

The Dominican Republic

Numbers
uno-1
dos-2
tres-3
quatro-4
cinco-5
seis-6
seite-7
ocho-8
nueve-9
diez-10
once-11
doce-12
trece-13
catorce-14
quince-15
diéz y seis-16
diéz y seite-17
diéz y ocho-18
diéz y nuevo-19
veinte-20
veinte y uno-21
treinta-30
uarenta-40
cincuenta-50
sesenta-60
setenta-70
ochenta-80
noventa-90
cien-100
ciento y uno-101
mil-1,000
mil uno-1,001

Days of the Week
Lunes-Monday
Martes-Tuesday
Miércoles-Wednesday
Juevos-Thursday
viernos-Friday
Sábado-Saturday
Domingo-Sunday
Ahora-Now

¿Quién? Who?
¿Qué? What?
¿Cuando? When?
¿Donde? Where?
¿Por qué? Why?
¿Cómo? How?
¿Qué lejos? How far is it?
   Está lejos. It's far.
   Está cerca. It's near.
¿Qué hora es? What time is it?
¿A qué hora? At what time?
Tengo hambre. I'm hungry.
Perdón. Excuse me.
¿Puede ayudarme? Can you help me?
¿Qué es eso? What is this (that)?
¿Cuánto cuesta? What does it cost?
Dame éste. Give me this one.
Dame eso. Give me that one.
No tengo dinero. I have no money.
¡No se mueva! Don't move!
¡Manos arriba! Put your hands up!

References

A Cruising Guide to the Caribbean and the Bahamas; Jerrems C. Hart and William T. Stone, Dodd, Mead and Company, New York, 1982

A General History of the Robberies and Murders of the Most Notorious Pirates: Daniel Defoe, (Capt. Charles Johnson). Routledge and Kegan Paul, Ltd., London, 1955

A History of the Turks and Caicos: Prof. Josiah A. Marvel, unpublished monograph

American Practical Navigator; Nathaniel Bowditch, LL.D., DMA Hydrographic Center, 1977

An Essay on the Constitutional History of the Turks & Caicos Islands: Prof. Josiah A. Marvel and Leonora Harvey Missick, unpublished monograph

A Shipwreck Guide to the Bahamas and the Turks and Caicos, Vol. I: Tony A. Jaggers, American Southern Printing, Sarasota, FL, 1994

Blackbeard the Pirate: Robert E. Lee and John Blair, Winston-Salem, NC, 1974

Coastal And Offshore Weather, The Essential Handbook; Chris Parker, Christopher Parker Jr., Green Cove Springs, FL. 2003.

Diving, Snorkeling, & Visitors Guide to the Turks and Caicos Islands: Capt. Bob Gascoine, Graphic Reproductions, Miami, FL, 1991

HF Radio E-Mail For Idi-Yachts, Captain Marti Brown, Cruising Companion Publications, Marathon, FL 2003.

Pirate Rascals of the Spanish Main: Addison B.C. Whipple, Doubleday and Co., New York, 1957

Pirates and Privateers of the Caribbean: Jennifer Marx, Krieger Publishing Company, Malabar, FL, 1992

Pirates of the Virgin Islands: Fritz Seyfarth, Spanish Main Press, St. Thomas, USVI, 1988

Sailing Directions For The Caribbean Sea; Pub. #147, Defense Mapping Agency, #SDPUB147

Secrets of the Bahamas Family Islands 1989; Nicolas Popov, Dragan Popov, & Jane Sydenham; Southern Boating Magazine, May 1989

The American Coast Pilot; Blunt, 1812

The Book of Pirates: Brian Innes, Bancroft and Co., Ltd., 1966

The Buccaneers of the Americas: A. O. Esquemelin, George Rutledge & Sons, London, 1893

The Diario of Christopher Columbus' First Voyage to the Americas, 1492-1493: Fray Bartolomé de Las Casas, Translated by Oliver Dunn and James E. Kelley Jr., Norman: University of Oklahoma Press, 1989

The Gentleman's Guide to Passages South: Bruce Van Sant, Cruising Guide Publications

The Great Days of Piracy in the West Indies: George Woodbury, W.W. Norton and Co.

The Log of Christopher Columbus: Robert H. Fuson, Tab Books, Blue Ridge Summit, PA, 1987

The Ocean Almanac; Robert Hendrickson, Doubleday, New York, 1984

The Pirates: Douglas Botting, Time-Life Books, Alexandria, VA, 1978

The Pirates Own Book; published by A. & C. B. Edwards, New York, and Thomas, Cowperthwait, & Co., Philadelphia, 1842

The Pirates Who's Who: Phillip Gosse, Rio Grande Press, 1988

The Turks and Caicos Islands, Lands of Discovery: Amelia Smithers, Macmillan Education, London, Second Edition, 1995

The Story of the Turks and Caicos Islands: C.D. Hutchings 1977

Turks and Caicos Islands: Paul G. Boultbee, World Bibliographical Series, Vol. 137, Clio Press, Oxford U.K./ABC Clio, Santa Barbara, CA, U.S.A.

Turks and Caicos Pocket Guide: Julia Blake, Domy Graphix Ltd., 1997

Turks Islands Landfall, Vol. 1-7: Herbert E. Sadler, Grand Turk

Where the Trade Winds Blow; Bill Robinson, Charles Scribner's Sons, New York, 1963

Appendices

Appendix A: Navigational Lights

Navigational lights in the Turks and Caicos should be considered unreliable at best. The actual characteristics of each light may differ from those published here and are subject to change without notice. It is not unusual for a light to be out of commission for long periods of time. Listing of lights reads from north to south. Please note that due to the efforts of Beryl Nelson of Providenciales, North West Point Light on Providenciales (Turks and Caicos Islands) is now working after years of disrepair.

LOCATION	LIGHT	COLOR	HT.	RANGE
The Southern Bahamas				
Hogsty Reef				
Northwest Cay	Fl ev 4 sec	W	29'	8 nm
Mayaguana				
Guano Pt., Abraham's Bay	Fl ev 3 sec	W	13'	8 nm
Northwest Point	Fl ev 5 sec	W	70'	12 nm
Great Inagua				
Matthew Town	Gp. Fl (2) 10 sec	W	120'	17 nm
The Turks and Caicos Islands				
The Caicos Islands				
North West Point, Providenciales	Gp Fl (3) 15 sec			14M
Providenciales, Bird Cay	Fl ev 10 sec	W		12M
Cape Comete, East Caicos	Gp Fl (2) 20 sec	W		12M
West Caicos, SW Point	Q	R	52'	
French Cay	Fl	R	10'	
South Caicos	Fxd	W	50'	9M
Long Cay, east end	Fl ev 2.5 sec	R		5M
Dove Cay, west end	Fl ev 2.5 sec	G		5M
Bush Cay	Gp Fl (2) 10 sec	W		14M
The Turks Islands				
Grand Turk Lighthouse	Fl ev 7.5 sec	W	108'	6M
Head of South Dock-front	Fl ev 3 sec	W & R	20'	3M
Head of South Dock-rear	Fl ev 3 sec		30'	3M
Salt Cay, NW Point	Gp Fl (4) 20 sec	W		8M
Great Sand Cay	Fl ev 2 sec	W	85'	10M
Dominican Republic				
Luperón - head of dock	GP Fl ev 10s	R	30'	3M
Ocean World Marina Sea Buoy	Fl	W		
Puerto Plata - sea buoy	Fl	R		
Punta Fortaleza	Fl ev 6 s	W	138'	8M
Puerto Plata Range	Fl	R		12M
Cayo Vigia	Fl	R	22'	8M

Appendix B: Marinas

Some of the marinas listed below may be untenable in certain winds and dockside depths listed may not reflect entrance channel depths at low water, check with the dockmaster prior to arrival. For cruisers seeking services "Nearby" may mean a walk or short taxi ride away.

MARINA	FUEL	GROCERY	DINING	E-MAIL or WEBSITE
The Caicos Islands				
Ambergris Cay				
Windward Marina	Still under construction - lack of financing			

MARINA	FUEL	GROCERY	DINING	E-MAIL or WEBSITE
Providenciales				
Blue Haven Marina	D & G	Nearby	Yes	http://www.bluehaventci.com/
Caicos Marina/Shipyard	D & G	No	No	http://www.caicosmarina.com/
Harbour Club Marina	Private			http://www.harbourclub.org/
South Side Marina	D & G	Nearby	Nearby	http://southsidemarina-tci.com/
Turtle Cove Marina	D & G	Nearby	Yes	http://www.tcmarina.com/
S. Walkin & Son Marina	None	Nearby	Nearby	
North Caicos				
North Caicos YC & Mar.	None	None	None	
South Caicos				
Seaview Marina	D & G	Yes	Nearby	
West Caicos				
West Caicos Marina	Closed, refinanced so expect construction to soon be underway			
The Turks Islands				
Grand Turk				
Flamingo Cove	D	No	Nearby	
Deane's Dock	Nearby	Nearby	Nearby	
The Dominican Republic				
Boca Chica				
Club Nautico Santo Dom.	D & G	Nearby	Nearby	www.clubnautico.com.do/
Marina Zarpar	D & G	Nearby	Yes	www.marinazarpar.com
Haina				
Club Nautico Haina	D & G	Nearby	Nearby	info@nauticohaina.cjb.net
La Romana				
Casa de CampoMarina	D & G	Yes	Yes	www.marinacasadecampo.com.do/
Las Salinas				
Salinas Hotel & Marina	D & G	Nearby	Nearby	
Luperón				
Luperón Marina & YC	None	Nearby	Yes	
Puerto Blanco Marina	None	Nearby	Yes	http://www.puertoblancomarina.com/
Tropical Marina	None	Nearby	Nearby	
Cofresi				
Ocean World Marina	D & G	Yes	Yes	www.oceanworldmarina.com
Punta Cana				
Cap Cana Marina	D & G	Yes	Yes	http://www.marinacapcana.com/
Marina de Punta Cana	D & G	Nearby	Yes	
Samaná				
Puerto Bahía Marina	D & G	Yes	Yes	www.puertobahiasamana.com/
Santo Domingo				
La Marina del Rio Ozama	D & G	Nearby	Yes	

Appendix C-1: Services Dominican Republic

All listings in the DR are area code 809, 829, or 849. As with any place, businesses come and go, sometimes seemingly overnight. Certain entries on this list may no longer exist by the time this is published or may have changed their names or phone numbers. All telephone numbers in the Dominican Republic are area code 809, 829, or 849.

FACILITY	LOCATION	TELEPHONE
Auto Rentals		
Avis: airport	La Romana	809-813-9099
Avis: airport	Puerto Plata	809-586-0214

Appendices

FACILITY	LOCATION	TELEPHONE
Avis: airport	Punta Cana	809-959-0534
Avis: airport	Santiago (airport)	809-233-8154
Avis: airport	Santo Domingo	809-549-0468
Avis: downtown	Santo Domingo	809-535-7191
Estelvina Felipe (Dentist)	Luperón	
Hertz-airport	Puerto Plata	809-586-0200
José	Luperón	809-458-9506
Lucke Car/Jeep Rental	Puerto Plata	809-568-0217
National- airport	Puerto Plata	877-222-9058
National- airport	Punta Cana	887-222-9058
National- airport	Santo Domingo	877-222-9058
National- Ave. Luperón	Puerto Plata	809-586-1366
Odalis	Luperón, DR	809-223-3580
Payless Car Rental	Puerto Plata (airport)	809-586-0108
Payless Car Rental	Punta Cana (airport)	809-959-0287
Payless Car Rental	Santo Domingo (airport)	809-549-8911
Thrifty Car Rental	Puerto Plata	809-333-4000
Thrifty Car Rental	Punta Cana	809-466-2046
Thrifty Car Rental	Santo Domingo	809-549-0930
Thrifty Car Rental	Sosúa	809-571-2215
Diesel Repair/Parts		
Cap Cana Marina	Cap Cana	809-695-5539
Casa de Campo Marina	La Romana	809-523-2111
Laboratorio Diesel	Puerto Plata	809-261-6394
Marina Zar-Par	Boca Chica	809-523-5858
Núñez & Núñez	Santiago	809-582-2200
Repuestos Maritimos	Puerto Plata	809-586-4728
Technical Marine	Santo Domingo	809-805-8125
Tony Rodamentes	Boca Chica	809-688-2151
Diving		
Caribbean Divers	Boca Chica	809-854-3483
Coral Point Diving	Bayahibe	829-574-9655
Diwa Dive Center	Puerto Plata	809-261-3150
Dressel Divers	Puerto Plata	321-392-2338
Northern Coast Aquasports	Sosúa	809-571-1028
Sea Pro Divers	Puerto Plata	809-710-3747
Sea Pro Divers	Punta Cana	809-754-3632
Scuba Fun Dive Center	La Romana	809-833-0003
Treasure Divers	Boca Chica	809-523-5320
Electrical Repairs		
Cap Cana Marina	Cap Cana	809-695-5539
Casa de Campo Marina	La Romana	809-523-2111
Centro Marino	Boca Chica	809-523-6720
Electro Nautica	Santo Domingo	809-328-1916
Manuel Electric	Boca Chica	809-523-9769
Marina Zar-Par	Boca Chica	809-523-5858
Repuestos Maritimos	Puerto Plata	809-586-4728
Tony Rodamentes	Boca Chica	809-688-2151
Wilson Marine	Boca Chica	809-743-9503
Fabrication/Welding		
Cap Cana Marina	Cap Cana	809-695-5539

FACILITY	LOCATION	TELEPHONE
Casa de Campo Marina	La Romana	809-523-2111
Kiko	Luperón	
Marina Zar-Par	Boca Chica	809-523-5858
Núñez & Núñez	Santiago	809-582-2200
Tony Rodamentes	Boca Chica	809-688-2151

Haul Out

Casa de Campo Marina	La Romana	809-523-2111
Club Náutico de Haina	Haina	
Club Náutico de Santo Domingo	Boca Chica	809-683-2582
Ocean World Marina	Cofresi	809-291-1000
Marina Zar-Par	Boca Chica	809-523-5858
Ocean World Marina	Cofresi	809-970-3373
Tropical Marine	Luperón	809-440-9926

Hull Repair/Painting

Cap Cana Marina	Cap Cana	809-695-5539
Casa de Campo Marina	La Romana	809-523-2111
Club Náutico de Haina	Haina	
Club Náutico de Santo Domingo	Boca Chica	809-683-2582
Marina Zar-Par	Boca Chica	809-523-5858
Tropical Marine	Luperón	809-440-9926

Internet

Hotel Salinas	Salinas	
Luperón Marina & YC	Luperón	809-771-2002
Marina Cap Cana	Cap Cana	809-688-5587
Marina Casa de Campo	La Romana	809-523-2111
Marina Zar-Par	Boca Chica	809-523-5858
Pharmacia Vanessa	Luperón	
R&V Comunicaciones	Santo Domingo	809-687-8565
Verizon	Luperón	

Marine Supplies

Auto Marina	Santo Domingo	809-565-6676
Casa de Campo Marina	La Romana	809-523-2111
Centro Marino	Boca Chica	809-523-6033
Luperón Marine Supplies	Luperón	
Repuestos Maritimos	Puerto Plata	809-586-4728

Outboard Repair

Cap Cana Marina	Cap Cana	809-695-5539
Casa de Campo Marina	La Romana	809-523-2111
Club Náutico de Haina	Haina	
Club Náutico de Santo Domingo	Boca Chica	809-683-2582
Marina Zar-Par	Boca Chica	809-523-5858
Tropical Marine	Luperón	809-440-9926

Propane

Any Motorconcho	Luperón	
Cap Cana Marina	Cap Cana	809-688-5587
Casa de Campo Marina	La Romana	809-523-2111
José	Luperón	809-458-9506
Papo	Luperón	

Propeller

Casa de Campo Marina	La Romana	809-523-2111
Marina Zar-Par	Boca Chica	809-523-5858

FACILITY	LOCATION	TELEPHONE
Refrigeration		
Cap Cana Marina	Cap Cana	809-695-5539
Casa de Campo Marina	La Romana	809-523-2111
Marina Zar-Par	Boca Chica	809-523-5858
Mercado del Sol	Luperón	
Tropical Marine	Luperón	809-440-9926
Zelltec	Puerto Plata	809-533-5019
Rigging		
Casa de Campo Marina	La Romana	809-523-2111
Marina Zar-Par	Boca Chica	809-523-5858
Sail and Canvas Repair		
Calamity Canvas	Luperón	809-523-6987
Casa de Campo Marina	La Romana	809-523-2111
Flaco	Luperón, DR	El Flaco, VHF ch. 68
Mare Sailmaker	Punta Cana	809-307-3426
Marina Casa de Campo	La Romana	809-523-2111
Marina Zar-Par	Boca Chica	809-523-5858

Appendix C-2: Services Turks and Caicos

All listings in the Turks and Caicos are area code 649.

FACILITY	LOCATION	TELEPHONE	VHF CALL OR E-Mail
Car Rentals			
AB's Rent a Car	North Caicos	331-1947	www.alsrentacar.com/
Avis (airport)	Providenciales	946-4705	reservations@avis.tc
Avis	Providenciales	941-7557	
Bayside Cars & Buggies	Providenciales	941-9010	www.baysidecarstci.com/
Budget	Providenciales	946-4079	budget@tciway.tc
Dickenson's Car Rental	Grand Turk	241-1549	
Dutchie's Car Rental	Grand Turk	946-2244	
Grace Bay Auto	Providenciales	941-8500	gracebaycarrentals.com
Grand Turk Adventures	Grand Turk	346-2450	grandturkadventures.com
Hertz (airport)	Providenciales	941-3910	www.hertz.com
Island Rent a Car	Providenciales	946-4993	
Karib Auto/Cart Rental	Grand Turk	346-8652	www.karibarentals.com/
KK & T's Auto Rentals	Providenciales	941-8377	http://kkntsautorentals.com/
Middle Caicos Rentals	Middle Caicos	946-6185	
Mitchell Car Rental	Grand Turk	946-1879	
Mystique	Providenciales	941-3910	www.mystiquecarrental.com
Old Nick Rental Cars	North Caicos	946-7358	
Pat Hamilton	North Caicos	946-7141	
Preferred Car Rental	Providenciales	941-3782	PreferredCar@tciway.tc
Provo Fun Cycles & Auto	Providenciales	946-5868	
Provo Rent a Car	Providenciales	946-4475	RentACar@provo.net
Rent a Buggy	Providenciales	946-4158	http://rentabuggy.tc/
Salt Cay Adventure Tours	Salt Cay	244-1407	http://saltcaydivers.com
Scooter Bob's	Providenciales	946-4684	http://scooterbobstci.com
Seaview Marina	South Caicos	946-3245	
Sierra Rent A Car	North Caicos	946-7317	
Sunrise Auto Rental	Providenciales	946-4705	
Superior Auto Rentals	North Caicos	232-2177	superiorautorentals.com

A Cruising Guide to the Turks and Caicos Islands

FACILITY	LOCATION	TELEPHONE	VHF CALL OR E-Mail
TC National Car Rental	Providenciales	946-4701	
Tony's Car Rental	Grand Turk	231-1806	
Tropical Auto Rental	Grand Turk	946-2095	
Tropical Auto Rental	Providenciales	946-5300	*tropicalautorentaltci.com*
Unique Taxi and VIP Serv.	Providenciales	244-7823	*uniquetaxiservice.com/*
Yellowman Car Rentals	Grand Turk	231-0167	
Diesel Repair/Parts			
Caicos Marina & Boatyard	Providenciales	946-5600	*caicosmarinashp@tciway.tc*
Caribbean Marine Diesel	S. Side Marina, Provo	941-5903	
MPL Enterprises	Grand Turk	431-0376	*yamaha@yamaha.tc*
Seaview Marina	South Caicos	946-3245	*seaviewm@tciway.tc*
Percy Tolbert	Salt Cay		
Diving			
Aqua TCI	Grace Bay	432-2782	*aquatci@live.com*
Art Pickering Turtle Divers	Providenciales	946-4232	*provoturtledivers.com*
Big Blue Divers	Grand Turk	946-5034	*bigblueunlimited.com*
Blue Water Divers	Grand Turk	946-2432	*info@bigblueunlimited.com*
Caicos Adventures	Providenciales	941-3346	*divucrzy@tciway.tc*
Dive Provo	Providenciales	946-5040	*diving@diveprovo.com*
Flamingo Divers	Providenciales	946-4193	*www.flamingodivers.com*
Grand Turk Diving	Grand Turk	946-1559	*http://www.gtdiving.com*
Oasis Divers	Grand Turk	946-1128	*www.oasisdivers.com/*
Provo Wall Divers	Providenciales	941-5441	
Salt Cay Divers	Salt Cay	241-1009	*www.saltcaydivers.tc*
Turtle Divers	Providenciales	946-4232	*provoturtledivers@provo.net*
Electronics/Electrical			
Walkin Marine	Providenciales	946-4411	*walkinmarine@tciway.tc*
Fabrication/Welding			
Caicos Marina & Shipyard	Providenciales	946-5600	*caicosmarinashp@tciway.tc*
Osprey Marine Services	Providenciales	946-5122	
Provo Steel	Providenciales	941-3112	*provosteel@tciway.tc*
Tibor's	Providenciales	941-5802	*tibor@express.tc*
Haul Out			
Caicos Marina & Shipyard	Providenciales	946-5600	*caicosmarinashp@tciway.tc*
Seaview Marina	South Caicos	946-3245	*seaviewm@tciway.tc*
Hull Repair/Painting			
Caicos Marina & Shipyard	Providenciales	946-5600	*caicosmarinashp@tciway.tc*
Internet			
Aqua Bar (Turtle Cove)	Providenciales	946-4763	
CompTCI	Providenciales	941-4266	*Ken@comptci.tc*
Computer Guys	Providenciales	946-4152	
Computer Line	Providenciales	941-5834	*info@computerline.ci*
Deluxe Business Center	Providenciales	941-8876	
Grace Bay Pharmacy	Providenciales	946-8242	
Turtle Cove Marina	Providenciales	941-3781	*tcmarina@provo.net*
Marine Supplies			
Caicos Marina & Shipyard	Providenciales	946-5600	*caicosmarinashp@tciway.tc*
MPL Enterprises	Grand Turk	431-0376	*yamaha@yamaha.tc*
Walkin Marine	Providenciales	946-4411	*walkinmarine@tciway.tc*
Outboard Repair			
Caicos Marina & Shipyard	Providenciales	946-5600	*caicosmarinashp@tciway.tc*

FACILITY	LOCATION	TELEPHONE	VHF CALL OR E-Mail
CMPL Enterprises	Grand Turk	946-2227	
MPL Enterprises	Grand Turk	431-0376	yamaha@yamaha.tc
Seaview Marina	South Caicos	946-3245	seaviewm@tciway.tc
Walkin Marine	Providenciales	946-4411	walkinmarine@tciway.tc
Propane			
Grand Turk Gas Depot	S. Dock, Grand Turk	946-2532	
Seaview Marina	South Caicos	946-3245	South Caicos Marina
South Side Marina	Providenciales	241-2439	southsidemarina@gmail.com
TC Gas	Grand Turk	946-2532	
TC Gas	Providenciales	941-3585	
Turtle Cove Marina	Providenciales	941-3781	tcmarina@provo,net
Rigging			
Osprey Marine Serv.	Providenciales	946-5122	

Appendix D: Waypoints

Caution: Waypoints are not to be used for navigational purposes. The following waypoints are intended to place you in the general area of the described position. All routes, cuts, and anchorages must be negotiated by eyeball navigation. The author and publisher take no responsibility for the misuse of the following waypoints. Waypoints are listed from north to south. Latitude is "**North**" and longitude is "**West**." Datum used is WGS84.

WAYPOINT DESCRIPTION	LATITUDE	LONGITUDE
Southern Bahamas		
Mayaguana		
Northwest Point - 1½ nm W of light	22° 27.10'	73° 09.90'
Abraham's Bay - inner waypoint at eastern entrance	22° 21.07'	72° 58.45'
Start Bay - ½ nm SW of best holding	22° 20.30'	73° 05.30'
Abraham's Bay - ¼ nm SSE of eastern entrance	22° 20.80'	72° 58.30'
Abraham's Bay - ¼ nm NE of western entrance	22° 19.80'	73° 02.50'
Abraham's Bay - ¼ nm SW of western entrance	22° 19.25'	73° 03.40'
Southeast Point - 1 nm WSW of anchorage	22° 16.70'	72° 48.40'
Inagua		
Little Inagua - ½ nm W of anchorage	21° 26.50'	73° 03.50'
Northwest Point - ½ nm NNW of point	21° 07.10'	73° 40.10'
Matthew Town - ¾ nm W of	20° 57.10'	73° 41.50'
Turks and Caicos Islands		
The Caicos Islands		
Ft. George Cut - ½ nm NW of cut	21° 53.70'	72° 07.90'
North West Point, Providenciales - ½ nm N of reef in deep water	21° 53.10'	72° 19.90'
Wheeland Cut - ½ nm NNE of cut	21° 52.65'	72° 17.65'
Leeward Cut - ½ nm NW of cut	21° 50.40'	72° 10.40'
Malcolm Roadstead - ½ nm W of anchorage	21° 49.85'	72° 20.80'
Stubb's Cut - ¼ nm NW of cut	21° 48.93'	72° 11.30'
Wiley Cut - ¼ nm NNW of cut	21° 48.85'	72° 21.35'
Leeward Going Through - S entrance, ¼ nm ESE of Bird Rock	21° 48.60'	72° 07.30'
Sellar's Cut - ½ nm N of cut	21° 48.40'	72° 12.40'
Jacksonville Cut, East Caicos - ¼ nm N of cut	21° 47.00'	71° 35.90'
Deep water on Banks for shortcut to Leeward	21° 45.50'	72° 07.00'
Cooper Jack Bight - ½ nm SW of entrance to Discovery Bay	21° 45.05'	72° 14.00'
Turning point to Boatyard -1 nm SSE of entrance channel	21° 44.80'	72° 10.30'
Sandbore Channel - ¾ nm W of entrance	21° 44.50'	72° 27.25'

WAYPOINT DESCRIPTION	LATITUDE	LONGITUDE
Sapodilla Bay - ¼ nm S of anchorage	21° 44.25'	72° 17.40'
Bay Cay - 1 nm ESE of, beginning of route to Boatyard	21° 43.75'	72° 14.00'
Pony Channel – ¼ nm W of	21° 43.40'	72° 27.30'
Pony Channel – ¼ nm E of	21° 43.40'	72° 26.75'
West Caicos Marina – ¼ nm NW of entrance channel	21° 42.00'	72° 28.00'
West Caicos, Clear Sand Road - ¾ nm S of Southwest Point	21° 36.75'	72° 29.00'
Freighter Channel - SW waypoint	21° 35.75'	72° 23.25'
French Cay - ½ nm W of anchorage	21° 30.60'	72° 12.70'
Starfish Channel	21° 30.25'	72° 06.75'
French Cay - ¾ SW of anchorage on edge of Caicos Bank	21° 29.75'	72° 12.65'
South Caicos, Cockburn Harbour - ¼ nm SE of entrance	21° 28.70'	71° 31.70'
Long Cay Cut - ½ nm NW of cut and anchorage area	21° 27.40'	71° 34.75'
Long Cay Cut - ½ nm SE of cut in Columbus Passage	21° 26.60'	71° 34.10'
Fish Cays - ¾ nm N of	21° 23.50'	71° 37.25'
West Sand Spit - 2 nm SW of	21° 20.50'	72° 10.05'
Big Ambergris Cay - 1 nm NW of anchorage	21° 19.75'	71° 39.75'

The Turks Islands

Grand Turk, North Creek - ¼ nm N of entrance channel at jetty	21° 31.10'	71° 08.50'
Grand Turk, Front Street anchorage - ¼ nm W of break in reef	21° 28.13'	71° 09.13'
Grand Turk, South Dock - ¼ nm WSW of end of dock	21° 25.90'	71° 09.20'
Big Cut - ¼ nm NW of	21° 24.60'	71° 09.25'
Salt Cay - ¼ nm W of Deane's Dock	21° 19.90'	71° 13.25'
Salt Cay - ¾ SW of S end, waypoint to take up course to DR	21° 17.60'	71° 14.10'
Great Sand Cay - ½ nm W of anchorage in West Bay	21° 11.65'	71° 15.50'
Great Sand Cay - ¾ SW of S end, waypoint to take up course to DR	21° 10.80'	71° 15.50'

The Dominican Republic

Northern Coast

Luperón - 1 nm N of entrance channel	19° 55.50'	70° 56.51'
Cofresi, *Ocean World Marina* - ½ nm NE of entrance	19° 50.05'	70° 43.65'
Puerto Plata - ¾ nm N of sea buoy	19° 49.10'	70° 41.55'
Sosúa anchorage - ¼ nm W of anchorage area	19° 45.60'	70° 31.40'
Rio San Juan - ¼ nm W of anchorage area	19° 38.60'	70° 05.50'
Puerto El Valle (Escondido) - 1¾ nm NNW of anchorage area	19° 19.00'	69° 20.50'

Eastern Coast

Samaná - ¼ nm S of Punta Gorda	19° 11.40'	69° 18.85'
Puerto Bahía Marina - ¼ nm SW of entrance channel	19° 11.40'	69° 21.40'
Bahía de San Lorenzo - ¼ nm W of Punta Arena	19° 05.50'	69° 29.00'

Southern Coast

Barahona - ¼ nm NE of sea buoy	18° 13.30'	71° 04.00'
Las Salinas - ½ nm NNW of Punta Calderas	18° 14.00'	70° 33.00'
Puerto de Haina - ¼ nm S of entrance between the jetties	18° 24.60'	70° 01.05'
Santo Domingo - ¼ nm S of entrance between the jetties	18° 27.50'	69° 53.50'
Boca Chica - 1¼ nm SE of marked entrance channel	18° 25.50'	69° 36.70'
Casa de Campo Marina - ¼ nm SW of marked entrance channel	18° 23.60'	68° 54.40'
Isla Saona - ½ nm NW of anchorage	18° 12.50'	68° 47.00'
Cap Cana Marina - ½ nm SE of entrance channel	18° 29.85'	68° 22.00'

Appendix E: Protected Areas

Historical Sites:
  Caicos Islands: Boiling Hole on South Caicos; Cheshire Hall ruins on Providenciales; Fort George Cay; Molasses Reef Wreck; Sapodilla Hill and West Harbour Bluff Rock Carvings on Providenciales.
  Turks Islands: Salt Cay; the wreck of H.M.S. Endymion south of Big Sand Cay.

National Parks:
  Caicos Islands: Admiral Cockburn Land and Sea Park at South Caicos; the Conch Bar Caves on Middle Caicos; the East Bay Islands off North Caicos; Fort George Land and Sea Park at Fort George Cay; Princess Alexandra on Providenciales; Chalk Sound on Providenciales; North West Point Marine Park on Providenciales; West Caicos Marine Park on West Caicos.
  Turks Islands: Grand Turk Cays Land and Sea Park; Columbus Landfall on Grand Turk; South Creek on Grand Turk.

Nature Reserves:
  Caicos Islands: Belle Sound and Admiral Cockburn Cays at South Caicos; Vine Point (Man O' War Bush); Ocean Hole at Middle Caicos; Cottage Pond on North Caicos; Pumpkin Bluff Pond on North Caicos; Dick Hill Creek and Bellefield Landing Pond on North Caicos; the Princess Alexandra Nature Reserve consisting of Little Water Cay, Mangrove Cay, and Donna Cay; North West Point Pond on Providenciales; Pigeon Pond and Frenchman's Creek on Providenciales; Lake Catherine on West Caicos.

Protected Buildings:
  North Caicos: The ruins of Wade's Green and the Bellefield Plantation.
  East Caicos: The ruins of the Jacksonville Plantation.
  West Caicos: The ruins at Yankee Town.
  South Caicos: DC's House and the Salt Sheds and Salt Works.
  Grand Turk: Guinep Tree Lodge (The National Museum); Police Station; Turk's Head Inn; Miss Wood's House; the Government House and the Governor's Mansion (Waterloo House); the Prison.

RAMSAR Site:
  The wetlands on the southern side of North, Middle and East Caicos are of international importance and is afforded protection under the RAMSAR Convention, an international treaty.

Sanctuaries:
  Caicos Islands: Three Mary's Cays; French Cay; Seal Cays; Bush Cay.
  Turks Islands: Big Sand Cay; Long Cay

UNESCO Heritage Site:
  Turks Islands: Salt Cay

Appendix F: Metric Conversion

Visitors to The Bahamas, Turks and Caicos Islands, and the Dominican Republic, will find the metric system in use and many grocery items and fuel measured in liters and kilograms.

1 centimeter (cm) = 0.4 inch	1 inch = 2.54 centimeters
1 meter (m) = 3.28 feet	1 foot = 30.48 centimeters
1 meter = 0.55 fathoms	1 fathom = 1.83 meters
1 kilometer (km) = 0.62 miles	1 yard = .92 meters
1 kilometer = 0.54 nautical miles	1 nautical mile = 1.852 kilometers
1 liter (l) = 0.26 gallons	1 gallon = 3.79 liters
1 gram (g) = 0.035 ounces	1 ounce = 28.4 grams
1 metric ton = 1.1 tons	1 pound = 454 grams

Appendix G: Flags

The Turks and Caicos Islands

The Dominican Republic

The Bahamas

Index

A

AAA Air Ambulance 19
Abraham's Bay 44, 45
Amber Coast 126
Ambergris Cays 83, 84, 88–90
Amber Museum 128
Armstrong Pond 79
Atlantic Village 48
Autonomous University of Santo Domingo 114

B

Bahamian moor 67
Bahía de las Aguilas 136
Balfour Town 107
Bambarra 19, 80
Barahona 136, 137, 138
Bay Cay 50, 57, 59, 61, 158
Bay Islands 78
Bayahibe 144
Beacon Hill 110
Bellefield 42, 43, 78
Bellefield Landing 78
Belvedere Plantation 78
Bermudez National Park 114
Bermudian Harbour 50, 76, 79
Bermudian Salt Rakers 42, 94, 99, 106
Bernard Bay 73
Big Ambergris Cay 76, 84, 89, 90, 158
Big Cut 79, 92, 103, 105, 158
Big Sand Cay 109, 110
Bimini 38
Bird Cay 44, 151
Bird Island 105
Bird Rock 36, 68, 69, 157
Blackbeard 40, 71
Blue Caicos 42, 46
Blue Hills 47, 54, 61
Blue Hills Road 54
Bluff Shoal 50
Boaby Rock Point 105
Boca Chica 141
Boiling Hole 84
Bottle Creek 19, 78
Boy Stubbs Shoal 69, 84
Breezy Point 80
Bridges to Nowhere. *See* Los Puentes
Brown House 108
Bush Cay 44, 90, 151

C

Cabarete 129, 131
Cable and Wireless 21, 65, 66, 84, 98, 100
Cabo Isabella 117
Caicos Bank 82, 83
Caicos Cays 65, 71
Caicos Marina and Shipyard 11, 16, 52, 56, 59, 69, 75
Calico Jack Rackham 40, 41, 71
Calle Las Damas 114
Cap Cana Marina 146, 147
Caribbean Marine Diesel 52, 59
Casa de Campo Marina 144
Castillo Mundo King 129, 130
Catalina Island 114
Cathedral of Santo Domingo 114
Centro de la Naturaleza 134
Chalk Sound 46, 53
Cheshire Hall 42, 46, 47
Ciboney Indians 115
Clear Sand Road 74, 158
Club Med Cut 65
Cockburn Harbour 17, 45, 46, 82–88, 92, 158
Cockburn Town 8, 12, 84, 94, 98, 99, 103
Codatel 121
Cofresi 112
Columbus' Castle 114
Columbus Lake 94
Columbus Passage 18, 45, 91, 106, 158
Columbus Square 114
Company Point 73
Conch Bar 19, 79, 80
Conch Bar Caves 79
Conch Farm 53, 56, 67, 68
Conch Ground 90
Cooper Jack Bight 57, 59
Cosmic Farm 78
Costambar 128
Cotton Cay 38, 103, 106
Cove Point 64, 74

D

Damn Fool Channel 7
DECR 12, 21, 23, 74, 77, 90, 105, 110
DECR Permit 77
Dellis Cay 16, 65, 70–72, 77
Delvin's Cove 72
Discovery Bay 16, 57, 58, 157
Divers Alert Network 19
Dolphin Project 18
Domingo, Autonomous University of Santo 114

Dominican Republic National Parks 114
Donna Cay 69
Dove Cay 44, 85, 151

E

Eagle's Nest 88
East Bays Cays 78
East Caicos 17, 38, 67, 77, 80–82, 151, 157
East Cay 103, 105
El Batey 129
El Faro a Colón (the Columbus Lighthouse) 114
El Limon Waterfall 134
El Presidente 22, 113
El Valle. *See* Puerto El Valle
Emerald Cloud 83
Endymion Reef 109, 110
Endymion Rock 109, 110
English Cut 62, 63, 65
Escondido 132
Esperanza 80
Estero Honda 124

F

False Cut 61
Ferguson Cut 79
Fish Cays 76, 88, 89, 158
Five Cays 47, 50, 55, 57, 59
Flamingo Cove Marina 97, 99
Flamingo Hill 82
Flamingo Pond 77
Fort George Cay 16, 65, 70–72, 80
Fort George Cut 66, 70–72
Fort San Felipe 114, 126, 128
Freighter Channel 72, 74, 158
French Cay 40, 44, 46, 74–76, 84, 151, 158
Front Street 12, 21, 45, 46, 92, 98–102, 158
Front Street anchorage 45, 46, 92, 98, 158

G

Gambia 80
Gamble Cut 79
Gambol Point 79
George Town 16, 59
Gibbs Cay 103, 105
Glowworms 44
Grace Bay 11, 18, 48, 54, 56, 61, 63, 64, 69
Grande Caicos 78
Grand Turk Landfall Theory 94
Great Sand Cay 23, 38, 46, 76, 91, 92, 109, 110, 117, 126, 151, 158
Guanahani 38, 94, 102
Guinep House 101

Gun Hill 105
Gun Reef 105
Gussie Point 52

H

Halfway Reef 50
Harbour Club Marina 57, 58
Haulover Point 82
Hawksnest Anchorage 98, 103, 105
Heaving Down Rock 67
Herrera 38
Hickory 114
H.M.S. Endymion 109
Horsestable Beach 78
House Bay 106

I

Iguana Cay 81
Indian Cave 79
International Ramsar Bureau 21
Isabel de Torres 126, 128
Isla Catalina 143
Island House 98
Island Pride 23, 54, 55
Isla Saona 114, 146

J

Jackson Cut Bay 81
Jacksonville Cut 81, 157
Jaragua-Bahoruco-Enriquillo Biosphere Reserve 137, 138
Jazz-Blues Merengue Festival 131
Joe Grant's Cay 81
Juba Point 57, 59, 75

K

Kew 19, 78
King Hill 79
King's Highway 76, 78
Kingston 40, 43, 56

L

La Caleta Underwater Park 114
La Isabella 124
Lake Enriquillo 137, 138
La Providentielle 46
La Romana 112, 114, 144
Leeward Cut 44, 45, 61, 62, 64–67, 157
Leeward Going Through 16, 18, 23, 48, 56, 61, 65–70, 80, 84, 105, 157
Leeward Highway 21, 46, 53–56

Index

Leeward Marina 12, 66, 67, 77
Lighthouse Park 95
Little Ambergris Cay 84, 89, 90
Little Cut 105
Little Man O War Bush 86
Little Water Cay 65, 67, 69, 105
Long Bar 86
Long Bay 16, 56, 61, 65
Long Bay Hills 16, 56, 61, 65
Long Cay 43, 44, 46, 76, 82–86, 88, 90, 92, 103, 105, 106, 151, 158
Long Point 46
Lorimers 80
Los Charamicos 129
Los Haitises National Park 114
Los Puentes 134
Loyalists 42, 46, 69, 80
Luperón 8, 10, 15, 17, 20, 23, 76, 90, 92, 109, 112, 116, 117, 119–124, 126, 128, 151, 152, 158

M

Major's Hill 78
Malcolm Roadstead 47, 48, 157
Mangrove Cay 67, 69
Man O War Bush 80, 86
Marina Punta Cana 147
Market Place 46, 54
Matthew Town 151, 157
Middle Caicos Expo 80
Middle Cay 52, 57, 59
Middleton Bar 83
Middleton Cay 84
Molasses Reef 74, 76, 101
Molasses Reef Wreck 76, 101
Mouchoir 12, 106
Mt. Torres 126, 128
Mudjian Harbour. *See* Bermudian Harbour
Museum of Royal Houses 114

N

Nature Reserve 21, 47, 90
New World 37, 38, 39, 94, 98, 102, 105, 124, 128
North Bay 107
North Beach 107, 109
North Caicos 17, 19, 42–44, 65, 67, 71, 76–79, 155
North Caicos Art Center 77
North Creek 17, 48, 86, 92, 94–99, 106, 158
Northeast Point 96
Northeast Reef 97, 98
North Wells 97
North West Point 45–48, 54, 61, 107, 151, 157
Northwest Cay 151

Northwest Point 47, 79, 91, 151, 157

O

Ocean World Marina 124, 126, 152, 158
Owen Rock 126
Ozama Fortress 114

P

Parrot Cay 16, 40, 41, 46, 65, 70–72, 77
Paso de Catuan 146
Pear Cay 105
Pearl Channel 84
Pelican Cay 80
Pelican Island 105
Penniston Cay 106
Phillip's Reef 82
Pillory Beach 98, 102
Pine Barrel Landing 79
Pine Cay 11, 16, 18, 65, 69–72
Pinzon Cay 103, 105
Pirate Cay 41
Playa Dorada 126, 128
Playa El Valle 132
Pony Channel 50, 72, 73, 158
Port of Silver 126
Port Royal 40
Princess Alexandra National Park 69
Proggin Bay 50
Propeller Cay 16
Provident Caicos 46
Provo International Billfish Tournament 63
Puerto Bahía Marina 134, 135
Puerto Blanco 23, 117, 119
Puerto de Haina 140
Puerto El Valle 132
Puerto Patillas 124
Puerto Plata 10, 15, 21, 92, 94, 109, 110, 151, 158
Punta 153
Punta Cana 112
Punta Chivato 20, 112–114, 116, 117, 121, 122, 126, 128, 152–155
Punta Fortaleza 112, 151
Punta Rucia 124
Pussey Cay 50, 57, 59

R

Ready Money 78
Rio San Juan 131
Ropier Cut 77
Round Cay 105
Rule of Twelfths 22

S

Salt Cay 19, 38, 39, 42, 46, 67, 91, 92, 94, 100, 103, 106–110, 151, 156, 158
Samaná 92, 112, 114, 134
Sanctuary 21, 114
Sandbore Channel 44, 45, 48, 50, 72, 73, 157
Sandy Point 19, 77
San Pedro de Macoris 143
San Salvador 94
Santiago 20, 21, 112, 116, 122–124, 154
Santo Doming 140
Santo Domingo 14, 112–115, 122, 140, 141
Sapodilla Bay 11, 45, 48, 50–53, 55, 57, 61, 69, 72–76, 83, 84, 88, 158
Sapodilla Hill 47, 52
Scape Park 147
Seal Cay 109
Seal Cays 88, 90
Sea View Marina 86–88
Sellar's Cut 36, 62, 63, 65, 157
Sellar's Pond 12, 16, 45, 47, 48, 61, 63–65
Silly Creek 50, 53
Silver Banks 92, 105, 106, 114
Silver Deep 67
Sim Cay 50, 57, 59
Sirus Cove 63
Six Hills Cays 82–84, 88
Smith's Reef 63
Sosúa 112, 130
South Base 9, 91, 96, 98, 100, 102, 103
South Caicos 17, 19, 22, 24, 38, 39, 44, 46, 47, 67, 76, 80, 82–88, 92, 94, 102, 121, 151, 155, 157, 158
South Caicos Regatta 88
South Creek 98, 103, 105
Southeast Point 44, 45, 157
Southern Cays 88
South Side Basin Marina 57
Southwest Beach 109
Southwest Point 44, 72, 74, 158
Southwest Reef 74
Star Channel 76
Star Town 74
Starfish Channel 84, 158
Start Bay 45, 157
Stella Maris 59
St. Francis Monastery 114
St. Thomas' Church 43
Stubbs Cay 71
Stubbs Cut 45, 61, 62, 65, 66
Sunset Reef 109
Suzie Turn 55

T

TACARS 13
Taylor House 106
The Looking Glass 109
Thompson Cove 16, 64, 65
Three Marys 92, 110
Three Mary's Cays 77
Turks and Caicos National Museum 101, 102
Turks Bank 91, 92, 109
Turks Island Passage 44, 45, 76, 83, 88–92, 94, 100
Turks Island Whaling Company 106
Turtle Channel 48
Turtle Cove 11, 12, 16, 47, 48, 55, 56, 61–64, 152, 156
Turtle Cove Marina 11, 12, 16, 47, 48, 55, 56, 61–64, 152, 156
Turtle Lake 58
Turtle Rock 50

U

UNESCO World Heritage Site 107

V

Village Cave 79

W

Walkin Marine 54, 156, 157
Water Cay 65, 67, 69, 70, 105
Waterloo 102
West Bay 109, 110
West Caicos 11, 38, 44, 50, 63, 72–74, 78, 80, 151, 152, 158
West Caicos Marina 72–74, 152
West Harbour Bluff 46, 48, 50
Whale Museum and Nature Center. *See* Centro de la Naturaleza
Wheeland Cut 61, 157
Whitby Plaza 77
White Cay 90
White House 107, 108
Wiley Cut 47, 48, 157
Wiley Point 48
William Dean Cay 50, 57, 59
Windsurfing World Cup 131
Windward Passage 40, 74, 76

Y

Yankee Town 72

About the Author

Photo Courtesy of Danielle Courteau

Stephen J. Pavlidis has been cruising and living aboard since the winter of 1989. He now cruises aboard the M/V *Swan Song*.

Starting in the Exuma Cays over 20 years ago, Steve began his writing career with guides to the many fascinating destinations he visited. Many of his books stand alone to this day as the quintessential guides to the areas he covers.

His books are different than most other cruising guides in some very significant ways. All of the charts in Steve's books were created using data personally collected while visiting each area using a computerized system that interfaces GPS and depth soundings.

You can find out more about this exceptional author by visiting his Web site, www.Seaworthy.com where there is current news and information about Steve's latest projects, as well as contact information.

Other books by Stephen J. Pavlidis:
Life at Sea Level, ISBN 978-1-892399-33-5
The Exuma Guide, 3rd Edition, ISBN 978-1-892399-31-1
A Cruising Guide to the Leeward Islands, 2nd Edition, ISBN 978-1-892399-36-6
The Northern Bahamas Guide, ISBN 978-1-892399-28-1
The Northwest Caribbean Guide, 2nd Edition, ISBN 978-1-892399-38-0
The Puerto Rico Guide, 3rd Edition, ISBN 978-1-892399-39-7
The Southern Bahamas Guide, ISBN 978-1-892399-29-8
A Cruising Guide to the Virgin Islands, 2nd Edition, ISBN 978-1-892399-35-9
A Cruising Guide to the Windward Islands, 2nd Edition, ISBN 978-1-892399-37-3

About Don Reynolds

Photo Courtesy of Don Reynolds

Don Reynolds whose sketches grace this publication, was born in 1944. Don's love of the sea began at the age of 18 months while crossing the *North Atlantic Ocean* from England to America aboard the *HMS Queen Mary*.

Subsequent voyages continued from Puerto Rico to New York via transport aboard the *Pvt William H. Thomas* and across the *Pacific Ocean* aboard the *USS Yorktown* and continuing on with his home-built 36' Roberts cutter, *Ppalu*.

Don met Steve during a shakedown cruise to the Exumas in 1996, sharing sketches and knowledge of the area. *Ppalu* eventually took Don & Lynn (wife) up to the coast of Maine and back before sailing for the Med the next year. Having always worked as an artist, a dream was fully realized in Italy by sculpting marble in Pietrasanta while living aboard *Ppalu* for three years.

The return voyage out of the Med and down to Cape Verde and across again to the Windward Islands began the island hop back through the turquoise and blue waters of the Bahama outer islands.

Private and public art commissions consume the present day activities, but the next dream voyage is still alive and with luck, should come true... while *Ppalu* patiently waits on her mooring.

www.ingramcontent.com/pod-product-compliance
Lightning Source LLC
Chambersburg PA
CBHW080540300426
44111CB00017B/2817